Children's Strategies

Children's Strategies

Contemporary Views of Cognitive Development

Edited by
David F. Bjorklund
Florida Atlantic University

LEA LAWRENCE ERLBAUM ASSOCIATES, PUBLISHERS
1990   Hillsdale, New Jersey   Hove and London

Lawrence Erlbaum Associates, Inc., Publishers
365 Broadway
Hillsdale, New Jersey 07642

Library of Congress Cataloging-in-Publication Data

Children's strategies: contemporary views of cognitive development /
edited by David F. Bjorklund.
    p.   cm.
Includes bibliographical references and index.
ISBN (invalid) 0-8058-0135-7
1. Problem solving in children.   2. Cognition in children.
I. Bjorklund, David F., 1949–
BF723.P8C45   1990
155.4'13–dc20   90-35934
                                                             CIP

Printed in the United States of America
10 9 8 7 6 5 4 3 2 1

To my wife Barbara.
Most of my best ideas are hers.

Contents

Preface

One of the issues central to both classic and contemporary theories of cognitive development is children's goal-directed behavior. How is it that children come to identify a goal and then execute the appropriate set of physical and mental operations to achieve that goal? In most contemporary approaches to cognitive development, children's goal-directed behavior is investigated in terms of *strategies*. At their most general, strategies are goal-directed, mental operations that are aimed at solving a problem. Historically, most researchers have also assumed that strategies are deliberate, or intentional.

The emphasis on strategies in cognitive development can be traced to the 1960s, beginning with work of John Flavell and his colleagues on mediated memory and with work of Jerome Bruner and his colleagues on children's problem solving. From this early research, much of the field of cognitive development during the 1970s became concerned with the development of strategies. In fact, it would not be too drastic an overstatement to say that, for many cognitive developmentalists during that time, cognitive development was equivalent to the development of strategies. It was thought that young children's deficits on hosts of tasks ranging from free-recall memory to conservation could be ameliorated simply by the introduction of the proper strategy. Young children were said to be *production deficient*, meaning that they were capable of using an effective mediator (that is, a strategy), but merely were unable to produce one spontaneously. To understand cognitive development, then, required an understanding of strategies—when they developed and what could be done to change production deficient children into children who produced efficient strategies on their own.

Much has changed over the past 20 years, but what has remained constant is an interest in children's strategies. Strategies are no longer seen as being limited to older children (and younger children who are instructed to use them), but are now seen even in the behavior of infants. Seven-month olds alter how hard they swing at mobiles over their playpens to produce slightly different outcomes from inanimate objects, and 18-month olds will deliberately stack boxes one on top of another to reach a desired object on a kitchen shelf. There is also general recognition that strategies vary not only with the developmental level of the child, but also with that child's familiarity with the testing context and the task materials. And strategies are no longer viewed as separate cognitive entities unto themselves, but are seen as important components in a developing cognitive system that includes both deliberate, effortful processes as well as automatic, effortless ones.

The papers in this volume describe up-to-date research and theory about the development of children's strategies for a variety of cognitive tasks. The first chapter (Harnishfeger & Bjorklund) provides an historical view of the concept of strategies in cognitive development. It further highlights many of the issues that concern contemporary developmental psychologists interested in strategies as well as setting the stage for the contributions that follow. The next nine chapters provide a detailed look at strategy development research and theory in a variety of areas. These include problem solving in infancy (Willatts, Chapter 2), memory (Folds, Footo, Guttentag, & Ornstein, Chapter 3; Bjorklund, Muir-Broaddus, & Schneider, Chapter 4; Howe & O'Sullivan, Chapter 5), selective attention (Miller, Chapter 6), mathematics (Ashcraft, Chapter 7; Bisanz & LeFevre, Chapter 8), analogical reasoning (Gholson, Morgan, Dattel & Pierce, Chapter 9), and reading (Garner, Chapter 10). The final chapter (Bjorklund & Harnishfeger, Chapter 11) looks back on these papers, integrating the diversity of ideas expressed by the contributors. This chapter focuses on the controversy regarding the definition of strategy (e.g., must a strategy be deliberate?) and the general concensus regarding the underlying mechanisms of strategy development.

As will be seen in reading the contributions to this volume, they all address the question of the development of children's techniques to solve problems, and there is much common ground on which the various contributors can stand. At the same time, there is no concensus concerning what exactly a strategy is (although I imagine that there is actually more agreement at a deep level than appears on the surface). This mixture of concensus and disagreement reflects both the explosion of research on the topic since the late 1960s and the complexity of the issues involved. It also reflects, I believe, some of the excitement developmental researchers feel when discussing the topic. On the one hand, we have a rich knowledge of children's developing strategies and good models for how they change. On the other hand, there are still many nagging questions remaining, with new approaches and new techniques to studying development causing us to re-evaluate our once sacred cows. Despite its long history and the plethora of papers written on the subject, it is a topic that is very much alive in cognitive development circles and one that will continue to stimulate research for years to come.

I would like to thank Barbara Bjorklund, Brandi Green, Katherine Kipp Harnishfeger, Katharine Lyon, and Jacqueline Muir-Broaddus for their assistance in preparing the manuscripts, and Wolfgang Schneider and Franz Weinert for their support during the summer of 1988 at the Max Planck Institute for Psychological Research in Munich, West Germany. Finally, I would like to thank the contributors who make the issues related to children's strategy development so vibrant.

Contributors

Mark H. Ashcraft
Department of Psychology
Cleveland State University
Cleveland, Ohio 44115

Jeffrey Bisanz
Department of Psychology
University of Alberta
Edmonton, Alberta
Canada T6G 2E9

David F. Bjorklund
Department of Psychology
Florida Atlantic University
Boca Raton, Florida 33431

Andrew R. Dattel
Department of Psychology
Memphis State University
Memphis, Tennessee 38152

Trisha H. Folds
Department of Psychology
University of North Carolina
 at Chapel Hill
Chapel Hill, North Carolina
 27599-3270

Marianna Footo
Department of Psychology
University of North Carolina at
 Chapel Hill
Chapel Hill, North Carolina
 27599-3270

Ruth Garner
College of Education
Washington State University
Buver Hall
Vancouver, Washington 98663

Barry Gholson
Department of Psychology
Memphis State University
Memphis, Tennessee 38152

Robert E. Guttentag
Department of Psychology
University of North Carolina
 at Greensboro
Greensboro, North Carolina
 27412

Katherine Kipp Harnishfeger
Department of Psychology
Florida Atlantic University
Boca Raton, Florida 33431

Mark L. Howe
Department of Psychology
Memorial University
St. John's, Newfoundland
Canada A1B 3X9

Jo-Anne LeFevre
Department of Psychology
Carleton University
Ottawa, Ontario
Canada K1S 5B6

Patricia H. Miller
Department of Psychology
University of Florida
Gainsville, Florida 32611

David Morgan
Department of Psychology
Memphis State University
Memphis, Tennessee 38152

Jacqueline E. Muir-Broaddus
Department of Psychology
Florida Atlantic University
Boca Raton, Florida 33431

Peter A. Ornstein
Department of Psychology
University of North Carolina at
    Chapel Hill
Chapel Hill, North Carolina
    27599-3270

Julia T. O'Sullivan
Department of Educational Psy-
    chology
Memorial University
St. John's, Newfoundland
Canada A1B 3X9

Karen A. Pierce
Department of Psychology
Memphis State University
Memphis, Tennessee 38152

Wolfgang Schneider
Max-Planck-Institute for Psycho-
    logical Research
Leopoldstrasse 24
D-8000, Munich, 40
West Germany

Peter Willatts
Department of Psychology
The University of Dundee
Dundee, DD1 4HN
Great Britain

CHAPTER 1

Children's Strategies: A Brief History

Katherine Kipp Harnishfeger
David F. Bjorklund
Florida Atlantic University

During the past 25 years, researchers have invested vast amounts of energy in the study of children's strategies. Although the definition of the term varies among researchers, all agree that strategies are goal-directed operations employed to facilitate task performance. Strategies are often viewed as being deliberately implemented and potentially available for conscious evaluation, although, as the chapters in this book show, there is much debate concerning these latter characteristics. The predominant views about the nature of children's strategies have changed frequently and dramatically over the decades. Despite disagreements among researchers concerning what constitutes a strategy and what children of different ages do when they behave strategically, there does seem to be a consensus that strategies develop. Whatever they are, they change in frequency of use, in effectiveness, and in form over the childhood years.

A BRIEF HISTORY OF STRATEGIES IN COGNITIVE DEVELOPMENT

Contemporary research and theory in developmental differences in children's strategies trace their ancestry back to the late 1950s and early 1960s. Two movements in psychology that were popular then had great influence on the course of cognitive development research, particularly research in strategy development. The first was *verbal mediation theory,* which was an extension of the behaviorism fashionable at the time. The second was the emerging science of *cognitive psychology,* developing out of information theory formulated in the 1940s. Later changes in perspective concerning the nature of strategies and their development (e.g., the importance of metacognition) can be seen as branches of these ancestral roots.

Strategies as Intervening Mediators

The beginnings of interest in children's strategies can be traced to the neobehaviorists. During the first half of this century, many researchers investigated stimulus–response explanations of learning (see Hilgard, 1987). Some theorists proposed that learning could better be explained in terms of intervening *mediators,* covert stimuli and responses that operated between observable stimuli and responses, represented by *S-r-s-R.* This first internal mechanism posited by the neobehaviorists paved the way for research in children's strategy development.

The Development of Verbal Mediators

An early demonstration of how mediators could be used to help explain developmental phenomena is seen in Kuenne's (1946) work with discrimination learning. On a near/far transposition test with children ages three to six, Kuenne found that children at all ages were able to consistently answer correctly the near test, but only the older children consistently answered correctly the far test. Kuenne proposed that the younger children's deficits were due to a failure to construct verbal mediators of their perceptual experiences in the task. Consequently, although they were able to complete the near transposition task on a perceptual basis, they were unable to apply the correct solution on the far test.

Mediational theorists in the 1960s had considerable influence on the burgeoning field of cognitive development in the United States. Perhaps most influential were the Kendlers (e.g., Kendler & Kendler, 1959, 1962; Kendler, Kendler, & Wells, 1960). They postulated that, in discrimination learning problems, young children respond to the absolute physical properties of a stimulus, whereas older children and adults respond to relational properties. The mechanisms permitting such relational, or conceptual, encoding were hypothesized to be covert, verbal mediators. Similar explanations of developmental differences in the use of verbal mediators to solve problems could be found in early research investigating crossmodal transfer (e.g., Birch

& Lefford, 1963; Blank & Bridger, 1964) and memory (e.g., Flavell, Beach, & Chinsky, 1966), among other tasks.

The neobehaviorists did not refer to covert, verbal mediators as strategies, however. The verbal mediators used by children were hypothesized to be mental, were used to facilitate task performance, were apparently available to consciousness, and were implemented deliberately (or at least could be used deliberately in certain situations). Thus, the verbal mediators postulated by the neobehaviorists of the 1960s would qualify as cognitive strategies. However, the significance of their work lies not in the fact that it provided discoveries and interpretations that have continued to be influential years after their publication, but rather because mediation theory was the impetus for a line of research and theorizing that was to dominate much of cognitive development for the next decade. (Developmental research on the verbal control of behavior by the Soviet psychologists Vygotsky, 1962, and Luria, 1961, was also influential and was integrated by some psychologists with the ideas of the neobehaviorists; for example, Miller, Shelton, and Flavell, 1970; Wozniak, 1972.)

Mediation and Production Deficiencies

Working in the tradition of the mediation theorists, Reese (1962) described young children as being *mediationally deficient,* or unable to use a mediator. In other words, a potentially effective strategy (or mediator) does not facilitate task performance. Mediationally deficient children, presumably, do not have the necessary mental apparatus (or hardware, using the computer metaphor) to use the mediator. Flavell (1970) furthered this line of reasoning. He coined the term *production deficiency* to describe children who are able to use strategies effectively when instructed, but do not use them spontaneously.

Flavell and his colleagues developed a unique method for investigating children's production of verbal mediation strategies (Flavell, Beach, & Chinsky, 1966). Children in the kindergarten, second, and fifth grades were instructed to remember the serial order of a set of items. During a 15-second delay between item presentation and recall, the children wore a space helmet with a visor that covered their eyes but exposed their lips. One of the experimenters trained himself to lip-read the semicovert verbalizations of the stimulus item names, and these observations were used to distinguish the children who produced verbal mediators, in the form of rehearsal, from those who did not. Using this method, Flavell et al. demonstrated that production of the rehearsal strategy in a serial recall task increased with age and was associated with level of performance.

Further research using this method provided stronger support for the contention that children's verbalizations do indeed mediate task performance, by showing that children who do not spontaneously produce such mediators can be trained to do so with a corresponding improvement in memory. For example, Keeney, Cannizzo, and Flavell (1967) classified first graders as Producers or Nonproducers based on whether they rehearsed in an initial testing session. In a subsequent session, the children were given instruction and practice in using verbal rehearsal, followed by a series of trials in which they were told to use the rehearsal strategy. Keeney et al. found that the Nonproducers did implement the strategy when instructed, and that this resulted in recall levels comparable to that of the Producers (see also Hagen & Kingsley, 1968).

Training Children To Be Strategic

This early work by Flavell and his colleagues, and the idea that children could often benefit from the imposition of a strategy that they had not used spontaneously, led to dozens of training studies on a variety of tasks. Basically, these studies were based on the logic (which we believe continues to be sound today) that by successfully training children to use a strategy, we can sometimes learn about the mechanisms involved in the ontogeny of strategy acquisition. The success of this approach can be seen clearly in the research most directly related to the original paper of Flavell et al. (1966)—the role of rehearsal in children's memory (e.g., Asarnow & Meichenbaum, 1979; Hagen, Hargrave, & Ross, 1973; Kennedy & Miller, 1976; Ornstein & Naus, 1978; Ornstein, Naus, & Stone, 1977).

The idea that young children are production deficient was used by investigators studying aspects of cognition other than rehearsal. Through a plethora of training studies, it became clear that young children could be instructed to use many of the strategies previously thought to be available only to older children. Training studies demonstrated that production-deficient children could be instructed to use memory strategies such as retrieval cues (e.g., Kobasigawa, 1974; Williams & Goulet, 1975), organization (e.g., Bjorklund, Ornstein, & Haig, 1977; Moely, Olson, Halwes, & Flavell, 1969), and elaboration (e.g., Danner & Taylor, 1973; Rohwer & Bean, 1973; Yuille & Catchpole, 1973). In other areas, researchers investigating phenomena brought to light by Piaget (e.g., conservation, transitive inferences, and class inclusion) demonstrated that, under the right instructional or stimulus conditions, young children could be trained to perform tasks previously thought to be beyond their abilities (e.g.,

Brainerd, 1974; Bryant & Trabasso, 1971; Gelman, 1969). The thrust of this research gave the impression that young children were far more competent than we had previously believed, and that by discovering the right strategy and proper instructional conditions, there were few cognitive tasks that young children could not be trained to perform.

Although young children could be encouraged by instructions to employ strategies, it became clear that the younger the child, the more intensive the training required to prompt effective strategy use (e.g., Bray, Justice, Ferguson, & Simon, 1977; Kobasigawa, 1974; Pressley, Levin, & Bryant, 1983; Rohwer, 1973). For instance, Moely et al. (1969) instructed children in kindergarten, first, third, and fifth grades to remember a group of categorically related pictures. The children were told they could move the pictures or do anything they wished to help them remember. Only the fifth graders spontaneously organized the pictures by categories. Subsequently, children were either instructed to use an organizational strategy or merely told the names of the categories by the experimenter. Moely et al. found that third graders produced the strategy under both conditions, whereas kindergarten and first-grade children required full instructions to use the strategy. Evidence of differential emphasis of training instruction as a function of age was not limited to memory, but was observed in a wide range of cognitive tasks (e.g., see Brown, Bransford, Ferrara, & Campione, 1983).

Not only were developmental differences discovered in the extent of prompting required to train children to use a strategy, but once younger children had learned a strategy they were less apt to transfer a strategy than older children (e.g., Bjorklund et al., 1977; Scribner & Cole, 1972). As with training, they required more prompting before any evidence of generalization was noted (e.g., Ringle & Springer, 1980). The problem of successful training but unsuccessful transfer raised the questions of what children were learning during these training experiments, and, if they were learning strategies, why were they apparently confined to the training task, at least for young children?

Issues of training and transfer, with their origins in the neobehaviorism of mediation theory, still concern developmental psychologists. One central concern of contemporary researchers is the issue of context specificity. Children who are capable of using a strategy effectively in some situations seem unable, or at least unwilling, to use one in similar situations. Opinions about what factors mediate children's acquisition and transfer of a strategy have changed over the years (e.g., Lodico, Ghatala, Levin, Pressley, & Bell, 1983;

Paris, Newman, & McVey, 1982), but many of the questions addressed by the early verbal mediation theorists continue to be posed
by developmental psychologists today.

The work of Flavell and his colleagues is the cornerstone for 2
decades of research in memory development, much of it dealing with
the development and modification of strategies. More than 20 years
after its publication, it is interesting to reread the original Flavell,
Beach, and Chinsky (1966) paper. This seminal article of the memory
and strategy development literature is steeped in the language of
mediation theory, making it clear that the origins of contemporary
research and theorizing in children's strategy development are in the
neobehaviorist tradition.

The Cognitive Revolution

Information-Processing Approaches to Thinking

About the same time that developmental psychologists were becoming enamored with verbal mediators, psychologists interested in adult
thinking were drawn to the computer as a metaphor, and modern
cognitive psychology was developing as a discipline. Psychologists
began thinking of humans as information processors and of human
behavior as following plans much as a computer follows a program
(Miller, Galanter, & Pribram, 1960). Inherent in this new focus was an
interest in strategic processing. For example, George Miller's (1956)
influential paper on the "magical number seven, plus or minus two,"
described how people facilitate their performance on memory tasks
by chunking discrete bits of information into meaningful units that
can then be stored as a single unit. Chunking, and other similar
means of organizing nonassociated information, became popular
topics for psychologists and were some of the first intensely investigated strategies of the information processing era (e.g., Bousfield, 1953; Mandler, 1967).

Theories of attention took center stage in early cognitive psychology (e.g., Broadbent, 1958) and became coupled with multistore information-processing models that distinguished structural features,
or "hardware," from processes, or "software." For example, Atkinson
and Shiffrin's (1968) memory system consisted of a sensory register
that receives information from the outside world and passes it into a
short-term store. Information may then be transferred from the
short-term to the long-term store, where it can be retained in-
definitely. Atkinson and Shiffrin proposed that controlled processes
such as rehearsal and organization are applied in the short-term store

to maintain information, to solve problems, and to transfer information to the long-term store.

The view of humans as information processors has remained in vogue, and the idea of controlled processes has been maintained in contemporary theory. For example, in the 1970s controlled processes, or strategies, were viewed as existing on a continuum with respect to the amount of one's limited mental resources that were required for an operation's execution (e.g., Hasher & Zacks, 1979; Kahneman, 1973; Posner & Snyder, 1975; Shiffrin & Schneider, 1977). At one extreme were highly effortful processes that were hypothesized to (a) be available to consciousness, (b) interfere with other processes, (c) improve with practice, (d) vary with individual differences in intelligence or motivation, and (e) require substantial amounts of mental effort (i.e., they use one's limited information-processing resources). At the other extreme were automatic processes that were hypothesized to (a) be unavailable to consciousness, (b) not interfere with the execution of other processes, (c) not improve with practice, (d) not vary as a function of individual differences in intelligence or motivation, and (e) require no mental effort (i.e., they use none of one's limited mental resources). Processes that began as effortful could become automatic via practice.

This concept of a continuum of mental effort requirement was greeted warmly by developmentalists, who proposed age-related changes in the amount of mental effort children required to implement a strategy (e.g., Bjorklund, 1987; Case, 1985). Developmental differences in the efficiency of processing (i.e., the amount of mental effort required to activate operations) have been hypothesized as central to strategy development on a wide range of tasks including arithmetic (e.g., Brainerd, 1983), reading (e.g., Daneman & Blennerhassett, 1984), selective attention (e.g., DeMarie–Dreblow & Miller, 1988), memory (e.g., Bjorklund & Harnishfeger, 1987; Guttentag, 1984), problem solving (e.g., Case, 1985), and search behavior in young children (e.g., DeLoache & Brown, 1983). These issues continue to guide research today.

Also developing out of the cognitive psychology of the late 1960s and early 1970s were questions concerning the nature of knowledge representation. For example, psychologists developed models of semantic memory (e.g., Collins & Loftus, 1975; Collins & Quillian, 1969) and postulated that the manner in which information was represented in semantic memory affected the way information was processed (e.g., Rosch, 1975; Smith, Shoben, & Rips, 1974). Developmental psychologists soon began to investigate age-related differences in children's representation of knowledge (e.g., Anglin,

1970, 1977; McCauley, Weil, & Sperber, 1976; Saltz, Soller, & Sigel, 1972), and proposed that developmental differences in children's knowledge base significantly influence cognitive task performance, including the use of strategies (e.g., Bjorklund, 1985; Chi, 1978, 1985; Ornstein & Naus, 1985; Siegler, 1981). The issue of knowledge-related differences in children's use of strategies continues to be central to many research programs today, and is highlighted in several chapters of this book.

The Development of Strategies

Researchers interested in adult thinking were not the only ones to jump on the cognitive bandwagon of the 1960s. Whereas cognitive psychologists were examining the ramifications of the computer metaphor for adult thought, groups of developmental psychologists became interested in illuminating the nature of children's knowledge and the processes children used to solve problems. For example, some of the first developmental "strategy" research was conducted by John Hagen and his colleagues, initially extending Broadbent's (1958) model of attention to children (e.g., Hagen, 1967; Hagen & Sabo, 1967; Maccoby & Hagen, 1965). This work eventually led Hagen to the study of children's memory strategies (e.g., Hagen & Kingsley, 1968; Kingsley & Hagen, 1969), an area that became the hotbed of strategy-development work in the 1970s.

Perhaps the most influential developmental work to arise from the early cognitive viewpoint of human thinking was that of Jerome Bruner and his colleagues (Bruner, Olver, & Greenfield, 1966). Approaching the problem of cognitive development from a neo-Piagetian perspective, Bruner and his colleagues proposed that, with development, the child's representational system is transformed. Following Piaget (1952), infants and toddlers were hypothesized to represent their world via enactive (i.e., sensorimotor) codes, which served as the basis for the ikonic (i.e., perceptually literal) representation of the preschool child. Sometime between the ages of 5 and 7 years, representation is transformed again and becomes symbolic, mediated primarily by language. (Notice the similarity here with the theorizing of the verbal mediationists, whose neobehavioral philosophy appears diametrically opposed to that of neo-Piagetians.) With the appearance of symbolic representation, children become capable of approaching problems strategically (Olson, 1966).

Initial evidence for a developing ability to behave strategically came from a study in which 6-, 8-, and 11-year-old children were shown an array of 42 pictures of common objects and asked to find which one the experimenter had in mind (Mosher & Hornsby, 1966). In this task, similar to the parlor game of Twenty Questions, children could only ask questions that could be answered with a yes or no. Mosher and Hornsby described two general types of strategies children used in approaching this task. Constraint-seeking strategists attempted to constrain the number of alternatives by asking questions that eliminated large numbers of the pictures (e.g., "Is it in the top half of the pictures?"). Hypothesis-scanning strategists tested a single hypothesis with each question (e.g., "Is it the duck?"). Mosher and Hornsby found that children over the age range studied showed a developmental pattern of increasing reliance on the more effective constraint-seeking strategy and less reliance on hypothesis scanning.

Research into children's hypothesis testing continued into the 1970s, expanding on the simple paradigm of Mosher and Hornsby (e.g., Gholson, 1980; Gholson & Danziger, 1975; Gholson, Levine, & Phillips, 1972; Phillips & Levine, 1974). For example, using discrimination-learning tasks, Gholson and his colleagues described a broader range of hypothesis-testing strategies than suggested by Mosher and Hornsby. They found age-related differences in the efficiency of strategies that children chose to use (see Gholson, 1980). The findings from the hypothesis-testing research were consistent with those of the verbal mediation research in that both found substantial changes in strategy selection between the ages of 5 and 7 years. Drastic changes in children's cognition during this age period had been noted previously by psychologists of a variety of orientations (e.g., Piaget, 1965; White, 1965). The new theorists, coming from a diversity of perspectives themselves, proposed that an important source of this change was in children's abilities and inclinations to use strategies.

The Importance of Metacognition

From the research done following the production-mediation metaphor, strategy development was seen as a progression from nonproduction to spontaneous production of effective strategies, made possible by the gradual development of increasing planfulness and the acquisition of the component strategic skills (e.g., Flavell, 1970). In the late 1970s and early 1980s, a different view of strategy development achieved prominence. This view emphasized higher order strategies or processes that control the use of various cognitive strategies. Flavell (1971) coined the term *metamemory* to refer to one's potentially verbalizable knowledge about memory storage and retrieval, and distinguished among several varieties of metamemory, including a sensitivity to the need for effortful memory strategies and a knowledge of the person, task, and strategy variables that influence memory performance (Flavell & Wellman, 1977). In a seminal study, Flavell and his colleagues (Kreutzer, Leonard, & Flavell, 1975) interviewed children about their knowledge of various memory situations and thereby demonstrated the developmental course of metamemory in young children. Following from the interest in children's knowledge about their memory processes came a focus on how children's metamemory knowledge might influence their memory performance (Brown & DeLoache, 1978). Corresponding with this, research interest shifted from a focus on teaching children a single strategy to employ in a single situation to a focus on examining children's arsenal of cognitive strategies and how children integrate and monitor strategy use.

The importance of knowledge about one's cognitive functioning is not limited to memory situations, but is central to theories of cognition and its development in general (e.g., Brown et al., 1983; Chi, 1978; Sternberg, 1985). In fact, there seems to be few cognitive phenomena today without a corresponding "meta." For example, children's metacognition has been investigated for attention (e.g., Miller, 1985), imitation (e.g., Green, Bjorklund, & Quinn–Cobb, 1988), reading comprehension (e.g., Paris & Oka, 1986), communication (e.g., Whitehurst & Sonnenschein, 1985), and self-monitoring (e.g., Wellman, 1977).

Despite its popularity, few contemporary developmental psychologists would propose that good metacognition causes good cognition, a connection that was implicitly searched for in the early days of metacognitive research. Metacognition today is seen as being integrally related to other aspects of strategy use and cannot be studied fruitfully without assessing other aspects of the learning situation. For example, Pressley and his colleagues proposed a model of the "Good Strategy User" (e.g., Pressley, Borkowski, & Schneider, 1987; Pressley, Forrest–Pressley, Elliot–Faust, & Miller, 1985; Schneider & Pressley, 1989), arguing that "just being able to execute a variety of cognitive processes [is] not sufficient to be considered a good strategy user, and that strategic, metacognitive, and knowledge variables [are] related in complex ways" (Pressley et al., 1987, p. 89). In this and other contemporary models (e.g., Brown, 1978; Flavell, 1978; Schneider, 1985), metacognition is seen both as a cause and consequence of other aspects of cognition, and researchers are striving to make more explicit the connection among metacognitive and cognitive variables with respect to children's strategy use.

NEW TOPICS IN STRATEGY DEVELOPMENT

Many of the issues that have influenced research in strategy development over the past 2 decades can be traced to related issues in adult cognition. These issues, which include the expenditure of mental resources and the role of knowledge base, have been transformed to fit the peculiar nature of developmental cognition and continue to guide the research of many contemporary developmental psychologists interested in strategy development. However, in the 1980s at least two new areas related to strategy development arose, and we end this section by reviewing them briefly. The first is the integration of developmental differences and individual differences in strategy use, and the second is the spontaneous use of strategies by young children.

Integrating Developmental with Individual Differences

Developmental psychologists are in the business of describing and explaining *developmental function,* the course that development takes over time; in the present case, the course of strategy development. However, any time we describe children of a given age as using a particular strategy, we are overstating our case. There is variability in the patterns of development. Different children of the same age will use different strategies (interindividual differences), and a single child may use a variety of strategies on similar tasks in different contexts (intraindividual differences).

Individual differences in strategy use is not a new topic in the study of child cognition. In fact, interindividual differences in children's problem-solving approaches filled the literature in the 1960s (e.g., Kagan, Rosman, Day, Albert, & Philips, 1964; Witkin, Goodenough, & Karp, 1967), and strategy differences have long been hypothesized to be important in distinguishing children of different intellectual levels or aptitudes (e.g., Campione, Brown, Ferrara, Jones, & Steinberg, 1985; Ceci, 1983; Worden, 1983). However, it has been only recently that psychologists studying developmental function have found it important to pay attention to individual differences in children's strategy use (see e.g., Bjorklund, 1989; Siegler, 1988).

Intraindividual differences in children's strategies have also not gone unnoticed, and attention to intraindividual differences has been particularly keen for children's arithmetic. Research in the past decade has well documented developmental changes in the strategies children use to solve addition and subtraction problems (e.g., Ashcraft, 1982; Groen & Parkman, 1972). Children's arithmetic computation was hypothesized to progress from using overt methods (e.g., counting on fingers), to simple covert methods (e.g., setting a mental counter for the first addend and increasing the counter by increments of one until the second addend has been counted), to fact retrieval (being able to retrieve the answer from long-term memory without need for computation). However, research by Siegler and his colleagues demonstrated that such a description of children's strategic approaches to arithmetic problems, arrived at by averaging over groups of children, did not reflect how any individual child solved a problem (e.g., Siegler, 1987, in press; Siegler & Shrager, 1984). Siegler demonstrated that there were intraindividual differences, with any given child using a variety of strategies depending on the difficulty of the arithmetic problem. Such an approach, which has been applied to nonarithmetic tasks as well (e.g., McGilly & Siegler, 1989), causes researchers to rethink exactly what is involved in strategy development. Not only do different children at a particular age use different strategies on a task (i.e., interindividual differences), but a given child has available to him or her a variety of strategies, which can be used as the task requires. The job of the psychologist becomes more complicated, having to describe not only ontogenetic changes in strategy use, but also the conditions under which children will use the variety of operations they possess.

Strategies in Infants and Young Children

Perhaps the greatest change in opinion concerning the development of children's strategies over the past 20 years involves the age at which children are believed to begin using strategies spontaneously. During the 1970s, the production-deficient view of strategy development led researchers to investigate strategy use by comparing older and younger children's use of strategies such as rehearsal and clustering. Very young children do not use these strategies. Not surprisingly then, the common view from this period was that children do not really use strategies (at least not spontaneously) before age six or so. Such ideas are now being challenged.

Wellman (1988) argued that very young children are frequently strategic, and that some of the age changes in memory performance throughout the early years are attributable to increasing mnemonic proficiency. He defined strategies as deliberate and as a means to produce an end. That is, strategies should be effective. Given this, Wellman proposed that many strategies of very young children are "faulty." Young children's strategies may be ineffective because they are inappropriate for a particular task. Wellman maintained that strategy development proceeds from the gradually increasing effectiveness of faulty strategies, rather than from a position of nonproduction to production of strategies. Ornstein, Baker–Ward, and Naus (1988) proposed a similar theory. They believe that strategy development should be seen as a broad continuum of skill and argued that strategic behavior is seen even in very young children, although such strategies will be different from those used by older children and often of limited effectiveness (see also Bjorklund & Muir, 1988).

Although the view that preschool children use strategies has only recently received wide acceptance, evidence that they are strategic has been available for over a decade. For instance, Wellman, Ritter, and Flavell (1975) asked 3-and 4-year-olds to remember the location of a toy dog for 40 seconds while the experimenter left the room. They found that children who were asked to remember the location looked at, pointed to, and touched the cup under which the dog was placed more than children who had not been told to remember the location. This strategic behavior was associated with greater recall. More recently, DeLoache, Cassidy, and Brown (1985) asked 18- to 23-month-old toddlers to remember the location of a stuffed Big Bird doll. They found that the children were strategic: They repeated the name of the toy or the location where it was hidden, looked at the hiding place, and pointed to it. Children who were not told to remember where Big Bird was did not do these things.

However, recent evidence also makes it clear that the strategies of young children often lack the effectiveness of those used by their older peers. For instance, Baker–Ward, Ornstein, and Holden (1984) asked some 4-, 5-, and 6-year-olds to remember a set of small toys, whereas others were simply told to play with the toys. During a 2-minute period in which the children were free to play with the toys, the experimenters observed more strategic behavior, such as naming, scanning, and covert rehearsal, for children in the "remember" condition than for children in the "play" condition. However, for the 4-year-olds, there was no difference in their level of recall between the "remember" and "play" conditions despite greater strategy use by the "remember" children. This suggests minimal effectiveness of these rudimentary strategies for the youngest group (see also De-Marie–Dreblow & Miller, 1988; Miller & Harris, 1988).

Even more surprising, perhaps, is the interpretation that strategies are not the sole preserve of language-possessing children, but can be observed in the preverbal infant. For example, Sophian and her colleagues (e.g., Sophian, Larkin, & Kadane, 1985; Sophian & Wellman, 1983) proposed that infants' search behaviors (as reflected by object permanence-type tasks) can be described in terms of strategies. Sophian argued that although there are certainly age differences in young children's search behaviors, there is a basic continuity in cognitive ability between infancy and childhood. Rather than viewing childhood cognition as a dramatic reorganization of conceptual skills, Sophian saw it as a development in capacities for consistency, memory, and attention (Sophian & Sage, 1985). In investigating the same search task with infants and children, Sophian proposed a rule-based model for infant search. This model takes into consideration infants' inconsistencies and tendencies to follow irrelevant and divergent rules simultaneously (Sophian et al., 1985). In this sense, Sophian and Wellman agreed that although infants are capable of strategic behavior, their strategies are often faulty.

CONTEMPORARY VIEWS OF STRATEGY DEVELOPMENT

Consistent with the "new" view that cognitive strategies are found early in development, this book begins with Willatt's (chapter 2) discussion of strategic behavior in infants and toddlers. Willatts proposes that very young infants have goals and engage in a form of problem solving. Their performance is always constrained by the limitations of their age, but Willatts contends that these young children do behave strategically, and if we approach the study of infancy with the appropriate methodology, we will be able to glimpse their problem-solving capabilities. Willatts proposes that infants are much more capable than Piaget believed, demonstrating goal-directed behavior in the first 6 months of life.

The next three chapters focus on the importance of interactions among the diverse factors that influence strategy development, particularly the development of memory strategies. The chapter by Folds, Foot, Guttentag, and Ornstein (chapter 3) examines strategy use in the preteen child. The authors propose that an expansion of earlier definitions of strategies is needed that addresses the component processes in strategy development. Metacognitive, motivational, contextual, and efficiency factors are deemed necessary for defining strategy development. Their chapter is concerned with three dimensions of strategy performance: consistency, effectiveness, and intentionality. Although a child's intention to reach a goal may be the key definitional characteristic of strategic behavior, the manner and situations in which he or she shows that intentionality are often difficult to demonstrate.

Bjorklund, Muir-Broaddus and Schneider (chapter 4) also deal with strategy development in preteen children. They discuss the relationships among a child's knowledge base, the efficiency of mental processing, a child's metacognitive knowledge, and the ways in which these factors interact with strategy development. Howe and O'Sullivan (chapter 5) take a similar approach to that of Bjorklund et al., although the conclusions they reach about the definition of strategies are quite different. They propose that the boundaries of strategic behavior should be widened to include all relevant cognitive behaviors used to maximize performance on a particular task.

Miller's chapter (chapter 6) outlines the development of selective attention strategies. The picture of strategy development is provided by Miller's research program involving an innovative methodology. In most studies, children are shown an array of stimuli that are covered by doors. The children are instructed to remember only some of the stimuli behind various doors, and the selective-attention task involves children's ability to attend to only the required information. Using this procedure, Miller is able to define strategies by observing the child's door-opening behaviors. Miller's chapter describes a developmental sequence in strategy attainment, and she proposes a resource explanation for improvements in strategy performance.

The chapters by Ashcraft (chapter 7) and Bisanz and LeFevre (chapter 8) discuss the development of strategic behavior within the realm of mental arithmetic. Similar patterns are discussed in these two chapters, although Ashcraft and Bisanz and LeFevre differ greatly in how they actually apply the term *strategy*. Ashcraft discusses some serious roadblocks to further research investigating children's mental arithmetic, and he proposes new avenues for future research in children's mathematical strategies. Following the recent trend in studies of children's arithmetic, Bisanz and LeFevre and Ashcraft concur that individual differences in strategy use need serious consideration.

Garner's chapter (chapter 9) examines children's strategic behavior in reading. Whereas adults frequently engage in various strategic attempts to aid the comprehension of text, children often fail to behave strategically. Garner demonstrates that this failure to use strategic processing in reading is due to a number of factors. Among these are children's poor comprehension-monitoring skills, poor understanding of expository text formats, inability to distinguish important from unimportant information, and failure to give up ineffective strategies to learn more effective ones.

Gholson, Morgan, Dattel and Pierce (chapter 10) examine strategic behavior in the form of analogical problem solving. They describe how children and adults learn to solve analogical reasoning problems of the sort typified by the missionaries/cannibals problem. Gholson et al. also examine generalization strategies, as children attempt to transfer their understanding of the training problem to a different, but closely related problem. Although strategic behavior in analogical reasoning occurs spontaneously only late in development, Gholson et al. propose that the rudimentary skills necessary for strategies are present even in preschoolers.

In the final chapter (chapter 11), we examine definitional issues relating to strategies as reflected by the contributors to this book. Although we do not assume to resolve the definitional conundrum, we view *strategy* in the context of contemporary research and forecast the future of this term and the concepts it connotes. We also look at the origins of children's strategies as reflected by the chapters herein, and propose that the development of self-awareness is one issue that has not been given the serious consideration it deserves as a key component in the development of strategic behavior.

ACKNOWLEDGMENTS

We would like to thank Barbara Bjorklund, Brandi Green, Katharine Lyon, and Jacqueline Muir-Broaddus for their comments on earlier versions of this chapter.

REFERENCES

Anglin, J. M. (1970). *The growth of word meaning.* Cambridge, MA: MIT Press.
Anglin, J. M. (1977). *Word, object, and conceptual development.* New York: Norton.
Asarnow, J. R., & Meichenbaum, D. (1979). Verbal rehearsal and serial recall: The mediational training of kindergarten children. *Child Development, 50,* 1173–1177.
Ashcraft, M. H. (1982). The development of mental arithmetic: A chronometric approach. *Developmental Review, 2,* 213–236.
Atkinson, R. C., & Shiffrin, R. M. (1968). Human memory: A proposed system and its control processes. In K. W. Spence & J. T. Spence (Eds.), *The psychology of learning and motivation: Advances in research and theory* (Vol. 2, pp. 90–197). New York: Academic Press.
Baker–Ward, L., Ornstein, P. A., & Holden, D. J. (1984). The expression of memorization in early childhood. *Journal of Experimental Child Psychology, 37,* 555–575.
Birch, H. G., & Lefford, A. (1963). Intersensory development in children. *Monographs of the Society for Research in Child Development, 28,* (5, Serial No. 89).
Bjorklund, D. F. (1985). The role of conceptual knowledge in the development of organization in children's memory. In C. J. Brainerd & M. Pressley (Eds.), *Basic processes in memory development: Progress in cognitive development research* (pp. 103–142). New York: Springer.

Bjorklund, D. F. (1987). How age changes in knowledge base contribute to the development of organization in children's memory: An interpretive review. *Developmental Review, 7,* 93–130.

Bjorklund, D. F. (1989). *Children's thinking: Developmental function and individual differences.* Pacific Grove, CA: Brooks-Cole.

Bjorklund, D. F., & Harnishfeger, K. K. (1987). Developmental differences in the mental effort requirements for the use of an organizational strategy in free recall. *Journal of Experimental Child Psychology, 44,* 109–125.

Bjorklund, D. F., & Muir, J. E. (1988). Children's development of free recall memory: Remembering on their own. In R. Vasta (Ed.), *Annals of child development* (Vol. 5, pp. 79–123). Greenwich, CT: JAI Press.

Bjorklund, D. F., Ornstein, P. A., & Haig, J. R. (1977). Development of organization and recall: Training in the use of organizational techniques. *Developmental Psychology, 13,* 175–183.

Blank, M., & Bridger, W. (1964). Crossmodal transfer in nursery school children. *Journal of Comparative and Physiological Psychology, 58,* 227–232.

Bousfield, W. A. (1953). The occurrence of clustering in recall of randomly arranged associates. *Journal of General Psychology, 49,* 229–240.

Brainerd, C. J. (1974). Training and transfer of transitivity, conservation, and class inclusion of length. *Child Development, 45,* 324–334.

Brainerd, C. J. (1983). Working-memory systems and cognitive development. In C. J. Brainerd (Ed.), *Recent advances in cognitive developmental theory: Progress in cognitive development research* (pp. 168–238). New York: Springer.

Bray, N. W., Justice, E. M., Ferguson, R. P., & Simon, D. L. (1977). Developmental changes in the effects of instructions on production deficient children. *Child Development, 48,* 1019–1026.

Broadbent, D. E. (1958). *Perception and communication.* London: Pergamon Press.

Brown, A. L. (1978). Knowing when, where, and how to remember: A problem of metacognition. In R. Glasser (Ed.), *Advances in instructional psychology* (pp. 77–165). New York: Halstead Press.

Brown, A. L., Bransford, J. D., Ferrara, R. A., & Campione, J. C. (1983). Learning, remembering, and understanding. In J. H. Flavell & E. M. Markman (Eds.), *Handbook of child psychology: Cognitive development* (Vol. 3, pp. 77–166). New York: Wiley.

Brown, A. L., & DeLoache, J. S. (1978). Skills, plans and self-regulation. In R. S. Siegler (Ed.), *Children's thinking: What develops?* (pp. 3–36). Hillsdale, NJ: Lawrence Erlbaum Associates.

Bruner, J. S., Olver, R. R., & Greenfield, P. M. (Eds.). (1966). *Studies in cognitive growth.* New York: Wiley.

Bryant, P. E., & Trabasso, T. (1971). Transitive inference and memory in young children. *Nature, 232,* 456–458.

Campione, J. C., Brown, A. L., Ferrara, R. A., Jones, R. S., & Steinberg, E. (1985). Breakdowns in flexible use of information: Intelligence related differences in transfer following equivalent learning performance. *Intelligence, 9,* 297–315.

Case, R. (1985). *Intellectual development: Birth to adulthood.* New York: Academic Press.

Ceci, S. J. (1983). Automatic and purposive semantic processing characteristics of normal and language/learning disabled (L/LD) children. *Developmental Psychology, 19,* 427–439.

Chi, M. T. H. (1978). Knowledge structure and memory development. In R. Siegler (Ed.), *Children's thinking: What develops?* (pp. 73–96). Hillsdale, NJ: Lawrence Erlbaum Associates.

Chi, M. T. H. (1985). Interactive roles of knowledge and strategies in the development of organized sorting and recall. In S. F. Chipman, J. W. Segal, & R. Glaser (Eds.),

Thinking and learning skills: Research and open questions (Vol. 2, pp. 457–483). Hillsdale, NJ: Lawrence Erlbaum Associates.

Collins, A. M., & Loftus, E. F. (1975). A spreading activation theory of semantic processing. *Psychological Review, 82,* 407–428.

Collins, A. M., & Quillian, M. R. (1969). Retrieval time from semantic memory. *Journal of Verbal Learning and Verbal Behavior, 8,* 240–248.

Daneman, M., & Blennerhassett, A. (1984). How to assess the listening comprehension skills of prereaders. *Journal of Educational Psychology, 76,* 1372–1381.

Danner, F. W., & Taylor, A. M. (1973). Integrated pictures and relational imagery training in children's learning. *Journal of Experimental Child Psychology, 16,* 47–54.

DeLoache, J. S., & Brown, A. L. (1983). Very young children's memory for the location of objects in a large scale environment. *Child Development, 54,* 125–137.

DeLoache, J. S., Cassidy, D. J., & Brown, A. L. (1985). Precursors of mnemonic strategies in very young children's memory for the location of hidden objects. *Child Development, 56,* 125–137.

DeMarie–Dreblow, D., & Miller, P. H. (1988). The development of children's strategies for selective attention: Evidence for a transitional period. *Child Development, 59,* 1504–1513.

Flavell, J. H. (1970). Developmental studies of mediated memory. In H. W. Reese & L. P. Lipsitt (Eds.), *Advances in child development and child behavior* (Vol. 5, pp. 181–211). New York: Academic Press.

Flavell, J. H. (1971). Stage-related properties of cognitive development. *Cognitive Psychology, 2,* 421–453.

Flavell, J. H. (1978). Metacognitive development. In J. M. Scandura & C. J. Brainerd (Eds.), *Structural/process theories of complex human behavior* (pp. 213–247). Alphen a.d. Rign, The Netherlands: Sijthoff & Noordhoff.

Flavell, J. H., Beach, D. R., & Chinsky, J. H. (1966). Spontaneous verbal rehearsal in a memory task as a function of age. *Child Development, 37,* 283–299.

Flavell, J. H., & Wellman, H. M. (1977). Metamemory. In R. V. Kail, Jr. & J. W. Hagen (Eds.), *Perspectives on the development of memory and cognition* (pp. 3–33). Hillsdale, NJ: Lawrence Erlbaum Associates.

Gelman, R. (1969). Conservation acquisition: A problem of learning to attend to relevant attributes. *Journal of Experimental Child Psychology, 7,* 167–187.

Gholson, B. (1980). *The cognitive-developmental basis of human learning: Studies in hypothesis testing.* New York: Academic Press.

Gholson, B., & Danziger, S. (1975). Effects of two levels of stimulus complexity upon hypothesis sampling systems among second and sixth grade children. *Journal of Experimental Child Psychology, 20,* 105–118.

Gholson, B., Levine, M., & Phillips, S. (1972). Hypotheses, strategies, and stereotypes in discrimination learning. *Journal of Experimental Child Psychology, 13,* 423–446.

Green, B. L., Bjorklund, D. F., & Quinn–Cobb, C. (1988, March). *Development of meta-imitation.* Paper presented at the Conference for Human Development, Charleston, SC.

Groen, G. J., & Parkman, J. M. (1972). A chronometric analysis of simple addition. *Psychological Review, 79,* 329–343.

Guttentag, R. E. (1984). The mental effort requirement of cumulative rehearsal: A developmental study. *Journal of Experimental Child Psychology, 37,* 92–106.

Hagen, J. W. (1967). The effect of distraction on selective attention. *Child Development, 38,* 685–694.

Hagen, J. W., Hargrave, S., & Ross, W. (1973). Prompting and rehearsal in short-term memory. *Child Development, 44,* 201–204.

Hagen, J. W., & Kingsley, P. R. (1968). Labeling effects in short-term memory. *Child Development, 39,* 113–121.

Hagen, J. W., & Sabo, R. A. (1967). A developmental study of selective attention. *Merrill–Palmer Quarterly, 13,* 159–172.

Hasher, L., & Zacks, R. T. (1979). Automatic and effortful processes in memory. *Journal of Experimental Psychology: General, 108,* 356–388.

Hilgard, E. R. (1987). *Psychology in America: A historical survey.* San Diego: Harcourt, Brace, Jovanovich.

Kagan, J., Rosman, B. L., Day, D., Albert, J., & Phillips, W. (1964). Information processing in the child: Significance of analytic and reflective attitudes. *Psychological Monographs, 78* (Serial No. 578).

Kahneman, D. (1973). *Attention and effort.* Englewood Cliffs, NJ: Prentice-Hall.

Keeney, T. J., Cannizzo, S. R., & Flavell, J. H. (1967). Spontaneous and induced verbal rehearsal in a recall task. *Child Development, 38,* 953–966.

Kendler, H. H., & Kendler, T. S. (1962) Vertical and horizontal processes in problem solving. *Psychological Review, 69,* 1–16.

Kendler, T. S., & Kendler, H. H. (1959). Reversal and nonreversal shifts in kindergarten children. *Journal of Experimental Psychology, 58,* 56–60.

Kendler, T. S., Kendler, H. H., & Wells, D. (1960). Reversal and nonreversal shifts in nursery school children. *Journal of Comparative and Physiological Psychology, 53,* 83–87.

Kennedy, B. A., & Miller, D. J. (1976). Persistent use of verbal rehearsal as a function of information about its value. *Child Development, 47,* 566–569.

Kingsley, P. R., & Hagen, J. W. (1969). Induced versus spontaneous rehearsal in short-term memory in nursery school children. *Developmental Psychology, 1,* 40–46.

Kobasigawa, A. (1974). Utilization of retrieval cues by children in recall. *Child Development, 45,* 127–134.

Kreutzer, M. A., Leonard, C., & Flavell, J. H. (1975). An interview study of children's knowledge about memory. *Monographs of the Society for Research in Child Development, 40* (Serial No. 159).

Kuenne, M. R. (1946). Experimental investigations of the relation of language to transposition behavior in young children. *Journal of Experimental Psychology, 36,* 471–490.

Lodico, M. G., Ghatala, E. S., Levin, J. R., Pressley, M., & Bell, J. A. (1983). The effects of strategy-monitoring on children's selection of effective memory strategies. *Journal of Experimental Child Psychology, 35,* 263–277.

Luria, A. R. (1961). *The role of speech in the regulation of normal and abnormal behavior.* New York: Liveright.

Maccoby, E. E., & Hagen, J. W. (1965). Effects of distraction upon central versus incidental recall: Developmental trends. *Journal of Experimental Child Psychology, 2,* 280–289.

Mandler, G. (1967). Organization and memory. In K. W. Spence & J. T. Spence (Eds.), *The psychology of learning and motivation* (Vol. 1, pp. 321–372). New York: Academic Press.

McCauley, C., Weil, C. M., & Sperber, R. D. (1976). The development of memory structure as reflected by semantic-priming effects. *Journal of Experimental Child Psychology, 22,* 511–518.

McGilly, K., & Siegler, R. S. (1989). How children choose among serial recall strategies. *Child Development, 60,* 172–182.

Miller, G. A. (1956). The magical number seven, plus or minus two: Some limits on our capacity for processing information. *Psychological Review, 63,* 81–97.

Miller, G. A., Galanter, E., & Pribram, K. (1960). *Plans and the structure of behavior*. New York: Holt, Rinehart & Winston.

Miller, P. H. (1985). Metacognition and attention. In D. L. Forrest–Pressley, G. E. MacKinnon, & T. G. Waller (Eds.), *Metacognition, cognition, and human performance* (Vol. 2, pp. 181–222). New York: Academic Press.

Miller, P. H., & Harris, Y. R. (1988). Preschoolers' strategies of attention on a same–different task. *Developmental Psychology, 24*, 628–633.

Miller, S. A., Shelton, J., & Flavell, J. H. (1970). A test of Luria's hypotheses concerning the development of verbal self-regulation. *Child Development, 41*, 651–665.

Moely, B. E., Olson, F. A., Halwes, T. G., & Flavell, J. H. (1969). Production deficiency in young children's clustered recall. *Developmental Psychology, 1*, 26–34.

Mosher, F. A., & Hornsby, J. R. (1966). On asking questions. In J. S. Bruner, R. R. Olver, & P. M. Greenfield (Eds.), *Studies in cognitive growth* (pp. 86–102). New York: Wiley.

Olson, D. R. (1966). On conceptual strategies. In J. S. Bruner, R. R. Olver, & P. M. Greenfield (Eds.), *Studies in cognitive growth* (pp. 135–153). New York: Wiley.

Ornstein, P. A., Baker–Ward, L., & Naus, M. J. (1988). The development of mnemonic skill. In M. Weinert & M. Perlmutter (Eds.), *Memory development: Universal changes and individual differences* (pp. 31–50). Hillsdale, NJ: Lawrence Erlbaum Associates.

Ornstein, P. A., & Naus, M. J. (1978). Rehearsal processes in children's memory. In P. A. Ornstein (Ed.), *Memory development in children* (pp. 69–99). Hillsdale, NJ: Lawrence Erlbaum Associates.

Ornstein, P. A., & Naus, M. J. (1985). Effects of the knowledge base on children's memory strategies. In H. W. Reese (Ed.), *Advances in child development and behavior* (Vol. 19, pp. 113–148). New York: Academic Press.

Ornstein, P. A., Naus, M. J., & Stone, B. P. (1977). Rehearsal training and developmental differences in memory. *Developmental Psychology, 13*, 15–24.

Paris, S. G., Newman, R. S., & McVey, K. A. (1982). Learning the functional significance of mnemonic actions: A microgenetic study of strategy acquisition. *Journal of Experimental Child Psychology, 34*, 490–509.

Paris, S. G., & Oka, E. R. (1986). Children's reading strategies, metacognition, and motivation. *Developmental Review, 6*, 25–56.

Piaget, J. (1952). *The origins of intelligence in children*. New York: Norton.

Piaget, J. (1965). *The child's conception of number*. New York: Norton.

Phillips, S., & Levine, M. (1974). Probing for hypotheses with adults and children: Blank trials and introtacts. *Journal of Experimental Psychology: General, 104*, 327–354.

Posner, M. I., & Snyder, C. R. P. (1975). Attention and cognitive control. In R. L. Solso (Ed.), *Information processing and cognition: The Loyola symposium* (pp. 55–85). Hillsdale, NJ: Lawrence Erlbaum Associates.

Pressley, M., Borkowski, J. G., & Schneider, W. (1987). Cognitive strategies: Good strategy users coordinate metacognition and knowledge. *Annals of Child Development, 4*, 89–129.

Pressley, M., Forrest–Pressley, D. L., Elliot–Faust, D., & Miller, G. (1985). Children's use of cognitive strategies: How to teach strategies, and what to do if they can't be taught. In M. Pressley & C. J. Brainerd (Eds.), *Cognitive learning and memory in children: Progress in cognitive development research* (pp. 1–47). New York: Springer.

Pressley, M., Levin, J. R., & Bryant, S. L. (1983). Memory strategy instruction during adolescence: When is explicit instruction needed? In M. Pressley & J. R. Levin (Eds.), *Cognitive strategy research: Psychological foundations* (pp. 25–49). New York: Springer.

Reese, H. W. (1962). Verbal mediation as a function of age level. *Psychological Bulletin,* *59,* 502–509.

Ringle, B. A., & Springer, C. J. (1980). On knowing how well one is remembering: The persistence of strategy use during transfer. *Journal of Experimental Child Psychology,* *29,* 322–333.

Rohwer, W. D., Jr. (1973). Elaboration and learning in childhood and adolescence. In H. W. Reese (Ed.), *Advances in child development and behavior* (Vol. 8, pp. 1–57). New York: Academic Press.

Rohwer, W. D., Jr., & Bean, J. P. (1973). Sentence effects and noun-pair learning: A developmental interaction during adolescence. *Journal of Experimental Child Psychology,* *15,* 521–533.

Rosch, E. (1975). Cognitive representations of semantic categories. *Journal of Experimental Psychology: General,* *7,* 192–233.

Saltz, E., Soller, E., & Sigel, I. E. (1972). The development of natural language concepts. *Child Development,* *43,* 1191–1202.

Schneider, W. (1985). Developmental trends in the metamemory–memory behavior relationship: An integrated review. In D. L. Forrest–Pressley, G. E. MacKinnon, & T. G. Waller (Eds.), *Cognition, metacognition, and human performance* (Vol. 1, pp. 57–109). New York: Academic Press.

Schneider, W., & Pressley, M. (1989). *Memory development between 2 and 20.* New York: Springer.

Scribner, S., & Cole, M. (1972). Effects of constrained recall training on children's performance in a verbal memory task. *Child Development,* *43,* 845–857.

Shiffrin, R. M., & Schneider, W. (1977). Controlled and automatic human information processing: II. Perceptual learning, automatic attending, and a general theory. *Psychological Review,* *84,* 127–190.

Siegler, R. S. (1981). Developmental sequences within and between concepts. *Monographs of the Society for Research in Child Development,* *46,* 631–683.

Siegler, R. S. (1987). The perils of averaging data over strategies: An example from children's addition. *Journal of Experimental Psychology: General,* *116,* 250–264.

Siegler, R. S. (1988). Individual differences in strategy choices: Good students, not-so-good students, and perfectionists. *Child Development,* *59,* 833–851.

Siegler, R. S. (in press). How content knowledge, strategies, and individual differences interact to produce strategy choices. In W. Schneider & F. E. Weinert (Eds.), *Interactions among strategies, knowledge, and aptitude in cognitive performance.* New York: Springer.

Siegler, R. S., & Shrager, J. (1984). Strategy choices in addition and subtraction: How do children know what to do? In C. Sophian (Ed.), *Origins of cognitive skills* (pp. 229–293). Hillsdale, NJ: Lawrence Erlbaum Associates.

Smith, E., Shoben, E., & Rips, L. (1974). Structure and process in semantic memory: A featural model for semantic decisions. *Psychological Review,* *81,* 214–241.

Sophian, C., Larkin, J. H., & Kadane, J. B. (1985). A developmental model of search: Stochastic estimation of children's rule use. In H. M. Wellman (Ed.), *Children's searching: The development of search skill and spatial representation* (pp. 185–214). Hillsdale, NJ: Lawrence Erlbaum Associates.

Sophian, C., & Sage, S. (1985). Infants' search for hidden objects: Developing skills for using information selectively. *Infant Behavior and Development,* *8,* 1–14.

Sophian, C., & Wellman, H. M. (1983). Selective information use and perseveration in the search behavior of infants and young children. *Journal of Experimental Child Psychology,* *35,* 369–390.

Sternberg, R. J. (1985). *Beyond IQ: A triarchic theory of human intelligence.* Cambridge, England: Cambridge University Press.

Vygotsky, L. S. (1962). *Thought and language.* Cambridge, MA: MIT Press.

Wellman, H. M. (1977). Tip of the tongue and feeling of knowing experiences: A developmental study of memory monitoring. *Child Development, 48,* 13–21.

Wellman, H. M. (1988). The early development of memory strategies. In F. Weinert & M. Perlmutter (Eds.), *Memory development: Universal changes and individual differences* (pp. 3–29). Hillsdale, NJ: Lawrence Erlbaum Associates.

Wellman, H. M., Ritter, K., & Flavell, J. H. (1975). Deliberate memory behavior in the delayed reactions of very young children. *Developmental Psychology, 11,* 780–787.

White, S. H. (1965). Evidence for a hierarchical arrangement of learning processes. In L. P. Lipsitt & C. C. Spiker (Eds.), *Advances in child development and behavior* (Vol. 2, pp. 187–220). New York: Academic Press.

Whitehurst, G. J., & Sonnenschein, S. (1985). The development of communication: A functional analysis. In G. J. Whitehurst (Ed.), *Annals of child development* (Vol. 2, pp. 1–48). Greenwich, CT: JAI Press.

Williams, K. G., & Goulet, L. R. (1975). The effects of cueing and constraint instructions on children's free recall performance. *Journal of Experimental Child Psychology, 19,* 464–475.

Witkin, H. A., Goodenough, D. R., & Karp, S. A. (1967). Stability of cognitive style from childhood to young adulthood. *Journal of Personality and Social Psychology, 7,* 291–300.

Worden, P. E. (1983). Memory strategy instruction with the learning disabled. In M. Pressley & J. R. Levin (Eds.), *Cognitive strategy research: Psychological foundations* (pp. 129–153). New York: Springer.

Wozniak, R. H. (1972). Verbal regulation of motor behavior: Soviet research and non-Soviet replications. *Human Development, 15,* 13–57.

Yuille, J. C., & Catchpole, M. J. (1973). Associative learning and imagery training in children. *Journal of Experimental Child Psychology, 16,* 403–412.

CHAPTER 2

Development of Problem-Solving Strategies in Infancy

Peter Willatts

University of Dundee, Great Britain

Anyone who has spent time with 2-year-old children can be in little doubt that they often show a formidable ability for overcoming obstacles to get what they want. The following two examples are typical of the everyday problems encountered by young children.

Katie is a determined little girl who is approaching her second birthday. She watches as her grandmother leaves the room and shuts the door behind her. Katie wants to follow, but the door is unfamiliar; it is much larger than the doors in her own home, and there is an old brass doorknob that is quite different from the doorknobs she is used to. She tries to push the door open, but nothing happens. She then grasps the doorknob and pulls, but the catch is firm and she gets nowhere. Kathie clenches her teeth, pulls harder, and while doing so manages to give the doorknob a little twist. Feeling the movement, she tries turning it again. The door opens slowly and Katie mutters "done it" as she sets off to find her grandmother.

Joanna is two-and-a-half and is playing with her doll on the couch. She likes to wrap the doll in a blanket, but recently she has started to use anything that is handy, especially Kleenex tissues. She goes over to the shelf where the Kleenex box is usually kept, but today it is missing. She looks around, then crouches down and opens the cupboard door below the shelf. There are plenty of other things inside, but no box. She shuts the door and begins looking along the shelf, but there is still no sign of the box. She turns to look back at her doll and spies a large basket full of newspapers next to the couch. She runs across the room and peers inside. There is nothing there but a few magazines, but when she pulls one out she sees the box in the place where her mother sometimes puts it. Grabbing some issues, Joanna returns to her doll.

It is clear that these children have definite goals, but it is also clear that they do not have a ready method for achieving their goals and are engaged in problem solving. As Newell and Simon (1972) put it, "a person is confronted with a problem when he wants something and does not know immediately what series of actions he can perform to get it" (p. 72), which is an accurate description of the state the aforementioned children are in. However, there are many ways of finding a series of actions that will lead to a goal, and only some of these methods or strategies suggest a growing intelligence and capacity for thought. By *strategy* I mean some regularity in the way infants organize their attempts to solve a problem, and the following definition captures this exactly: "A strategy refers to a pattern of decisions in the acquisition, retention, and utilization of information that serves to meet certain objectives, i.e. to insure certain forms of outcome and to insure against certain others" (Bruner, Goodnow, & Austin, 1956, p. 54). The crucial part of this definition is the phrase, *pattern of decisions*. Problem solving that is goal directed but disorganized is not strategic because it lacks a definite pattern. The function of a strategy is to aid the decision of what to do next, which typically is achieved through the reasonably efficient management of information-processing resources, and through the imposition of constraints on choices. This chapter examines the development of strategies that infants use, and in keeping with the foregoing definition, it focuses more on the underlying processes that control problem-solving behavior rather than on the behavior alone.

The preceding examples give us some clues about what may develop during the first 2 years of life. First, both children maintained their goal for a period of time and in the face of various potential distractions. Both recognized when their goal had been achieved; Katie signaled this with her exclamation, a characteristic at this age (Gopnik & Meltzoff, 1986), and Joanna by ending the search and resuming her original play. Both children tried out several different procedures but stopped when each failed to work; they did not repeat unsuccessful methods, but moved on to something new. Their choice of what to try appeared to be constrained by both the goal and the current situation. Katie's attention was initially focused on the door and then shifted to the doorknob, whereas Joanna at first searched for the missing box in what seemed to her the most likely places. Both responded quickly to some opportunity that assumed significance in the context of what they were doing; Katie by pulling open the door as soon as she noticed the movement, and Joanna by crossing the room when she saw the basket as another possible hiding place. Both children appeared to organize their search; Katie by first trying out simple and direct methods, such as pushing the door, before exploring other possibilities. Joanna's search was guided by a representation of the box and where it was most likely to be. When she failed to locate it in the cupboard, she went on to search in related places (DeLoache & Brown, 1984) and finally considered a spot where the box was not usually to be found.

These characteristics suggest strategies for problem solving that are considerably more sophisticated than any method based on random trial and error. They point to some degree of task analysis by the child, careful monitoring of the solution, effective use of memory to retain the goal and subgoals, organization of successive attempts, and the use of discovered information to guide further efforts. These features of problem solving tap a range of different cognitive abilities that may each undergo considerable change during infancy. However, the orchestration of these abilities is this chapter's primary concern, and the next section considers the main characteristics of strategies that could be available in infancy.

PROBLEM-SOLVING STRATEGIES

There are two general types of strategies for solving problems. The first is *forward search*, which entails trying out a sequence of methods one at a time until the goal is attained (Nilsson, 1971; Winston, 1984). An example is trying to find an address in a housing development when you have no idea of the route. One method is to find the house through exhaustive forward search of all the roads; each time you arrive at a junction you choose an exit, drive along it to the next junction, and repeat the process. If you encounter a dead end, you must return to the previous junction, and when you do find the correct street you can then look for the house with the right number. This kind of forward search will eventually lead to the goal, but it is generally slow and laborious.

Forward search may be structured in different ways, such as breadth first or depth first, but whichever is adopted the main problem is choosing which method or step to try next. The simplest approach is to choose randomly, but a more efficient way is to make the selection with the aid of heuristic information, which can substantially reduce the search space but does not guarantee that a solution will be found. It would probably help you find the house if you had an idea of its direction, so that you would only follow roads that appeared to go in that direction and avoid those that do not. Notice also that heuristic information may guide a solution in two ways; first, in the selection of what to try next, and second, in the evaluation of that choice when its outcome is known. Heuristic information can be used to select among a discrete set of options (such as which road to follow or which act to perform), but can also be used to shape performance when the range of choice is continuous. This is the principle you use to help children find a hidden object by telling them whether they are getting warm or cold. This temperature heuristic does not tell the child exactly where to look, but suggests how they should vary their search.

A different type of strategy is problem reduction, or subgoaling. The best known example is means–end analysis, in which you identify a difference between your current state and goal state and choose a method for reducing it (Newell & Simon, 1972). You may be able to act directly to produce the desired reduction, but typically there is some further obstacle, and you will need to repeat the process and carry out additional problem solving. This will generate a sequence of subgoals that must each be achieved before the original difference can be reduced and the goal attained. Means–ends analysis therefore requires the formulation of a plan in which the initial problem is redefined as a sequence of subproblems. At some point it becomes possible to take a direct action, and this in turn triggers a series of actions that will lead to the goal.

Although these strategies are quite different in structure, forward search and problem reduction share several features. They both make demands on memory, and the more complex the task, the greater the demands. With forward search it is necessary to remember what has been tried, and the outcome, where in the sequence you have reached, and what remains to be attempted. With problem reduction it is necessary to remember what has already been considered, and of course it is essential that the whole plan be remembered until the goal is achieved. Operation of either strategy will be enhanced if there has been an appropriate task analysis, which can suggest heuristic information for selecting the most useful actions to try out first. Thus, both strategies will be more effective if the problem solver has a fund of knowledge relevant to the task.

The two kinds of strategies also differ in several ways. Each is suited to a particular kind of problem. Search is effective when the set of possible actions at any step is small, but can become unmanageable if the set is large. It will take too long to work through each step one at a time, and the large number of alternate sequences of steps will place an excessive load on memory. Problem reduction is more appropriate when the set of possible actions is undefined and potentially very large. The advantage of a problem-reduction strategy is that it narrows the range of choice to those specific subgoals that are most likely to lead to a solution.

A further difference is whether the strategy can be carried out in a planning mode. A planned solution is one in which the problem solver looks beyond the first step and considers further steps in the sequence (Wellman, Fabricius, & Sophian, 1985). Planned solutions should therefore be distinguised from planful solutions, which only entail consideration of a single step. Forward search is planful when each step is tried out, the result evaluated, and the next step determined on the basis of the information gathered. Such a procedure is typically referred to as *trial and error,* a term that is frequently taken to mean elementary and mindless. This may be very misleading, given that forward search can be highly efficient when it incorporates high-powered heuristics. Forward search may also be planned if the problem solver can anticipate the effect of each step and does not need to resort to overt trial and error. In contrast, problem-reduction strategies can only be planned in advance, because no action is taken until the sequence of subgoals has first been established. Consideration of these strategies is relevant to understanding the development of problem solving in infancy for several reasons. First, it is possible to see how strategies that on the surface look quite different are in fact related. This applies particularly to forward search, where there may be considerable overlap in the basic structure of two strategies, but marked differences in the solutions that each strategy generates. The significance of this for a theoretical account is that there may be much underlying continuity, so that our task is not to explain how new strategies appear, but instead to show how existing strategies become modified. Second, we can consider how changes in cognitive abilities interact with the execution of strategies. It is highly probable that improvements in memory capacity and knowledge play an important role. Third, we can see how mental representation in infancy determines problem-solving methods. Planning is possible only when the infant can represent the effects of actions and can coordinate sequences without any need for overt action. This is one issue considered by Piaget, and the main features of his theory are presented in the next section.

PIAGET'S THEORY OF STRATEGY DEVELOPMENT

Piaget's (1953) account of the growth of sensorimotor intelligence is the only theory that attempts to explain the development of problem-solving strategies in infancy. Piaget did not use the term *strategy*, but instead discussed the organization of sensorimotor schemes. However, given that his main concern was to characterize the structures that regulate behavior, and bearing in mind the afore-mentioned definition of a strategy, it seems appropriate to refer to strategies in connection with his theory. Piaget's descriptions of problem solving are certainly clear enough for us to identify the strategies outlined in the previous section. With this contemporary interpretation, Piaget's theory states that strategies appear in a definite sequence, with new ones arising when the infant enters another developmental stage.

Stages I–III

Piaget saw that intentional, goal-directed behavior was a necessary condition for problem solving, but because he did not think that infants in Stages I and II could have goals, he did not consider the possibility that they could solve problems. Early behavior consists of the exercise of single sensorimotor reflexes (Stage I) or schemes (Stage II), and the infant is unable to understand the relation between its own activity and any effects that arise from that activity. However, in Stage III infants do start to coordinate separate sensorimotor schemes and thus develop structures (secondary circular reactions) that could support intentional behavior. A good example was provided by Piaget (1953, obs. 97) when one of his children discovered how to shake a rattle that was hanging above her cot. The rattle was tied to the baby's arm with a piece of string, and after discovering that movements of her arm were accompanied by movements of the rattle she quickly came to repeat the arm movements. This led to the creation of a new scheme in which existing schemes for controlling arm movements, looking, and hearing were all coordinated.

Although such a coordination appears to be intentional, Piaget did not regard secondary circular reactions in this way and did not consider the formation of coordinations in Stage III to be an early form of problem solving. He argued that the infant merely regards the effect of an action as part of the action itself and is unable to distinguish the means from the ends. As Piaget put it, "means and ends are inseparable from one another and, consequently, produced in the same entity" (Piaget, 1953, p. 208).

However, Piaget did report several observations that seem to contradict this account, and one appeared to show a heuristically guided search for a solution. When Laurent was 4.5 months old he was waving a stick about and accidentally knocked a toy that was hanging above his crib. The sight of the movement of the toy attracted his attention, but instead of continuing to wave the stick he stopped, moved it closer to the toy, then moved it away a little, and finally he struck the toy again. He repeated this cautious behavior several times with the stick kept close to the toy and the movements becoming increasingly faster (Piaget, 1953, obs. 105). This observation is very interesting because it suggests that Laurent had a definite goal of making the toy move and that he was using the goal to regulate his behavior. The slow and deliberate way that he maneuvered the stick to strike the toy is suggestive of a forward-search strategy that was guided by information of the sort, "Keep the stick near to the toy."

Stage IV

The next stage is entered when the infant begins to display clear signs of planful means–ends behavior. Infants in Stage IV have a variety of means–ends skills; they remove obstacles to get to toys; search for hidden objects; use supports and strings to recover distant objects; manipulate objects in order to gain visual information about their structure; and use gestures as an early form of communication.

The strategy for solving these means–ends problems is unplanned forward search, and Piaget's (1955) account of the development of search behavior is a good illustration. Early in Stage III, infants would make no effort to search if the object was hidden under a cover, but later they began to run through a series of activities such as scratching, striking, or pushing the cover. Each activity was familiar to the infant and had previously appeared in a different context, but Piaget did not think they were generally performed with the intention of recovering the hidden object. He noticed that variations in the method of hiding disrupted the infant, and even when the cover was removed, the infant might not look for the object and was surprised when it was finally noticed (Piaget, 1955, obs. 38). Following this transitional period in which the infant's activity gradually became directed toward the goal, the infant's actions were reorganized and became more efficient. Irrelevant activities such as scratching were discarded, and the infant started to pack up the cover while looking for the object.

Although problem solving in Stage IV shows a clear advance, it is limited by a lack of flexibility that takes two different forms. One is that infants can solve a problem only if they already have a method in their repertoire, and the problem will be intractable if its solution requires either the modification of an existing method or the creation of a new one. Forward search in Stage IV is therefore more goal terminated than goal directed (Rutkowska, 1985), and the infant is unable to use heuristic information to home in on a goal.

A second type of inflexibility arises when infants are required to adapt a previously successful performance to some modification in a task. Spatial modifications are especially problematic, and the infant typically persists in repeating the original performance. The classic example of such a failure to adjust is the *A*-not-*B* search error, where the infant who searched accurately for an object hidden at place *A* returns to the original place when the object is later hidden at place *B*. Piaget's explanation for this error was that the infant is egocentric in its understanding of the relation between its own behavior and the effect of that behavior on objects. This conceptual limitation leads the infant to regard the existence of the object as dependent on its own actions, and therefore it returns to search at place *A* because that activity will recreate the object. It is not difficult to see how such egocentrism rules out the use of a flexible strategy for searching for objects. Stage IV infants are therefore unable to modify means–ends coordinations (Frye, 1980), and other examples appear to support this view. Piaget noted that Stage IV infants would pull a cloth to retrieve an object resting on it, but continued to pull it even when the object was placed alongside the cloth or held above (Piaget, 1955).

Stage V

These limitations are overcome when the infant enters Stage V. The characteristic of this stage is that infants deliberately vary their behavior so that instead of simply repeating familiar actions with toys, they experiment with new actions. For example, the Stage V infant is not content to just pick up objects and throw them; instead it alters the distance, direction, and force of its throwing and observes the effects. This deliberate experimentation produces a new strategy that Piaget termed *directed groping*. An illustration of this strategy was provided by the way Piaget's children discovered how to use a stick to draw in a distant object. Whereas the Stage IV infant could only learn that the stick made the object move, in Stage V the infant produced a controlled investigation of the relation between the movements of the stick and the object (Piaget, 1953, obs. 157–161). The result was that the infant could slowly find a way to manipulate the stick and recover the object. These solutions were not planned in advance, but neither could the activity be described as random trial and error. Instead, the infant was guided by what happened, and groped its way to the solution.

Piaget's directed groping strategy is really unplanned forward search that incorporates heuristic information in the selection and evaluation of actions. This strategy means that infants can now be more flexible and are able to modify methods that were initially unsuccessful. The infant can solve problems that defeated the more limited strategy of Stage IV, such as retrieving long objects through the narrow bars of a playpen or inserting blocks into a shape sorter. The infant no longer makes A-not-B search errors, and will refuse to pull a cloth if there is no object resting on it.

Stage VI

Despite these advances, infants in Stage V lack the capacity for mental representation, which means that all problem solving is unplanned and must be carried out in real time by trying each action and observing the result. The ability to solve new problems without any need for trial and error first appears in Stage VI, and Piaget reported a number of occasions when solutions came about through the use of a new strategy. Piaget referred to this new method as "the invention of new means through mental combinations" (Piaget, 1953, p. 331), but this rather inelegant expression corresponds with what we now prefer to call *planning* (Wellman, Fabricius, & Sophian, 1985).

One of the clearest examples in Piaget's investigations was provided by Lucienne, who was attempting to get a long chain into a small box through a narrow opening. She first tried to fit one end of the chain into the box, but after three attempts in which it fell out each time she stopped, put the chain down, waited a moment, then rolled it into a ball and succeeded in placing it in the box (Piaget, 1953, obs. 179). Her performance can be contrasted with the clumsy efforts of Jacqueline, who in Stage V also managed eventually to get the chain in the box, but only after a long sequence of 22 attempts. Similar planned solutions were reported by Piaget for other tasks, such as using a stick to retrieve a distant toy and removing an object from inside a partially open box.

Planned solutions are made possible because the Stage VI infant has a newly developed capacity for mental representation that allows schemes to be coordinated in the absence of overt action. Piaget ruled out the possibility of planning occurring any earlier, because he maintained that mental representation is only acquired at the end of infancy.

SUMMARY

Piaget's theory is attractive because it appears to explain how problem-solving strategies gradually come into existence. The sequence is plausible because there is progression in the complexity of strategies and thus a basis for continuity. Random forward search may be converted into a more powerful strategy with the inclusion of heuristic information to evaluate the outcome after each attempt, and the shift from Stage IV to Stage V could be made by simply adding a new stage-linked component to an existing strategy. Finally, the development of representation in Stage VI would provide the infant with a new method of implementing problem-solving strategies and could promote the use of problem reduction methods.

However, the strategies themselves are neutral with regard to the issue of development. The sequence that Piaget proposed is not derived from any characteristics of the strategies, but from other changes brought about as the infant passes through successive sensorimotor stages. Random search, heuristic search, and problem reduction are alternative methods, and there is no special reason why any one should develop before another. Another account of sensorimotor development could lead to a very different interpretation of how problem-solving strategies develop.

PIAGET'S THEORY IN LIGHT OF RECENT EVIDENCE

There are a number of difficulties with Piaget's theory. There are inconsistencies, and some of the interpretations he made of key observations are questionable. In addition, Piaget's methodology is often weak and inadequate for revealing the changes in problem solving that he claimed are present. The findings of recent research suggest a very different account of the way problem solving develops in infancy.

Stages I–III

Piaget's views on the early stages of development have been challenged by a considerable number of studies, and our current understanding is quite different. Many of the coordinations that Piaget thought took several months to appear are present in the neonate, and there is much evidence for the existence of the intermodal relations that are required for early means–ends behavior (Harris, 1983).

Although it is now clear that young infants possess cognitive structures that could support goal-directed behavior, the important question is whether young infants can and do act with the intention of achieving goals. It is difficult to identify intentionality using only behavioral criteria; but different researchers agree that intention is shown when the infant selects from among alternative actions those that are appropriate for the goal, persists in his or her efforts to achieve the goal, makes corrections for errors, and finally stops acting when the goal is achieved (Bruner, 1973, 1981; Harding, 1982; Piaget, 1953; Wellman, 1977). This implies that problem solving may occur whenever behavior is directed toward a goal, and is not restricted to situations requiring the use of intermediaries and tools. For example, Bruner (1970, 1972, 1973) argued convincingly that early skilled behavior is regulated by goals, and the acquisition of skills requires the application of problem-solving strategies. If we accept this argument, then it becomes feasible to examine behavior in the earliest stages for evidence of problem solving.

One important decision that must be made is whether an infant is acting intentionally to make an event happen or is merely expecting an outcome. If young infants can only acquire expectancies, then Piaget's account of early development would not be seriously challenged. One method of distinguishing between an expectancy and an intention is to observe the infant's reactions to a violation of the expected outcome. If the infant has only an expectation, then he or she might show this in some way (such as displaying surprise reactions), but would do nothing else. If the infant has been acting with an intention, then we should observe some attempt to achieve the desired goal.

Evidence for early goal-directed behavior comes from studies of reaching. Bower, Broughton, and Moore (1970) showed infants as young as 6 days an illusory object produced by a stereoscopic shadow caster. All infants became distressed when they were unable to touch the virtual object, and there was an increase with age in the number of attempts to try and contact it. Bower et al. reported that at 5 months, infants not only tried to touch the virtual object, but also engaged in a variety of exploratory tactile behaviors such as feeling around the edges. This result suggests that intentional reaching may take several months to appear, because only older infants showed persistence when they failed to achieve the desired outcome.

In one of our own studies we were also able to show intention and persistence in the reaching behavior of 5-month-olds (Hood & Willatts, 1986). Infants were presented with an attractive object at one side while their hands were restrained by the mother. The lights were then turned out, the object was removed, and the mother let go of the baby's hands. Behavior in the dark was recorded using an infrared video system, and the recordings showed that infants made significantly more reaches to the place where the object had been seen than to a corresponding control place on the opposite side that had previously been empty. The precaution of removing the object ruled out any chance that these reaches were the result of accidental contacts with the object, a flaw in the design of an earlier study by Bower and Wishart (1972). This result therefore shows that 5-month-olds will make efforts to attain a remembered goal and persist when their first attempts are unsuccessful.

Perhaps the most convincing evidence for early goal-directed behavior comes from studies of contingency learning. In one experiment, Fagen and Rovee (1976) showed that 3-month-old infants could rapidly learn to kick a leg in order to move a mobile containing six component parts. When the number of components was later reduced to two, the kicking rate increased rapidly. This increase has been interpreted as a "strategy by which the infant conserves the amount of stimulus change in the moving mobile" (Rovee–Collier, 1983, p. 79). The claim that rate of kicking is goal determined and not simply goal terminated is supported by a further observation of Fagen and Rovee (1976) that infants who underwent a change from 10 components to 2 also increased their kicking but quickly gave up and resorted to crying. It could not have been the fact that the mobile contained only two components, because infants in the other condition had the same mobile and showed a very different reaction. Instead, this result suggests that the infants who experienced the large reduction in components gave up and became distressed because their goal was unattainable. This finding was replicated by Mast, Fagen, Rovee–Collier, and Sullivan (1980) and provides compelling evidence that early contingency learning is aimed at achieving a goal.

One final study suggests that even newborns are capable of goal-directed behavior. Butterworth and Hopkins (1988) found that about 32% of the spontaneous arm movements of neonates took the infants' hands directly to the mouth. Butterworth and Hopkins argued that these movements were intentional because the mouth was open more often for episodes of hand contact than for episodes of no contact with the mouth. Mouth opening occurred before the start of the hand movement as if in anticipation of the arrival of the hand. Even more surprising was their observation that when the infant missed the target and their hand touched some other part of their face, a corrective movement was made that more often took the hand toward the mouth than away. However, this accuracy was restricted to the perioral region of the face; hand movements following contact with areas such as the forehead or ears were as likely to be away from the mouth as toward it. Success was not due to the infant setting off a rooting reflex, because the hand reached the mouth by being taken there, rather than by the infant turning its head. This finding suggests that newborn infants have access to some spatial representation of their own face and can use this information to regulate what may be a very early form of guided or heuristic search for a goal. As Butterworth and Hopkins concluded, "goal-directed behaviors or even proto-intentional activities may be a part of our innate endowment that has been overlooked until now" (Butterworth & Hopkins, 1988, p. 314). In addition, Case (1984, 1985) argued on theoretical grounds that a capability for setting goals must be innate.

These studies tell us several things about the kind of strategy that infants can use during the first 6 months of life. First, there is no doubt that they have goals and produce activity that is directed toward these goals. Second, they are able to detect whether a goal has been achieved, and will repeat an activity when unsuccessful. Third, they are able both to detect and use information about their failure to regulate further attempts. Infants who were trying to grasp a virtual object altered their behavior and started to explore the edges of the "object." Infants who were trying to reinstate the original level of movement of a mobile did not simply repeat their original pattern of kicking but started to increase the rate. Newborns who were trying to put their fingers in their mouth did not withdraw their hand and start all over again when they missed, but made a corrective movement. Infants who were trying to reach for an object in the dark continued to reach to the correct place. All these reactions suggest that young infants can employ a simple type of forward search strategy for achieving a goal and use information about the difference between what was achieved and what was intended to guide subsequent activity. We even have some clues as to the nature of this guidance. One approach is to increase the level of performance by "turning up the volume" in some appropriate way. Another is to achieve guidance within a spatial context, which was apparent in the hand-to-mouth behavior reported by Butterworth and Hopkins (1988), and the use of a stick, which was observed by Piaget (1953). Other examples are found in the reactions of infants to the disruption of distress–relief behavior (Lamb & Malkin, 1986), and their ability to learn complex sequences of head turns (Papousek & Bernstein, 1969), or acquire visual anticipations (Canfield, 1988; Haith, Hazan, & Goodman, 1988). All these features of early strategies were found in the strategies used by the 2-year-olds described at the beginning of this chapter. This suggests that infants start out with a basic problem-solving strategy that will be expanded in a variety of ways as development proceeds. Although the evidence for such early abilities is still rather sketchy, these findings are sufficient to cast serious doubts on Piaget's account.

Stage IV

Piaget's view that a change in problem solving occurs between 6 and 8 months is supported by my own research into the development of early means–ends skills. One study examined the development of search in infants aged 6 to 8 months (Willatts, 1984a). A group of infants was tested at 6, 7, and 8 months on a simple search task in which a toy was hidden behind a cup. In addition, infants were also tested on a control task in which only a cup was presented and no toy was hidden. Intentional search was identified by rating different aspects of the infants' behavior. The first activity with the cup was scored as intentional if it was only picked up and moved away. Any behavior that suggested the infant was interested in the cup for its own sake (such as examining behavior or play) was scored as showing no intention to search. Fixation was scored as intentional if the infant looked for the hidden toy after the cup had been removed, and behavior with the toy was rated as intentional if the infant picked it up. In addition, the interval between first contacts with the cup and the toy was scored.

If retrieval of the toy was the sole criterion for search, then there was no significant improvement, because infants at each age successfully recovered the toy. However, there were clear changes in the method by which this was accomplished. At 6 months, search was a series of unrelated acts in which the screen was picked up for the purpose of play, the toy was only noticed once it had been uncovered, and it was finally picked up after a long interval (see Fig. 2.1). Scores for intention were low and unaffected by whether or not a toy was hidden. There was an improvement at 7 months, and by 8 months the majority of infants were showing intentional search on at least one trial. There was now a clear difference between search trials on which a toy was hidden and control trials on which only the cup was presented.

One finding of special interest was that infants at each age showed a significantly higher level of intention for fixation than they did for behavior with the cup. This can be interpreted as evidence that infants had the goal of finding the hidden toy (revealed by their fixation), but were still trying to discover the means for achieving it. Lower intention scores for cup behavior came about because infants produced a wide range of activities; they picked up the cup and shook it, waved it around, passed it from hand to hand, banged it on the table, examined it visually, or put it in their mouth and explored it orally. Although each method did reveal the hidden toy, the behavior of deliberately removing the cup developed gradually.

It may seem surprising that infants who at 5 months can reach out

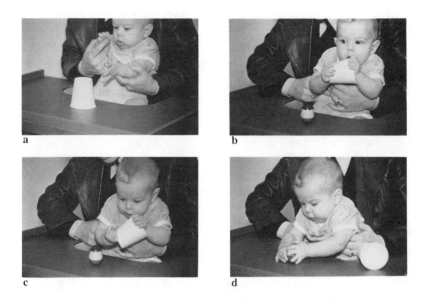

FIG. 2.1. Search by 6-month-old infants is usually a sequence of un-related acts. (a) Infant reaches for the cup; (b) takes cup to mouth and looks away; (c) then notices the toy; (d) and finally reaches for the toy. (Photographs by Peter Willatts.)

in the dark for an invisible object are unable at 6 months to search for a hidden object. One possible reason is that manually guided reaching is a relatively new skill that makes heavy demands on attention so that infants are unable to keep the goal in mind while simultaneously monitoring hand and arm movements (Bushnell, 1985). A similar idea was developed by Bruner (1973), who suggested that infants deliberately restrict their degrees of freedom for action when at-tempting to master a new skill. As each component of the skill is mastered, the restrictions are progressively relaxed so that new methods may be incorporated. Restricting degrees of freedom for action would clearly impose a severe limitation on problem-solving ability and could well account for this apparent contradiction in search competence. However, difficulty in controlling manual skills while keeping in mind a goal cannot be the whole story, because the higher intention scores for fixation showed that the infants were thinking about the toy while they were manipulating the cup. The fact that intention scores were lower for cup behavior suggests that infants were unclear about what to do to achieve the goal. Younger infants may reach for an object in the dark because this method is direct and familiar. With a means–ends problem like search, the infant must first deal with something else and does not immediately understand how this will help to reach the goal.

Similar changes are found in the development of other means–ends skills, such as use of a support (Willatts, 1985a). Infants at 6, 7, and 8 months were presented with a long cloth on which a toy was placed either at the center (near position), or twice as far from the infant at the end of the cloth (far position). Intentional performance was identified by the following criteria: The infant should pull the cloth and not play with it in any way; should maintain fixation on both the cloth and the toy and not lose interest; and finally should retrieve the toy. The interval between first contacting the cloth and the toy was also recorded, and efficient pulling was identified when the toy was brought within reach with a single uninterrupted movement of the cloth or with a succession of pulls with intervening pauses of no more than half a second.

Six-month-olds could retrieve the toy, but their performance was not often intentional; they frequently played with the cloth and looked away from the toy, the cloth–toy interval was long, and the cloth was pulled inefficiently because the toy moved slowly across the table while the infant was engrossed with the cloth. As with search, success at 6 months tended to be the result of a sequence of independent activities (see Fig. 2.2). Performance improved at 7 months, although intention scores for fixation were significantly higher than scores for cloth behavior (as they had been with search). By 8 months the irrelevant activities with the cloth had largely

a   b

FIG. 2.2. A 6-month-old infant using a cloth support to retrieve a toy. (a) The infant first picks up the cloth in order to put it in his mouth. (b) When he sees the toy is within reach, he grasps it. As with search, the toy is retrieved but performance does not often appear intentional. (Photographs by Peter Willatts.)

dropped out and intentionality scores for cloth behavior and fixation were equal; performance was much faster, highly efficient, and direct. The cloth was pulled immediately regardless of the distance of the object, and often the infant held out its other hand in anticipation of grasping the toy. At 6 and 7 months the overall level of intention was somewhat lower when the toy was at the far position, but by 8 months infants were able to use the support effectively regardless of the distance. The finding that infants also come to use supports at first by means of inappropriate methods reinforces the conclusion that early performance on these means–ends problems stems from a lack of knowledge about what to do and not from difficulty in mastering new reaching skills.

Do infants use heuristic information to guide their early means–ends problem solving? As noted, it is possible that infants younger than 6 months carry out a rudimentary kind of heuristic search, but there are no studies that have specifically looked at this issue. Despite this gap in our knowledge, some observations of Kaye and Marcus (1978, 1981) are relevant. Their studies looked at the ability of infants to learn a complex series of actions by imitating an adult model. An example of such a series would be opening and closing the mouth five times. Infants as young as 6 months are normally unable to imitate such a complex sequence (Piaget, 1951; Uzgiris, 1972), but the adult model provided repeated demonstrations of the sequence of acts. Infants did not imitate the sequence immediately, but gradually "worked up" a performance over a series of trials. The infant might first open its mouth only once and follow this later with a burst of arm movements. At some point the burst of movements would shift from arm to mouth and the infant would manage to put together a fair copy of the target behavior. This achievement indicates a marked capacity for goal-directed search in which random trial and error appears to play no part.

Given these accomplishments, we might question whether Stage IV infants do lack flexibility in adjusting means–ends coordinations. If this is a conceptual problem, then it should be possible to demonstrate a failure to make adjustments on other means–ends tasks as well as search. In one of my own studies (Willatts, 1985b), I tested this idea by comparing the performance of 9-month-old infants on a standard A-not-B search task and a comparable A-not-B support task. Infants were presented with two cloths, and a toy was either hidden under one for the search task, or placed on the top and beyond reach for the support task. Performance on the A trials was accurate on both tasks, but many more errors were made on the B trials with the search task.

In contrast, infants were able to switch immediately from pulling one cloth to pulling the other.

One possible reason for this successful adjustment is that infants were simply drawn to the side where there were more objects (a cloth and a toy). A further study showed that infants can still make adjustments when the number of objects remains constant (Willatts, 1985a). In this study, described earlier, infants were tested on their use of supports with objects placed at two distances. It was predicted that a failure to adjust means–ends performance would be apparent in two ways. Infants who had first learned to retrieve the toy in the far position would accomplish this with either a single long pull or a rapid series of shorter pulls. If this method was repeated with the object in the near position, then the toy would be carried over the edge of the table and fall on the floor. Alternatively, infants who started out with the object in the near position would retrieve it by means of a short pull on the cloth. Repetition of this method with the toy in the far position would fail to bring it within reach, and the infant would need to pause to discover its error and pull the cloth again. The effect on performance would be to make it slower and less efficient. The results showed that infants had no difficulty in adjusting their performance when the distance of the object was changed. The toy was hardly ever pulled over the edge of the table, and there was no sign that this occurred more frequently when the near position followed the far. Efficiency of pulling and cloth–toy contact interval were both unaffected when the toy was presented at a new distance (see Fig. 2.3).

Infants do not appear to have any of the difficulties in adjusting to changes on support tasks that they do with search tasks. They can switch from pulling one support to pulling another, and alter their style of pulling to allow for the distance of the object. However, it is also clear from a number of studies that in certain circumstances infants can also adjust their search and do not make errors (Harris, 1989). Contextual factors are important, and infants can search accurately when the tasks are presented against spatially distinct backgrounds (Butterworth & Jarrett, 1982; Butterworth, Jarrett, & Hicks, 1982), so that lack of flexibility may depend more on the characteristics of tasks than the characteristics of infants (Corrigan & Fisher, 1985). A further discussion of this question of flexibility and some other aspects of early means–ends performance may be found in Willatts (1989).

Means–ends performance appears between 6 and 8 months, because infants are discovering how their recently acquired manual skills may be employed in new ways to achieve goals. The develop-

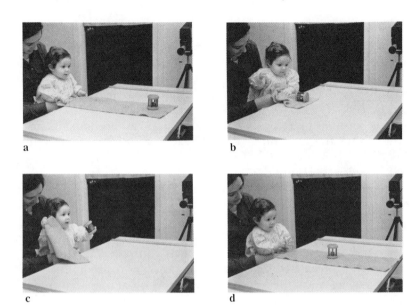

FIG. 2.3. An 8-month-old infant uses a cloth efficiently as a means for retrieving a distant toy. (a) The toy is presented at the far position; (b & c) the infant pulls the cloth in a single uninterrupted movement and recovers the toy; (d) she was equally successful with the toy at the near position and adapted to the change in distance of the goal. (Photographs by Peter Willatts.)

ment of reaching and grasping opens up a whole set of different goals that the infant must struggle to achieve. This is accomplished with a strategy that is available throughout the first 6 months, so it is not the onset of a whole new strategy that produces the change, but the application of an existing strategy to a whole new domain. This differs from Piaget's account in two ways. First, the reason for the appearance of means–ends behavior around the middle of the 1rst year is not that the infant has just begun to have goals and is producing intentional behavior in order to achieve them; as we have seen, goal-directed behavior is a feature of infant cognition from birth. Second, infants do not need to develop a strategy for solving means–ends problems, because they can employ existing methods that have been available from the start. It is possible that this shift to a new realm of problem solving is accompanied by changes in the organization of the infant's forward search, but as yet we do not have sufficient information to identify any such changes. However, this possibility would not alter the conclusion that Piaget's account does not fit the data.

Stage V

There is a good deal of evidence to support Piaget's claim that infants become more effective at solving problems during their 2nd year. Detour behavior improves, and there is a noticeable reduction in attempts to either reach or locomote through a barrier (Bruner, 1970; Jarrett, 1988; Lockman, 1984; McKenzie & Bigelow, 1986). The use of tools becomes more proficient, and infants can use implements to retrieve toys that are either out of reach or inside a narrow tube (Goldfield, 1983; Kopp, O'Connor, & Finger, 1975; McCrickard, 1982; Uzgiris & Hunt, 1975).

One feature of cognition at the end of the first year is that infants start to coordinate relationships between different sets of sensory-motor relations or "mappings" (Fischer, 1980). Instead of simply learning that action A leads to effect B, the infant establishes a range of parameters for actions and their effects and systematically coordinates this information, thus making it possible to predict new outcomes. For instance, the infant might discover that a small throw will send an object a small distance, and a large throw will send it a large distance. The capacity to coordinate these relations would allow the Stage V infant to predict that a medium throw will send the object a medium distance. Support for this view comes from a study by Mounoud and Hauert (1982), who showed that by 14 months, infants are able to relate variations in the size of objects with variations in weight and can predict an object's weight from its size. This was revealed when infants correctly adjusted their grasp of a new object in anticipation of its weight.

This capacity to systematically coordinate actions and effects would certainly have an impact on the infant's conduct of a forward search. After a preliminary exploration, the infant could have enough information to narrow the range of possible actions considerably. There is little research on problem solving that addresses this possibility, but some observations of Rieser and Heiman (1982) on the use of spatial reference systems to guide search are relevant. Infants aged 18 months were placed in a circular enclosure with eight identical windows equally spaced around the wall. Only one of the windows could open to reveal an attractive display. Infants were helped by a parent to locate this window from a constant starting position when given a signal. They were then rotated away from this constant position, and the signal was given to find the display window. The infants were prevented from gazing at the target window during this rotation, so they would have to remember where it was positioned.

Rieser and Heiman found that infants could locate the correct window with only a modest level of accuracy (though better than chance), but more interestingly, the magnitude of turning toward the correct window was related to the magnitude of the initial rotation away. Often they would check one of the wrong windows first, but persisted in searching and found the correct one unaided on 69% of trials. In a second experiment, Rieser and Heiman went on to demonstrate that following the initial rotation, both 14- and 18-month-old infants would turn in the direction of the shorter route to the target. These results show that infants could coordinate their own movements with the spatial arrangement of their surroundings and used this information to guide their search. Piaget was correct to identify an improvement in problem solving, though the source of this improvement is not the use of heuristic information for the first time, but the use of a different type of heuristic information.

Stage VI

Piaget's claim that toward the end of the 2nd year infants start to plan or invent solutions without any need for active experimentation may be contested. First, in all the examples of planning that Piaget reported there is not a single instance of a solution appearing without the infant previously having resorted to some action that failed. In the example of Lucienne and the chain, she had three failures with a simple method before she rolled up the chain and put it in the box. Similarly, when she tackled the problem of removing the chain from a box with a narrow opening, she tried to grasp it directly before she thought of pulling the drawer to make the opening larger (Piaget, 1953, obs. 180). The same pattern is found with all of Piaget's examples, and this means that the critical difference between Stage V and Stage VI solutions was never really observed. Instead of planning their solutions, it is just as likely that infants were solving the tasks by some form of trial and error.

A second difficulty with Piaget's analysis is that he placed too much emphasis on the speed and success of solutions in Stage VI (e.g., Piaget, 1953, obs. 178). These two criteria are unsatisfactory for distinguishing whether or not a solution was planned, because differences in speed may have more to do with the infant's level of skill than with the strategy adopted, and planning does not necessarily guarantee success. An infant who planned to use a method that was unsuitable and led to failure would not be identified as using a Stage VI strategy.

The third criticism of Piaget (1953) concerns the familiarity of the infant with the materials used to solve the problem. A younger infant may fail to plan because the materials are unfamiliar and their potential functions are therefore not understood. The infant may become more involved in exploring or playing with the materials so that the task is solved by a trial-and-error method. Familiarity with the materials may account for several of Piaget's examples of planning, such as that of Laurent, who produced a Stage VI solution with a stick but who had played with it on at least eight previous occasions. Given that familiarity with task materials is known to affect dramatically performance in older children (Smith & Dutton, 1979; Sylva, Bruner, & Genova, 1976), poorer performance by infants may not reflect a difference in their strategies but a difference in their knowledge.

THE 2ND YEAR:
AN ALTERNATIVE TO PIAGET'S ACCOUNT

Piaget's observations suggest that there is an improvement in infants' problem solving during the 2nd year of life, but it is not obvious that this comes through the use of new strategies based on planning. An alternative explanation is that infants start to use a more sophisticated form of unplanned forward search. There are several reasons why forward search should become more effective; and three likely influences are improvements in monitoring performance, an increased capacity to inhibit errors and avoid repeating earlier mistakes, and a growing ability to generalize and transfer methods to new situations. The question of when infants are first able to plan solutions to problems is considered in the next section.

Monitoring Performance

Effective forward search requires that infants can remember which methods have already been tried, can detect errors and diagnose their cause, and can organize a search using some nonrandom approach. Problems that require infants to try several different methods will therefore prove difficult to solve if monitoring skills are limited.

Keeping Track

There is very little research that shows whether infants do have trouble keeping track of what they have already done, but some evidence from studies of object search suggests that improvements occur during the 2nd year. Webb, Massar, and Nadolny (1972) tested 14- and 16-month-olds on a search task in which an object was hidden under one of three covers. Infants of both ages were accurate on their first search even after a delay of 15 seconds, but often made the error of searching at the original location when the object was hidden at a new place on a later trial (resembling the A-not-B error). However, Webb et al. allowed their infants to correct these errors and discovered that 16-month-olds were far more likely to go to the correct place on their second search than were 14-month-olds. This finding suggests that 16-month-olds can keep in mind several possible locations and will search through them, though in a sequence that is unlike that of older children.

Another technique is to look for the occurrence of redundant searches when there is a choice of several places to search (redundant searches being returns to a place that has already been examined). Bertenthal and Fischer (1983) found that infants aged 16 and 24 months made very few redundant searches, and there was no difference between the ages. However, they also reported that older infants were more likely to search persistently through a series of five locations, and although this may mean that younger infants give up sooner, it could also mean that younger infants are poorer at remembering which locations remain to be tried. A high level of search competence was also reported by Wellman, Somerville, Revelle, Haake, and Sophian (1984), who tested children aged 30 months to 54 months on a game of hide-and-seek involving three different arrays of eight locations. The children did not see where the toy was hidden but were asked to find it, and measures of search performance were taken from trick trials on which no toy was actually hidden. Although the youngest children did well, they searched less exhaustively than older children and showed a higher level of redundant searches. Such studies of search competence with multiple locations would appear to be a promising way of studying the development of monitoring skills, and the topic deserves a more systematic examination.

The clearest evidence that older infants do keep track of their progress while solving a problem comes from a study of forward-search strategy by Willatts, Domminney, and Rosie (1989). A total of 40 children with a mean age of 26 months were tested on two types of platform-rotation tasks. One was a straight lever and the other was a circular tray, and the problem for the child was to discover how to rotate the platform to retrieve a toy that was fastened to the opposite side. Children used a variety of methods, and nine different types were identified that were based on an earlier scheme devised by Koslowski and Bruner (1972). These fell into four categories: (a) direct approaches, where the child tried to reach for the toy, or pointed at it, or tried to climb on the table; (b) attempts to move the platform by pulling, lifting, or fiddling with the pivot screw; (c) methods in which the platform was partially rotated; and (d) methods in which the platform was rotated and the toy captured. Of those children who made at least two attempts to solve the task, 47% did so with a mean of 2.8 attempts, but without repeating any method they had tried previously. The remaining children solved the problems with a mean of 7.7 attempts, of which 42% were repetitions. However, it is unlikely that these repetitions occurred because the children had forgotten what they had already done. The chances that a method would be repeated were unequal across the categories, and the proportion of repetitions for the direct-approach methods (50%) was significantly higher than for the move platform (36%) or rotate platform (10%) methods. One reason why 2-year-olds continue to try using a direct approach may be that they see it as a method that could work if executed properly. Lifting or pulling the platform will clearly not work if the platform fails to move, but a direct reach might if the child tried a bit harder. Such a basis for the different level of repetitions would indicate a subtle appreciation by young children of the reason for failure, and not a problem with monitoring performance.

One final aspect of remembering what has been tried is knowing how to return to a previous state in the event of failure. Again, there is little information about the emergence of such a skill, but some informal observations by Heth and Cornell (1980) suggest that although this may be a problem for 12-month-olds, such backtracking does sometimes occur. Heth and Cornell tested infants on a two-choice maze in which only one path went to the goal. Infants who chose the wrong path would often persist in trying to break through the barrier and eventually became quite fussy. However, some would quickly head back to the starting area to take the other route. A very different study by DeLoache, Sugarman, and Brown (1985) considered the ability of children aged between 18 and 42 months to fit together a set of nested cups. DeLoache et al. identified six different correction strategies that were used after the child made an error. Three of these entailed backtracking, where the set of cups was taken apart and fitted together again in some way. Children younger than 30 months were unlikely to resort to these methods, but there was a highly significant increase with age.

Piaget (1955) also described a form of backtracking that he took to be a strong indication that infants were basing their search on a representation. The task was the invisible displacement of an object through three different locations, and Piaget claimed that infants would search by working backward through each location until the object was found. However, attempts to reproduce this observation have met with repeated failure, and even 2-year-olds rarely backtrack in this way (Bertenthal & Fischer, 1983; Corrigan, 1981). It is too early on the strength of these few examples to know whether infants are unable to back up to a previous level in the course of solving problems, but this is obviously another topic that deserves the attention of researchers.

Error Detection

The quality of problem solving will also be affected by the ability of infants to detect errors. The study by DeLoache et al. (1985) considered this issue, and they showed that error detection depends in part on the child's goal. In addition to the set of nested cups, children were given a set of rings that had to be stacked on an upright rod. It was clear that children did attempt to fit the cups together in order of size, because they took some corrective action when trying to place a cup into another that was too small. However, there was little evidence for any corrective action when the children were fitting the rings onto the rod. Once a ring had been placed, it was left in position regardless of its size. The authors noted that, "whether children will detect and attempt to correct their own errors depends on the extent to which that task informs them that they have erred" (DeLoache et al., 1985, p. 937). Changes in performance may not be determined so much by changes in strategy, but more by changes in the structure of goals. One reason why younger infants either take longer to solve a problem or fail could be that they are more easily distracted and forget the goal, so that even if they managed to produce appropriate behavior its significance would not be understood.

Differences in tasks will determine how much information the infant receives about the cause of errors. One possible reason for 9-month-olds' poorer performance with the A-not-B search task in comparison with the support version is availability of information about why performance is correct in some cases and incorrect in others (Willatts, 1985b). When the wrong support is pulled, the stationary toy can be seen on the other cloth; and when the infant corrects the error, the movement of the toy can be watched while the appropriate cloth is pulled in. Less information will be available in search, because once a cloth is picked up the relation that existed between it and the toy is no longer available. Some extra data that were not reported by Willatts (1985b) suggest that the two tasks do offer different opportunities for discovering the reason for errors. Infants making an error on the support task were far more likely to look across to the correct cloth than were infants making an error on the search task, who confined their attention to the cloth they grasped and rarely looked at the correct location of the toy. To understand why on some occasions search is successful and on others it is not, the infant must remember where the toy was located, which cloth it was under, and link that memory to success or failure. Learning to solve search problems is more difficult than learning to solve support problems because of difference in the available information.

Organizing Search

A third aspect of monitoring performance concerns the way that infants organize and structure their sequence of attempts. Keeping track of progress will be easier if attempts are organized, because it is less important to remember exactly what has already been tried. For example, if you group your attempts into categories and try out methods in one category before proceeding to the next, then you need only remember which category has been attempted instead of all the individual methods. This is another important topic about which we have little information, but there are indications that infants can organize their problem solving during the 2nd year.

Koslowski and Bruner (1972) found that children aged 12 to 24 months organized their search for a solution to a lever-rotation problem by starting with simple methods and moving on to something more complex when they failed. Stronger evidence for an organized search was obtained by Willatts, Domminney, and Rosie (1989) in their platform-rotation study. They reported a significant increase in the complexity of methods used by 2-year-olds over a series of attempts during the first trial, with the simplest being tried first, intermediate next, and most complex last of all (see Fig. 2.4). A similar shift was also reported by McKechnie (1987) in another study of lever rotation problems in which the performance of infants between 12 and 24 months was examined over a series of trials. McKechnie obtained a trial-by-age interaction with the youngest infants (12–14 months) using only simple methods and showing no change across trials. Older infants started out with the same methods, but progressed to more complex ones on later trials. In a second study, McKechnie also tested infants on a number of different problems that consisted of a brightly colored object suspended on a bent wire (Davis, 1974; Hollis, 1962; Whitecraft, Cobb, & Davis, 1959). The infant's task was to find a way of removing the object from the wire by sliding it around the series of bends. McKechnie reported that infants of 14 months or older also started out with simple methods such as spinning or hitting the object, but advanced to more complex methods such as moving the object to and fro on later trials.

a

b

c

d

FIG. 2.4.   A 2-year-old attempts a sequence of different methods before finding the solution to a lever-rotation problem. (a) She first tries a simple and direct approach by reaching for the toy. (b) Having failed, she then fiddles with the pivot screw, which does not move. (c) Shifting attention to the lever, she rotates it 45° and lets go. (d) Finally, she turns the lever and recovers the toy. This sequence shows a steady increase in complexity of method attempted with each new method being tried only once. Unsuccessful methods were discarded and did not get repeated. (Photographs by Peter Willatts.)

One final example comes from the study of spatial reference systems by Rieser and Heiman (1982). Although 18-month-old infants were eventually able to find a target window following a rotational movement, very often they began by heading toward the nearest window, which was directly in front. Rieser and Heiman suggested that infants are predisposed to search straight ahead, but they also noted that there was an increase in this tendency between 14 to 18 months. An alternative explanation is that infants selected a simple approach to try out first and postponed doing something more demanding until later. The fact that most infants still knew which direction to turn after their straight-ahead search showed that they had not forgotten the task, and the increase in this approach with age supports the proposal that this represents a change in strategy. Although data are available from only these few tasks, a tentative conclusion is that organization of attempts to solve problems appears gradually during the 2nd year of life.

Error Inhibition

Careful monitoring of performance will be of no use if the infant is unable to prevent an error from being repeated. Error inhibition is an essential feature of heuristic search so that failed methods are dropped and new possibilities can be tried out. A number of researchers have suggested that response inhibition is a major difficulty for young infants and that progress may be related to neurological development (Diamond & Goldman–Rakic, 1985; Diamond, in press). Evidence for improvement comes from several different paradigms. Studies of search behavior on the A-not-B task have shown that infants often know where the object is hidden at place B (Baillargeon & Graber, 1988; Harris, 1989), but may be unable to inhibit an approach to place A. One influence on response inhibition with the A-not-B task is delay that was examined in a longitudinal study by Diamond (1985). She found that all infants aged between 7 and 12 months could inhibit an approach to place A and would search accurately, but that younger infants could only maintain this inhibition for relatively short periods when a delay was imposed between the object being hidden at place B and the infant being allowed to search. At 7 months infants could manage only to inhibit their approach to A for about 2 seconds, but this increased steadily to about 12 seconds at the end of the year. Diamond suggested that this increase reflected a change in the ability to use recall to guide behavior while overcoming the tendency to be guided by habit.

Changes in error inhibition can also be shown in tasks that do not rely on recall memory. In another study, Diamond (1988) presented infants with a toy that was covered by a transparent box with one open side. The task for the infant was to make a detour reach to retrieve the toy, but the youngest (aged 6–7 months) failed to do this and reached persistently along the line of sight. There was no sign that they could stop this behavior, and Diamond commented that "no clue, no coaxing, no amount of failure could persuade infants of this age to try anything other than reaching straight to where they saw the toy" (Diamond, 1988, p. 32). Infants between 7 and 10 months of age found an ingenious means–ends solution for this problem by shifting their position so they could reach into the box along the line of sight. Finally, at 12 months they were able to inhibit any attempt to reach along the line of sight and instead made successful detour reaches. However, we should be cautious in accepting this finding as evidence for the development of response inhibition during the 1st year because of the findings of an experiment by Jarret (1988). This research also confirmed that younger infants were unable to make a detour around a screen, but Jarrett found that if he used a screen that prevented infants from shifting their body position to accomplish a line-of-sight reach, then even 12-month-olds could not inhibit a direct reach and failed to make a detour. Whether or not an infant can inhibit an error may therefore depend on task factors as well.

A study by Fagen (1977) also shows that infants of 10 months can begin to inhibit errors in a learning set paradigm (Harlow, 1949). Infants received a series of trials over several days in which they had to learn which of two stimuli to contact in order to produce an interesting visual display. Despite interference from stimulus and position preferences, Fagen reported a steady improvement in success from 50% correct (chance) on Day 1 to 76.5% on Day 10. The method by which infants solved these problems was to select a stimulus at random on Trial 1, discover the outcome, and then select stimuli on remaining trials according to a win-stay, lose-shift strategy, which is a simple form of heuristic search. In addition, Fagen noted that response latency was significantly longer on trials that were correct than on trials where the infant made an error. This study is important because it reveals two types of inhibitory control; one is the capacity to delay responding, which is associated with greater accuracy; and the other is the ability to switch a response when the intended outcome is not obtained.

Although these findings do suggest that ability to inhibit one activity and perform another develops slowly during the 1st year, it would be a mistake to conclude that this is a general age-related capacity that affects performance on all tasks. In several different studies of infants' use of supports, I have not found any evidence for difficulties in inhibiting inappropriate actions, even in infants as young as 6 months (Willatts, 1985a; 1985b). There is also evidence that 2- and 3-month-olds can inhibit unsuccessful actions in contingency learning tasks. For example, Kalnins and Bruner (1973) showed that infants could learn to increase their rate of sucking to bring a picture into focus, and were able to reduce the rate of sucking when the contingency was altered and sucking produced blurring. In a different study, Rovee–Collier, Morrongiello, Aron, and Kupersmidt (1978) trained 3-month-olds to kick one leg to activate a mobile. Once criterion performance was achieved, the mobile was disconnected and reattached to the other leg. Infants rapidly learned to kick this leg as well, but Rovee–Collier et al. noticed that although infants started off by kicking both legs, activity with the unattached leg steadily declined. This is a surprising result, because it was not necessary for the infant to stop kicking with the unattached leg in order to jiggle the mobile. The fact that it happened shows that very young infants can inhibit actions that do not produce expected outcomes.

Although young infants may be able to inhibit errors, Willatts and Scott (1988) reported a study in which 2- and 3-year-olds did not. Children sat at a table and were offered a choice of two strings to pull, one of which was in contact with a toy at the end of the table and one of which was not. However, this arrangement was really a trick, because the string that was in contact with the toy was not attached and parted from the toy when it was pulled. The string that appeared unattached was connected by means of an invisible thread, and despite appearances to the contrary could be used to retrieve the toy. Each child was encouraged to get the toy for a series of 16 trials. All children started by attempting to pull the string that was in contact with the toy, and when it came adrift they were encouraged to try pulling the other string as well. Many appeared surprised when this resulted in the movement of the seemingly unattached toy, and some even looked for the invisible thread. However, there was no adjustment of their initial approach on later trials, and children at both ages persisted in pulling the contact string first. There was one age difference that showed in the behavior after the contact string had been grasped. Two-year-olds pulled it right across the table as if it ought to drag the toy behind (and some even tried to reattach the string), but 3-year-olds became more cautious over trials and only pulled it a short distance as if testing its properties rather than assuming it would work, a finding that was also reported in a similar study by Brown (1987). Despite this interesting change in performance, even 3-year-olds seemed unable to inhibit behavior that led to an error, and in this respect showed a degree of persistence comparable to that of 9-month-olds attempting to retrieve a toy by reaching through a transparent screen.

Although ability to inhibit errors is undoubtedly an important influence on problem solving, these studies present a confusing picture. It seems unlikely that inhibition is a general characteristic that affects all behavior in the same way. Instead, it appears to be necessary to take into account the nature of the response that must be inhibited. Where the infant has learned some arbitrary association (as in the Fagen [1977], Kalnins & Bruner [1973], and Rovee–Collier et al. [1978] studies), then inhibition can occur at all ages. The difficulty seems to lie with tasks that tap a deeper level of understanding. Infants may refuse to give up on one method, not because they are unable to inhibit an error, but because they do not see the need to stop. The infant who keeps on trying to reach through the transparent screen or persists in pulling the string that is in contact with the toy may do so because of a deep-seated belief that these methods are correct and constitute a "theory in action" (Karmiloff–Smith, 1979). Progress at solving problems that tap such theories will depend on the current level of the child's knowledge and his or her capacity to test and modify these theories.

Representation of Solutions

Infants who have solved a problem will only benefit from their success if they can add the new method to their repertoire. This may be difficult if the solution has appeared from a series of errors and false starts, and it would be inefficient for the infant to remember the entire sequence and reproduce it when the problem is encountered again. An infant who struggles to reach directly through a screen for an object, then locates the edge, tries to pull the screen, and eventually discovers how to reach around, needs only to remember how to make the final detour and can forget the other activity that preceded the solution. We know that infants as young as 5 months can rapidly learn sequences of events and can remember parts of those sequences (Smith, 1984; Smith, Arehart, Haaf, & de Saint Victor, 1989). However, knowing which part of a sequence comprises the solution requires that the infant can separate the entire episode into relevant and irrelevant segments, and the ability to make such distinctions may develop only slowly. Infants of 12 months who first tried to reach through a barrier and then discovered how to reach around it continued to start with a direct approach on later trials, but older infants learned to produce only the detour movement (Jarrett, 1988; Willatts, 1987). However, little is known about the development of skills that would achieve such segmentation, although there might be innate procedures for detecting consistent sequences, eliminating redundancies, and reorganizing a performance to achieve efficiency (Case, 1984, 1985; Karmiloff–Smith, 1979; Klahr, 1984; Klahr & Wallace, 1976).

One technique that might reveal the development of such skills is to model a solution with the inclusion of actions that are both relevant and irrelevant to the task. A study that used this method was reported by Harnick (1979), who found that infants aged between 12 and 24 months could ignore irrelevant actions if the task was an easy one, but would imitate these actions if the task had a moderate or high level of difficulty. This effect was apparent on the very first trial, and this method can provide a useful way of showing whether infants can extract the parts of an event that are relevant to solving the problem.

Once an infant has learned a new method, it is important to know whether it is retained in a form that is specific to the context in which the problem originally arose, or whether it can be generalized to new situations. Koslowski and Bruner (1972) argued that transfer was built into the solution of their lever-rotation task, but they offered no evidence to support their claim. There have been almost no studies of transfer of learning in infants and preschool children, but some recent research does show that 2-year-olds are able to show transfer. Willatts, Domminney, and Rosie (1989) tested children on two types of platform-rotation tasks, of which one was a rotating lever and the other a circular tray. The children made a series of errors on their first trial, but produced a near flawless performance on their second trial. Clearly, they were able to identify that portion of their sequence of attempts that was relevant to solving the task; but they were also able to transfer what they had learned to the other version of the task, which was solved quickly and with few errors. In contrast, children who had initially been given an unrelated problem to solve took much longer with these platform-rotation problems and had many more unsuccessful attempts.

Other studies by Crisafi and Brown (1986) show that 2-year-olds can transfer solutions on inferential reasoning tasks when offered some adult assistance, but it is still unclear whether this is a new skill that appears toward the end of the 2nd year. Certainly, 12-month-olds do not immediately transfer their detour skills when the position of a barrier is changed (Jarrett, 1988; McKenzie & Bigelow (1986); Willatts, 1987). However, younger infants are able to search in a wide range of situations, such as under cloths and cups, in containers, behind screens, and even after crawling across the floor (Benson & Uzgiris, 1985). Piaget noted that string-pulling could occur in novel situations, and he thought that such behavior "surely constitutes an early form of true generalization" (Piaget, 1950, p. 102). Generalization may be yet another example of a capacity that appears in some form at all developmental levels.

This discussion of possible influences on forward search during the 2nd year of life suggests several ways in which Piaget's children might have achieved their improved performance in Stage VI. Solutions may have been discovered more quickly because older infants have better monitoring skills. They may have remembered more about which methods they had already tried, could appreciate the significance of errors and were therefore better informed, and perhaps also understood why certain methods failed and should not be repeated. Additionally, they may have been able to transfer other solutions and so could borrow techniques that had been learned in different contexts. Having achieved a solution, they were then in a better position to identify what produced the result and could reproduce it immediately when tested on the same problem again. Piaget's (1953) descriptions look very much like the kind of performance of children on platform-rotation tasks (Willatts, Domminney, & Rosie, 1989), and this suggests that Piaget did not observe planning but a more effective form of forward search.

PLANNING IN INFANCY

Piaget's (1953) evidence for the occurrence of strategies based on planning in infancy was ambiguous, but this means that the use of such methods by young infants may have gone unnoticed. The possibility that planning could be available much earlier is supported by recent research that points to the operation of mental representation throughout infancy and well before Stage VI. This evidence comes from studies of imitation (Meltzoff, 1988; Meltzoff & Moore, 1983); recall memory (Mandler, 1984); object permanence (Baillargeon, Spelke, & Wasserman, 1985; Hood & Willatts, 1986); and making inferences (Haake & Somerville, 1985; Sophian & Adams, 1987; Sophian & Sage, 1983).

Some of my own research has been aimed at showing that strategies that use planning appear at around the same time as planful means–ends performance. One study considered whether 9-month-old infants could plan a sequence of actions that entailed the coordination of existing means–ends skills (Willatts, 1984b). The infants had to retrieve a toy by first removing a barrier (a large block of foam) and then pulling a support cloth. A control group was tested on a similar task, but the toy was placed beside the cloth and could not be retrieved. If the infants were unable to make plans, then it was expected that both groups would approach these tasks in the same way, working through each step in the sequence until the support was pulled and the toy either retrieved or left behind on the table. However, if 9-month-olds were able to use their knowledge of supports and barriers to plan a solution, differences should be apparent at the outset because only one of the tasks could be solved. The results supported a planning interpretation because the group given the planning task removed the barrier, quickly pulled the support, and recovered the toy. In contrast, the control group picked up the barrier, played with it, and generally ignored the cloth on many trials. These differences suggest that the infants had planned a sequence of actions, and their first activity with the barrier was determined by what they intended to do next.

Although infants may have planned how to retrieve the toy, Wellman et al. (1985) suggested an alternative interpretation. Perhaps the planning group did not really care that the toy and support were separate and simply regarded the two as a combined toy–object. The task would then have been a more straightforward means–ends problem of removing a barrier to obtain a goal, and the differences in performance between the groups could have arisen from the greater attractiveness of the cloth toy in comparison with the less interesting cloth on its own. Infants solving the planning task might have set aside the barrier to grasp the cloth toy, and at that point decided to use the cloth to retrieve the toy. This decision would then have been taken after the barrier was removed and not before, and the solution, though planful, would not have been planned.

More recently, we completed a further experiment that was designed to avoid this criticism and that provides clearer evidence for early planning (Willatts & Rosie, 1988). Twelve-month-old infants were tested on an extended version of the original task, which required three steps for solution. In the planning condition there was a barrier and a cloth with a string resting on it at the far end. A toy was attached to the other end of the string and was placed on the table at some distance from the cloth. To retrieve the toy the infant had to remove the barrier, pull the cloth, grasp the string, and pull it. In the control condition the barrier, cloth, and string were all in the same arrangement, but the toy was visibly separate from the string and could not be retrieved.

An important feature of these tasks was that the appearance of the cloth was equivalent, so that once the first step of removing the barrier had been accomplished (by whatever means), the infant had access to the same combination of cloth and string in both conditions. This means that differential attractiveness could not be responsible for any differences in performance. In addition, it was hoped that presenting a task needing three steps for solution would provide a more rigorous test of planning ability. Each infant was given several trials on both conditions, with order of presentation counterbalanced. There were clear differences in the way infants set about the tasks; in the planning condition they were more likely to remove the barrier without any play, were quicker to contact the cloth, and retrieved the string more frequently. The order of the tasks had no influence, and the infants' behavior was adjusted as soon as the condition was changed (see Fig. 2.5).

This study (Willatts & Rosie, 1988) shows that 12-month-old infants are capable of planning a series of actions to obtain a goal. When the toy was fastened to the string, they were quicker to get the barrier out of the way and grasp the cloth. This rapid approach could not have been a response to a more attractive appearance, because the cloth and string looked the same in both conditions. It also seems highly unlikely that these infants could have been so successful because they regarded the cloth, string, and toy as a single object. We know from work by Wishart and Bower (1984) that 12-month-old infants regard objects resting on supports as separate and distinct. The infants in this study watched the placement of each object; and the different colors, dimensions, and position of the string at right angles to the cloth provided substantial information that they were separate items. In fact, means–ends problem solving is impaired when the goal and intermediary do resemble a single unit (Bates, Carlson–Luden, & Bretherton, 1980). However, it is unclear exactly how much of the sequence was planned in advance. The infants must have considered at least two steps and planned to remove the barrier and pull the cloth to recover the string. Whether they also included the final step of pulling the string in the plan, or thought about it after they had grasped the cloth, remains uncertain. It is also unclear whether planning was based on a problem reduction or forward-search approach. A means–ends analysis account seems more accept-

a   b

FIG. 2.5. Twelve-month-old infants are able to plan a series of actions to achieve a goal. (a) Typical reaction on the planning task; the infant removes the barrier and quickly reaches for the cloth in order to retrieve the string which is fastened to the toy. (b) The infant shows no interest in recovering the string on the control task, and instead examines the barrier. (Photographs by Peter Willatts.)

able, but I do not yet know of any empirical way of distinguishing these two alternatives. Nevertheless, these results confirm that 1-year-old infants can think beyond the first step of a means–ends problem.

We should not be too surprised that infants of less than a year can make some progress in planning series of actions, because there are at least two situations in which this would be an advantage, if not a necessity. One is to increase efficiency when locomoting. Infants who are able to crawl or walk may cover a considerable distance, and it would be an advantage to plan a route that prevents extensive detours and ensures that objects are collected at the appropriate places. This is not simply to avoid expending too much effort, but has a more practical implication. An infant who can follow a planned route and knows how each substage leads on to the next will have a better chance of attaining the goal than an infant who has to spend time negotiating unnecessary detours and who may become distracted by unanticipated events. The other role for planning is in communication where the infant may need to work out a sequence of steps to achieve a goal. For example, the baby who looks at his or her mother, then across the room to a toy, and points to the toy and vocalizes while looking back to the mother, may have planned a sequence of events just as effectively as the infant who retrieves a toy by manipulating the barrier, cloth, and string (Harding & Golinkoff, 1979). The fact that one of the steps is performed by another person is irrelevant if the infant has the intention to make the person act in a particular way.

CONCLUSIONS

Where do problem-solving strategies come from in infancy and how do they develop? Piaget's answer to this question was that the characteristics of strategies are identical with the characteristics of sensori-motor stages, and therefore strategy development is linked directly to the development of sensorimotor intelligence. Indeed, one of Piaget's major contributions was to assign problem solving a central role in infant cognition (Gratch & Schatz, 1987). For Piaget there was an integrity to development such that no single domain could be considered independently of any other. His achievement was to show how problem solving in infancy could be studied, but more importantly, why it should be studied.

We now realize that development shows far more diversity, and new evidence demands a new explanation. A variety of studies point to the existence in the earliest months of intentional behavior and a primitive form of heuristic search by which infants can accomplish their goals. This is at a stage when Piaget denied even the existence of goals and intentions. We also have evidence that representation in certain elementary forms is present from the earliest months, and that planning, which should signal the final stage of infancy, is available toward the end of the 1st year. It is simply not possible to modify Piaget's theory to accommodate this new evidence; we are not seeing more rapid development through the six stages, but a new developmental sequence.

The development of problem solving in infancy does not come about through the appearance of radically new strategies, but mostly through the development of new abilities that increase the power and range of existing strategies. In the final sections of this chapter I indicated how some of these abilities would allow infants to conduct their problem solving with greater effectiveness. Improvements in monitoring, task analysis, error detection, recall of solutions, and transfer between tasks each have a dramatic effect on performance, even though the basic strategy remains much the same. Piaget was therefore correct to the extent that he saw problem solving limited by the infant's current state of knowledge.

There are good reasons why very young infants should be able to function strategically. The role of strategy in problem solving is to organize use of knowledge, information, and action. We see this clearly with puzzles like the Tower of Hanoi (Klahr & Robinson, 1981), where the level of motor skill is trivial and progress can only be made when a strategy has been formulated for organizing complex sequences of moves. Strategy is not just important for knowing what to do, but also when to do it. A strategy serves to overcome the limitations of the human information-processing system, which is constrained by time, memory capacity, attention, and even motivation and affect. Infants are far more limited in their processing capacity than are older children or adults, so the opportunity of functioning with a strategy may be a decisive factor in early development. The rapidity of development in the early months may in part reflect the operation of an innate agenda, but may equally be a consequence of the operation of strategies for achieving goals.

There is nothing in the aforementioned view that rules out developmental change. The newborn's strategies can serve a dual role of organizing goal-directed behavior and also providing a core structure from which new methods may develop. Changes will occur when the infant acquires new competence and needs to solve problems of a higher level of complexity. For example, there is little doubt that the 2-year-old has more effective strategies than the 1-year-old, and we are now in a position to identify these differences with some precision. However, it is also obvious that the 2-year-old inhabits a more complex world that requires more complex strategies if the child is to function adquately. Thus, the 1-year-old does not need to try out simple methods before more complex ones, because the possible range of methods is too limited to encourage the use of such an approach. For the 2-year-old, however, the opportunity to think of several different methods at the same time demands some new technique. This explanation is therefore the reverse of Piaget's; new strategies emerge to cope with the demands imposed by other developmental advances. For Piaget, strategy change is at the leading edge and signals the advance to a new stage. The position I advocate is more in keeping with neo-Piagetian theories, which view development as constrained by some upper limit or level that undergoes regular increases (Case, 1984, 1985; Fischer, 1980).

At present we have little idea about how these changes in strategies come about. Some are probably the result of a simple replacement when the infant switches to a new source of information. Others are more difficult to explain. The approach of trying out simple methods first and more difficult ones later is new and does not appear to build on anything that has gone before. One possible explanation for this approach is that the infant simply begins with methods that are most familiar and practiced. However, this does not fit the facts, because children solving the lever tasks started off by trying methods, such as pointing, that have a more recent developmental history than other methods, such as pulling (which they turned to later on). At some point, the child must know that there are several ways of approaching a problem, that some are simpler than others, and that it is a good idea to start with the simpler ones first. But how the child comes by this information and puts it together as part of a strategy is a mystery.

One possible way of learning new strategies is through collaboration with another person (Kaye, 1982; Vygotsky, 1978). The advantage of an adult tutor who can provide a scaffold is that this person can organize the infant's activity in a way that the child is unable to manage for itself. For example, the child may be unable to inhibit its activity, but a tutor can achieve this by redirecting the child's attention to a substitute activity (Wood, Bruner, & Ross, 1976). Recently, I observed in a pilot study how parents assist their children to play with a shape-sorter, and I was struck by the emphasis that they placed on teaching the right strategy. The children were encouraged to search exhaustively for the correct slot for a shape, to monitor their sequence of attempts, and to try to narrow the range of choices by matching features of the shape with features of the slots. These procedures have a wider application than solving shape-sorter problems, and it might be possible to see children learning some general principles of a strategy in one context and applying it to another.

Our theories of strategy development in infancy, like infants' use of strategies, are constrained by an upper limit that is set by a lack of data. Despite the rich variety of studies that have appeared in recent years, there is still much that we do not understand. The mechanisms by which new strategies are formed are unclear; and until we have a better idea of what develops, we will continue to have little to say about how it develops. We need more research into the range of newborns' goal-directed activity; better descriptions of the information infants use to guide their search; and above all, detailed accounts of the way that infants come to achieve their goals over successive attempts. This is especially important because we need insights not just into which problems infants can solve but the methods they use to solve them. This work will require much search and a good deal of trial and error, but the prospect of achieving a foundation for understanding the early growth of one of the major accomplishments of later childhood seems well worth the effort.

ACKNOWLEDGMENTS

This chapter was completed during a sabbatical visit to the Department of Psychology at the University of Denver. I am grateful to Janette Benson, Denise Arehart, Rob Roberts, and Marshall Haith for all their helpful advice and assistance in its preparation.

REFERENCES

Baillargeon, R., & Graber, M. (1988). Evidence of location memory in 8-month-old infants in a nonsearch AB task. *Developmental Psychology, 24,* 502–511.

Baillargeon, R., Spelke, E. S., & Wasserman, S. (1985). Object permanence in five-month-old infants. *Cognition, 54,* 191–208.

Bates, E., Carlson–Luden, V., & Bretherton, L. (1980). Perceptual aspects of tool using in infancy. *Infant Behavior and Development, 3,* 127–140.

Benson, J. B., & Uzgiris, I. C. (1985). The effects of self-initiated locomotion on infant search activity. *Developmental Psychology, 21,* 923–931.

Bertenthal, B. L., & Fischer, K. W. (1983). The development of representation in search: A social-cognitive analysis. *Child Development, 54,* 846–857.

Bower, T. G. R., Broughton, J. M., & Moore, K. M. (1970). The coordination of visual and tactual input in infants. *Perception and Psychophysics, 8,* 51–53.

Bower, T. G. R., & Wishart, J. G. (1972). The effects of motor skill on object permanence. *Cognition, 1,* 28–35.

Brown, A. (1987, April). *Strategies in the very young.* Paper presented at the Biennial Meeting of the Society for Research in Child Development, Baltimore, MD.

Bruner, J. S. (1970). The growth and structure of skill. In K. Connolly (Ed.), *Mechanisms of motor skill development* (pp. 63–92). London: Academic Press.

Bruner, J. S. (1972). Origins of problem solving strategies. In R. Rudner & I. Scheffler (Eds.), *Logic and art: Essays in honor of Nelson Goodman* (pp. 100–126). New York: Bobbs–Merrill.

Bruner, J. S. (1973). Organization of early skilled action. *Child Development, 44,* 1–11.

Bruner, J. S. (1981). Intention in the structure of action and interaction. In L. P. Lipsitt (Ed.), *Advances in infancy research* (Vol. 1, pp. 41–56). Norwood, NJ: Ablex.

Bruner, J. S., Goodnow, J. J., & Austin, G. A. (1956). *A study of thinking.* London: Wiley.

Bushnell, E. W. (1985). The decline of visually guided reaching during infancy. *Infant Behavior and Development, 8,* 139–155.

Butterworth, G., & Hopkins, B. (1988). Hand-mouth coordination in the new-born baby. *British Journal of Developmental Psychology, 6,* 303–314.

Butterworth, G. E., & Jarrett, N. (1982). Piaget's Stage 4 error: Background to the problem. *British Journal of Psychology, 73,* 175–185.

Butterworth, G. E., Jarrett, N., & Hicks, L. (1982). Spatiotemporal identity in infancy: Perceptual competence or conceptual deficit? *Developmental Psychology, 18,* 435–449.

Canfield, R. L. (1988). *Visual anticipation and number development in early infancy.* Unpublished doctoral dissertation, University of Denver, Denver, CO.

Case, R. (1984). The process of stage transition: A neo-Piagetian view. In R. J. Sternberg (Ed.), *Mechanisms of cognitive development* (pp. 19–44). New York: Freeman.

Case, R. (1985). *Intellectual development from birth to adulthood.* London: Academic Press.

Corrigan, R. (1981). The effects of task and practice on search in invisibly displaced objects. *Developmental Review, 1,* 1–17.

Corrigan, R., & Fischer, K. W. (1985). Controlling sources of variation in search tasks: A skill theory approach. In H. M. Wellman (Ed.), *Children's searching: The development of search skill and spatial representation* (pp. 287–318). Hillsdale, NJ: Lawrence Erlbaum Associates.

Crisafi, M. A., & Brown, A. L. (1986). Analogical transfer in very young children: Combining two separately learned solutions to reach a goal. *Child Development, 57,* 953–968.

Davis, R. T. (1974). *Primate behavior: Development in field and laboratory research. Monkeys as perceivers* (Vol. 3). London: Academic Press.

DeLoache, J. S., & Brown, A. L. (1984). Where do I go next? Intelligent searching by very young children. *Developmental Psychology, 20,* 37–44.

DeLoache, J. S., Sugarman, S., & Brown, A. L. (1985). The development of error correction strategies in young children's manipulative play. *Child Development, 56,* 928–939.

Diamond, A. (1985). Development of the ability to use recall to guide action as indicated by infants' performance on AB̄. *Child Development, 56,* 868–883.

Diamond, A. (1988). *Retrieval of an object from an open box: The development of visual-tactile control of reaching in the first year of life.* Manuscript submitted for publication.

Diamond, A. (in press). *Frontal lobe involvement in cognitive changes during the first year of life.* In K. Gibson, M. Konner, & A. Peterson (Eds.), *Brain and behavioral development.* New York: Aldine Press.

Diamond, A., & Goldman–Rakic, P. S. (1985). Evidence for involvement of prefrontal cortex in cognitive changes during the first year of life: Comparison of human infants and rhesus monkeys on a detour task with transparent barrier. *Society for Neuroscience Abstracts (Part II), 11,* 832.

Fagen, J. W. (1977). Interproblem learning in ten-month-old infants. *Child Development, 48,* 786–796.

Fagen, J. W., & Rovee, C. K. (1976). Effects of quantitative shifts in a visual reinforcer on the instrumental response of infants. *Journal of Experimental Child Psychology, 22,* 349–360.

Fischer, K. W. (1980). A theory of cognitive development: The control and construction of hierarchies of skills. *Psychological Review, 87,* 477–531.

Frye, D. (1980). Stages of development: The stage IV error. *Infant Behavior and Development, 3,* 115–126.

Goldfield, E. C. (1983). The development of control over complementary systems during the second year. *Infant Behavior and Development, 6,* 257–262.

Gopnik, A., & Meltzoff, A. N. (1986). Relations between semantic and cognitive development in the one-word stage: The specificity hypothesis. *Child Development, 57,* 1040–1053.

Gratch, G., & Schatz, J. A. (1987). Cognitive development: The relevance of Piaget's infancy books. In J. D. Osofsky (Ed.), *Handbood of infant development, 2nd. Ed.* (pp. 204–237). New York: Wiley.

Haake, R., & Somerville, S. (1985). The development of logical search skills in infancy. *Developmental Psychology, 21,* 176–186.

Haith, M. M., Hazan, C., & Goodman, G. (1988). Expectation and anticipation of dynamic visual events by 3.5-month-old babies. *Child Development, 59,* 467–479.

Harding, C. G. (1982). The development of the intention to communicate. *Human Development, 25,* 140–151.

Harding, C. G., & Golinkoff, R. M. (1979). The origins of intentional vocalizations in prelinguistic infants. *Child Development, 49,* 209–212.

Harlow, H. F. (1949). The formation of learning sets. *Psychological Review, 56,* 51–65.

Harnick, F. S. (1979). The relationship between ability level and task difficulty in producing imitation in infants. *Child Development, 49,* 209–212.

Harris, P. L. (1983). Infant cognition. In P. H. Mussen (Series Ed.), M. M. Haith, & J. J. Campos (Volume Eds.), *Handbook of child psychology. Infancy and developmental psychobiology* (4th ed., Vol. 2, pp. 689–782). London: Wiley.

Harris, P. L. (1989). Object permanence. In A. Slater & J. G. Bremner (Eds.), *Infant development* (pp. 103–121). Hillsdale, NJ: Lawrence Erlbaum Associates.

Heth, C. D., & Cornell, E. H. (1980). Three experiences affecting spatial discrimination learning by ambulatory children. *Journal of Experimental Child Psychology, 30,* 246–264.

Hollis, J. H. (1962). Solution of bent-wire problems by severely retarded children. *American Journal of Mental Deficiency, 67,* 463–472.

Hood, B., & Willatts, P. (1986). Reaching in the dark to an object's remembered position: Evidence for object permanence in 5-month-old infants. *British Journal of Developmental Psychology, 4,* 57–65.

Jarrett, N. L. M. (1988). *The origins of detour problem solving in human infants.* Unpublished master's thesis, University of Southampton, Southampton, England.

Kalnins, I. V., & Bruner, J. S. (1973). The coordination of visual observation and instrumental behavior in early infancy. *Perception, 2,* 307–314.

Karmiloff–Smith, A. (1979). Micro- and macrodevelopmental changes in language acquisition and other representational systems. *Cognitive Science, 3,* 91–118.

Kaye, K. (1982). *The mental and social life of babies.* Chicago: University of Chicago Press.

Kaye, K., & Marcus, J. (1978). Imitation over a series of trials without feedback: Age six months. *Infant Behavior and Development, 1,* 141–155.

Kaye, K., & Marcus, J. (1981). Infant imitation: The sensory-motor agenda. *Developmental Psychology, 17,* 258–265.

Klahr, D. (1984). Transition processes in quantitative development. In R. J. Sternberg (Ed.), *Mechanisms of cognitive development* (pp. 101–139). New York: Freeman.

Klahr, D., & Robinson, M. (1981). Formal assessment of problem-solving and planning processes in preschool children. *Cognitive Psychology, 13*, 113–148.

Klahr, D., & Wallace, J. G. (1976). *Cognitive development: An information-processing view.* Hillsdale, NJ: Lawrence Erlbaum Associates.

Kopp, C. B., O'Connor, M. J., & Finger, I. (1975). Task characteristics and a Stage 6 sensorimotor problem. *Child Development, 46*, 569–573.

Koslowski, B., & Bruner, J. S. (1972). Learning to use a lever. *Child Development, 43*, 790–799.

Lamb, M. E., & Malkin, C. M. (1986). The development of social expectations in distress-relief sequences: A longitudinal study. *International Journal of Behavioural Development, 9*, 235–249.

Lockman, J. J. (1984). The development of detour ability in infancy. *Child Development, 55*, 482–491.

Mandler, J. M. (1984). Representation and recall in infancy. In M. Moscovitch (Ed.), *Infant memory: Its relation to normal and pathological memory in humans and other animals* (pp. 75–101). London: Plenum Press.

Mast, V. K., Fagen, J. W., Rovee–Collier, C. K., & Sullivan, M. W. (1980). Immediate and long-term memory for reinforcement context: The development of learned expectancies in early infancy. *Child Development, 51*, 700–707.

McCrickard, D. (1982). *Some aspects of tool use in infancy.* Unpublished master's thesis, University of Dundee, Dundee, Scotland.

McKechnie, J. (1987). *Problem solving in infancy: A study of infants' performance on tasks of spatial manipulation.* Unpublished doctoral dissertation, University of Stirling, Stirling, Scotland.

McKenzie, B. E., & Bigelow, E. (1986). Detour behaviour in young human infants. *British Journal of Developmental Psychology, 4*, 139–148.

Meltzoff, A. N. (1988). Infant imitation and memory: Nine-month-olds in immediate and deferred tests. *Child Development, 59*, 217–225.

Meltzoff, A. N., & Moore, M. K. (1983). Newborn infants imitate adult facial gestures. *Child Development, 54*, 702–709.

Mounoud, P., & Hauert, C. A. (1982). Development of sensorimotor organization in young children: Grasping and lifting objects. In G. E. Forman (Ed.), *Action and thought: From sensorimotor schemes to symbolic operations* (pp. 3–35). London: Academic Press.

Newell, A., & Simon, H. A. (1972). *Human problem solving.* Englewood Cliffs, NJ: Prentice-Hall.

Nilsson, N. J. (1971). *Problem-solving methods in artificial intelligence.* London: McGraw-Hill.

Papousek, H., & Bernstein, P. (1969). The functions of conditioning stimulation in human neonates and infants. In A. Ambrose (Ed.), *Stimulation in early infancy* (pp. 229–252). London: Academic Press.

Piaget, J. (1950). *The psychology of intelligence.* London: Routledge & Kegan Paul.

Piaget, J. (1951). *Play, dreams, and imitation in childhood.* London: Heinemann.

Piaget, J. (1953). *The origins of intelligence in the child.* London: Routledge & Kegan Paul.

Piaget, J. (1955). *The construction of reality in the child.* London: Routledge & Kegan Paul.

Rieser, J., & Heiman, M. L. (1982). Spatial self-reference systems and shortest route behavior in toddlers. *Child Development, 53*, 524–533.

Rovee–Collier, C. K. (1983). Infants as problem solvers: A psychobiological perspective. In M. D. Zeiler & P. Harzem (Eds.), *Advances in analysis of behavior* (Vol. 3, pp. 63–101). London: Wiley.

Rovee–Collier, C. K., Morrongiello, B. A., Aron, M., & Kupersmidt, J. (1978). Topographical response differentiation and reversal in 3-month-old infants. *Infant Behavior and Development, 1,* 323–333.

Rutkowska, J. C. (1985). *A computational alternative to Piaget's theory of infant knowledge: Action is non-trivially represenational.* Unpublished manuscript, Cognitive Studies Programme, School of Social Sciences, University of Sussex, Sussex, England.

Smith, P. H. (1984). Five-month-old infant recall and utilization of temporal organization. *Journal of Experimental Child Psychology, 38,* 400–414.

Smith, P. H., Arehart, D. M., Haaf, R. A., & de Saint Victor, C. M. (1989). Expectancies and memory for spatiotemporal events in 5-month-old infants. *Journal of Experimental Child Psychology, 47,* 210–235.

Smith, P. K., & Dutton, S. (1979). Play and training on direct and innovative problem solving. *Child Development, 50,* 830–836.

Sophian, C., & Adams, N. (1987). Infants' understanding of numerical transformations. *British Journal of Developmental Psychology, 5,* 257–264.

Sophian, C., & Sage, S. (1983). Developments in infants' search for displaced objects. *Journal of Experimental Child Psychology, 35,* 143–160.

Sylva, K., Bruner, J. S., & Genova, P. (1976). The role of play on the problem-solving of children 3–5 years old. In J. S. Bruner, A. Jolly, & K. Sylva (Eds.), *Play: Its role in development and evolution* (pp. 244–257). Harmondsworth: Penguin.

Uzgiris, I. C. (1972). Patterns of vocal and gestural imitation in infants. In F. Monks, W. Hartup, & J. deWit (Eds.), *Determinants of behavioral development* (pp. 467–471). New York: Academic Press.

Uzgiris, I. C., & Hunt, J. M. (1975). *Assessment in infancy: Ordinal scales of psychological development.* London: University of Illinois Press.

Vygotsky, L. S. (1978). *Mind in society: The development of higher psychological processes.* Cambridge, MA: Harvard University Press.

Webb, R. A., Massar, B., & Nadolny, T. (1972). Information and strategy in the young child's search for hidden objects. *Child Development, 43,* 91–104.

Wellman, H. M. (1977). The early development of intentional memory behavior. *Human Development, 20,* 86–101.

Wellman, H. M., Fabricius, W. V., & Sophian, C. (1985). The early development of planning. In H. M. Wellman (Ed.), *Children's searching: The development of search skill and spatial representation* (pp. 123–149). Hillsdale, NJ: Lawrence Erlbaum Associates.

Wellman, H. M., Somerville, S. C., Revelle, G. L., Haake, R. J., & Sophian, C. (1984). The development of comprehensive search skills. *Child Development, 55,* 472–481.

Whitecraft, R. A., Cobb, H. V., & Davis, R. T. (1959). Supplementary report: Solution of bent-wire detour problems by preschool children. *Psychological Reports, 5,* 609–611.

Willatts, P. (1984a). Stages in the development of intentional search by young infants. *Developmental Psychology, 20,* 389–396.

Willatts, P. (1984b). The Stage IV infant's solution of problems requiring the use of supports. *Infant Behavior and Development, 7,* 125–134.

Willatts, P. (1985a, July). *Development and rapid adjustment of means–ends behavior in infants aged six to eight months.* Paper presented at the Biennial Meeting of the International Society for the Study of Behavioral Development, Tours, France.

Willatts, P. (1985b). Adjustment of means–ends coordination and the representation of spatial relations in the production of search errors by infants. *British Journal of Developmental Psychology, 3,* 259–272.

Willatts, P. (1987). *Development of infants' manual detour skills.* Unpublished manuscript, University of Dundee, Department of Psychology, Dundee, Scotland.

Willatts, P. (1989). Development of problem solving in infancy. In A. Slater & J. G.

Bremner (Eds.), *Infant development* (pp. 143–182). Hillsdale, NJ: Lawrence Erlbaum Associates.

Willatts, P., Domminney, C., & Rosie, K. (1989, April). *How two-year-olds use forward-search strategy to solve problems.* Paper presented at the Biennial Meeting of the Society for Research in Child Development, Kansas City, MO.

Willatts, P., & Rosie, K. (1988, September). *Planning by 12-month-old infants.* Paper presented at the British Psychological Society Developmental Section Conference, Harlech, Wales.

Willatts, P., & Scott, H. (1988). *Young children's understanding of causal connections.* Unpublished manuscript, University of Dundee, Department of Psychology, Dundee, Scotland.

Winston, P. H. (1984). *Artificial intelligence* (2nd ed.). London: Addison-Wesley.

Wishart, J. G., & Bower, T. G. R. (1984). Spatial relations and the object concept: A normative study. In L. P. Lipsitt & C. K. Rovee–Collier (Eds.), *Advances in infancy research* (Vol. 3, pp. 57–123). Norwood, NJ: Ablex.

Wood, D., Bruner, J. S., & Ross, G. (1976). The role of tutoring in problem solving. *Journal of Child Psychology and Psychiatry, 17,* 89–100.

CHAPTER 3

When Children Mean to Remember: Issues of Context Specificity, Strategy Effectiveness, and Intentionality in the Development of Memory

Trisha H. Folds
Marianna M. Footo
University of North Carolina at Chapel Hill

Robert E. Guttentag
University of North Carolina at Greensboro

Peter A. Ornstein
University of North Carolina at Chapel Hill

Over the course of the elementary school years, children become increasingly facile users of an impressive array of techniques for remembering information (Schneider & Pressley, 1989). Indeed, much of the literature on children's memory focuses on the emergence of skills in the deployment of strategies such as rehearsal, organization, and elaboration (Brown, Bransford, Ferrara, & Campione, 1983; Schneider & Pressley, 1989). But what is the nature of the progression toward the flexible use of multiple strategies? More basically, what are the defining features of mature strategic behavior, and when can a child be said to behave in a strategic fashion? Athough these issues seem to be rather simple, recent research suggests that they are actually quite complex (e.g., Bjorklund, 1985, 1987; Ornstein, Baker-Ward, & Naus, 1988; Ornstein & Naus, 1985).

Previous discussions of the "diagnosis" of strategic behavior have focused on three dimensions of performance. First, at the most fundamental level, it should be evident that strategic activities are *intentionally* directed toward a particular goal (Brown, 1975; Flavell, 1970; Wellman, 1977, 1988). Second, it is expected that children progress toward a *consistent* application of mnemonic techniques across a range of contexts (Brown et al., 1983; Pressley, Borkowski, & Schneider, 1987). Finally, it is assumed that accompanying the consistent use of strategies is an increase in the *effectiveness* of the techniques used to satisfy a memory goal (Pressley, Borkowski, & Schneider, 1987; Wellman, 1988).

A major question facing researchers in the area of cognitive development concerns the manner and extent to which these variables should be considered when attempting to describe mnemonic growth. For example, with respect to consistency, how is a child to be characterized when he or she demonstrates seemingly strategic behavior under some task conditions, but not under others? Furthermore, are behaviors that are deliberately initiated during a memory task, but that fail to facilitate the goal of memory, to be considered strategic? Moreover, what "level" of intentionality is required in order for goal-directed behavior to be defined as strategic? Specifically, how should behaviors be characterized if they occur incidentally or are automatically driven by the stimulus materials, but still result in improved memory performance?

It is our view that little is gained by labeling adults as *"strategic"* and children as *"nonstrategic."* Not only is this characterization often incorrect, but it serves to direct attention away from a careful analysis of the development of strategic competence. This change in perspective has led researchers to view strategies in more complex terms than had been the case previously, recognizing the myriad factors that can serve to orchestrate their use (Pressley, Borkowski, & Schneider, 1987; Schneider & Pressley, 1989; Weinert & Perlmutter, 1988).

In this chapter, we present a treatment of the literature on children's memory that focuses on the diagnosis of strategic behavior according to the three dimensions of performance just indicated. We first focus on the progression toward consistent strategy use, emphasizing material that suggests a context-specific view of the development of memory. This view serves as an essential background to the subsequent discussions of questions of strategy effectiveness and intentionality. In the process, a developmental perspective is articulated that draws upon a consideration of metacognitive, motivational, knowledge, and attentional (i.e., effort) factors.

CONTEXT SPECIFICITY IN STRATEGY DEVELOPMENT

As a framework for examining the complexities of children's strategy use, consider two seemingly simple classes of strategies: rehearsal and organization. By using paradigms to "externalize" rehearsal and organization, much has been learned about the transition of children's performance from relatively "passive" to relatively "active" styles of memorization (see Ornstein & Naus, 1985).

For example, when children between the ages of 9 and 14 are given a list of to-be-remembered words and asked to rehearse aloud as each item is presented, there are clear age-related changes in the types of rehearsal techniques that are employed (e.g., Ornstein, Naus, & Liberty, 1975). Indeed, children of different ages appear to approach the task of remembering in quite different ways, with 9-year-olds focusing their rehearsal on each item as it is presented, and 14-year-olds rehearsing each word along with several previously displayed items. Paralleling these changes in rehearsal are comparable differences in the use of organizational strategies. For example, when presented with a set of low-associated items and asked to form groups that will help them remember, young children (up to third grade) will rarely create groupings based on semantic relationships, whereas older children (sixth grade and above) will do this spontaneously (e.g., Bjorklund, Ornstein, & Haig, 1977). These age differences in rehearsal and organization are clearly related to differences in recall success.

A rich literature documents these developmental differences in the use of rehearsal, organization, elaboration, and other strategies (Schneider & Pressley, 1989). However, the literature also attests to the fact that variations in task conditions can readily influence children's use of these mnemonic techniques. For example, if second and third graders are specifically instructed to engage in active, multi-item rehearsal, they can demonstrate that they are capable of doing so, although they expend more attentional effort than do older children and adults (Guttentag, 1984). In addition, if the information-processing demands of the task are reduced by permitting children visual access to all previously presented items, some typically passive rehearsers appear to spontaneously engage in active rehearsal (Guttentag, Ornstein, & Siemens, 1987). Moreover, variations in children's understanding of the materials to be remembered and the metacognitive information that is provided by the experimenter can result in corresponding variations in the age at which children first spontaneously engage in strategies such as active rehearsal, organization, and elaboration (Borkowski, Peck, Reid, & Kurtz, 1983; Ornstein & Naus, 1985; Paris, Newman, & McVey, 1982).

How shall these variations in task performance be understood? What are their implications for the definitional issues raised previously? Until recently, these variations in children's performance would have been interpreted as production deficiencies (Brown & DeLoache, 1978; Moely, Olson, Halwes, & Flavell, 1969). This term suggests that young children may possess knowledge concerning particular strategies but nonetheless fail to spontaneously invoke these techniques in appropriate situations. More recent theorizing (e.g., Ornstein, et al., 1988) places less emphasis on the nature of children's failures and more stress on documenting the conditions that facilitate successful strategy use. By focusing on contextual variations in children's performance, it may be possible to more precisely characterize children's mnemonic capabilities. The result of this reconceptualization of the nature of memory development has yielded demonstrations that even young preschoolers are capable of strategiclike behaviors under certain, highly supportive conditions (Baker–Ward, Ornstein, & Holden, 1984; DeLoache & Todd, 1987; DeLoache & Brown, 1983; Wellman & Somerville, 1982).

Given the variability in children's memory performance across tasks, it would be helpful to develop some means of describing the salient features of those contexts that affect the nature and "degree" of children's strategic behavior. A taxonomy of memory tasks would be ideal, because it could then be used to systematically inform our understanding of age-related changes in task performance (Ornstein & Folds, 1988). However, even in the absence of such a taxonomy, it would be useful to articulate some of the critical task dimensions that influence strategic behavior. As we see it, the context in which the memory task is presented can be defined in terms of the following characteristics: (a) the explicit goal of the activity, (b) the materials to be remembered, (c) the instructions provided, (d) the information-processing demands of the task, and (d) the child's knowledge and understanding of the materials.

Although we discuss each of these dimensions separately, it should be noted that we do not consider them to be independent. Rather, it is our belief that they interact in complex ways to influence strategic behavior. Moreover, even though we treat features of the context here as if they can be organized along a set of dimensions, we recognize that context effects must ultimately be considered in relative terms, with respect to characteristics of the individual subject. That is, reflecting the operation of individual differences in knowledge and existing cognitive skills, what is a highly supportive context for strategy use by one child may be less so for another.

The Explicit Goal of the Activity

The quality of young children's strategic behavior varies substantially with the goal set by the experimenter. Indeed, a number of studies have documented contrasting behaviors resulting from the explicit specification of different goals. For example, Baker–Ward et al. (1984) presented 4-, 5- and 6-year-old children with either instructions to remember or to play with a set (or a subset) of items and noted that subjects exhibited different behaviors with respect to the articulated goal of the task. Most interestingly, when asked to remember, even the 4-year-olds appeared to be studiously trying to meet this goal.

Other studies illustrate that even when the specified goals of two tasks are the same, differences in the structure of the task presentation may alter the child's understanding of the goal, thus eliciting variations in strategic activities. For example, in a paradigm developed by Istomina (1975), it has been shown that preschoolers exhibit strategylike behaviors and improved recall if the memory task is embedded in a gamelike context as opposed to the typical laboratory setting (Schneider & Brun, 1987). Istomina suggested that the reason for the different behaviors in the two situations is that the goal of remembering is intrinsic to the gamelike setting; the child does not have to explicitly adopt the memory goal. Instead, recall naturally emerges from participation in the "game." On the other hand, children's performance is not always superior in more informal settings. For example, Newman (1980) reported that 5-year-olds who prepared for a recall task under relatively informal conditions (i.e., a relaxed situation with the child sitting with the experimenter on the floor) actually recalled less than did peers tested under more standard conditions (see also Weissberg & Paris, 1986).

The Materials To Be Remembered

Assuming that children are expecting to be tested for recall, various characteristics of the materials to be remembered affect the likelihood they will appear strategic and that they will be successful in their efforts to remember information (Best & Ornstein, 1986; Corsale & Ornstein, 1980; Folds, Ornstein, & Bjorklund, 1989). For example, when third graders and younger children are given instructions to sort so that the groups formed will help them remember, they will readily make placements on the basis of meaning when presented with taxonomic materials, but not with low-associated items (Best & Ornstein, 1986; Corsale, 1978; Corsale & Ornstein, 1980; Lange, 1973; 1978). These differences in strategy use as a function of materials (i.e., meaning-based sorting with one type of materials but not another) have recently been replicated by Folds, Ornstein, & Bjorklund (1989) using a within subjects design that permits the observation of an *individual's* behavior across multiple contexts. In addition, other illustrations of materials effects can be seen in the ample demonstrations of young children's superior performance when they are presented with pictures versus words (e.g., Ghatala & Levin, 1981), objects versus pictures (e.g., Newman, 1980), highly typical versus less typical category exemplars (e.g., Rabinowtiz, 1984), and highly meaningful versus less meaningful words (e.g., Tarkin, 1981).

In contrast to the performance of young children, the performance of sixth graders and older children appears less dependent on the nature of the to-be-remembered stimulus materials. That is, when asked to remember, they will use an organizational strategy across a wider set of materials than do young children. Thus, these children will sort on a semantic basis even when presented with low-associated items (Best & Ornstein, 1986; Corsale & Ornstein, 1980; Folds, Bjorklund, & Ornstein, 1987).

The Instructions Provided

The instructions given to subjects represent a significant feature of the memorization context, and variations in the instructions can markedly influence the level of children's strategic activities (e.g., Corsale & Ornstein, 1980; Ornstein, Medlin, Stone, & Naus, 1985). For example, when second graders were instructed to use an active, multi-item rehearsal strategy, they were able to use this technique, although they were better able to do so when given additional time or continued visual access to the to-be-remembered materials (Ornstein, Naus, & Stone, 1977; Ornstein, et al., 1985). Moreover, improvements in recall were noted as a function of these changes in the strategies utilized. Comparable findings are observed with organizational and elaboration strategies (see Schneider & Pressley, 1989). For example, using a sort/recall task, Corsale and Ornstein (1980) demonstrated that third graders instructed to group items based on meaning did do so and subsequently displayed higher levels of recall than peers instructed to group items to facilitate recall. Findings such as these suggest that even subtle changes in the context can lead to significant increases in effective strategic performance.

The Information-Processing Demands of the Task

When memory is the explicit goal, the information-processing requirements of the task can easily affect the likelihood that school-age children will appear to be strategic. Thus, for example, visual access to to-be-remembered items increases the frequency with which third graders rehearse in an active manner, even without explicit instruction to do so (Guttentag et al., 1987). These authors suggested that the effect of visual access to items is to lessen the demands on the subject's information-processing capabilities. Less effort is required for maintaining the to-be-remembered items in immediate memory, so that more effort can be devoted to strategic behaviors to enhance recall. Moreover, the "simplification" of memory tasks for young children is generally presumed to involve a reduction in the information-processing demands of strategic performance, resulting in even preschoolers' appearing to perform in a strategic manner (Wellman, 1988; Wellman & Somerville, 1980; DeLoache & Todd, 1987).

The Child's Knowledge
and Understanding of the Materials

Beginning with the demonstrations of Chi (1978) and Lindberg (1980) there is now ample evidence of children's superior recall of materials about which they have substantial prior knowledge. Indeed, Chi (1978) indicated that the influence of knowledge can be so strong that under some conditions, child experts in a particular domain can exhibit performance that is superior to that of adult novices. Current debate on the influence of prior knowledge centers on the degree to which these demonstrations can be interpreted in terms of the direct (i.e., unmediated by strategies) influence of the knowledge system on memory performance (e.g., Bjorklund, 1985, 1987; Ornstein & Naus, 1985; Ornstein et al., 1988). Nonetheless, there are a number of reports of an interaction between knowledge and strategies, such that superior strategic performance is obtained when children are given materials about which they have greater knowledge than when they are asked to remember less familiar items (see Ornstein & Naus, 1985; Rabinowitz & Chi, 1987). Zembar and Naus (1985), for example, found that typical age differences in rehearsal-strategy use and recall were eliminated when the younger children were presented a list of highly familiar words to learn (e.g., milk) and the older children were presented a list of difficult, less familiar words (e.g., galleon).

THE DEVELOPMENT OF EFFECTIVE STRATEGY USE

Our characterization of the context specificity of children's strategic deployment indicates that with increases in age, children broaden the range of situations in which their efforts can be viewed as strategic.

Paralleling this generalization across contexts, there are also increases in the effectiveness of children's strategic activities, measured in terms of improvements in recall performance. Moreover, this increased effectiveness appears to reflect two different developmental patterns. First, there are substantial changes in what children actually do while trying to remember. Whereas younger children engage in more passive, rote memorization techniques, as they get older, their mnemonic activities involve a more active integration of to-be-remembered information with existing knowledge. Second, even when a seemingly identical strategy is used by children of different ages, the technique seems to be more effective in facilitating the recall of older as opposed to younger children. In this section, we discuss both of these types of "effectiveness," and then turn to a treatment of factors that may account for these developmental changes.

Changes in the Form of Children's Strategies

With increases in age, not only are children more likely to engage in some form of strategy to meet a goal of remembering, but what they do to meet the goal changes substantially. For example, as previously suggested, during the course of the elementary school years, children's rehearsal changes from relatively simple single-item techniques to substantially more complex multi-item rehearsal procedures (e.g., Ornstein & Naus, 1978). Comparable age-related changes are observed in children's use of other mnemonic techniques, and there is ample evidence that the more active strategies of older children are more effective in facilitating memory performance. Indeed, evidence for the strategy–recall linkage is seen in numerous training studies in which the recall performance of younger children is enhanced as a result of instruction and practice in the techniques of older children (e.g., Footo, Guttentag, & Ornstein, 1988; Ghatala, Levin, Pressley, & Lodico, 1985; Paris, et al., 1982). For example, Paris et al. (1982) found that providing young children with extensive training and feedback concerning a variety of mnemonic strategies spontaneously used by older individuals increased performance on a subsequent recall task and also improved metamnemonic awareness.

To some extent, the greater strategic effectiveness of older children reflects the incorporation of an increasing number of mnemonic techniques into their strategic repetoire and a growing ability to select the most effective strategy for any particular task (Schneider & Pressley, 1989). In a series of studies, Ghatala, Levin, Pressley, and their colleagues (Ghatala et al., 1985; Lodico, Ghatala, Levin, Pressley, & Bell, 1983; Pressley, Levin, & Ghatala, 1984) trained children to use several techniques that varied in their effectiveness for supporting recall. Training was accompanied by feedback focused on the effectiveness of the strategy for improving recall. Following training, subjects were presented with test materials and allowed to choose which of the trained strategies they perceived as most task appropriate. The results demonstrated that the children selected the strategy that had been indicated as most effective during training. The authors concluded that children understand the importance of choosing the most effective strategy and are more likely to do so when they have specific information about the comparative effectiveness of various strategies.

Increases in the Effectiveness of Identical Strategies

An additional component of the age-related trend in increased strategic effectiveness is seen in the enhanced benefit that children derive from any given mnemonic procedure. For instance, it was previously indicated that the recall performance of younger children improves when they are trained to utilize the same procedures spontaneously deployed by older children. However, age differences in recall performance are rarely eliminated by such training, even though subjects at each age appear to be using the same procedures (e.g., Ornstein, et al., 1977). Often, the mnemonic technique appears to simply work more effectively for older children, although reducing the information-processing demands can facilitate the performance of younger children (Ornstein, et al., 1985). Of course, under some conditions it can be shown that children are actually utilizing somewhat different forms of the strategy and that these variations are responsible for the failure to eliminate age differences (see, e.g., Naus, Ornstein, & Aivano, 1977).

Other examples of age differences in the effectiveness of specific procedures can be seen in Wellman's (1988) descriptions of "faulty" strategies, that is, strategies that young children utilize but which do not benefit their performance. Clearly, in some cases, the problem is that the strategy selected is simply inappropriate for the task (e.g., Heisel & Ritter, 1981). In other cases, however, the strategy is indeed appropriate, but for unknown reasons the children are not yet able to implement it in a manner that benefits memory performance. For example, consider the Baker-Ward, et al. (1984) demonstration that children as young as 4 years of age spontaneously used techniques such as naming and visual examination of target objects in response to an instruction to remember. However, these 4-year-olds failed to recall more times than comparison groups that had been instructed to play with the items. In contrast, although the 6-year-olds appeared to be using the same strategy as the 4-year-olds in the "remember" condition, the older children exhibited superior recall. Thus, Baker–Ward et al. (1984) found that children may, under some conditions, evidence strategic behavior that fails to benefit recall. Comparable demonstrations of ineffective attentional strategies have been reported by Miller and Harris (1988).

As a general rule, then, with increases in age, children's mnemonic techniques have a correspondingly greater "payoff" in terms of enhanced remembering, both as a result of the incorporation and selection of increasingly effective mnemonic procedures, and as a consequence of the increasing effectiveness with which specific techniques are deployed. Of course, the distinction drawn here between age differences in the nature of the strategies deployed and age differences in the effectiveness of specific procedures may be more apparent than real. With more refined techniques of assessment, it may be found that even when subjects of different ages seem to be using the same strategy, in fact there may be subtle, but important differences, in the functional elements of strategic deployment (Naus, et al., 1977).

What Factors Underlie These Changes?

How can these age-related trends in strategy effectiveness be understood? In this section we consider four possible contributors to this developmental progression: (a) increases in metamnemonic understanding, (b) experiences in school, (c) the growth of the knowledge base, and (d) the increased efficiency of strategy use.

Metamnemonic Understanding

Correlated with the developmental changes previously discussed is a corresponding growth of metamemory. That is, there is an increase in children's understanding of the demands of tasks involving memory and of the operation of their own memory systems (Cavanaugh & Perlmutter, 1982; Kreutzer, Leonard, & Flavell, 1975; Schneider, 1985; Wellman, 1983). Given that both strategic understanding and competence develop during the elementary school years, there has been much speculation about a causal linkage. Indeed, numerous investigators have suggested that an increase in metamnemonic knowledge is a crucial element in the child's increasing tendencies to use good mnemonic strategies in an appropriate and effective fashion (Cavanaugh & Borkowski, 1980; Schneider, 1985).

Although metamemory has often been suggested as being of critical importance for mnemonic growth, convincing empirical evidence in support of the linkage between knowledge about strategies and strategy use is lacking. Interestingly, the importance of the connection between metamemory and strategy use has been demonstrated more convincingly in training studies than in research correlating existing levels of mnemonic knowledge with spontaneous strategy use. More specifically, the incorporation of metamnemonic instruction in strategy training programs has contributed to better understanding of the impact of metamnemonic knowledge on strategic performance (e.g., Paris et al., 1982), than have studies of the memory–metamemory connections under conditions of spontaneous strategy use, which often show the connection to be weak or nonexistent, especially for younger children (e.g., Cavanaugh & Perlmutter, 1982; Schneider, 1985). Examples of the difficulties in documenting the importance of metamemory in correlational studies include cases in which young children verbalize knowledge of a mnemonic technique but fail to actually use it (Sodian, Schneider, & Perlmutter, 1986) and cases in which subjects use what might be viewed as a deliberate strategy but who are unable to demonstrate any corresponding metamnemonic awareness (Bjorklund & Zeman, 1982).

To some extent, this problem may be traceable to methodological difficulties in the assessment of metamnemonic understanding (e.g., Cavanaugh & Perlmutter, 1982; Schneider, 1985). If this is the case, then the use of other methodologies (e.g., Best & Ornstein's, 1986, peer tutoring technique) may yield different outcomes. On the other hand, it is possible that general motivational or attributional processes may influence the likelihood that younger children in particular will make reference to their existing mnemonic knowledge when selecting a mnemonic strategy (see Pressley, Borkowski, & Johnson, 1987; Pressley, Borkowski, & Schneider, 1987). Lange, Guttentag, and Nida (1988), for instance, found evidence for a strong correlation between memory knowledge and strategy use among 6- and 7-year-olds, but only for those children classified by their teachers as having higher mastery orientations; that is, children who were rated to be more self-directed and intent on succeeding in challenging tasks. Kurtz and Borkowski (1984) also found that of the children in their training study who showed strategy transfer, those who attributed success in the task to their own effort were more likely to profit from use of the strategy.

Experience in School

A second factor that has been linked to the increased effectiveness of children's mnemonic techniques is exposure to tasks requiring the use of memorization. For example, as children proceed through the elementary school years, there are increasing demands placed upon their memory abilities, and these demands may result in the development of task-appropriate techniques. Also, teachers begin to gradually remove organizational supports and repetitions from their lessons and place more of the burden for the use of learning strategies on the child (e.g., Rogoff & Mistry, 1985). Although effective strategy use may in some cases be explicitly instructed, the evidence for this is still weak, and it appears more likely that strategies are induced as a consequence of the more general task demands placed on children in school (Best & Ornstein, 1986; Morrison, 1987).

The role of formal schooling has been implicated in numerous comparative-cultural studies of memory development (e.g., Rogoff, 1981; Wagner, 1978; Wagner & Spratt, 1987), and in a recent "natural experiment" reported by Morrison (1987). Morrison (1987) was able to compare two groups of children who were matched on chronological age and gender, but who differed in terms of the amount of exposure to a school setting. The groups were composed of children whose birthdays were clustered around the cut-off date used for entry into school; a group of "old kindergarteners" who had just "missed" the cut-off date for first grade, and a comparison group of "young first graders" who had just "made" the cut-off-date. With these groups, Morrison (1987) could document the impact of one year of formal schooling on a variety of memory and other cognitive tasks. Most interestingly, despite teacher reports suggesting that strategies were not explicitly taught, Morrison found that the children with a year of school experience were superior in terms of recall and strategy use.

The Knowledge Base

A third factor thought to be relevant to the developmental progression toward more effective mnemonic activity is an increase in the content and complexity of the child's general fund of knowledge, or knowledge base. With increases in age, children learn more about their native language, about specific bodies of information, and indeed about the world. There are ample demonstrations that this increased knowledge is related to corresponding changes in recall performance, although there has been considerable debate concerning the mechanisms by which knowledge influences performance (e.g., Bjorklund, 1985, 1987; Chi, 1978; Ornstein & Naus, 1985; Ornstein et al., 1988). For example, Bjorklund (1985) initially argued that prior to adolescence, children's memory performance could best be viewed as an automatic by-product of an increasingly more articulated knowledge system. In contrast to these strong claims about the direct (i.e., not mediated by strategies) effects of the knowledge base on memory performance, there now seems to be a growing consensus concerning the importance of both knowledge and strategies (e.g., Ornstein, in press; Ornstein et al., 1988; Muir & Bjorklund, in press; Rabinowitz & Chi, 1987). Indeed, there is some evidence to suggest that the impact of the knowledge base may under some conditions be mediated by effects on strategy implementation (Ornstein & Naus, 1985; Rabinowitz & McAuley, in press).

This interactional perspective stresses the extent to which the current state of a child's knowledge system may enable the execution of particular strategies (e.g., Ornstein, et al., 1988). Examples of this influence of the knowledge base on strategy execution were presented previously in the treatment of variations in strategic performance as a function of the child's knowledge of the materials. Thus, when presented with highly salient categorical items, third graders were able to utilize a semantically based sorting strategy, whereas they did not do so with low associated items (Corsale, 1978; Corsale & Ornstein, 1980; Folds et al., 1989). In this situation, the highly organized nature of the third graders' taxonomic knowledge facilitated the execution of the more effective mnemonic strategy. Moreover, it is thought that with increases in age, the knowledge system in general becomes more articulated and richly interconnected, thereby further contributing to the ease of access that is required for efficient strategy execution (Bjorklund, 1987; Muir & Bjorklund, in press; Ornstein & Naus, 1985)

Efficiency of Strategy Use

An additional factor hypothesized to influence strategic effectiveness is the resource efficiency of strategy use. The findings from several recent studies suggest that, with increasing age, children become capable of executing specific strategic procedures in a manner that is less demanding of attentional resources. For example, Guttentag (1984) showed that, although second graders are capable of executing an active rehearsal strategy, deployment of the strategy is more demanding of their limited attentional resources than is the case for older children or adults (see also Bjorklund & Harnishfeger, 1987; Kee & Davies, 1988). Guttentag hypothesized that age differences in the resource demands of strategy use may contribute to age differences in the deployment of effective, but resource-demanding, strategies such as active rehearsal. To test this contention, Guttentag et al. (1987) examined the effects on strategy use of presenting list items in a manner that reduced the resource demands of active rehearsal. They found that some children who utilized a passive strategy under normal presentation conditions switched to the utilization of more active procedures under conditions in which the resource demands of the more active procedures was reduced.

Whereas Guttentag emphasized the role of strategy execution efficiency on the selection of effective strategies, Bjorklund and Harnishfeger (1987) and Kee and Davies (1988) stressed potential effects on the benefits to be derived from the deployment of particular strategies. These authors have argued that, because younger children need to allocate more attentional resources than do older children to the mechanics of strategy execution, younger children will have fewer resources left over for other storage and encoding operations, thereby reducing the mnemonic benefit derived from strategy use (see also Miller & Harris, 1988). Thus, age differences in the resource demands of strategy use may be a further factor contributing to the age differences in memory performance under conditions in which strategy use is held constant across age.

INTENTIONALITY

The complexities of mnemonic growth just illustrated reinforce the perspective that intentionality must be viewed at several levels of analysis and that there are likely to be substantial age-related changes in children's understanding of what it means to be intentional and goal oriented. For many researchers, intentionality is the defining feature of strategic behavior (see Schneider & Pressley, 1989). At the core of most conceptions of intentionality are (a) an individual's awareness of a goal and (b) an explicit awareness of a specific means–end relationship for achieving that goal (Bullock & Lütkenhaus, 1988; Paris, 1978; Wellman, 1977). Moreover, it is often assumed that the subject selects a strategy for deployment on the task based on an awareness of a goal and knowledge of a procedure thought to be appropriate for reaching that goal (Pressley, Borkowski, & Johnson, 1987; Wellman, 1977). Although these considerations seem compelling, there are numerous potential problems, particularly when we are considering strategy use in young children.

Definitional Complexities

The difficulties with this view of intentionality appear at each of the three steps included in past definitions: (a) awareness of the goal, (b) knowledge of a means–end relationship, and (c) the selection of a technique.

Awareness of a Goal

Awareness of a mnemonic goal is perhaps the fundamental aspect of intentionality. Nonetheless, it is important to realize that this awareness may vary markedly as a function of the complexity of the task. Even quite young children may demonstrate an awareness of the goal when the task is simplified and familiar (e.g., DeLoache & Todd, 1987; Wellman, 1988), but yet seem unaware of the goal when the task is more complex and adultlike. In addition, it seems possible, particularly with more complex tasks, that there may be a discrepancy between the experimenter's goal and that of the child; consequently, there may be a difference between the task that is intended and the task that is perceived (for parallels in the Piagetian literature, see, e.g., McGarrigle, Greive, & Hughes, 1978). Nonetheless, it seems likely that with simple tasks of remembering, there will be a substantial overlap between the adult's and the child's goals.

Knowledge of Means–Ends Relationship

Although awareness of a mnemonic goal is a basic feature of intentionality, one must also know that certain procedures (i.e., strategies) should be carried out in order to reach that goal. In addition, for the use of a specific procedure to be labeled deliberate, there must be explicit awareness that the procedure is being used to achieve the intended goal. This knowledge, of course, may exist at several different levels, ranging from the young child who thinks that one simply has to "work hard" in order to remember, to the adolescent who is able to manipulate a range of complex strategies.

Specific knowledge of means-ends relationships varies to a considerable extent over a dimension that could be labeled "preplanning." In some situations, a subject may be quite aware of techniques that are applicable to a given situation, and may use the techniques in a preplanned manner. Indeed, some children's knowledge of means–ends relationships is so detailed that they are able to use feedback from task performance in order to modify their strategies (Pressley, et al., 1984; Pressley, Borkowski, & Schneider, 1987). In other situations, however, the child may develop strategic insights while in the midst of attempting to reach the goal (e.g., Bjorklund & Zeman, 1982). Indeed, in the majority of situations, the child's performance may be governed by a combination of prior metamnemonic understanding and "ah ha" experiences during the task itself. This set of "on line" experiences may include the use of feedback from task performance and the discovery of features of the materials that are conducive to the deployment of particular procedures. Thus, children can demonstrate knowledge of means–ends relations at many different levels, and these likely change as a function of age and experience with particular types of memory tasks.

Selection and Execution of a Procedure

This discussion seems to imply that knowledge of a goal and of a particular means–goal relation will lead a child into mnemonic action. However, this also assumes that the child's knowledge is matched by corresponding motivation, but this is not always the case. Thus, the final component of intentionality that we discuss is described by Wellman (1977) as the difference between "can" and "try" and by Paris and Byrnes (1989) as the difference between "competence" and "performance." "Can" and "competence" basically refer to what we have already discussed as the child's underlying metamnemonic knowledge and skills in the utilization of strategies. In contrast, "try" and "performance" are more tied to the individual's motivational system. A child can understand the prescribed goal, can have the requisite metamnemonic knowledge, and still not be motivated to use the strategy.

Although there are certainly external factors, such as task difficulty (Weiner, 1974, 1979), that influence a person's desire to exert effort, a significant amount of the drive to engage in a particular behavior has its source in certain characteristics of the individual. Many researchers (e.g., Bandura, 1982; Brophy, 1983; McCombs, 1984; Schunk, 1988) believe that this internal drive state is a result of the individual's set of beliefs about what behaviors he or she will be able to execute successfully in a given situation. Bandura and Schunk (1981) and McCombs (1984) argued that a person with a higher level of self-efficacy (defined as "personal judgments about one's capabilities to organize and implement behaviors in specific situations," Schunk, 1984, p. 48) is more likely to engage in task-relevant activities. Similarly, a person who perceives his or her performance to be improved by the exertion of effort (Andrews & Debus, 1978; Kurtz & Borkowski, 1984; Weiner, 1979) would be more likely to actually exert effort. These motivational and attributional variables fit with conceptions of intentionality because of the presumption that children do not use skills in their cognitive repertoires if they do not believe that there would be a pay off for the effort exerted (e.g., Paris, Newman, & Jacobs, 1985).

Are Children Intentional?

Given this analysis of component features of intentionality, how can we characterize the developing child? From our perspective, with relatively simple tasks, even preschoolers show clear signs of being intentional at the level of demonstrating an awareness of a memory goal and an understanding that *something* should be done in order to reach that goal. Of course, what is done is not always effective, but it does represent deliberately initiated strategic behavior in the service of a memory goal. Older children, in turn, evidence a deeper understanding of what it means to be intentional; their strategies are more complex and effective, although the execution of these techniques may sometimes be influenced by the associative properties of the to-be-remembered materials. Still older children demonstrate the most sophisticated behavior in that their memorization efforts can be characterized by preplanning, skillful selection of strategies, and monitoring of their strategic effectiveness.

We feel that awareness of a mnemonic goal in and of itself is sufficient to credit the young child with intentionality. Our evidence for claims about preschoolers' goal awareness stems from studies that use "differentiation" paradigms (Wellman, 1977; Yussen, Gagné, Gargiulo, & Kunen, 1974). These experiments are designed to contrast the performance of children in situations in which different goals are specified by the experimenter. If children's behavior varies as a function of the goal that is set, it is assumed that they share some understanding of what is meant by the goals. For example, consider the study of Baker–Ward et al. (1984) in which 4-, 5-, and 6-year-olds were instructed either to play with a group of toys or to try to remember the toys. Even among the 4-year-olds, children who were instructed to remember the materials engaged in activities such as naming and visual examination that were relevant to the goal of remembering, whereas children receiving play instructions did just that, that is, they tended to play with the toys. Comparable inferences concerning intentionality emerge from studies of preschooler's performance in simple tests of spatial memory (DeLoache & Brown, 1979, 1983; Wellman, Ritter, & Flavell, 1975).

Although the methodology of the differentiation paradigm has not been employed in studies with school-age children, the compliance of older children with requests to externalize their strategic efforts seems consistent with a shared understanding of the goal of remembering. Nonetheless, as previously discussed, what children do when they are asked to remember changes markedly during the course of the elementary school years, and these changes are associated with increases in effectiveness. Thus, children's command of means–ends relations changes substantially from the level of the third grader who executes a simple single-item rehearsal strategy to the level of the seventh grader who monitors his or her performance, adjusting the procedures as necessary. Further, the adolescent is able to apply strategies and abstract general principles so that they can be transferred to other situations (see Cox, Ornstein & Valsiner, in press).

It is important to emphasize that judgments of intentionality—and particularly competence in means–ends relations—may vary substantially as a function of task parameters. Consider, for example, the performance of third graders in tasks that use sorting procedures to examine organizational strategies (e.g., Corsale & Ornstein, 1980). When presented with low associated items to be remembered, and requested to form groups that will help them remember the items, third graders seem to engage in a random sorting pattern; they do not utilize their command of interitem relationships to form groups of related items. These children are clearly intentional in the sense of being goal oriented, but their behavior provides no hint of an understanding that the use of associative relations might facilitate recall. On the other hand, when the materials are changed to taxonomically related items (Best & Ornstein, 1986; Corsale, 1978; Folds, et al., 1989), children of the same age engage in categorized sorting in the service of the memory goal. This finding thus suggests that not only will children's knowledge of means–ends relations seem to vary as a function of task parameters, but also that strong interitem associations may actually facilitate the execution of a particular strategy. In this situation, there is a deliberate strategy in the sense that the child is goal oriented and makes specific placements of items in particular groups, but these placements are driven by the strong organizational properties of the stimuli.

These results suggest that strategy execution may involve a mixture of intentional and automatic procedures, with the exact nature of the mix changing with age (Bjorklund, 1985). The simple classification of the components of strategy execution as intentional or automatic may not, however, fully capture the dynamics of strategy use. In many cases, the automatic processes may not occur independently of the intentional ones. That is, some components of strategy use may occur as automatic by-products of other, more deliberate or intentional procedures. Guttentag (1989), for instance, found evidence for "automatic" elaboration during the paired associate learning of "easy to elaborate" word pairs (e.g., star/telescope), but these elaborations occurred only when subjects deliberately engaged in semantic processing of the individual words within each item pair.

These findings highlight again the different levels of intentionality that may be operative in any particular case of strategy use. For example, in some cases, taxonomic organization during the memorization of categorized lists may result from a deliberate and pre-planned intent to search for taxonomic relations among items. In other cases, however, taxonomic organization may result from a de-liberate on-line search for meaningful relations among items without any preplanned intent to organize in a particular way, or may simply occur as an automatic by-product of deliberate attentiveness to the presented materials.

SUMMARY AND CONCLUSION

In this chapter, we have examined the literature on the development of memory strategies, focusing on three dimensions of strategic per-formance: consistency, effectiveness, and intentionality. It is clear from the research discussed that children's strategy use and resulting recall performance vary dramatically as a function of the context. Therefore, a child cannot simply be characterized as either strategic or nonstrategic; rather, children seem to be more strategic in certain settings and less so in others. Moreover, an analysis of settings in which remembering is required suggests that task requirements vary widely; hence, the very definition of what it means to be strategic may change markedly according to the targeted task. And most critically, in some situations, certain features of the task—such as the materials to be remembered—seem to elicit in an automatic or "obligatory" fashion, behaviors that would otherwise be viewed as strategic, mak-ing rather difficult the determination of whether the behaviors in question were deployed in a deliberate sense.

Demonstrations of context specificity could be viewed as produc-tion deficiencies and perhaps dismissed as frequent examples of this ubiquitous (and presumably uninteresting) concept (Brown & De-Loache, 1978). However, to do so would be to ignore important information concerning the development of children's skills. Rather than being bored or distressed by young children's differing perfor-mance across settings, we suggest that this variability offers unique opportunities for charting the course of mnemonic growth and for learning about factors that may be of critical developmental im-portance. In particular, we argue that children's memory skills should be discussed in terms of a profile of performance in contrasting contexts, and that developmental changes in memory abilities should be measured in terms of variations in the profile across age.

Consistent with other recent perspectives on strategy development (e.g., Muir & Bjorklund, in press Ornstein, et al., 1988; Waters & Andreassen, 1983), we propose that children may initially demonstrate goal-directed memory strategies in the context of highly sup-portive task environments and then show gradual generalization to other less supportive contexts. Young children may initially demon-strate mnemonic strategies when asked to remember strongly related materials, or materials in which an underlying structure is made very explicit, particularly when the stimuli remain available for prolonged visual inspection. Children may gradually generalize these strategic approaches to less "hospitable" environments (cf., Rowher, 1973). Paralleling this generalization process is a corresponding increase in the effectiveness of children's strategies.

Central to this approach is the notion that young children need more contextual supports for the execution of mnemonic techniques than do older children and that with the provision of appropriate supports, young children may demonstrate mnemonic competence earlier than would typically be the case. As such, this view has much in common with Brown and Reeve's (1987) "bandwidths of competence" approach and Vygotsky's (1978) "zone of proximal development" (see also Cox et al., in press).

Our consideration of the growing generality and effectiveness of children's mnemonic strategies led to a treatment of the complex question of intentionality. Given the resulting multicomponential analysis of what it means to be a deliberate strategy user, it is not surprising that the literature contains conflicts concerning strategy diagnosis. For example, contrast Bjorklund's (1985) claim that chil-dren do not appear to be strategic until adolescence with our view (see also Ornstein & Naus, 1985; Ornstein et al., 1988) that even pre-schoolers can be deliberately strategic. It seems likely that this dis-agreement reflects attention to different features of intentionality. Thus, Bjorklund (1985) seemed to require a fully-developed-in-ad-vance plan for strategic activities, whereas we are willing to accept mere awareness of a mnemonic goal.

Differential use of the concepts such as intentionality, however, should not distract us from acknowledging the fundamental agree-ment that exists in the field concerning descriptions of developmental change. That is, it is less important that concensus be reached about where to draw the line between strategic and nonstrategic behavior than it is to examine, with increasing precision, the nature of de-velopmental change in mnemonic skill. It is hoped that analyses of the component features of strategy use, such as that attempted here, will facilitate the adoption of a common classification scheme for the discussion of children's use of strategies in the service of memoriza-tion goals.

REFERENCES

Andrews, G. R., & Debus, R. L. (1978). Persistence and the causal perception of failure: Modifying cognitive attributions. *Journal of Educational Psychology, 70* 154–166.

Baker–Ward, L., Ornstein, P. A., & Holden, D. J. (1984). The expression of memorization in early childhood. *Journal of Experimemtal Child Psychology, 37,* 555–575.

Bandura, A. (1982). Self-efficacy mechanism in human agency. *American Psychologist, 37,* 122–147.

Bandura, A., & Schunk, D. (1981). Cultivating competence, self-efficacy, and intrinsic interest through proximal self-motivation. *Journal of Personality and Social Psychology, 41,* 586–598.

Best, D. L., & Ornstein, P. A. (1986). Children's generation and communication of mnemonic organizational strategies. *Developmental Psychology, 22,* 845–853.

Bjorklund, D. F. (1985). The role of conceptual knowledge in the development of organization in children's memory. In C. J. Brainerd & M. Pressley (Eds.), *Basic processes in memory development: Progress in cognitive development research* (pp. 103–142). New York: Springer-Verlag.

Bjorklund, D. F. (1987). How age changes in knowledge base contribute to the development of children's memory: An interpretive review. *Developmental Review, 7,* 93–130.

Bjorklund, D. F., & Harnishfeger, K. K. (1987). Developmental differences in the mental effort requirements for the use of an organizational strategy in free recall. *Journal of Experimental Child Psychology, 44,* 109–125.

Bjorklund, D. F., Ornstein, P. A., & Haig, J. R. (1977). Developmental differences in organization and recall: Training in the use of organizational techniques. *Developmental Psychology, 13,* 175–183.

Bjorklund, D. F., & Zeman, B. R. (1982). Children's organization and metamemory awareness in their recall of familiar information. *Child Development, 53,* 799–810.

Borkowski, J. G., Peck, V. A., Reid, M. K., & Kurtz, B. E. (1983). Impulsivity and strategy transfer: Metamemory as a mediator. *Child Development, 54,* 459–473.

Brophy, J. (1983). Conceptualizing student motivation. *Educational Psychologist, 18,* 200–215.

Brown, A. L. (1975). The development of memory: Knowing, knowing about knowing, and knowing how to know. In H. W. Reese (Ed.), *Advances in child development and behavior.* (Vol. 10, pp. 103–152). New York: Academic Press.

Brown, A. L., Bransford, J. D., Ferrara, R. A., & Campione, J. C. (1983). Learning, remembering, and understanding. In J. H. Flavell & E. M. Markman (Eds.), *Handbook of child psychology: Cognitive development* (Vol. 3, pp. 77–166) New York: Wiley.

Brown, A. L., & DeLoache, J. S. (1978). Skills, plans, and self-regulation. In R. S. Siegler (Ed.), *Children's thinking: What develops?* (pp. 3–36). Hillsdale, NJ: Lawrence Erlbaum Associates.

Brown, A. L., & Reeve, R. R. (1987). Bandwidths of competence: The role of supportive contexts in learning and development. In L. Liben (Ed.), *Development and learning* (pp. 173–223) Hillsdale, NJ: Lawrence Erlbaum Associates.

Bullock, M., & Lütkenhaus, P. (1988). The development of volitional behavior in the toddler years. *Child Development, 59,* 664–674.

Cavanaugh, J. C., & Borkowski, J. G. (1980). Searching for metamemory–memory connections: A developmental study. *Developmental Psychology, 16,* 441–453.

Cavanaugh, J. C., & Perlmutter, M. (1982). Metamemory: A critical examination. *Child Development, 53,* 11–28.

Chi, M. T. H. (1978). Knowledge structure and memory development. In R. Siegler (Ed.), *Children's thinking: What develops?* (pp. 73–96). Hillsdale, NJ: Lawrence Erlbaum Associates.

Corsale, K. (1978). *Factors affecting children's use of organization in recall.* Unpublished doctoral dissertation, University of North Carolina at Chapel Hill.

Corsale, K., & Ornstein, P. A. (1980). Developmental changes in children's use of semantic information in recall. *Journal of Experimental Child Psychology, 41,* 18–37.

Cox, B., Ornstein, P. A. & Valsiner, J. (in press). The role of internalization in the transfer of mnemonic strategies. In L. Oppenheimer & J. Valsiner (Eds.), *The origins of action: International perspectives.* New York: Springer.

DeLoache, J. S., & Brown, A. L. (1979). Looking for Big Bird: Studies of memory in very young children. *The Quarterly Newsletter of the Laboratory of Comparative Human Cognition, 1,* 53–57.

DeLoache, J. S., & Brown, A. L. (1983). Very young children's memory for the location of objects in a large-scale environment. *Child Development, 20,* 37–44.

DeLoache, J. S., & Todd, C. M. (1987). *Young children's use of spatial organization as a mnemonic strategy.* Paper presented at the biannual meeting of the Society for Research in Child Development, Baltimore.

Flavell, J. H. (1970). Developmental studies of mediated memory. In H. W. Reese & L. P. Lipsitt (Eds.), *Advances in child development and behavior* (pp. 182–213). London: Academic Press.

Folds, T. H., Bjorklund, D. F., & Ornstein, P. A. (1987). *The effects of taxonomic relatedness on third and sixth graders' use of an organizational strategy.* Unpublished manuscript, University of North Carolina at Chapel Hill.

Folds, T H., Ornstein, P. A., & Bjorklund, D. F. (1989). *Context specificity in mnemonic strategy use.* Paper presented at the biannual meeting of the Society for Research in Child Development, Kansas City.

Footo, M. M., Guttentag, R., & Ornstein, P. A. (1988). *Capacity demands of strategy execution: Effects of training and practice.* Paper presented at the annual meeting of the American Educational Research Association, New Orleans.

Ghatala, E. S., & Levin, J. R. (1981). Children's incidental memory for pictures: Item processing versus list organization. *Journal of Experimental Child Psychology, 33,* 504–513.

Ghatala, E. S., Levin, J. R., Pressley, M., & Lodico, M. G. (1985). Training and cognitive strategy monitoring in children. *American Educational Research Journal, 22,* 199–216.

Guttentag, R. E. (1984). The mental effort requirement of cumulative rehearsal: A developmental study. *Journal of Experimental Child Psychology, 37,* 92–106.

Guttentag, R. E. (1989). Age differences in dual-task performance: Procedures, assumptions, and results. *Developmental Review, 9,* 146–170.

Guttentag, R. E., Ornstein, P. A., & Siemens, L. (1987). The mental effort requirements of cumulative rehearsal: Transitions in strategy acquisition. *Cognitive Development, 2,* 307–326.

Heisel, B. E., & Ritter, K. (1981). Young children's storage behavior in a memory for location task. *Journal of Experimental Child Psychology, 31,* 250–364.

Istomina, M. (1975). The development of voluntary memory in preschool-age children. *Soviet Psychology, 13,* 5–64.

Kee, D. W., & Davies, L. (1988). Mental effort and elaboration: A developmental analysis. *Contemporary Educational Psychology, 13,* 221–228.

Kreutzer, M. A., Leonard, C., & Flavell, J. H. (1975). An interview study of children's knowledge about memory. *Monographs of the Society for Research in Child Development, 40*(1, Serial No. 159).

Kurtz, B. E., & Borkowski, J. G. (1984). Children's metacognition: Exploring relations among knowledge, process, and motivational variables. *Journal of Experimental Child Psychology, 37,* 335–354.

Lange, G. (1973). The development of conceptual and rote recall skills among school age children. *Journal of Experimental Child Psychology, 15,* 394–406.

Lange, G. (1978). Organization-related processes in children's recall. In P. A. Ornstein (Ed.), *Memory development in children* (pp. 101–128). Hillsdale, NJ: Lawrence Erlbaum Associates.

Lange, G., Guttentag, R. E., & Nida, R. E. (1988). Metamnemonic predictors of young children's acquisition and use of organizational strategies. Paper presented at the Conference on Human Development, Charleston, SC.

Liberty, C., & Ornstein, P. A. (1973). Age differences in organization and recall: The effects of training in categorization. *Journal of Experimental Child Psychology, 15,* 169–186.

Lindberg, M. A. (1980). Is knowledge base development a necessary and sufficient condition for memory development? *Journal of Experimental Child Psychology, 30,* 401–410.

Lodico, M. G., Ghatala, E. S., Levin, J. R., Pressley, M., & Bell, J. A. (1983). The effects of strategy-monitoring on children's selection of effective memory strategies. *Journal of Experimental Child Psychology, 35,* 263–277.

McCombs, B. L. (1984). Processes and skills underlying continuing intrinsic motivation to learn: Toward a definition of motivational skills training interventions. *Educational Psychologist, 19,* 199–218.

McGarrigle, J., Grieve, R., & Hughes, M. (1978). Interpreting inclusion: A contribution to the study of the child's cognitive and linguistic development. *Journal of Experimental Child Psychology, 26,* 528–550.

Miller, P. H., & Harris, Y. R. (1988). Preschoolers' strategies of attention on a same-different task. *Developmental Psychology, 24,* 628–633.

Moely, B. E., Olson, F. A., Halwes, T. G., & Flavell, J. H. (1969). Production deficiency in young children's clustered recall. *Developmental Psychology, 1,* 26–34.

Morrison, F. (1987). *Making the cut: Contrasting developmental and learning influences on cognitive growth.* Paper presented at the annual meeting of the Psychonomics Society, Seattle.

Muir, J. E., & Bjorklund, D. F. (in press). Developmental and individual differences in children's memory strategies: The role of knowledge. In W. Schneider & F. E. Weinert (Eds.), *Interactions among strategies, knowledge, and aptitude in cognitive performance.* New York: Springer-Verlag.

Naus, M. J., Ornstein, P. A., & Aivano, S. (1977). Developmental changes in memory: The effects of processing time and rehearsal instructions. *Journal of Experimental Child Psychology, 23,* 237–251.

Newman, L. S. (1980). *Intentional and unintentional memory in young children: remembering vs. playing.* Unpublished master's thesis, University of North Carolina at Chapel Hill.

Ornstein, P. A. (in press). Knowledge and strategies: A discussion. In W. Schneider & F. Weinert (Eds.), *Interactions among aptitudes, strategies, and knowledge in cognitive performance.* New York: Springer-Verlag.

Ornstein, P. A., Baker–Ward, L., & Naus, M. J. (1988). The development of mnemonic skill. In F. E. Weinert & M. Perlmutter (Eds.), *Memory development: Universal changes and individual differences* (pp. 31–50). Hillsdale, NJ: Lawrence Erlbaum Associates.

Ornstein, P. A., & Folds, T. H. (1988). *Context specificity in young children's strategy use.* Paper presented at the Conference on Human Development, Charleston, SC.

Ornstein, P. A., Medlin, R. G., Stone, B. P., & Naus, M. J. (1985). Retrieving for rehearsal: An analysis of active rehearsal in children's memory. *Developmental Psychology, 21,* 633–641.

Ornstein, P. A., & Naus, M. J. (1978). Rehearsal processes in children's memory. In P. A. Ornstein (Ed.), *Memory development in children* (pp. 69–99). Hillsdale, NJ: Lawrence Erlbaum Associates.

Ornstein, P. A., & Naus, M. J. (1985). Effects of the knowledge base on children's memory strategies. In H. W. Reese (Ed.), *Advances in child development and behavior* (Vol. 19, pp. 113–148). New York: Academic Press.

Ornstein, P. A., Naus, M. J., & Liberty, C. (1975). Rehearsal and organizational processes in children's memory. *Child Development, 46,* 818–830.

Ornstein, P. A., Naus, M. J., & Stone, B. P. (1977). The effects of list organization and rehearsal activity in memory. *Child Development, 48,* 292–295.

Paris, S. G. (1978). Coordination of means and goals in the development of mnemonic skills. In P. A. Ornstein (Ed.), *Memory development in children* (pp. 259–273). Hillsdale, NJ: Lawrence Erlbaum Associates.

Paris, S. G., & Byrnes, J. P. (1989). The constructivist approach to self-regulation and learning in the classroom. In B. J. Zimmerman & D. H. Schunk (Eds.), *Self-regulated learning and academic achievement: Theory, research, and practice* (pp. 169–200). New York: Springer-Verlag.

Paris, S. G., Newman, R. S., & Jacobs, J. E. (1985). Social contexts and functions of children's remembering. M. Pressley & C. J. Brainerd (Ed.), *Cognitive learning and memory in children* (pp. 81–115). New York: Springer-Verlag.

Paris, S. G., Newman, R. S., & McVey, K. A. (1982). Learning the functional significance of mnemonic actions: A microgenetic study of strategy acquisition. *Journal of Experimental Child Psychology, 34,* 490–509.

Pressley, M., Borkowski, J. G., & Johnson, C. J. (1987). The development of good strategy use: Imagery and related mnemonic strategies. In M. A. McDaniel & M. Pressley (Eds.), *Imagery and related processes: Theories, individual differences, and applications* (pp. 274–301). New York: Springer-Verlag.

Pressley, M., Borkowski, J. G., & Schneider, W. (1987). Cognitive strategies: Good strategy users coordinate metacognition and knowledge. In R. Vasta & G. Whitehurst (Eds.), *Annals of Child Development* (Vol. 5, pp. 89–129), New York: JAI.

Pressley, M., Levin, J. R., & Ghatala, E. S. (1984). Memory strategy monitoring in adults and children. *Journal of Verbal Learning and Verbal Behavior, 23,* 270–288.

Rabinowitz, M. (1984). The use of categorical organization: Not an all-or-none situation. *Journal of Experimental Child Psychology, 38,* 338–351.

Rabinowitz, M., & Chi, M. T. H. (1987). An interactive model of strategic processing. In S. J. Ceci (Ed.), *Handbook of the cognitive, social, and neuropsychological aspects of learning disabilities* (Vol. 2, pp. 83–102). Hillsdale, NJ: Lawrence Erlbaum Associates.

Rabinowitz, M., & McAuley, R. (in press). Conceptual knowledge processing: An oxymoron? In W. Schneider & F. Weinert (Eds.), *Interactions among aptitudes, strategies, and knowledge in cognitive performance.* New York: Springer-Verlag.

Rogoff, B. (1981). Schooling and the development of cognitive skills. In H. C. Triandis & A Heron (Eds.), *Handbook of cross-cultural psychology* (Vol. 4, pp. 233–294). Boston: Allyn & Bacon.

Rogoff, B., & Mistry, J. (1985). Memory development in cultural context. In M. Pressley & C. J. Brainerd (Eds.), *Cognitive learning and memory in children* (pp. 117–142). New York: Springer-Verlag.

Rowher, W. D. (1973). Elaboration and learning in childhood and adolescence. In H. W. Reese (Ed.), *Advances in child development and behavior* (Vol. 8, pp. 2–57). New York: Academic Press.

Schneider, W. (1985). Developmental trends in the metamemory-memory behavior relationship: An integrative review. In D. L. Forrest–Pressley, G. E. MacKinnon, & T. G. Waller (Eds.), *Cognitive, metacognition, and human performance* (Vol. 1, pp. 57–109). New York: Academic Press.

Schneider, W., & Brun, H. (1987). The role of context in young children's memory performance: Istomina revisited. *British Journal of Developmental Psychology, 5,* 333–341.

Schneider, W., & Pressley, M. (1989). *Memory development between 2 and 20.* New York: Springer-Verlag.

Schunk, D. (1984). Self-efficacy perspective on achievement behavior. *Educational Psychologist, 19,* 48–58.

Schunk, D. (1988). *Perceived self-efficacy and related social cognitive processes as predictors of student academic performance.* Paper presented at the annual meeting of the American Educational Research Association, New Orleans.

Sodian, B., Schneider, W., & Perlmutter, M. (1986). Recall, clustering, and metamemory in young children. *Journal of Experimental Child Psychology, 41,* 395–410.

Tarkin, B. (1981). The effects of stimulus meaningfulness on children's spontaneous rehearsal strategies. Unpublished senior honors thesis, University of Massachusetts.

Vygotsky, L. S. (1978). *Mind in society.* Cambridge, MA: Harvard University Press.

Wagner, D. A. (1978). Memories of Morocco: The influence of age, schooling, and environment on memory. *Cognitive Psychology, 10,* 1–28.

Wagner, D. A., & Spratt, J. E. (1987). Cognitive consequences of contrasting pedagogies: The effects of Quaranic preschooling in Morocco. *Child Development, 58,* 1207–1219.

Waters, H. S., & Andreassen, C. (1983). Children's use of memory strategies under instruction. In M. Pressley & J. R. Levin (Eds.), *Cognitive strategy research: Psychological foundations* (pp. 3–24). New York: Springer-Verlag.

Weiner, B. (1974). *Achievement motivation and attribution theory.* Morristown, NJ: General Learning Corporation.

Weiner, B. (1979). A theory of motivation for some classroom experiences. *Journal of Educational Psychology, 71,* 3–25.

Weinert, F. E., & Perlmutter, M. (1988). *Memory development: Universal changes and individual differences.* Hillsdale, NJ: Lawrence Erlbaum Associates.

Weissberg, J. A., & Paris, S. G. (1986). Young children's remembering in different contexts: A developmental study of memory monitoring. *Child Development, 57,* 1123–1129.

Wellman, H. M. (1977). The early development of intentional memory behavior. *Human Development, 48,* 1720–1723.

Wellman, H. M. (1983). Metamemory revisited. In M. T. H. Chi (Ed.), *Trends in memory development research* (pp. 31–51). Basel: Karger.

Wellman, H. M. (1988). The early development of memory strategies. In F. E. Weinert & M. Perlmutter (Eds.), *Memory development: Universal changes and individual differences* (pp. 3–29), Hillsdale, NJ: Lawrence Erlbaum Associates.

Wellman, H. M., Ritter, K., & Flavell, J. H. (1975). Deliberate memory behavior in the delayed reactions of very young children. *Developmental Psychology, 11,* 780–787.

Wellman, H. M., & Somerville, S. C. (1980). Quasi-naturalistic tasks in the study of cognition: The memory-related skills of toddlers. *New Directions in Child Development, 10,* 33–48.

Wellman, H. M., & Somerville, S. C. (1982). The development of human search ability. In M. E. Lamb & A. L. Brown (Eds.), *Advances in developmental psychology* (Vol. 2, pp. 41–84). Hillsdale, NJ: Lawrence Erlbaum Associates.

Yussen, S. R., Gagné, E., Gargiulo, R., & Kunen, S. (1974). The distinction between perceiving and memorizing in elementary school children. *Child Development, 45,* 457–551.

Zembar, M. J., & Naus, M. J. (1985). *The combined effects of knowledge and mnemonic strategies on children's memory.* Paper presented at the biennial meeting of the Society for Research in Child Development, Toronto.

CHAPTER 4

The Role of Knowledge in the Development of Strategies

David F. Bjorklund
Jacqueline E. Muir-Broaddus
Florida Atlantic University

Wolfgang Schneider
Max-Planck-Institute

Cognition always occurs in some context. When children (or adults) have performed in a particular setting before or have dealt previously with the materials or information pertinent to the task at hand, levels of performance are typically higher than when the context is less familiar. Fischer (1980), in his theory of cognitive development, made much of this fact, postulating that children function at their optimal level (which is set by maturation) only when the environment is maximally supportive.

This dependency upon context is central to issues in the development of children's strategies. Children display high levels of performance and apparently use sophisticated strategies, but only under specific conditions. The environment must be supportive to the extent that it provides prompts or cues for children to use a particular strategy or to the extent that task-relevant information is well known to the children, presumably permitting them to process that information efficiently. When children are presented with similar tasks without prompts or involving less familiar information, task performance and strategy use decline (see Bjorklund & Muir, 1988).

One of the major factors in the development of strategies, we believe, is children's acquisition of knowledge. Children are universal novices (Brown & DeLoache, 1978), knowing relatively little about most of the things they encounter. With age and experience they develop expertise in certain areas; but development of knowledge is rarely uniform across domains, and children find themselves with more pockets of ignorance than of expertise. As a result, when strategies are used effectively, they are typically limited to specific knowledge-defined contexts, rarely generalizing to other situations in which they could be useful.

Although knowledge can be defined very broadly, in this chapter unless otherwise stated, we define content knowledge in terms of information in a modified network model of semantic memory (see Bjorklund, 1987). Each item in semantic memory is defined by a node that is connected to other nodes in semantic memory. In addition to connections with other items, each node also has associated with it features that characterize it. In development, the number of nodes changes, as do the number and strength of connections among items. Also, the number of features associated with an item changes developmentally, as does the feature hierarchy (i.e., the priority given to various features associated with an item, cf., Gibson, 1971). When referring to a "domain" of knowledge, we refer to semantic knowledge that is highly interrelated, such as a knowledge of the game of chess, the rules of soccer, or the composition of one's school class. Strategies and their development can best be understood when one considers the domain of knowledge to which a strategy is applied.

Of course, we do not mean to imply that all there is to development is the acquisition of knowledge. Rather, knowledge represents a center stage around which both more elementary and specific and more complex and global processes revolve. Factors that influence the encoding of stimuli, the selective attention to relevant features of events, and the ease with which information can be represented in memory all affect the state of a person's knowledge. Similarly, one's knowledge base will influence (and will be influenced by) effortful strategies and metastrategies for operating on information. The effects on performance of developmental differences in the knowledge base cannot in and of themselves adequately explain age differences in thinking; however, we believe that an understanding of developmental differences in the knowledge base and their effects on cognition are central to understanding strategy development, and cognitive development generally.

DEVELOPMENTAL DIFFERENCES IN KNOWLEDGE, MENTAL EFFORT, AND STRATEGY USE

The Relation Between Knowledge and Mental Effort

There is little controversy in the statement that a child's knowledge of the world increases over the course of development. What is more controversial is the assumption that these quantitative differences in content knowledge determine developmental differences in cognition (e.g., Carey, 1985). We do not make this strong claim here. We believe that many aspects of cognitive development are qualitative in nature (although the mechanisms underlying these qualitative changes may be quantitative). However, we also contend that quantitative changes in knowledge play a critical role in shaping children's cognitions, and many of the differences found on a wide range of cognitive tasks between children of different ages can be attributed to differences in their knowledge bases (see Bjorklund, 1989; Carey, 1985; Chi, 1985).

With respect to the development of strategies, having detailed knowledge for a particular domain permits a person to process information from that domain more efficiently, with knowledge (and processing efficiency) increasing developmentally (e.g., Bjorklund, 1985, 1987; Bjorklund & Harnishfeger, 1989, 1990; Muir-Broaddus & Bjorklund, in press). Basically, similar to Case (1985), we propose that cognitive resources are limited, with children becoming more effective in allocating their limited pool of resources for the execution of cognitive operations with age.

One aspect of information processing that involves a portion of these shared, mental resources is the activation (or identification) of the information. When children are highly familiar with the items on a cognitive task or the relations among items, less in the way of mental resources is required to activate those items. By expending less of one's limited cognitive capacity for the activation of relevant task information, more resources can be allocated to the short-term storage of information or to the execution of resource-expensive *strategies*. Thus, as children's knowledge becomes more detailed and better integrated, individual items and sets of related items can be accessed with reduced amounts of mental effort, affording more resources for the execution of effortful strategies.

Figure 4.1 presents a schematic representation of how having substantial knowledge for a particular domain may result in increased strategy use, and in turn, increased task performance. The primary effect that an elaborated knowledge base has on cognitive processing is to increase speed of processing for domain-specific information. Individual items can be accessed more quickly from the long-term store, as can relations among related items in the knowledge base. In the current model, faster processing is equated with more efficient processing, which results in greater availability of mental resources. These mental resources can then be applied to retrieving specific items (item-specific effects, Bjorklund, 1987; Muir-Broaddus & Bjorklund, in press), to domain-specific strategies, or to metacognitive processes. Domain-specific strategies can directly facilitate task

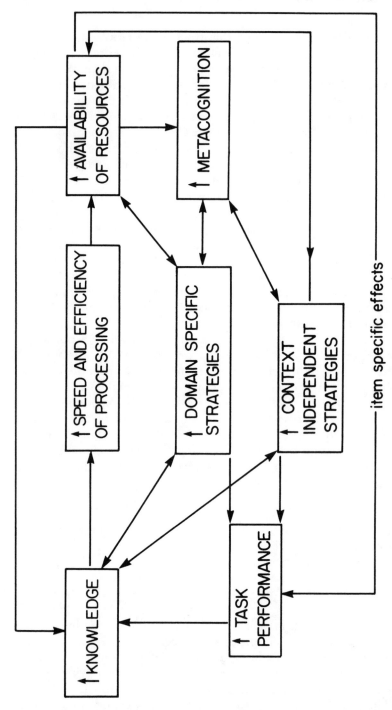

FIG 4.1. Model of the effects of knowledge on information processing and acquisition of subsequent knowledge.

performance, as can context-independent strategies, both of which can in turn affect subsequent metacognitive processes. This feedback loop between metacognitive processes and strategy use can take many forms. For example, in a free-recall task, children may begin to recall items according to categorical relations, with such clustering being guided primarily by strong interitem associations. In monitoring their recall, they may note some of these relations and more systematically guide their subsequent retrieval by this categorical scheme (see Bjork-lund & Zeman, 1982).

This, of course, represents merely a brief sketch of the relation between knowledge, mental effort, and strategy use. Having detailed knowledge can facilitate task performance in ways other than via strategies, but strategies are the emphasis of this chapter. Our point in the review that follows is to illustrate how developmental differences in knowledge play an important role in the development of strategies.

Strategies as Effortful Processes

In this chapter, strategies are defined as being effort consuming. They are goal directed in that they are not ends in themselves but deliberate means to an end, the end being enhanced task performance. Strategies achieve cognitive purpose and are potentially conscious and controllable activities (cf. Flavell, 1985). When tasks can be successfully completed without the use of strategies, there is no reason to expect effortful operations to be used. Thus, when children can use relatively automatic and thus effortless processes to solve a problem, there is no need for the use of strategies. And when a process has been exercised so thoroughly that it is executed without conscious awareness, bringing the specific procedures involved in that operation to consciousness can actually impede cognition. Whether these formerly conscious and effortful but now unconscious and effortless procedures should be called strategies is certainly arguable (see Paris, Lipson, & Wixson, 1983; Schneider & Pressley, 1989). However, in the present context, we use the term *strategy* to refer to cognitive operations that are effortful and subject to consciousness.

Strategies then, as defined here, are not necessary for all forms of complex cognition and may not always facilitate task performance, although this is the intent of using them. In fact, based on the assumption that the use of strategies requires large amounts of a child's limited mental resources, there should be situations where task performance will actually be hindered (or at least not greatly facili-tated) by the use of a strategy. This occurs when the execution of the strategy depletes so much of a child's information-processing capacity that too little remains for allocation to other aspects of the task. Older children and adults, by comparison, are able to take advantage of the greater efficiency that a strategy affords because they have sufficient mental resources available (e.g., Bjorklund & Harnishfeger, 1987; DeMarie-Dreblow & Miller, 1988; Guttentag, 1984; Kee & Howell, 1988).

Evidence of developmental changes in efficiency of strategy execution has been obtained in dual-task experiments, in which performance on a secondary task (finger tapping, for example) is evaluated as a function of performance on a primary task (free recall, for example). Using dual-task paradigms, there is evidence that when performance is equivalent across different age groups there may nevertheless be age-related differences in the mental resources consumed by strategy implementation (e.g., Bjorklund & Harnishfeger, 1987; Guttentag, 1984; Kee & Davies, 1988; Kee & Howell, 1988; for a review of this work see Guttentag, 1989). Although we are confident that one of the reasons for these increases in efficiency with age is related to maturationally based changes in the speed with which information can be processed (e.g., Dempster, 1985; Kail, 1986, 1988), we are equally confident that age-related differences in knowledge also contribute significantly to this developmental change (e.g., Roth, 1983).

The greater efficiency afforded by a strategy must be weighed against the depletion of limited resources required for the execution of that strategy. This trade-off has consequences that will vary with the age (and thus processing efficiency) of the child. In general, children can execute a strategy more efficiently with age (i.e., using less in the way of mental resources), making that strategy more likely to be beneficial to task performance.

KNOWLEDGE AND THE DEVELOPMENT OF STRATEGIES

Evidence from Nonmemory Research

A developmental relationship between knowledge, mental effort, and strategy use has been demonstrated for a broad range of tasks, including mathematics, reading, and problem solving.

Mathematics

In the domain of mathematics, increases in strategy sophistication and factual and procedural knowledge act to increase processing efficiency, and thereby decrease the mental effort requirements of mathematical operations. Although children as young as 5 and 6 years demonstrate some fact retrieval, as shown by their fast performance of simple operations with small whole numbers (e.g., Hamann & Ashcraft, 1985), they quickly revert to overt strategies such as finger counting as problem difficulty increases (Siegler & Shrager, 1984). For the most part, then, young children rely on simple but relatively effortful strategies, such as counting each element separately in order to determine the total (Siegler, 1987). Another early strategy is the *min* procedure, which entails setting one's "mental counter" at the larger of two numbers to be added, and then counting by increments of one until the second smaller number has been added to the first (Ashcraft & Fierman, 1982; Siegler, 1987). As predicted by the min model, reaction times are proportional to the size of the numbers being added (Groen & Parkman, 1972; Groen & Resnick, 1977), attesting to the laborious nature of this early counting procedure.

Although Ashcraft and Fierman (1982) found that the transitional stage between the min strategy and fact retrieval occurs around the third grade level, Siegler (1987) has provided evidence that as early as first and second grade, children performed more fact retrieval and decomposition (transforming a problem into two or more simpler ones) than their kindergarten counterparts. Though decomposition is an effortful strategy, it has the effect of reducing the mental effort requirements of the necessary computations. Thus, with age, there is a gradual transition from the use of "labor-intensive" to "labor-efficient" techniques, and from effortful (strategies) to automatic (fact retrieval) processes in the domain of arithmetic. As these processes become more efficient, moreover, their mental effort requirements are further lessened.

Reading

The significance of mental effort has also been emphasized in the domain of reading. Following a model of mental resources similar to what we have ascribed (Case, 1985), Daneman and her colleagues have examined the interplay between the processing and storage functions of working memory in an attempt to understand developmental and individual differences in reading comprehension (e.g., Daneman & Blennerhassett, 1984; Daneman & Carpenter, 1980; Daneman & Green, 1986). Basically, they proposed that it is necessary for information to be retained in working memory for as long as possible so that each newly read word in a passage can be integrated with the words and concepts that preceded it. Younger or less proficient readers have less available capacity to store and maintain information in working memory because it is necessary for them to devote considerable capacity to the processes involved in comprehension (Daneman & Blennerhassett, 1984). These include anything from letter decoding to concept integration. Alternately, young children also have fewer resources to devote to comprehension processes because more capacity is consumed by storage and maintenance functions.

This trade-off between processing, storage, and comprehension was examined across a variety of age groups. For example, in a study of prereaders, Daneman and Blennerhassett (1984) provided convincing evidence that listening span, defined as the number of successive short sentences that could be recalled verbatim, correlated significantly with comprehension. The second experiment of this two-part study was especially convincing because of the systematic variations made in the level of integration required for comprehension. They reasoned that the greater the required level of integration, the greater the processing demands on working memory and thus the less capacity remaining for storage. As expected, the greater the required level of integration, the greater was the performance advantage of large-span over small-span listeners in terms of comprehension. Daneman and her colleagues have arrived at similar interpretations in experiments with older children and adults (e.g., Daneman & Carpenter, 1980; Daneman & Green, 1986).

One factor believed to influence the efficiency of text processing is knowledge. Anderson and his colleagues (Anderson, Hiebert, Scott, & Wilkinson, 1984) defined reading as "a process in which information from the text and the knowledge possessed by the readers act together to produce meaning" (p. 8). In other words, "reading is a constructive process" (p. 9), in which the background knowledge that one brings to a text interacts with its literal content to produce inferences and interpretations of varying degrees of concordance with the author's intended purpose. Anderson et al. cited considerable evidence from the research literature to support these claims. In a study by Pearson, Hansen, and Gordon (1979), for example, second graders who were equated in reading skill were tested for their knowledge of spiders and then given a passage about spiders to read. The children who knew more about spiders at the outset were better at answering subsequent questions about the passage, especially those questions that involved reasoning. Instructional efforts aimed at increasing background knowledge have also been found to enhance reading comprehension (e.g., Hansen, 1981; Hansen & Pearson, 1983; Omanson, Beck, Voss, & McKeown, 1984). In more recent research, Schneider, Körkel, and Weinert (in press) compared the text comprehension of soccer expert with soccer novice third-, fifth-, and seventh-grade children on stories related to soccer. The soccer experts showed significantly greater comprehension, with performance being unrelated to individual differences in intelligence. In other words, domain-specific knowledge was more important for comprehension than intelligence (see also Recht & Leslie, 1988; Walker, 1987). Knowledge, then, clearly makes reading more accurate and meaningful. It also makes reading less effortful, in that knowledge provides "ready made" inferences and interpretations to the reader.

Problem Solving

The relationship between knowledge, mental effort, and strategy use is also evident in the study of problem solving. Considerable research has explored the role of knowledge by comparing the problem-solving characteristics of experts and novices. One robust finding has been that the two groups categorize problems differently (e.g., Chi, Feltovich, & Glaser, 1981; Chi, Glaser, & Rees, 1982), with novices tending to categorize problems by their surface features and experts tending to categorize them by their underlying principles. A study comparing novices and experts in the domain of physics, for example, found that novices grouped the problems according to characteristics of the problem statement, such as all those problems involving a certain object (such as a rotating disk), or containing certain physics-related keywords (such as "friction"). Experts, on the other hand, categorized problems according to their "deep structure," such as the relevance of Newton's second law (Chi et al., 1981). These differences between novices and experts have been interpreted as reflecting characteristics of the "problem schema" by which problems are encoded and represented (Chi & Greeno, 1987). For the expert, schemas include secondary procedural knowledge about the applicability of existing strategies to the specific demands of the problem, thereby enabling inferences about the problem (i.e., the relations among problem components) and its solution to be drawn. In this way, strategies can be viewed as simply one component of a rich knowledge base. With experience, problem and solution become increasingly intertwined in a single problem schema, so that the activation of appropriate problem-solving strategies becomes increasingly automatic.

Knowledge, then, plays a considerable role in determining the mental effort requirements of a problem-solving task. Unlike experts, who can attack a problem armed with a well developed schema and pre-existing problem representation, the problem solving of novices is carried out on line (Chi & Greeno, 1987). That is, solutions must be derived from the problem itself instead of being selected from an available schema, and resources are consumed in the ongoing process of developing a schema where none or next-to-none existed before.

There is considerable evidence from research in nonmemory domains of the interrelationships between knowledge, mental effort, and strategy use. Common themes that emerge from the domains of arithmetic, reading, and problem solving are that knowledge provides the necessary background information and context to appropriately and efficiently guide the comprehension of a passage or problem. It also frees mental effort for the implementation of strategies appropriate for carrying out the task at hand. As these strategies become more efficient, more of one's mental capacity remains for higher level comprehension, increasingly complex strategies, and the acquisition of more detailed and integrated knowledge.

Evidence from Memory Research

Knowledge and the Development of Rehearsal Strategies

Recent work by Ornstein, Naus, and their colleagues suggests that the much cited change in rehearsal style over childhood (from passive to active, or cumulative, e.g., Ornstein, Naus, & Liberty, 1975) is attributed, in part, to changes in children's knowledge base. For example, Tarkin, Myers, and Ornstein (cited in Ornstein & Naus, 1985), compared third graders' overt rehearsal for two word lists that differed in meaningfulness, with *meaningfulness* defined in terms of the extent to which the words elicited associations. Large differences in spontaneous rehearsal were observed, in that fewer than two words were typically rehearsed together when the list was low in meaningfulness, whereas more than three words tended to be grouped together during rehearsal of the highly meaningful list.

In related research, Zembar and Naus (1985) reported more sophisticated rehearsal for sixth versus third grade children when a standard set of words served as the stimulus list. However, differences in rehearsal style and recall were eliminated when the third graders were given a list of highly familiar words (e.g., *shoe, doll*) and the sixth graders were given a list of difficult, unfamiliar words (e.g., *limpet, galleon*). In other research, soccer expert and novice college students were given lists of categorized words to rehearse and recall (cited in Ornstein & Naus, 1985). One list consisted of soccer-related words, whereas a control list consisted of nonsoccer words. No group differences emerged for the control list; on the soccer list, however, experts grouped together more items from each category during rehearsal than the novices, and subsequently showed superior recall.

Findings such as these indicate a potent relationship between knowledge and strategy use. When subjects are familiar with the to-be-processed items, they are apt to use a more sophisticated rehearsal strategy that results in enhanced levels of performance. The experiments by Ornstein and Naus clearly indicate that patterns of strategy use can be manipulated by varying the materials with which subjects are presented. They also indicate that the age-related changes typically observed in children's rehearsal activities are influenced by similar developmental changes in knowledge.

Knowledge and the Development of Organizational Strategies

Perhaps the area of memory research that has contributed most to our understanding of the developmental relationship between knowledge and strategy use concerns organization. There have been a number of studies in which children's familiarity for sets of related items has been manipulated, with investigators assessing levels of recall and strategy use (usually categorical clustering). Although several studies have examined children's tendencies to use taxonomic/conceptual versus complementary schemes in memory tasks (e.g., Bjorklund & Zaken-Greenberg, 1981; Lange & Jackson, 1974; Worden, 1976), more recent studies have manipulated children's knowledge of categorical relations in terms of *category typicality* (e.g., Ackerman, 1986; Bjorklund, 1988; Bjorklund & Bernholtz, 1986; Corsale & Ornstein, 1980; Rabinowitz, 1984, 1988). In general, the results of these studies indicate that children are more apt to use a strategy effectively when the stimulus items are highly representative (i.e., typical) of their categories.

Category Typicality and Children's Strategy Use. Research by Rabinowitz (1984, 1988) provides a good example of the relationship between category typicality and strategy use. In one experiment, second and fifth grade children were presented with sets of highly typical (e.g., *cat, horse*) or moderately typical (e.g., *fox, goat*) category exemplars for free recall (Rabinowitz, 1984). Subjects in the category condition were told of the categorical nature of the list and instructed to remember the items by categories. Subjects in the standard condition were given conventional free-recall instructions. Rabinowitz reported that differences in recall between the category and standard conditions were greater (in favor of the category condition) for the highly typical than the moderately typical list items. In other words, subjects were better able to take advantage of the categorical instructions to benefit recall for the highly typical items. These findings were supported in a later experiment with adults (Rabinowitz, 1988), in which greater awareness of an instructed organizational strategy and greater transfer of that strategy was demonstrated for items rated as high as opposed to medium or low in category typicality. In both of Rabinowitz's experiments, overall recall was greater for the high than for the less typical items, as were the benefits of strategy use and transfer, clearly illustrating an interaction between knowledge base and strategy use.

In related research, Bjorklund and his colleagues (Bjorklund, 1988; Bjorklund & Buchanan, 1989) assessed children's acquisition and generalization of an organizational strategy for sets of typical and atypical items over repeated trials. As in previous research, levels of recall and clustering were greater for the sets of typical than atypical items, with age differences being most apparent for the atypical items. Children were also classified as using an organizational strategy on each trial, separately for the typical and atypical items, using a procedure developed by Bjorklund and Bernholtz (1986). Children were classified as strategic if they had at least one long intracategory cluster (three words or more) and fast within-category interitem latencies (i.e., their mean within-category interitem latencies were faster than their mean between-category interitem latencies).

The number of fourth and seventh grade children classified as strategic using this dual criterion is shown for the typical and atypical items over trials in Table 4.1. As shown in the table, seventh graders were more apt to be classified as strategic than the fourth graders,

TABLE 4.1   Number and Percentage of Subjects Classified as Strategic by Grade, Typicality, and Trial

	Trial			
	1	2	3	4
Fourth Grade				
Typical	11 (32%)	10 (29%)	17 (50%)	22 (65%)
Atypical	2 (6%)	10 (29%)	11 (32%)	18 (53%)
Seventh Grade				
Typical	16 (50%)	25 (78%)	24 (75%)	29 (91%)
Atypical	7 (21%)	18 (56%)	20 (63%)	24 (75%)

Note. From "Acquiring a Mnemonic: Age and Category Knowledge Effects" by D. F. Bjorklund, 1988, *Journal of Experimental Child Psychology, 45*, p. 80. Copyright 1988 by Academic Press.

children were more apt to be classified as strategic for the typical than for the atypical items, and there was a dramatic increase in strategic classification over trials. As can be seen from the table, most children were not classified as strategic on the initial trial. This is especially apparent for the atypical items. However, the situation was substantially different by the fourth trial. Most seventh grade children were classified as strategic for both the typical and atypical items. In fact, *every* seventh grade child was classified as strategic on Trial 4 for either the typical or atypical items. The pattern was similar although less pronounced for the fourth graders, with 74% of these children being classified as strategic for at least one set of items on the final trial.

The findings of the Bjorklund (1988) study were bolstered by a training experiment by Bjorklund and Buchanan (1989), in which third, fifth, and seventh grade children were trained to use an organizational strategy on sets of either typical or atypical items (Experiment 2). Following training, children were given a second list of items on a generalization task, with half of the children receiving category-typical items and half receiving category-atypical items. The training lists (typical or atypical) were orthogonal to the generalization lists (typical or atypical). As in the Bjorklund (1988) investigation, children were classified as strategic using the dual criterion of at least one long intracategory cluster and fast within-category latencies.

The results of training were impressive in that there were no grade differences in the percentage of children classified as strategic for the typical items by the final (third) training trial (88%, 94%, and 94% for the third, fifth, and seventh graders, respectively). Grade differences were apparent, however, for the atypical items (56%, 63%, and 91% classified as strategic for each grade, respectively), although more than half of the third grade children tested were classified as strategic for these items. In assessing generalization, it was found that children at each grade level showed higher levels of recall and clustering when they had been trained on the category-typical items (cf. Rabinowitz, 1988). Patterns of results were similar for the strategy-classification measure. Moreover, grade differences in strategy classification on the generalization trials were limited to the atypical items.

Bjorklund and Buchanan (1989) proposed that the greater saliency of the typical categories, and the increased ease of accessing one category member given another, resulted in higher levels of recall relative to children who received training with sets of atypical items. This heightened performance may have provided children with the opportunity to assess more intently the organizational mnemonic they were being taught, resulting in greater inculcation of the strategy than found for children who were given the atypical lists. This, in turn, led to greater generalization. Bjorklund and Buchanan (1989) concluded that using highly typical items makes the training of a strategy easier and the generalization of that strategy more likely. "Children's earliest successful memory strategies begin with highly familiar information and so do successful training efforts" (p. 469). They also commented that, although children of all ages display greater levels of performance and strategy use with sets of typical as opposed to atypical items, younger children's strategy use is especially affected by the use of atypical items. "The less sophisticated children are with respect to strategy use, the more important knowledge base factors are to their performance" (p. 470).

Associative Versus Categorical Relations. Other research has examined developmental differences in strategy use when list items can be related on the basis of both associative *and* categorical relations (e.g., Bjorklund & de Marchena, 1984; Bjorklund & Jacobs, 1985; Frankel & Rollins, 1982, 1985; Lange, 1973; Schneider, 1986). Associative relations are believed to be formed prior in development to categorical relations (Bjorklund & Jacobs, 1984), with the activation of one item eliciting its associate in an automatic (i.e., effortless) fashion.

In one experiment by Schneider (1986), second and fourth grade children were given a sort/recall task, with categorizable pictures serving as stimuli. Four different types of lists were used that varied in degree of category and interitem relatedness (cf. Frankel & Rollins, 1985). One list contained items that were highly related to the category with high interitem associations among some of the items on the list (high related–high associated). A second list was composed of items highly related to the category but with low interitem associations (high related–low associated). A third list was composed of items that were weakly related to the category, although some were highly associated (low related–high associated), and a fourth list consisted of words low in both category relatedness and interitem associativity (low related–low associated). Examples from the category "animals" for each list type are shown in Table 4.2.

In general, more clustering was found for the highly associated lists, and the fourth graders had higher levels of recall and clustering and sorted items according to categorical membership to a greater degree than the second graders. Most importantly, there was a striking age-by-list associativity interaction in the clustering data, such that low associativity especially penalized the younger children. There were also significant correlations between sorting at study, clustering, and recall, with particularly high correlations (all $rs > .5$) for the older

TABLE 4.2   Examples of Items by List-Type

High related-high associated list:	dog, cat, pig, horse, cow, mouse
High related-low associated list:	tiger, elephant, cow, pig, bear, dog
Low related-high associated list:	goat, deer, buffalo, hippopotamus, monkey, lamb
Low related-low associated list:	beaver, rat, alligator, camel, squirrel, giraffe

Note. From "The Role of Conceptual Knowledge and Metamemory in the Development of Organizational Processes in Memory" by W. Schneider, 1986, *Journal of Experimental Child Psychology, 42,* p. 222. Copyright 1986 by Academic Press.

children. Overall, what emerges from this study is a portrait of second graders who use organizational strategies much less than fourth graders. This is a qualified conclusion, however, in that younger children's use of the clustering strategy can be evoked when the categories contain highly associated items.

In a related experiment by Bjorklund and Jacobs (1985), children from Grades 3, 5, 7, and 9 were given categorized lists of words to recall that varied in the associative strength among items within a category. Within each five-item category, two pairs of items were high associates of each other (e.g., *cat, dog* and *lion, tiger*). A fifth item (e.g., *cow*) was not strongly associated with any of the other list items. Thus, in remembering category items together, a subject could recall items contiguously that are high associates of one another (e.g., *dog, cat*), or could recall items that are related to one another strictly on the basis of category relationship (i.e., not high associates, e.g., *dog, lion; cow, tiger*). Lists of items were presented to subjects in one of three ways: randomly, blocked by categories with highly associated items separated within the list (blocked), and blocked by categories with highly associated items presented contiguously (blocked associate).

Patterns of recall and clustering varied with grade and presentation condition, with performance being greatest in the blocked-associate condition and least in the random condition for all grades. More interesting than levels of recall, however, was the pattern of correlations between recall and clustering. Bjorklund and Jacobs argued, as have others (e.g., Frankel & Rollins, 1985; Jablonski, 1974), that high, positive correlations between recall and clustering are indicative of strategic functioning. These correlations, presented in Table 4.3, were significant for all grade levels for subjects in the blocked condition, indicating that the blocking manipulation resulted in the identification and use of an organizational strategy even by the youngest subjects tested here (8- to 9-year-olds). However, these correlations were nonsignificant for the third, fifth, and seventh graders

TABLE 4.3   Correlations Between Recall and Clustering by Grade
and Condition: Experiment 1

| | Condition | | |
Grade	Random	Blocked	Blocked Associate
Third	.16	.45*	.08
Fifth	.13	.56*	−.04
Seventh	.32	.69*	.28
Ninth	.59*	.66*	.51*

* $p < .05$.
Note 1. All $df = 18$.
Note 2. From "Associative and Categorical Processes in Children's
Memory: The Role of Automaticity in the Development of Organization
in Free Recall by D. F. Bjorklund and J. W. Jacobs, Journal of Experimental
Child Psychology, 1985, 39, p. 605. Copyright 1985 by Academic Press.
Reprinted by permission.

in both the random and blocked-associate conditions. Only for the
ninth graders were the correlations between recall and clustering
significant for these two conditions. Thus, despite the high levels of
recall and clustering observed in the blocked-associate condition, the
organization observed here for the third, fifth, and seventh graders
was apparently mediated by the relatively effortless activation of
associative relations, and not by strategic (i.e., deliberate) processes.

A similar pattern of correlational results has been reported in a
recent study by Hasselhorn (1989). Second and fourth grade children
were presented with lists varying in categorical relatedness (high
versus low) and associativity (high versus low) (cf. Schneider, 1986).
In a free-recall condition, Hasselhorn reported nonsignificant correlations between recall and clustering for both the high and low
associated lists, and for the low categorical lists for both the second
and fourth grade subjects. For the high categorical lists, the correlation between recall and clustering was again low for the second
graders ($r = .08$) but higher and approaching significance for the
fourth graders ($r = .30$). Thus, using the relationship between clustering and recall as an indication of strategic processing, only the oldest
children could be considered to be strategic, and this only for the high
categorical lists.

Knowledge and Organization at Output

With respect to the development of organizational strategies,
Bjorklund and his colleagues have proposed that the organization
that is initially seen in the recall of most young children is mediated
not by a deliberately imposed strategy, but rather by the relatively

automatic activation of well established semantic memory relations. In the process of this associatively mediated retrieval, children may notice categorical relations in their recall, and may then proceed to use this fortuitously discovered organizational strategy to guide the remainder of their recall (Bjorklund, 1985, 1987; Bjorklund & Jacobs, 1985; Bjorklund & Zeman, 1982, 1983).

Such a process was inferred in experiments by Bjorklund and Zeman (1982, 1983), who asked children to recall the members of their current school class. Although levels of recall and clustering were high for children of all grades (first, third, and fifth) when asked to retrieve the well known names of their classmates, metamemory interviews indicated that few children at any grade were aware of using an organizational strategy. Moreover, examination of children's clustering for each *half* of recall indicated that many children apparently switched organizational schemes in the course of recall. Bjorklund and Zeman concluded that few children began the class-recall task in a strategic (i.e., deliberate) way. However, because of the associative nature of their recall, organizational schemes (e.g., recalling children by seating arrangements, sex) were discovered by some children and used to direct the remainder of their recall. Children who, during the metamemory interview, were able to profess accurately a strategy they had used in recalling their classmates' names (as reflected by their clustering scores) had higher overall levels of recall and clustering than children who were unable to accurately profess a strategy. These data suggest that the use of a strategy does facilitate performance (although even the performance of the nonstrategic children was high in an absolute sense), with the strategy being "discovered" because of the familiar (and highly associative) nature of the to-be-remembered material.

More direct evidence for this position comes from an experiment by Bjorklund and Jacobs (1985), outlined briefly above. To reiterate the design, third, fifth, seventh, and ninth grade children were given categorized lists to recall consisting of items related on the basis of both categorical and associative relations (e.g., *dog, cat, cow, lion, tiger*). Children's intracategory clusters of three words or more were examined as a function of whether these clusters were led by an associative pair (e.g., *dog, cat, cow*) or not (e.g., *dog, cow, cat*). In the random condition, where subjects were not biased by order of item presentation to recall words either by categories or by associates, a nonmonotonic developmental relationship was observed. As shown in Fig. 4.2, the proportion of category clusters led by a high associate peaked for the seventh and ninth grade children. These values were significantly lower for the younger children and for a group of adults (who were run in the random condition only).

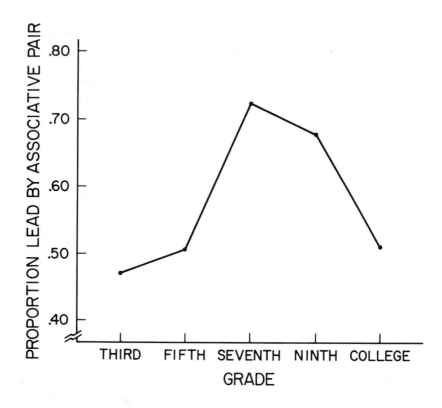

FIG 4.2.   Proportion of total number of intracategory word strings of
length three, four, and five to those leading with a high-associative word
pair by grade. Data from "Associative and Categorical Processes in Children's Memory: The Role of Automaticity in the Development of Organization in Free Recall" by D. F. Bjorklund and J. W. Jacobs, *Journal of
Experimental Child Psychology*, 1985, *39*, p. 613. Copyright 1985 by Academic Press. Reprinted by permission.

Bjorklund and Jacobs (1985) interpreted these results as reflecting
the fact that the seventh and ninth grade children were making use of
the high associative relations to instigate categorical recall. As a result
of the relatively automatic activation of associative relations, pairs of
categorically related items were retrieved contiguously. These older
children then used these associatively retrieved pairs as prompts for
other categorically related items. The proportion of category clusters
led by associative pairs was less for the adults, presumably, because
they were sufficiently strategic so that they did not require high
associativity to prompt categorical recall. In contrast, nonassociated
category relations were not easily activated by the third and fifth

graders, making the associative prompts relatively ineffective in eliciting subsequent clustering.

What may cause children, who apparently begin the task in a nondeliberate manner, to begin to use an organizational strategy in the course of recall? Bjorklund and his colleagues suggested a process akin to Piaget's (1971) idea of *reflective abstraction* (Bjorklund, 1980, 1985, 1987; Bjorklund & Jacobs, 1985; Bjorklund & Zeman, 1982). Preadolescent children have the ability to reflect upon the outcomes of their own cognitions. In the present context, children are able to examine the products of their recall efforts and, in the process, may recognize previously unnoticed relations among the recalled items. Reflective abstraction is a conscious and effortful process, although it is likely not planful, in that children do not enter a task with the idea of evaluating the products of their recent cognitions. However, because it is resource consuming, children are not likely to engage in reflective abstraction until other aspects of task processing can be executed efficiently. Accordingly, children's "discovery" of an organizational strategy should be most apt to occur for sets of items that are well represented in their semantic memories, such as the names of their classmates and highly associated words. It is primarily in this way, we believe, that deliberate and effective strategies are typically mediated in development.

We must emphasize here that this picture of the acquisition of an organizational strategy is meant to describe the developmental progression for tasks where children are not biased to organize information at time of presentation. For example, in sort/recall paradigms, where children are allowed (and sometimes required) to group items according to meaning prior to recall, there is clear evidence of spontaneous strategy use in preadolescent, and even preschool, children (e.g., Bjorklund & de Marchena, 1984; Bjorklund & Zaken-Greenberg, 1981; Kee & Bell, 1981; Schneider, 1986; Schneider, Borkowski, Kurtz, & Kerwin, 1986; Sodian, Schneider, & Perlmutter, 1986). The discrepancy between these results and those reported when sorting prior to testing is not possible, can be attributed to differences in task difficulty. Sort/recall tasks are easier to handle for young children because children usually have sufficient time to encode the stimulus items, and the instructions often bias children to form meaningful groupings of items, which is not the case in most free-recall (nonsorting) experiments. In general, adequate encoding strategies (i.e., sorting according to categories) greatly facilitates subsequent retrieval.

Success in nonsorting free-recall tasks, on the other hand, heavily depends on the efficiency of the retrieval strategies. There is evidence that young elementary school children's problems with semantic categorization tasks are due more to deficiencies in retrieval strategies than to deficiencies in encoding relevant information (cf. Ackerman, 1985, 1987; Brainerd, 1985). It is not surprising, then, that elementary school children seem able to spontaneously use organizational strategies during encoding in sort/recall tasks, but fail to employ organizational strategies at retrieval in free-recall tasks where sorting is not permitted. It is only for the latter type of task that spontaneous use of organizational strategies is rarely observed in preadolescent children. However, we should note that differences in the familiarity of the task materials also influences children's tendencies to organize information at input in sort/recall tasks. Younger children require more obvious and strongly associated relations among items (e.g., Corsale & Ornstein, 1980; Schneider, 1986) or more explicit prompts from the experimenter (e.g., Bjorklund, Ornstein, & Haig, 1977) before displaying strategic organization.

STRATEGIES, THE KNOWLEDGE BASE, AND METAMEMORY

So far, we have restricted our review to studies that examined the role of semantic knowledge on children's strategies. There are other aspects of knowledge that can affect strategies as well. Since the early seventies, research on metamemory has explored the relevance of knowledge about memory for strategy use and performance in various tasks (see Cavanaugh & Perlmutter, 1982; Flavell, 1985; Schneider, 1985; Wellman, 1983, for reviews of the literature).

In most taxonomies of metamemory, a distinction is made between *declarative* and *procedural* knowledge components. The declarative component taps factual knowledge about memory by using metamemory questionnaires or interview procedures. More specifically, declarative metamemory includes knowledge about mnemonic persons, tasks, and strategies. The person category addresses the child's mnemonic self-concept, including ideas about his or her own memory strengths and weaknesses. Task variables include factors that make a memory task easier (e.g., familiarity with learning materials, high interitem associations). Finally, the strategies variable refers to verbalizable knowledge about encoding and retrieval strategies.

Although measures of declarative metamemory are taken without concurrent memory assessment (independent measures), measures of procedural knowledge are collected simultaneously with the measurement of memory activity (concurrent measures). They tap awareness of ongoing processes (memory monitoring) and mostly consist of judgments or feelings about the ease or difficulty of remembering something. Examples of memory monitoring measures include performance predictions and recall-readiness assessments.

It has been shown in numerous studies that both declarative and procedural metamemory components are developing rapidly during the elementary school years (see Schneider & Pressley, 1989). Although this seems to be an interesting finding in its own right, the question crucial for most researchers in the field has been how and to what degree increases in metamemory influence children's strategy use and performance in memory tasks.

Interrelations Among Organizational Strategies, Semantic Knowledge, and Metamemory

We have stated earlier in this chapter that most young children do not use organizational strategies spontaneously. Given that strategy use, as defined in this chapter, is principally conscious and intentional, the expectation is that strategy usage should covary with the ability to verbally describe and explain strategic behavior (i.e., declarative metamemory). Theoretically, all children applying an organizational strategy should also possess the relevant declarative strategy knowledge, but not necessarily vice versa (cf. Wimmer & Tornquist, 1980). In the aforementioned study by Schneider (1986), this assumption was tested by assessing different aspects of children's declarative metamemory. Metamemory measures included an interview tapping general metamemory, an interview dealing with knowledge about organizational strategies, and a paired-comparison judgment task developed by Justice (1986) to assess children's judgments of strategy effectiveness.

The data showed that the different components of metamemory were related to memory performance in fourth graders but not in second graders. Moreover, individual differences in task-related metamemory (i.e., knowledge about organizational strategies) were important predictors of strategy use and recall for the fourth-grade children. In contrast, second graders' task-related metamemory was not related to sorting at study or clustering during recall. These findings demonstrate that second graders are relatively unaware of the importance of organizational strategies for facilitating recall on sort/recall tasks, indicating that output organization (i.e., clustering during recall) is involuntarily guided by associations between items rather than by category grouping principles (cf. Bjorklund & Jacobs,

1985; Bjorklund & Zeman, 1982). Deliberate use of organizational strategies is typically not found in this age group.

On the other hand, fourth graders seem to be in a transitional state concerning the flexible use of organizational strategies. About half of the sample of fourth graders in Schneider's (1986) study showed strategic behavior, and those children were also able to verbalize their knowledge about organizational strategies. The remaining subjects seemed to be unaware of task requirements. It is important to note that the degree of interitem associativity in the sort/recall lists also affected strategy use and recall of those children with high metamemory scores. Apparently, these children are "transitional" concerning deliberate strategy use because they required salient learning materials to capitalize on their declarative knowledge. It appears, then, that the knowledge base and metamemory jointly contribute to the acquisition of organizational strategies.

Significant correlations between the use of organizational strategies and declarative metamemory are occasionally found for children even younger than those recruited by Schneider (1986). In our view, this may be due to the interplay between the knowledge base and declarative metamemory. That is, only rudimentary knowledge about the advantage of organizational strategies may be sufficient to elicit sorting in a sort/recall task, provided that the children are highly familiar with stimulus materials. Given these preconditions, even young children (i.e., preschoolers and kindergarteners) can behave strategically in tasks of this nature (cf. Fabricius & Hagen, 1984; Paris, Newman, & McVey, 1982; Sodian et al., 1986).

However, in concluding that there can be correlational relationships between knowledge about the efficacy of organizational strategies and memory behaviors in young children, it must also be pointed out that samples of young children typically include very few subjects who know a lot about organizational strategies and their advantages. For example, a closer inspection of the Wimmer and Tornquist (1980) data shows that only three out of the 24 first grade children possessed adequate knowledge of organizational strategies and used semantic categorization. Sodian et al. (1986) obtained a statistically significant correlation ($r = .37$) among 6-year-olds between reported preference for sorting strategies and their use in a sort/recall task. However, perceptual sorting strategies were preferred over semantic organizational strategies overall, even though they are less effective in mediating performance for this age group (Schneider, Körkel, & Vogel, 1987). Instead, the positive correlation reflects the fact that the few subjects who reported a preference for semantic sorting in their metamemory interview also used this strategy to a large extent. Taken together, the results of these studies indicate that most children between four and eight years of age do not know about the effectiveness of semantic organizational strategies.

Retrieval Strategies, Knowledge Base, and Metamemory

Although research on organizational strategies reveals that young children do not know much about these strategies and consequently rarely apply them spontaneously, it has been shown in several studies that young children do have a rudimentary knowledge of memory strategies (cf. Baker-Ward, Ornstein, & Holden, 1984; Fabricius & Cavalier, 1989; Fabricius & Hagen, 1984; Sodian et al., 1986).

If young children possess a metacognitive understanding of the behaviors they display on memory tasks, this understanding should be clearer and more articulate the more natural a memory task is for the child. Even very young children (2-year-olds) are familiar with hide-and-seek tasks, and memory-for-location tasks have been successfully used with children of that age (e.g., DeLoache, 1980). Among other purposes, these tasks have been employed to study the development of a particular type of retrieval strategy, namely, cueing strategies. Geis and Lange (1976) found that even 4-year-olds, when hiding pictures of people in houses, made spontaneous use of the fact that the houses were marked with pictures of objects that were semantically related to the people's social roles (e.g., crown–king). Young children's use of cueing strategies seems to be dependent, however, on the strength of the semantic association between cue and target items (cf. Ritter, 1978; Whittaker, McShane, & Dunn, 1985). Thus, it could be that young children's behavior in hide-and-seek tasks, where there are strong semantic relations between cues and hidden objects, reflects an automatic tendency to group pictures with related objects rather than a deliberate, truly strategic attempt at remembering.

One way to find out whether young children employ retrieval cues in a deliberate attempt to aid prospective retrieval is to investigate their metacognitive understanding of retrieval-cue utilization. Studies by Beal (1985) and Whittaker et al. (1985) reveal that 5- and 6-year-olds are aware of some of the basic requirements for retrieval cues, such as that the cue should be associated with the target item, and that an encounter with the cue is necessary for retrieval to occur. However, it is not clear from these studies if this knowledge is closely related to preschoolers' and kindergarteners' use of cueing strategies. In a more recent study (Schneider & Sodian, 1988), the relationships among planful behaviors, metacognitive awareness of the functions of these behaviors, and memory performance were investigated in 4- and 6-year-old children. Using a memory task similar to that of Geis and Lange (1976), pictures of people were hidden in and retrieved from houses. Half of the houses were marked with a picture of an object that was conceptually related to one of the people's social roles, whereas the other half were marked with pictures that were not related in a conventional way to the people. The question was whether and to what extent preschoolers and kindergarteners would make use of the semantic association between cues and targets, and whether the use of related cues would improve their performance on two memory tasks (relocating the hidden pictures and free recall). A task-related metamemory interview was also given to explore whether the use of retrieval cues was accompanied by an awareness of their function.

Schneider and Sodian (1988) found significant correlations between metamemory and memory behavior (i.e., use of retrieval cues) and memory performance (i.e., relocating hidden objects and free recall). The results thus showed that even very young children's planful behaviors in memory tasks are accompanied by some degree of conscious awareness of the usefulness of these behaviors. Intercorrelations among metamemory, memory behavior, and memory performance were generally substantial, a result rarely found for this age group. In addition to metamemory, semantic knowledge positively affected recall. When children created their own relationships between target items and unrelated cues, they were less successful in relocating the items than when they relied on pre-established semantic relationships. Again, it appears that it is the interaction of the two knowledge components that leads to optimal performance.

Strategies, Knowledge, and Metamemory in Text Processing

From a theoretical perspective, it seems particularly interesting to analyze interactions between the knowledge base and metamemory in complex cognitive activities such as text processing. There is plenty of evidence in the literature that metacognitive knowledge concerning text recall and comprehension develops rather late in childhood (Baker & Brown, 1984; Brown, Bransford, Ferrara, & Campione, 1983; Garner, 1987). The impact of older children's metacognitive knowledge about text processing on text recall and comprehension has also been consistently demonstrated (Forrest-Pressley & Waller, 1984; Jacobs & Paris, 1987; Pressley, Forrest-Pressley, & Elliott-Faust,

1988). Similarly, strong effects of the knowledge base on text processing have been frequently shown, particularly impressively in research using the expert–novice paradigm (cf. Chi & Ceci, 1987; Chiesi, Spilich, & Voss, 1979). However, research on the interaction of the knowledge base and metacognitive knowledge in determining text recall and comprehension is rare.

In a first attempt to address this complicated issue, the research group at the Munich Max-Planck-Institute for Psychological Research conducted a series of developmental studies all dealing with the impact of soccer expertise and metacognitive knowledge on recall and comprehension of a story dealing with a soccer game (Hasselhorn & Körkel, 1986; Körkel, 1987; Schneider, Körkel, & Weinert, in press). Although the story was generally easy to understand even for novices, there were a few exceptions to this rule. That is, occasionally important information was omitted that had to be inferred by the reader. Moreover, several contradictions were built into the text that could only be detected by careful reading. Although knowledge about soccer was important in order to draw correct inferences, it was not always necessary to detect the contradictions in the text. The soccer experts and novices in these studies (mostly third, fifth, and seventh graders) were presented with an extensive battery of memory and metamemory measures.

Interactions between metamemory and the knowledge base were analyzed separately for declarative and procedural metacognitive knowledge. The declarative metamemory questionnaire tapped general metacognitive knowledge not restricted to a specific domain. Thus, the expectation was that the soccer experts and novices would not differ on this measure. However, if individual differences in metacognitive knowledge are indeed important for text recall, this should be evident in within-group comparisons. Accordingly, the assumption was that in both the soccer expert and novice groups, children with high metacognitive knowledge should outperform those with low metacognitive knowledge.

As can be seen from Fig. 4.3, the empirical findings confirmed this prediction. Recall was greater for the experts than the novices overall. In both the expert and novice groups, furthermore, children with high metacognitive knowledge recalled significantly more text units than their metacognitively unknowledgeable counterparts. Again, this result demonstrates that it is the combination of a rich knowledge base and high metacognitive knowledge that leads to optimal performance.

The expectations concerning the relationship between the knowledge base and procedural metacognitive knowledge differed from

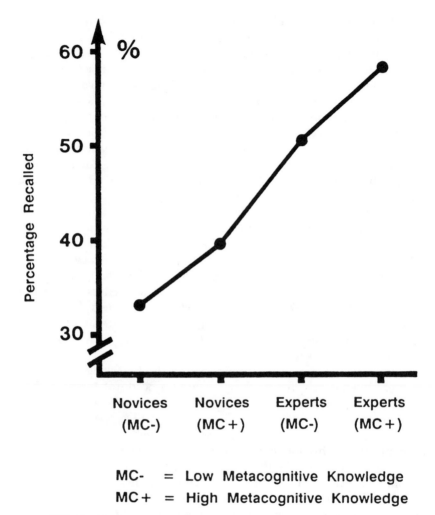

MC- = Low Metacognitive Knowledge
MC+ = High Metacognitive Knowledge

FIG 4.3.   Mean text recall (percentage correct), as a function of expertise and metacognitive knowledge. Data from "Die Entwicklung von Gedächtnis-und Metagedächtnisleistungen in Abnägigkeit von Bereich sspezifischen Vorkenntnissen" by J. Körkel, 1987. Copyright 1987 by J. Körkel. Reprinted by permission.

those for the interaction between the knowledge base and declarative metacognitive knowledge. Although the declarative metamemory measure assessed general metacognitive knowledge, the measures tapping procedural metacognitive knowledge were closely linked to the domain of interest. In a performance-prediction task, subjects had to predict how many sentences of the soccer story they could correctly remember. The second measure of procedural knowledge consisted of "feeling-of-knowing" judgments that were given after responding to each item of a cloze test. That is, children had to indicate how certain they were that they filled in the blanks correctly. Results were straightforward in that soccer experts outperformed soccer novices on both tasks, regardless of age.

Taken together, these results indicate that expert knowledge strongly affects the quality of procedural metacognitive knowledge, and that both expert knowledge and declarative metamemory greatly facilitate text recall. One of the most interesting findings from the soccer expertise studies concerns the fact that metamemory significantly contributes to cognitive performance even in those cases where the knowledge base is very rich.

KNOWLEDGE AND THE DEVELOPMENT OF STRATEGIES: SOME CONCLUDING COMMENTS

The research reviewed in this chapter makes clear the developmental relationship between knowledge and strategy use, particularly in memory tasks. Preadolescent children can and do use memory strategies, but only when the task stimuli are highly familiar to them or when biased by the experimental context (e.g., as in sort/recall tasks). Older children are also affected by their knowledge of the to-be-remembered materials, but will behave strategically even with sets of atypical or low-associated items, especially if repeated trials are administered. Children's content knowledge influences the quality of their procedural metacognitive knowledge, with children being more apt to show metacognitive competence for highly familiar sets of items. The benefits of strategy training are greater and generalization is more likely to be found when highly familiar (e.g., category typical) items serve as stimuli.

Despite our firm beliefs about the relationship between knowledge and strategy development, we must temper our conclusions somewhat because of ambiguities in just exactly what we mean by *strategies* and *knowledge*. We briefly discuss some of these definitional problems in the following section.

Defining Strategies

In this chapter we have used a traditional definition of strategy, stating that it is an effortful, deliberately implemented, goal-directed process that is potentially available to consciousness (e.g., Flavell,

1985; Pressley, Forrest-Pressley, Elliot-Faust, & Miller, 1985). From this definition, processes that are activated automatically, that are not planful, and that we are not aware of, are not considered to be strategic, even if they greatly facilitate task performance.

The most notable advantage of this definition is that it limits the range of cognitive operations to which the term can be applied. When *strategy* includes all processes involved in the execution of some task, it becomes a generic term, no different from any one of a number of synonyms for *thought* (e.g., cognitive operation, mental processing). By restricting the definition of strategy as we have, other processes that are not strategic can be studied, unencumbered by the connotations of an overused label.

This does not imply, however, that strategies should be viewed as being independent of nonstrategic processes. Our view of strategies makes it clear that they are intricately related to nonstrategic processes. The selection and execution of a strategy involves many nonstrategic operations, and understanding these nonstrategic components is necessary if we are to understand the nature and development of the strategy itself.

Furthermore, there must be the recognition that strategies exist on a continuum in terms of complexity, effectiveness, and the amount of mental effort required for their execution. When we state that few preadolescent children spontaneously use memory strategies such as organization or rehearsal, it is not tantamount to saying that these children are incapable of strategy use. Rather than simply labeling children as *strategic* or *nonstrategic*, it is instead much more fruitful to determine the type and nature of strategies used by children of a given age and how those strategies develop into more effective operations.

Our definition is not without its own problems, however. The requirement that strategies be potentially available to consciousness biases one to notice them more in older children and adults than in younger children. Consciousness itself is a sticky problem, and insisting that children of any age (but especially young ones) prove that they are aware of what they are doing before declaring them strategic is a serious shortcoming of our definition. Equally problematic is the fact that many adults are rarely at a loss to explain their cognitions, sometimes inventing reasons for unconsciously motivated behavior (e.g., Gazzaniga, 1985), potentially causing us to overestimate their strategicness.

We do not offer a solution for this definitional conundrum here. We do think it is important, however, to maintain a definition of strategy that makes it distinct from other terms describing cognitive activity. Regardless of how one defines strategy, it is imperative that that definition be made explicit, making it clear what the writer considers to be strategic and what he or she does not when making claims or interpreting research findings.

Measuring Knowledge

Knowledge is an equally problematic concept. Knowledge-base theorists usually specify the general type of knowledge they are concerned with (declarative, procedural), but, at least with respect to declarative knowledge, often fail to provide a detailed description of the nature of the knowledge base. There are exceptions to this trend, such as the work by Chi and her colleagues for children's knowledge of dinosaurs (Chi, 1985; Chi & Koeske, 1983; Gobbo & Chi, 1986), research dealing with people's knowledge of the procedures of familiar games such as chess (e.g., Roth, 1983), and studies focusing on children's knowledge of the small and highly familiar set of their classmates (e.g., Bjorklund & Zeman, 1982; Chi, 1985). However, when discussing children's knowledge for broader categories, such as words and real-world events, estimates of what children know is less precise. Moreover, terms such as *semantic knowledge, world knowledge,* and *domain-specific knowledge* often go undefined, permitting readers to provide their own meanings for these terms.

Norms of children's word knowledge do exist and are used in memory and learning experiments. These include norms of category frequency (Posnansky, 1978), word associations (Bjorklund & Jacobs, 1984; Entwistle, 1966), and category typicality (Bjorklund, Thompson, & Ornstein, 1983). However, these norms are based on small samples, both of children and words, and although they are useful, they do not provide the level of detail we need to make more accurate predictions about the developmental relationship between knowledge and cognitive processing.

Despite the recognition of the importance of such descriptive information, we fear that this paucity of normative data will not soon be rectified. Because the main contribution of normative studies is descriptive and not theoretical, they excite few researchers, and, when they are done, they rarely find their way into the most prestigious journals. Yet it is only with more detailed descriptions of children's declarative knowledge that we can develop more sophisticated models, and we encourage researchers to collect and report normative data in their studies examining the role of knowledge on children's cognition.

The need for more precise measures of children's knowledge is not restricted to the important but limited domain of word meanings. If knowledge is as potent a mediator of strategy use as we propose, we must extend our work beyond list-learning experiments and investigate real-world topics, such as children's knowledge of history, literature, and geography. These and related topics have important implications for communication, reading (e.g., Anderson et al., 1984), and, more generally, success in a technological society (see Hirsch's, 1987, discussion of cultural literacy). Recent research investigating reading comprehension as a function of intelligence and knowledge has provided important steps in the right direction (e.g., Recht & Leslie, 1988; Schneider et al., in press; Walker, 1987). However, as topics of research interest become broader and more contextually relevant, the knowledge base with which we are dealing becomes, necessarily, less well defined.

Research and theorizing cannot wait until we can describe precisely the nature of children's knowledge, particularly considering that much of what any particular child knows will be idiosyncratic to that child alone. An alternative is to administer knowledge pretests to subjects, and, although time consuming, to use them to develop test materials individually tailored to each specific child's knowledge base (cf. Bjorklund & Bernholtz, 1986). Even if such an idiographic approach were to prove successful and become widespread, we must also continue with research that outlines what children at any one age tend to "know," and how this knowledge influences other aspects of cognition.

CONCLUDING REMARKS

Despite the definitional problems, the relation between knowledge and strategy use seems unambiguous to us. Age-related changes in children's content knowledge are integrally related to their tendency to use a memory strategy, the quality of their metacognitive knowledge about such strategies, the likelihood that a strategy will enhance performance, the success of strategy training, and the transfer of a strategy once acquired. Much more needs to be done, however, in terms of describing more precisely what children know and extending our theorizing to socially important content. Although much of this work may be tedious, it will be necessary if we are to attain a clearer understanding of the nature of knowledge development and how it interacts with other aspects of cognition.

ACKNOWLEDGMENTS

We would like to thank Brandi L. Green, Katherine Kipp Harnishfeger, Katherine Lyon, and Donna Watson for comments on earlier versions of this manuscript. Portions of this manuscript were done while the first author was a Visiting Professor at the Max-Planck-Institute for Psychological Research in Munich, West Germany, and he thanks Franz Weinert and the Institute's staff for their support during this time.

REFERENCES

Ackerman, B. P. (1985). Children's retrieval deficits. In C. J. Brainerd & M. Pressley (Eds.), *Basic processes in memory development* (pp. 1–46). New York: Springer-Verlag.

Ackerman, B. P. (1986). Retrieval search for category and thematic information in memory by children and adults. *Journal of Experimental Child Psychology, 42*, 355–377.

Ackerman, B. P. (1987). Descriptions: A model of nonstrategic memory development. In H. W. Reese (Ed.), *Advances in child development and behavior* (Vol. 20, pp. 143–183). Orlando, FL: Academic Press.

Anderson, R. C., Hiebert, E. H., Scott, J. A., & Wilkinson, I. A. G. (1984). *Becoming a nation of readers: The report of the commission on reading*. Washington, DC: U.S. Department of Education.

Ashcraft, M. H., & Fierman, B. A. (1982). Mental addition in third, fourth, and sixth graders. *Journal of Experimental Child Psychology, 33*, 216–234.

Baker, L., & Brown, A. L. (1984). Metacognitive skills and reading. In P. D. Pearson, M. Kamil, R. Barr, & P. Mosenthal (Eds.), *Handbook of reading research* (pp. 353–394). New York: Longman.

Baker-Ward, L., Ornstein, P. A., & Holden, D. J. (1984). The expression of memorization in early childhood. *Journal of Experimental Child Psychology, 37*, 555–575.

Beal, C. R. (1985). Development of knowledge about the use of cues to aid prospective retrieval. *Child Development, 56*, 631–642.

Bjorklund, D. F. (1980). Developmental differences in the timing of children's awareness of category relations in free recall. *International Journal of Behavioral Development, 3*, 61–70.

Bjorklund, D. F. (1985). The role of conceptual knowledge in the development of organization in children's memory. In C. J. Brainerd & M. Pressley (Eds.), *Basic processes in memory development: Progress in cognitive development research* (pp. 103–142). New York: Springer.

Bjorklund, D. F. (1987). How age changes in knowledge base contribute to the development of children's memory: An interpretative review. *Developmental Review, 7*, 93–130.

Bjorklund, D. F. (1988). Acquiring a mnemonic: Age and category knowledge effects. *Journal of Experimental Child Psychology, 45*, 71–87.

Bjorklund, D. F. (1989). *Children's thinking: Developmental function and individual differences*. Pacific Grove, CA: Brooks/Cole.

Bjorklund, D. F., & Bernholtz, J. E. (1986). The role of knowledge base in the memory performance of good and poor readers. *Journal of Experimental Child Psychology, 41*, 367–393.

Bjorklund, D. F., & Buchanan, J. J. (1989). Developmental and knowledge base differences in the acquisition and extension of a memory strategy. *Journal of Experimental Child Psychology, 47*, 451–471.

Bjorklund, D. F., & de Marchena, M. R. (1984). Developmental shifts in the basis of organization in memory: The role of associative versus categorical relatedness in children's free-recall. *Child Development, 55,* 952–962.

Bjorklund, D. F., & Harnishfeger, K. K. (1987). Developmental differences in the mental effort requirements for the use of an organizational strategy in free recall. *Journal of Experimental Child Psychology, 44,* 109–125.

Bjorklund, D. F., & Harnishfeger, K. K. (1989). In defense of resources. *Journal of Experimental Child Psychology, 47,* 19–25.

Bjorklund, D. F., & Harnishfeger, K. K. (1990). The resources construct in cognitive development: Diverse sources of evidence and a theory of inefficient inhibition. *Developmental Review, 10.*

Bjorklund, D. F., & Jacobs, J. W. (1984). A developmental examination of ratings of associative strength. *Behavior Research Methods, Instruments & Computers, 16,* 568–569.

Bjorklund, D. F., & Jacobs, J. W. (1985). Associative and categorial processes in children's memory: The role of automaticity in the development of organization in free recall. *Journal of Experimental Child Psychology, 39,* 599–617.

Bjorklund, D. F., & Muir, J. E. (1988). Children's development of free recall memory: Remembering on their own. In R. Vasta (Ed.), *Annals of Child Development* (Vol. 5, pp. 79–123). Greenwich, CN: JAI.

Bjorklund, D. F., & Ornstein, P. A., & Haig, J. R. (1977). Development of organization and recall: Training in the use of organizational techniques. *Developmental Psychology, 13,* 175–183.

Bjorklund, D. F., Thompson, B. E., & Ornstein, P. A. (1983). Developmental trends in children's typicality judgments. *Behavior Research Methods & Instrumentation, 15,* 350–356.

Bjorklund, D. F., & Zaken-Greenberg, F. (1981). The effects of differences in classification style on preschool children's memory. *Child Development, 52,* 888–894.

Bjorklund, D. F., & Zeman, B. R. (1982). Children's organization and metamemory awareness in their recall of familiar information. *Child Development, 53,* 799–810.

Bjorklund, D. F., & Zeman, B. R. (1983). The development of organizational strategies in children's recall of familiar information: Using social organization to recall the names of classmates. *International Journal of Behavioral Development, 6,* 341–353.

Brainerd, C. J. (1985). Model-based approaches to storage and retrieval development. In C. J. Brainerd & M. Pressley (Eds.), *Basic processes in memory development: Progress in cognitive development research* (pp. 143–207). New York: Springer-Verlag.

Brown, A. L., Bransford, J. D., Ferrara, R. A., & Campione, J. C. (1983). Learning, remembering, and understanding. In J. H. Flavell & E. M. Markman (Eds.), *Cognitive development: Vol. 3. Handbook of child psychology* (4th ed., pp. 77–166). New York, NY: Wiley.

Brown, A. L., & DeLoache, J. S. (1978). Skills, plans, and self-regulation. In R. S. Siegler (Ed.), *Children's thinking: What develops?* (pp. 3–35). Hillsdale, NJ: Lawrence Erlbaum Associates.

Carey, S. (1985). *Conceptual changes in childhood.* Cambridge, MA: MIT Press.

Case, R. (1985). *Intellectual development: Birth to adulthood.* New York: Academic Press.

Cavanaugh, J. C., & Perlmutter, M. (1982). Metamemory: A critical examination. *Child Development, 53,* 11–28.

Chi, M. T. H. (1985). Interactive roles of knowledge and strategies in the development of organized sorting and recall. In S. F. Chipman, J. W. Segal, & R. Glaser (Eds.), *Thinking and learning skills: Vol. 2. Research and open questions* (pp. 457–483). Hillsdale, NJ: Lawrence Erlbaum Associates.

Chi, M. T. H., & Ceci, S. J. (1987). Content knowledge: Its role, representation, and restructuring in memory development. In H. W. Reese (Ed.), *Advances in child development and behavior* (Vol. 20, pp. 91–142). Orlando, FL: Academic Press.

Chi, M. T. H., Feltovich, P. J., & Glaser, R. (1981). Categorization and representation of physics problems by experts and novices. *Cognitive Science, 15,* 121–152.

Chi, M. T. H., Glaser, R., & Rees, E. (1982). Expertise in problem solving. In R. J. Sternberg (Ed.), *Advances in the psychology of human intelligence,* (Vol. 1, pp. 7–75). Hillsdale, NJ: Lawrence Erlbaum Associates.

Chi, M. T. H., & Greeno, J. G. (1987). Cognitive research relevant to education. *Annals of the New York Academy of Sciences, 517,* 39–57.

Chi, M. T. H., & Koeske, R. D. (1983). Network representation of a child's dinosaur knowledge. *Developmental Psychology, 19,* 29–39.

Chiesi, H. L., Spilich, G. J., & Voss, J. F. (1979). Acquisition of domain-related information in relation to high and low domain knowledge. *Journal of Verbal Learning and Verbal Behavior, 18,* 257–274.

Corsale, K., & Ornstein, P. A. (1980). Developmental changes in children's use of semantic information in recall. *Journal of Experimental Child Psychology, 30,* 231–245.

Daneman, M., & Blennerhassett, A. (1984). How to assess the listening comprehension skills of prereaders. *Journal of Educational Psychology, 76,* 1372–1381.

Daneman, M., & Carpenter, P. (1980). Individual differences in working memory and reading. *Journal of Verbal Learning and Verbal Behavior, 19,* 450–466.

Daneman, M., & Green, I. (1986). Individual differences in comprehending and producing words in context. *Journal of Memory and Language, 25,* 1–18.

DeLoache, J. S. (1980). Naturalistic studies of memory for object location in very young children. In M. Perlmutter (Ed.), *New directions for child development: Children's memory* (pp. 17–32). San Francisco: Jossey–Bass.

DeMarie-Dreblow, D., & Miller, P. H. (1988). The development of children's strategies for selective attention: Evidence for a transitional period. *Child Development, 59,* 1504–1513.

Dempster, F. N. (1985). Short-term memory development in childhood and adolescence. In C. J. Brainerd & M. Pressley (Eds.), *Basic processes in memory development: Progress in cognitive development research* (pp. 209–248). New York: Springer.

Entwisle, D. R. (1966). *Word associations of young children.* Baltimore: Johns Hopkins Press.

Fabricius, W. V., & Cavalier, L. (1989). The role of causal theories about memory in young children's memory strategy choice. *Child Development, 60,* 298–308.

Fabricius, W. V., & Hagen, J. W. (1984). Use of causal attributions about recall performance to assess metamemory and predict strategic memory behavior in young children. *Developmental Psychology, 20,* 975–987.

Fischer, K. W. (1980). A theory of cognitive development: The control and construction of hierarchies of skills. *Psychological Review, 87,* 477–531.

Flavell, J. H. (1985). *Cognitive development* (2nd ed.). Englewood Cliffs, NJ: Prentice–Hall.

Forrest-Pressley, D. L., & Waller, T. (1984). *Cognition, metacognition, and reading.* New York: Springer-Verlag.

Frankel, M. T., & Rollins, H. A. (1982). Age-related differences in clustering: A new approach. *Journal of Experimental Child Psychology, 34,* 113–122.

Frankel, M. T., & Rollins, H. A. (1985). Associative and categorical hypotheses of organization in the free recall of adults and children. *Journal of Experimental Child Psychology, 40,* 304–318.

Garner, R. (1987). *Metacognition and reading comprehension.* Norwood, NJ: Ablex.

Gazzaniga, M. S. (1985). *The social brain: Discovering the networks of the mind.* New York: Basic Books.

Geis, M. F., & Lange, G. (1976). Children's cue utilization in memory-for-location task. *Child Development, 47,* 759–766.

Gibson, E. J. (1971). Perceptual learning and the theory of word perception. *Cognitive Psychology, 2,* 351–368.

Gobbo, C., & Chi, M. T. H. (1986). How knowledge is structured and used by expert and novice children. *Cognitive Development, 1,* 221–237.

Groen, G. J., & Parkman, J. M. (1972). A chronometric analysis of simple addition. *Psychological Review, 79,* 329–343.

Groen, G. J., & Resnick, L. B. (1977). Can preschool children invent addition algorithms? *Journal of Educational Psychology, 69,* 645–652.

Guttentag, R. E. (1984). The mental effort requirement of cumulative rehearsal: A developmental study. *Journal of Experimental Child Psychology, 37,* 92–106.

Guttentag, R. (1989). Age differences in dual-task performance: procedures, assumptions, and results. *Developmental Review, 9,* 146–170.

Hamann, M. S., & Ashcraft, M. H. (1985). Simple and complex mental addition across development. *Journal of Experimental Child Psychology, 40,* 49–72.

Hansen, J. (1981). The effects of inference training and practice on young children's reading comprehension. *Reading Research Quarterly, 16,* 391–417.

Hansen, J., & Pearson, P. D. (1983). An instructional study: Improving the inferential comprehension of good and poor readers. *Journal of Educational Psychology, 75,* 821–829.

Hasselhorn, M. (1989). *The emergence of strategic knowledge activation in categorical clustering during retrieval.* Manuscript submitted for publication.

Hasselhorn, M., & Körkel, J. (1986). Metacognitive vs. traditional reading instructions: The mediating role of domain-specific knowledge on children's text-processing. *Human Learning, 5,* 75–90.

Hirsch, E. D. (1987). *Cultural literacy: What every American needs to know.* Boston: Houghton Mifflin.

Jablonski, E. M. (1974). Free recall in children. *Psychological Bulletin, 81,* 522–539.

Jacobs, J. E., & Paris, S. G. (1987). Children's metacognition about reading: Issues in definition, measurement, and instruction. *Educational Psychologist, 22,* 255–278.

Justice, E. M. (1986). Developmental changes in judgements of relative strategy effectiveness. *British Journal of Developmental Psychology, 4,* 75–81.

Kail, R. (1986). The impact of extended practice on rate of mental rotation. *Journal of Experimental Child Psychology, 42,* 378–391.

Kail, R. (1988). Developmental functions for speeds of cognitive processes. *Journal of Experimental Child Psychology, 45,* 339–364.

Kee, D. W., & Bell, T. S. (1981). The development of organizational strategies in the storage and retrieval of categorical items in free-recall learning. *Child Development, 52,* 1163–1171.

Kee, D. W., & Davies, L. (1988). Mental effort and elaboration: A developmental analysis. *Contemporary Educational Psychology, 13,* 221–228.

Kee, D. W., & Howell, S. (1988, April). *Mental effort and memory development.* Paper presented at the meeting of the American Educational Research Association, New Orleans, LA.

Körkel, J. (1987). *Die Entwicklung von Gedächtnis-und Metagedächtnisleistungen in Abhnägigkeit von bereichsspezifischen Vorkenntnissen.* Frankfurt/Main: Lang.

Lange, G. W. (1973). The development of conceptual and rote recall skills among school age children. *Journal of Experimental Child Psychology, 15,* 394–407.

Lange, G. W., & Jackson, P. (1974). Personal organization in children's free recall. *Child Development, 45,* 1060–1067.

Muir-Broaddus, J. E., & Bjorklund, D. F. (in press). Developmental and individual differences in children's memory strategies: The role of knowledge. In W. Schneider & F. E. Weinert (Eds.), *Interactions among strategies, knowledge, and aptitudes in cognitive performance.* New York: Springer–Verlag.

Omanson, R. C., Beck, I. L., Voss, J. F., & McKeown, M. G. (1984). The effects of reading lessons on comprehension: A processing description. *Cognition & Instruction, 1,* 45–67.

Ornstein, P. A., & Naus, M. J. (1985). Effects of the knowledge base on children's memory strategies. In H. W. Reese (Ed.), *Advances in child development and behavior* (Vol. 19, pp. 113–148). New York: Academic Press.

Ornstein, P. A., Naus, M. J., & Liberty, C. (1975). Rehearsal and organizational processes in children's memory. *Child Development, 46,* 818–830.

Paris, S. G., Lipson, M. Y., & Wixson, K. K. (1983). Becoming a strategic reader. *Contemporary Educational Psychology, 8,* 293–316.

Paris, S. G., Newman, R. S., & McVey, K. A. (1982). Learning the functional significance of mnemonic actions: A microgenetic study of strategy acquisition. *Journal of Experimental Child Psychology, 34,* 490–509.

Pearson, P. D., Hansen, J., & Gordon, C. (1979). The effect of background knowledge on young children's comprehension of explicit and implicit information. *Journal of Reading Behavior,* 201–209.

Piaget, J. (1971). *Biology and knowledge.* Chicago: University of Chicago Press.

Posnansky, C. J. (1978). Category norms for verbal items in 25 categories for children in grades 2–6. *Behavior Research Methods & Instrumentation, 10,* 819–832.

Pressley, M., Forrest–Pressley, D. L., & Elliott–Faust, D. J. (1988). What is strategy instructional enrichment and how to study it: Illustrations from research on children's prose memory and comprehension. In F. E. Weinert & M. Perlmutter (Eds.), *Memory development: Universal changes and individual differences* (pp. 101–130). Hillsdale, NJ: Lawrence Erlbaum Associates.

Pressley, M., Forrest–Pressley, D. L., Elliot–Faust, D., & Miller, G. (1985). Children's use of cognitive strategies: How to teach strategies, and what to do if they can't be taught. In M. Pressley & C. J. Brainerd (Eds.), *Cognitive learning and memory in children* (pp. 1–47). New York: Springer-Verlag.

Rabinowitz, M. (1984). The use of categorical organization: Not an all-or-none situation. *Journal of Experimental Child Psychology, 38,* 338–351.

Rabinowitz, M. (1988). On teaching cognitive strategies: The influence of accessability of conceptual knowledge. *Contemporary Educational Psychology, 13,* 229–235.

Recht, D. R., & Leslie, L. (1988). Effect of prior knowledge on good and poor reader's memory for text. *Journal of Educational Psychology, 80,* 16–20.

Ritter, K. (1978). The development of knowledge of an external retrieval cue strategy. *Child Development, 49,* 1227–1230.

Roth, C. (1983). Factors affecting developmental changes in the speed of processing. *Journal of Experimental Child Psychology, 35,* 509–528.

Schneider, W. (1985). Developmental trends in the metamemory-memory behavior relationship: An integrative review. In D. L. Forrest–Pressley, G. E. MacKinnon, & T. G. Waller (Eds.), *Metacognition, cognition, and human performance* (Vol. 1, pp. 57–109). Orlando, FL: Academic Press.

Schneider, W. (1986). The role of conceptual knowledge and metamemory in the development of organizational processes in memory. *Journal of Experimental Child Psychology, 42,* 218–236.

Schneider, W., Borkowski, J. G., Kurtz, B. E., & Kerwin, K. (1986). Metamemory and motivation: A comparison of strategy use and performance in German and American children. *Journal of Cross-Cultural Psychology, 17,* 315–336.

Schneider, W., Körkel, J., & Vogel, K. (1987). Zusammenhänge zwischen Metagedächtnis, strategischem Verhalten und Gedächtnisleistungen im Grundschulalter: Eine entwicklungspsychologische Studie. *Zeitschrift fur Entwicklungspsychologie und Pädagogische Psychologie, 19,* 99–115.

Schneider, W., Körkel, J., & Weinert, F. E. (in press). Expert knowledge, general abilities, and text processing. In W. Schneider & F. E. Weinert (Eds.), *Interactions among aptitude, strategies, and knowledge in cognitive performance.* New York: Springer-Verlag.

Schneider, W., & Pressley, M. (1989). *Memory development between 2 and 20.* New York: Springer–Verlag.

Schneider, W., & Sodian, B. (1988). Metamemory-memory relationships in preschool children: Evidence from a memory-for-location task. *Journal of Experimental Child Psychology, 45,* 209–233.

Siegler, R. S. (1987). The perils of averaging data over strategies: An example from children's addition. *Journal of Experimental Psychology: General, 116,* 250–264.

Siegler, R. S., & Shrager, J. (1984). Strategy choices in addition and subtraction: How do children know what to do? In C. Sophian (Ed.), *Origins of cognitive skills* (pp. 229–293). Hillsdale, NJ: Lawrence Erlbaum Associates.

Sodian, B., Schneider, W., & Perlmutter, M. (1986). Recall, clustering, and metamemory in young children. *Journal of Experimental Child Psychology, 41,* 395–410.

Walker, C. H. (1987). Relative importance of domain knowledge and overall aptitude on acquisition of domain-related information. *Cognition and Instruction, 4,* 25–42.

Wellman, H. M. (1983). Metamemory revisited. In M. T. H. Chi (Ed.), *Trends in memory development research* (pp. 31–51). Basel: Karger.

Whittaker, S., McShane, J., & Dunn, D. (1985). The development of cueing strategies in young children. *British Journal of Developmental Psychology, 3,* 153–161.

Wimmer, H., & Tornquist, K. (1980). The role of metamemory and metamemory activation in the development of mnemonic performance. *International Journal of Behavioral Development, 3,* 71–81.

Worden, P. E. (1976). The effects of classification structure on organized free recall in children. *Journal of Experimental Child Psychology, 22,* 519–529.

Zembar, M. J., & Naus, M. J. (1985, April). *The combined effects of knowledge base and mnemonic strategies on children's memory.* Paper presented at meeting of the Society for Research in Child Development, Toronto.

CHAPTER 5

The Development of Strategic Memory: Coordinating Knowledge, Metamemory, and Resources

Mark L. Howe
Julia T. O'Sullivan
Memorial University

For many cognitive developmental psychologists, improvements in children's long-term memory have been viewed traditionally as the outcome of corresponding increases in the spontaneous application of sophisticated memorization strategies. Recently, however, there has been a growing awareness that memory development, like cognitive development, consists of the independent and aggregate effects of changes in strategy effectiveness, conceptual knowledge, metamemorial knowledge, and processing efficiency. Associated with this change in perspective is a number of troublesome matters related to the definition and measurement of these factors. First, there is little consensus on what constitutes a strategy. For example, should we restrict the definition of strategic behavior to those situations in which conscious and effortful mnemonic devices are employed, or should we allow for more automatic organizational schemes to be incorporated into the definition of what is strategic? Second, is metamemory a distinct form of knowledge that contributes to memory development by directing strategic operations? Third, and more generally, how can we measure the properties, development, and restructuring of children's knowledge base (see Bjorklund, 1987; Chi & Ceci, 1987; Rabinowitz & Chi, 1987) in order to determine how different forms of knowledge (e.g., declarative, procedural, etc.) contribute to changes in children's strategy use and memory performance? Fourth, what role do changes in the efficiency of children's processing resources (see Bjorklund & Harnishfeger, 1987; Guttentag, 1984, 1985;

Pressley, Cariglia–Bull, Deane, & Schneider, 1987) play in the execution of strategies?

In this chapter, we address each of these areas in turn and discuss the relevant definitional, methodological, and/or measurement problems associated with each factor. It is only when these issues have been adequately addressed that we can proceed with the business of developing theories that enumerate the independent and combined influences of strategies, metamemory, knowledge base, and processing resources on memory development. Throughout the chapter, we try to do just that by integrating automatic and purposive aspects of strategic processing with changes in conceptual and metamemorial knowledge, as well as changes in processing efficiency. We begin with a brief historical sketch of the research that contributed to the current perspective on memory development.

HISTORICAL SKETCH

Research in memory development during the 1970s was focused primarily on strategic mnemonic behavior. Indeed, a review of the literature from that time could lead to the conclusion that strategy development was considered to be almost synonymous with memory development. A large body of research now exists that indicates that strategies are commonly employed by school age children in a variety of situations, that the sophistication of strategies and their application increases with age, and that developments in strategy use accompany age differences in memory performance (see Pressley, Heisel, McCormick, & Nakamura, 1982).

The importance attributed to the role of strategy development was reflected in the large body of instructional studies designed to teach memory strategies to children. The instructional method provided the opportunity to reconstruct empirically how the developmental progression from memory novice to memory expert might occur. This was done by testing the sufficiency of specific variables, in this instance strategies, to account for improvements in performance following instruction. The working hypothesis here was that if young children could be taught to use strategies that they do not currently employ, subsequent improvements in memory performance could be expected and this, in turn, would demonstrate the importance of strategies in memory development (for a review, see Pressley et al., 1982). Findings from instructional research clearly indicated that a variety of child populations benefit from strategy training. However, despite sophisticated instructional technology, it proved difficult to train strategies such that children would continue to use them following training or generalize them to new memory situations. It was apparent by the mid 1970s that the ability to execute a strategy was not sufficient to insure intelligent generalized use of that strategy (Pressley, Borkowski, & Schneider, 1987).

These findings prompted a great deal of research aimed at identifying the determinants of competent strategy use. The initial focus of much of this research was directed at the role of metamemory in strategy development. Metamemory is defined as knowledge and awareness of memory or of anything pertinent to information storage and retrieval (Flavell & Wellman, 1977). There are several categories of metamemorial knowledge including knowledge about strategies. Metamemory about strategies (Pressley, Borkowski, & O'Sullivan, 1985) can play various causal roles in strategy selection, implementation, and monitoring activities (Borkowski, Carr, & Pressley, 1987). The link between metamemory about strategies and strategy use has been investigated in both correlational and instructional studies (for a review, see Pressley, Borkowski, & O'Sullivan, 1985). As the evidence accumulated linking developments in strategy use with metamemory, developmental models of memory that incorporated both of these components began to appear in the literature (e.g., Pressley, Borkowski, & O'Sullivan, 1985).

In these early models the structure and content of the knowledge base (other than the metamemory component) received scant attention. However, as research findings on the important role of knowledge base in memory development accumulated, it became clear that models of strategy use should be expanded to incorporate more general features of knowledge. Of particular relevance here were the findings that (a) knowledge base can facilitate efficient memory performance without strategic assistance (e.g., Bjorklund, 1987; Chi, 1981) and (b) strategy application depends on the state (structure and content) of the knowledge base (e.g., Corsale, 1978; Corsale & Ornstein, 1980). In addition, because the development of knowledge base is thought to increase processing efficiency (e.g., Sternberg, 1985), a number of investigators have emphasized the importance of considering the differential allocation of resources in strategic processing (e.g., Bjorklund & Harnishfeger, 1987; Guttentag, 1985). Although both of these factors have been acknowledged as important in the development of strategic memory (e.g., Pressley, Borkowski, & Schneider's, 1987, "Good Strategy User" model), a complete specification of their roles is still at the formative stage.

DEFINING STRATEGIES TODAY

From an information-processing perspective, strategies are task-appropriate behaviors used in the service of maximizing performance. In this context, memory strategies can be defined as specific sets of processes (involving both automatic and controlled subcomponents) that determine the content and order of execution of essential memory operations (e.g., encoding, storage, search, and retrieval). It is this set of behaviors (both overt and covert) that is strategic and that serves to optimize memory performance in a given task.

Although few would disagree with this simple definition, there is debate concerning whether these cognitive/behavioral sets, or components of sets, are strategic when executed in an effortless automatic fashion, or only when executed in a deliberate conscious manner. Previously, researchers adopted the latter position and defined strategies as being deliberate plans that were subject to conscious evaluation (e.g., Naus & Ornstein, 1983; Pressley, Borkowski, & O'Sullivan, 1985). All more or less automatic memory processes, both overt (e.g., pointing, looking, or touching the materials to be remembered) and covert (e.g., categorizing, associating, and drawing inferences concerning the to-be-remembered material), were traditionally relegated to the "nonstrategic" category. As the distinction between automatic and controlled processing became more engrained in the memory development literature, a number of behaviors that had previously been classified as "strategic" (e.g., category clustering) were now considered strategic in some circumstances and "nonstrategic" in others (e.g., Lange, 1978). The distinction was predicated on whether the process was used with (strategic) or without (nonstrategic) conscious intent.

As it turns out, this distinction is both artificial and theoretically counterproductive. Specifically, the extent to which processing is effortful is more a matter of degree, with different processes or processing components lying on a continuum ranging from *predominantly automatic* to *predominantly controlled*. When aspects of memory development are dissected in an all-or-none manner, rather than viewed as variation on a continuum, we effectively isolate (both empirically and theoretically) what are integral components of the behavior under study. In order to understand how an individual "solves" a memory problem, we must take into account those processes that are executed more or less automatically, those that are executed more or less effortfully, and the way in which processes that vary in degree of effortfulness conjoin to produce organized (strategic) behavior. By simply focusing on one set of processes at a time, we may tend to ignore the emergent properties inherent in strategy use.

More recently, several authors (Ackerman, 1987; Pressley, Borkowski, & Schneider, 1987) have suggested that the critical distinction between strategic and nonstrategic behavior lies in whether the target process is basic to carrying out the task (nonstrategic behaviors such as looking at the material to be memorized) or involves higher order cognitive operations (strategic behaviors such as rehearsal or elaboration). Unfortunately, this definition raises a series of new problems, in particular, the need to construct some sort of complexity scale for cognitive operations (with nonstrategic operations being at the lower end and strategic operations being at the high end). Assuming such a scale can be constructed, we must also be able to distinguish scale levels empirically. Because overt and covert behavior from a number of different (potentially independent) sources conjoin to determine memory performance, it may not be as easy to segregate empirically the individual components of a task without the help of formal modeling techniques (see later discussion).

More importantly, however, these different "levels" of processing involved in mnemonic performance interact dynamically. Indeed, developmental changes occur in the degree to which different aspects of a memory task are executed automatically or effortfully, and how responsive these changes are to varying task demands. What is important in memory development is not only whether particular isolated aspects of strategic behavior become automatic or remain effortful, but also the overall efficiency of the entire constellation of behaviors required to maximize memory performance in numerous different contexts.

Today's touchstone for decifering what is and what is not strategic is becoming increasingly blurred. In addition to whether the process under scrutiny is automatic or controlled, current theorizing has added the requirement that strategies be "potentially conscious" or "potentially controlled" (see Pressley, Borkowski, & Schneider, 1987). From this point of view, automatic components of strategic behavior are potentially subject to conscious reflection and control. In particular, well mastered skills in a subject's knowledge base can be automatically and "unconsciously" recruited in the service of memory goals (e.g., Brown, Bransford, Ferrara, & Campione, 1983). For example, the relatively automatic process of "semantic capture" (in which subjects can take advantage of taxonomic organization inherent in a to-be-remembered list to facilitate performance) which occurs spontaneously in older children and adults, is not necessarily accompanied by conscious mentation, although certainly we could reflect on this process and report on its use. As Pressley, Borkowski, and Schneider (1987) pointed out, "Even though strategic processing that is driven by the knowledge base probably does not qualify as consciously intentional or planful, it accomplishes cognitive purposes, can be reflected on, and probably could be controlled if the subject wanted to do so. Thus, we consider this type of processing strategic . . ." (pp. 111–112).

The central problem here is that what is strategic and what is not strategic hinges on a subject's ability to reflect on his or her own cognitive operations. Traditionally, this has been viewed as a component of metamemory rather than a defining feature of strategies themselves. Therefore, by definition, developmental changes in awareness of cognitive processes (metacognition) is unnecessarily tied to whether a behavior is diagnosed as being strategic. What this means is that this definition can be both underinclusive and overinclusive. For very young children who have relatively limited powers of reflection, many behaviors would be classified as nonstrategic. For older children and adults who have considerably greater powers of reflection, just about any behavior could be classed as strategic.

An important question that arises concerns whether young children's behavior in memory tasks should be described as strategic or nonstrategic when the behavior is directed at the specific goal of remembering (e.g., Baker-Ward, Ornstein, & Holden, 1984; De-Loache, Cassidy, & Brown, 1985). Recently, the traditional view that very young children behave nonstrategically has been challenged. In fact, there is considerable evidence indicating that preschoolers (children under 6 years of age) do use a variety of mnemonic strategies (e.g., DeLoache et al., 1985; Pressley, Borkowski, & Schneider, 1987). Although these strategies require deliberate mnemonic effort, many of them have been classified as primitive action-control strategies (i.e., very general strategies that simply regulate attention so that subjects attend to only those items that are to be remembered and ignore nonmemory components of the display, see Pressley, Borkowski, & Schneider, 1987).

The question remains as to whether preschoolers can use more sophisticated strategies (e.g., rehearsal and categorization). There has been a recent accumulation of research that indicates that the answer to this question is yes. There are a number of instances in which young children exhibit behavior that is analogous to more mature forms of rehearsal. That is, even 2- (DeLoache et al., 1985) and 3-year-olds (Wellman, Ritter, & Flavell, 1975) repeatedly look at a hiding place of a to-be-remembered object during a retention interval. More specifically, DeLoache et al. (1985) found evidence that even 18- to 24-month-old children exhibit ostensibly strategic behavior in a memory-for-location task. Like mature memorizers, strategylike behaviors occurred differentially depending on the familiarity of the setting (with three times more strategic behavior occurring in the unfamiliar and, hence, more memory demanding, laboratory setting than in the familiar home environment). Similarly, strategic behavior was sensitive to variations in the memory demands of the tasks. When the memory load was low (i.e., the to-be-located object remained visible during the retention interval or the experimenter was to retrieve the toy at the end of the retention interval), substantially fewer target behaviors were observed than when memory load was high (i.e., when the object remained hidden and the child was to retrieve it following the retention interval).

Although DeLoache et al. (1985) did not interpret these outcomes as indicating that very young children have full-fledged memory strategies, it is clear that very young children are strategic, although conscious evaluation of the rationale for these behaviors is unlikely in children of this age. However, these behaviors may represent reasonably sophisticated precursors of more elaborate, consciously available strategies that develop as children mature. The critical point is that like the strategies used by older children, these early strategies are sensitive to differential task and memory demands, and appear to be executed without conscious awareness. As Brown et al. (1983) suggested these early task-oriented behaviors evolve (i.e., becoming more reliable, systematic, and refined), with development gradually becoming flexible and generalizable. With practice, many of these skills become automatic components of larger, more sophisticated routines. Thus, the primary differences between immature and mature strategies lies in the latter's stability and transituational characteristics (also see Brown et al., 1983).

Potential skeptics could, of course, argue that these behavioral analogs of rehearsal are very general forms of strategic behavior and that mature strategy use requires the tailoring of cognitive operations to the specific task at hand. Like older children, more specific strategic behavior in very young children is most likely to be observed in cognitive domains that preschoolers have already mastered (e.g., Brown et al., 1983). That is, young children will be more likely to exhibit sophisticated mnemonic behavior in areas in which they already have considerable experience and knowledge. Recognizing this intimate relationship between what a child knows and the application of that knowledge in the service of mnemonic behavior, DeLoache and Todd (1988) examined preschooler's (2- to 5-year-olds) ability to use spatial organization (a cognitive skill that even 2-year-olds possess) to categorize to-be-remembered from not-to-be-remembered items. In all three of their experiments, preschoolers were able to seriate spatially items for future retrieval from those not to be retrieved. Developmental differences were also observed, primarily in the area of sustaining goal-directed mnemonic efforts. That is, although all of the children were able to use spatial categorization to mediate memory performance, younger children had greater difficulty executing the strategy effectively (e.g., they lost track of what they were doing perhaps because their planning was inadequate and/ or they failed to monitor their progress). Again, these results highlight the fact that even young children are relatively sophisticated strategy users when the mnemonic requirements are congruent with the child's current cognitive or knowledge base structure.

To summarize, we have argued that the distinction between "strategic" and "nonstrategic" aspects of memory behavior is not theoretically productive. Rather, in order to understand strategic behavior, we must consider both the automatic and purposive components of that behavior in children of all ages, as well as the types of knowledge structures children of different ages (and abilities) possess. We prefer to define strategic behavior as any mnemonic effort that either takes advantage of inherent structure or imposes structure on the to-be-remembered information. We are using the term *structure* in a very general and liberal sense, referring simply to the manner in which the contents of long-term memory are organized. To us, taking advantage of mnemonic properties inherent in some material (e.g., using categorical or associative relations in a list, using spatial properties, drawing inferences in reading prose, and so on) is just as strategic as imposing one's own structure on material that does not contain such mnemonic assistance. Whether this process occurs automatically or requires considerable effort is irrelevant to whether the process is strategic or not strategic. The relative difficulty of executing the strategy is important in determining performance, but regardless of the level of effort, the behaviors themselves can be interpreted as being strategic. Similarly, the question of whether strategies are "potentially conscious and controllable" is not of concern in determining what does and what does not constitute a strategy. Although this is certainly an important consideration in strategy development, it is perhaps best addressed in the arena of developmental changes that occur in metamemorial knowledge.

Given this rather broad definition of what a strategy is we could be accused of being overinclusive. That is, we have left little or no room for the existence of nonstrategic behavior. In fact, however, we believe that this is an advantage. To our knowledge, there are few, if any, instances in which children fail to exhibit strategic behavior, at least when their current cognitive level is taken into account. That is, "nonstrategic" behaviors tend to be observed when the knowledge required for the execution of the anticipated strategy is inconsistent with the child's current knowledge (i.e., they are observed only in circumstances in which an experimenter's expectation of how the information should be organized is not met). This does not mean that the child is nonstrategic, but rather, that the expected behavior is not in the child's repertoire. As has been pointed out numerous times now (e.g., DeLoache & Todd, 1988), when children are given the opportunity to organize materials in a manner consistent with their knowledge base, their behaviors tend to be strategic. It is feasible, then, that we are inherent organizers and that all children, given the opportunity, are strategic, especially when the requirements of the task allow children to use the knowledge they possess. It is only when the task demands are outside of the child's knowledge range that "nonstrategic" performance occurs.

Like other theorists (e.g., Brown et al., 1983; DeLoache & Todd, 1988), our definition of strategic behavior tightly interweaves the observation of organized behavior with the child's current cognitive or knowledge base structures. That is, both the type of organized behavior exhibited and the efficiency with which the behaviors are executed is determined by the structure and type of knowledge a child possesses. As this knowledge changes, so too will the type of organization used to mediate mnemonic performance.

From this perspective, the role of strategies in memory development must be considered in a larger context, one that includes an understanding of concomitant changes in underlying cognitive functioning. More specifically, changes in strategy use (including the relative effortfulness of various subcomponents of these strategies) are accompanied by developments in conceptual and metamemorial knowledge as well as the efficiency with which various cognitive operations are executed. It is only when we consider all of these components in unison that a complete picture of memory development will emerge.

THE ROLE OF KNOWLEDGE IN STRATEGY DEVELOPMENT

Because the structure and contents of the knowledge base are inextricably linked to the types of strategic behavior children of different ages are likely to exhibit, it is paramount that we formulate some idea of what constitutes this knowledge bank. In general, the knowledge base consists of declarative knowledge (e.g., semantic relations),

procedural knowledge (e.g., rules of association), strategies themselves, and metacognitive knowledge. The task facing theorists is to
determine how these different types of knowledge are stored and
organized, and how this knowledge is reorganized as development
proceeds. In this section we consider the development of metamemorial knowledge first and more general aspects of the knowledge base
second.

Metamemory

Metamemory (Flavell, 1971) is a specialized form of metacognition
that refers to the individual's knowledge and awareness of memory.
Flavell and Wellman (1977) proposed that metamemory includes at
least four content categories: (a) knowledge that some memory situations require intentional mnemonic behavior and some do not, (b)
knowledge about one's own memory limitations and capacities, as well
as the ability to monitor cognitive experiences in a memory task, (c)
knowledge about the influence of task demands or properties of the
input information on memory performance, and (d) knowledge
about storage and retrieval strategies. This taxonomy was not intended to be exhaustive and the authors pointed out that they did not
set out to define the concept precisely. Although the concept of
metamemory is an inherently "fuzzy" one (Wellman, 1983), with little
consensus concerning the definitional boundary, there is agreement
that the central components of metamemory include knowledge
about the properties of memory and knowledge about the current
memory state. As Flavell (1979) pointed out, metamemory is fun-
damentally identified as a form of knowledge and is no different than
any other form of knowledge one possesses. Moreover, as Wellman
(1983, p. 36) suggested,

> What distinguishes metamemory is its referent—it is knowledge
> about the human-information processing system. Otherwise it has no
> special status. It is stored in long-term memory like other knowledge; it
> may be neither more nor less consciously accessible than any other
> knowledge; it has, on the average, no greater nor fewer implications for
> behavior than any other knowledge.

The major hypothesized function of metamemory is to inform and
regulate mnemonic routines and strategies (Brown, 1978). The sophisticated memorizer is assumed to integrate metamemorial knowledge with strategic behaviors in solving problems. This interchange
enables the memorizer to select, modify, and invent strategies and

also to modify the contents of metamemory through successful problem solving (Brown, 1978). This hypothesized link has explanatory potential when considered in the context of strategy development. For example, even though children have the competence to execute certain strategies, they may lack the knowledge concerning when, how, and why the strategies are useful, knowledge that may be essential for competent generalized strategy use (Flavell & Wellman, 1977). However, although this theoretical position about metamemory as a driving force in strategic behavior is plausible, empirical demonstrations of metamemory–strategy links have been relatively difficult to obtain (Cavanaugh & Perlmutter, 1982).

One reason frequently cited as contributing to this outcome is that early studies used an overly simplistic model of metamemory–strategy relations (Wellman, 1983) and used unreliable measures of metamemory (Rushton, Brainerd, & Pressley, 1983). This line of research was subsequently deemphasized, largely because of the suggestion that investigators were looking for relations in tasks where they were unlikely to be observed (i.e., tasks thought to involve only automatic processing). For example, Borkowski (1985) argued that metamemory–strategy relations were more likely to be observed when the correct strategy was less obvious (e.g., maintenance and generalization of trained strategies), and processing was more effortful. Recently, many researchers have focused their attention on more deliberate and effortful tasks involving strategy training studies (for a review, see Pressley, Forrest–Pressley, Elliot–Faust, & Miller, 1985), and new multicomponent models of metamemory about strategies (Pressley, Borkowski, & O'Sullivan, 1985; Pressley, Borkowski, & Schneider, 1987) are based on this work.

Although we applaud this paradigm shift and the related theoretical developments, we are concerned that research on metamemory–strategy relations is overly focused on relatively effortful strategic processing, with little or no attention paid to relatively automatic components. If metamemory is knowledge about memory, then, by definition, it must include at least some knowledge about automatic processes as well as knowledge about effortful processes. Although we do not have a well-articulated idea regarding the contents of metamemory for automatic processes, we can offer two suggestions.

First, we suspect that knowledge about the specific *procedural* aspects of automatic processing is much less detailed than procedural knowledge about effortful processing. This is because automatic processes are, by definition, less available to conscious inspection affording us little opportunity to develop an elaborated knowledge base about them. Second, metamemory must include *declarative* knowledge concerning the relative difficulty of memory problems, including the understanding that an "effort" continuum (automatic to controlled) exists with respect to memory strategies—that is, some tasks require more strategic effort than others. It is this knowledge that influences our appraisal of the memory task at hand, at least in terms of the degree of strategic effort required. For example, when confronted with a memory task, one must first recognize whether that task requires considerable deliberate strategic effort, or whether the task can be accomplished with relative ease in an automatic fashion. The outcome of this appraisal, together with motivational factors, is the cornerstone of deliberate strategy deployment. We suspect that the increasing accuracy of these appraisals accompanies improvements in memory performance and that sophisticated memorizers probably have an integrated understanding of the combined effects of effort, person, strategy (automatic and controlled), and task variables. Our definition of strategic behavior (i.e., one that stresses both automatic and controlled aspects of strategic memory), and our conceptualization of metamemory as knowledge about all aspects of strategic behavior, requires that metamemory research be expanded to include knowledge about the role of automatic processing.

At a more general level, what we are saying is that metamemory research must keep pace with current theoretical refinements in models of children's memory development. Specifically, because metamemory is knowledge about the memory-processing system, and because recent proposals concerning the development of this system include knowledge-base and processing resources as pivotal components that contribute to age changes in memory, we suggest that metamemory also contains knowledge about these factors. It is because these factors appear to play a central role in memory development that metamemory research must be expanded to include knowledge about the knowledge base and the efficient allocation of resources, in addition to knowledge about strategies. Where the focus of research should be, therefore, is on disentangling the different components of knowledge and determining their separate and aggregate effects on the developing memory system. We are aware that the nature of these aspects of metamemory, and the degree to which they are consciously accessible, are empirical questions, ones that require addressing methodological and measurement issues. However, we believe that if we expand our idea of the nature of strategies and expand our concept of metamemory about strategies and the other contents of the knowledge base, we will be better equipped to study the emergence of metamemory–strategy relations in very young children.

Knowledge Base

The importance of knowledge-base development has been recognized by investigators who are concerned with both the "strategic" end of the memory development continuum (e.g., Bjorklund, 1985, 1987; Ornstein & Naus, 1985) as well as those concerned with the "nonstrategic" end of the memory development continuum (e.g., Ackerman, 1987). In much of the research in this area, attention has been focused on the semantic information (declarative memory) that strategies operate on, as well as on the strategies themselves. Because both semantic and strategic information are contained in the knowledge base, it has often been noted that the presence of organized recall does not always signal the presence of *deliberate* strategy use (e.g., Brown et al, 1983; Lange, 1978). Associative and taxonomic clustering can occur as an *automatic* consequence of the interitem associative structure of information in a subject's knowledge base. As Brown et al. (1983) pointed out, however, it is often difficult to partition those effects that are the consequence of automatic "semantic capture" and those that are attributable to the use of effortful organizational strategies. As mentioned in the preceding section, the distinction between deliberate and automatic components is frequently of limited usefulness. This is particularly germane here as it is often difficult to consider strategic operations in the absence of content knowledge (e.g., Chi & Ceci, 1987).

Research on the role of the declarative content of the knowledge base in memory development has focused on changes in the structure of information (e.g., Chi, 1985; Chi & Ceci, 1987; Rabinowitz & Chi, 1987) as well as on changes in the accessibility of knowledge structures (e.g., Bjorklund, 1987; Rabinowitz, 1988; Rabinowitz & Chi, 1987). Although evidence concerning qualitative changes in knowledge structure across development is somewhat sketchy owing to a number of measurement problems (for a review of different representational systems, see Chi & Ceci, 1987), there is evidence that both the number and strength of featural links (both within and between entries in the knowledge base) vary developmentally (e.g., Bjorklund, 1987, 1988; Rabinowitz & Chi, 1987). As featural links increase in strength and number, individual items are encoded on more dimensions (leading to more elaborate item traces) and activation is said to spread further between items within the semantic structure.

One way in which the impact of knowledge base on memory performance has been investigated is to "equate" knowledge levels across different subjects by using age- and/or ability-appropriate category norms (e.g., Bjorklund & Bernholtz, 1986), or to compare "experts" in a particular knowledge domain with "novices" (e.g., Chi & Koeske, 1983). In either case, differences in knowledge, not age, account for most of the performance differences. Similar results have recently been reported for text recall (Recht & Leslie, 1988).

A second approach has been to provide repeated recall attempts with the same material (e.g., Bjorklund, 1988). The rationale underlying this approach is that younger children may take longer than older children to access and/or activate semantic relations in the knowledge base. Thus, in the usual one-trial memory procedure, age differences in clustering may reflect differences in accessibility of categorical structures in younger children's memory and not the absence of these relations. Consistent with this suggestion, Bjorklund (1988) found an Age × Trial interaction in which the use of an organizational strategy unfolded more slowly across trials for younger (Grade 4) than older (Grade 7) children. Similarly, we have found that when a criterion-learning design is used, even younger (Grade 2) children exhibit what would be classified as spontaneous (organizational) strategy use (Howe, Brainerd, & Kingma, 1985; Howe, O'Sullivan, Brainerd, & Kingma, 1989). It would appear, then, that previous one-trial designs provide only a conservative estimate of children's use of organizational strategies. When multiple learning opportunities are permitted, even young children can take advantage of categorical relations to optimize memory performance.

Finally, Brainerd, Kingma, and Howe (1986) used a criterion-learning design to investigate age differences in spread of encoding. Recall that both within-item and between-item featural integrity play a role in making information more available and accessible for use as organizational schemes facilitating performance in memory tasks. What Brainerd et al. (1986) examined was the extent to which children encode categorical features of individual items and the degree to which the activation of these categorical features spreads to other, same category items within a list. The results showed that while both second- and sixth-grade students encoded the individual concepts in terms of their category features, it was not until adolescence that this category encoding spread to same category members within the list. Developmentally, then, access to category features in the knowledge base initially enhances item-by-item learning of list members, with spread of activation among same category members occurring later in development. Consistent with recent theorizing, these developmental increases in spread of activation may improve memory performance by freeing up resources (see the following section) for the execution of cognitive activities required for improved memory performance (e.g., Bjorklund, 1987) including the execution of more complex mnemonic strategies (e.g., Ornstein & Naus, 1985).

Before turning to an examination of this resources hypothesis, it is important to note that although considerable progress has been made in mapping declarative aspects of the knowledge base, there is much work left to be done in this area as well as on the other constituents (procedural, strategic, and metacognitive). As both the contents and their representation are thought to alter as development proceeds, it is important not only to map static aspects of knowledge, but also the inherent, dynamic changes that occur as a function of experience. With the advent of increasingly sophisticated measurement procedures (e.g., Chi & Ceci, 1987) progress in this area should be rapid.

THE ROLE OF RESOURCES IN STRATEGY DEVELOPMENT

One theoretical perspective that has gained credence in cognitive psychology during the past decade is *resource theory*. Simply stated, information-processing tasks are said to be executed in working memory, a system that contains stored representations of the task at hand and can draw on long-term memory representations or other data sources as required in the completion of the task. Although some theorists contend that the number of resources is not a fixed commodity changing with practice and experience (see discussion on attentional resources in Hirst & Kalmar, 1987), most theorists agree that the "fuel" that drives working memory is a limited-capacity pool of resources where the limitations are assumed to be analogous to those of short-term memory (e.g., Klapp, Marshburn, & Lester, 1983). Although considerable debate exists concerning whether these resources are generic in nature (being allocated to any component, e.g., encoding, storage, retrieval, computation, etc., of the processing task) or are specialized pools of dedicated resources (Baddeley, 1986; Brainerd & Kingma, 1984, 1985; Brainerd & Reyna, 1988; Klapp et al., 1983), most theorists agree that there exists an interaction between the individual and the task such that the required processing effort can vary in the degree to which it is resource draining. That is, depending on the expertise and age of the individual, the effort required to complete a task can range from being very demanding and resource dependent (or effortful) to very easy and resource independent (or automatic).

Naturally, the resources theory often serves as a pivotal concept in the construction of models of cognitive development (e.g., Case, 1985). Here, changes in cognitive development are ascribed to alterations in the efficiency with which children allocate resources in various information-processing tasks (e.g., Baddeley, 1986; Case, 1985).

Some theorists propose that the *actual capacity* of the system increases with age (e.g., Pascual-Leone, 1970) while others suggest that it is the efficiency of processing or *functional capacity* that develops (e.g., Case, 1985). As children mature and gain expertise in the execution of cognitive processes, resources become freed permitting increased storage of information (Case, 1985) or execution of more sophisticated operations (e.g., Bjorklund, 1985, 1987).

Reliance on resource theory in explanations of children's cognitive development has become practically ubiquitous. Capacity differences have been used to "explain" changes in speed of processing (e.g., Kail, 1988), problem solving and reasoning (e.g., Brainerd & Kingma, 1984, 1985; Case, 1985; Chapman, 1987; Halford, Maybery, & Bain, 1986), and memory (e.g., Bjorklund, 1987; Guttentag, 1985). In the domain of strategy development, there have been several recent demonstrations of the utility of resource theory. One approach has been to examine the relationship between individual differences in measures of functional capacity (working memory, short-term memory) and the ability to execute different strategies. For example, Pressley, Cariglia-Bull et al. (1987) reasoned that because the construction of imaginal representations requires the simultaneous execution of several cognitive steps, limitations in imagery-generation skill may be tied to functional capacity limitations. In order to test this hypothesis, they examined individual and age differences in measures of short-term memory and verbal competence and the execution of an imagery strategy in children from Grades 1 through 6. The most interesting results concerned the pattern of individual differences. Here, regardless of age, children with higher estimates of functional (short-term memory) capacity were more successful in the execution of an imagery strategy than those children with lower estimates of functional capacity. As Pressley, Cariglia-Bull et al. (1987) pointed out, children's failures to use imagery in the service of memory is not strictly a production deficiency that can be altered by imagery instructions. Rather, such failures may also be rooted in limitations in functional capacity.

A second approach, adapted from the attention literature, has been to *increase* resource demands using the dual-task procedure. Here, children execute two tasks, a primary activity (e.g., memory) and a secondary, irrelevant activity (e.g., finger tapping), in isolation and concurrently. The important outcome is interference between the two tasks such that performance on either task alone is superior to performance when both tasks are executed simultaneously. This datum has been used to argue that different tasks draw on a central bank of generic resources and that when the aggregate demand for an individual's resources exceeds the limitations of this commodity, competition for resources (interference) occurs. The putative advantage of this procedure is that it provides an estimate of the resource requirements of different cognitive activities.

To date, three types of strategies have been investigated using this procedure, rehearsal (Guttentag, 1984), organization (Bjorklund & Harnishfeger, 1987), and elaboration (Kee & Davies, 1988). In a series of three experiments, Guttentag (1984) exploited the dual-task procedure to examine the resource requirements of a trained cumulative rehearsal strategy with second-, third-, and sixth-grade children. While the children were rehearsing a list of unrelated words they were required to perform a secondary task of tapping their index finger as quickly as they could. This tapping rate during rehearsal was compared to a baseline rate established when children were tapping only. Specifically, a dual-task deficit is computed according to the following formula:

$$\frac{\text{Baseline Tapping Rate} - \text{Concurrent Tapping Rate}}{\text{Baseline Tapping Rate}} \qquad (1)$$

Consistent with the general dual-task framework, Guttentag reasoned that the magnitude of a reduction in tapping that occurred during cumulative rehearsal, relative to baseline, would be indicative of the mental resource demands of the cumulative rehearsal strategy. His results showed that all of the children successfully executed the cumulative rehearsal strategy and that recall levels were comparable across grades. Importantly, dual-task deficits were present at all grades, but the magnitude of this interference declined with age, with the percent deficits being 41% (Grade 2), 31% (Grade 3), and 17% (Grade 6). Guttentag interpreted these results as showing that younger children allocated more of their pool of generic resources to execute a simple cumulative rehearseal strategy than older children did.

In two subsequent experiments, Guttentag (1984) repeated the dual-task procedure and trained either a one-word rehearsal strategy (Experiment 2, Grades 2 and 6 only) or both cumulative and one-word rehearsal strategies (Experiment 3, Grades 2, 3, 4, and 5). Unlike the first experiment, reliable age differences were observed in both recall (Experiments 2 and 3) and rehearsal frequency (Experiment 3). Dual-task deficits, though present and in the right direction, failed to reach statistical significance. These failures to replicate can be viewed as consistent with the position that age differences in functional (resource) capacity mediate, and thus trade-off against, efficient strategy use and recall performance. That is, in order to achieve comparable levels of strategy use and memory performance across age (as in Experiment 1), there is a cost, namely, younger children must expend greater mental effort than older children. When levels of mental effort expenditure are "equated" (as in Experiments 2 and 3), the cost is in terms of poorer recall and less frequent strategy use by younger than older children. Thus, failures by younger children to use a cumulative rehearsal strategy spontaneously may not originate in a production deficiency, but rather, may be the result of the large mental effort expenditure needed to execute it successfully in a limited resource environment.

Bjorklund and Harnishfeger (1987) used the dual-task procedure to examine children's use of organizational strategies. In their first experiment, Grade 3, Grade 7, and college students were given a single study-test trial on a list of unrelated words and a list of categorized words. Unlike Guttentag's (1984) procedure, subjects in Bjorklund and Harnishfeger's (1987) first experiment were not instructed in strategy use, and dual-task performance was measured at three different points in the experiment: (a) during study, (b) during test, and (c) during the postrecall interval (i.e., after recall of the last word but before the recall interval was terminated). The important results were that although recall increased with age, the magnitude of dual-task deficits was developmentally invariant.

In a similar second experiment, third and seventh grade children were instructed to use an organizational strategy on the second of two categorized lists. Although the same global pattern of results emerged here as in Experiment 1, there was the added finding that dual-task deficits tended to be larger when subjects used the clustering strategy than when they did not. Again, these findings are consistent with resource theory. In addition, the results of Experiment 2 indicate that the use of a sophisticated strategy such as clustering has a cost in terms of resource consumption. (Brainerd and Reyna, 1989, noted that because the strategic list always followed the nonstrategic list the observed increase in dual-task deficits might represent fatigue rather than increased resource load due to mnemonic effort. We return to this and other problems with the resource approach in a more detailed discussion following.)

Kee and Davies (1988) used this procedure to compare Grade 6 and college students' use of an elaboration strategy with their use of a simpler rehearsal strategy. Unlike previous studies where the secondary task was executed unimanually with the subject's dominant hand (usually the right), Kee and Davies (1988) required bimanual finger tapping. The reason for this manipulation is that in recent neuropsychological studies, it has been theorized that two independent pools of resources exist, one for each of the cerebral hemispheres (e.g., Friedman, Polson, & Dafoe, 1988). Because finger tapping is controlled by the contralateral hemisphere, and because subjects in the previous studies were required to execute their strategy use aloud, there is a potential confound between estimates of effort expenditure and the cognitive (strategy execution) and speech production (which is usually controlled by the same hemisphere as finger tapping with the dominant hand) components of dual-task performance.

In two experiments, Kee and Davies (1988) manipulated bimanual tapping (left versus right hand) and task requirements (tapping only, tapping plus rehearsal versus tapping plus elaboration). In the first experiment, subjects were required to rehearse and elaborate aloud, whereas they were instructed to execute their strategies silently in the second experiment. The results of the first experiment indicated that although elaboration was superior to rehearsal in recall performance, no differences in finger tapping emerged as a function of age or type of strategy. However, greater interference was observed when tapping was executed by the right than the left hand. The results of the second experiment showed only minimal age differences in interference when subjects were using the rehearsal strategy, whereas interference declined with age with the elaboration strategy. Importantly, tapping asymmetries were not found in this latter experiment. It would seem that, consistent with the idea that there are separate resource pools for the different hemispheres, tapping asymmetries occur only when speech production is involved in strategy deployment. Moreover, consistent with previous results, older subjects use fewer resources when executing mnemonic strategies.

Finally, a third approach has been to try to *decrease* the resource demands associated with strategy use. If children fail to use strategies spontaneously because the enormous expenditure of resources exceeds their functional capacity, then strategy use should increase when the resource cost is reduced. Guttentag (1985) reviewed several studies designed to examine this question in the context of children's spontaneous cumulative rehearsal. In general, these studies revealed that for most Grade 2, 3, and 4 children, the lowering of the resource demands associated with the use of cumulative rehearsal strategies (e.g., by having all of the to-be-remembered items remain visible during the study interval) resulted in an increase in the spontaneous deployment of this strategy. Similarly, Ryan, Ledger, and Weed (1987) found enhanced memory performance with kindergarten children when elaborative imagery-based strategies were augmented with external supports (e.g., with part of the image provided in external pictures). It would appear that when environmental support is provided for the implementation of a strategy, thereby reducing its resource cost, even very young children exhibit spontaneous strategy use.

The general picture that emerges from these studies is that whereas the number of available resources remains developmentally invariant, the allocation of those resources changes with age. That is, as memory processes and strategies (or components of strategies) become more automatic with age, resources are freed up and can be allocated to auxilliary tasks (e.g., finger tapping) or to the execution of more sophisticated strategies. The reason younger children perform more poorly on memory tasks than older children is because they must devote more resources to the task as fewer of the component routines necessary for the task have become automatized. Whereas seemingly simple memory problems may be well within the capacity limits of the older child, this is not so for younger children who must expend considerable effort.

Despite the attractiveness of resource theory, there are serious theoretical and empirical problems associated with its implementation. First, at a general level, it is not exactly clear what a resource is and how one would go about measuring it. As Salthouse (1988) pointed out, the processing-resource concept can be considered vacuous because it has rarely been operationalized sufficiently to permit empirical inspection. Because this construct has never been adequately quantified, critical assumptions concerning the number of resources needed for various tasks or available to different individuals remain unverified in resource theories. What this implies in dual-task situations, for example, is that it is not clear that the relationship between resource quantity and secondary-task performance is the same across individuals. That is, regardless of developmental status, adding a one-resource-unit demand by introducing a concurrent secondary task might result in a two-unit decrement in performance for one child but a six-unit decrement in another child (also see Howe & Rabinowitz, 1989).

Second, the resource theory has been challenged empirically. For example, we noted earlier that limitations on a generic pool of resources may be related to the capacity restrictions of short-term memory (e.g., Pressley, Cariglia-Bull et al., 1987). What this implies is that the ability to retain information in short-term memory and to process it adequately must be related as both activities consume the same generic resources (e.g., see Brainerd & Reyna, 1988). Obviously, it follows that in problem-solving paradigms (e.g., class inclusion, conservation, mental arithmetic, transitivity), the degree of success in solving the problem and recognizing or recalling the background problem information should be interrelated.

Unfortunately, the evidence concerning this prediction is ambiguous at best. On the one hand, perhaps the most important evidence infirming this line of reasoning has been presented by Brainerd and Kingma (1984, 1985). In a series of experiments designed to measure reasoning (e.g., class inclusion, transitivity, etc.) and remembering (short-term memory probes) relationships, these researchers found that the adequacy of a subject's short-term retention of background problem facts was stochastically independent of the adequacy of their problem solutions. Thus, contrary to the generic resource hypothesis in which reasoning/remembering dependencies are always anticipated, Brainerd and Kingma's findings indicate that reasoning/remembering independence does, in fact, occur with some regularity (also see Brainerd & Reyna, 1988, for conditions where reasoning/remembering dependencies are predicted from other than a generic resource hypothesis).

On the other hand, Rabinowitz, Howe, and Lawrence (1989) discovered very strong dependencies between strategies for solving class-inclusion problems and memory. In fact in Experiment 2, variation in memory load affected the type of problem-solving strategy employed, not the accuracy of memory. What these results indicate is that the quality of reasoning depends directly on memory. Although it is not clear why our results are so discrepant from those of Brainerd and Kingma (1985), one key difference between the studies concerns the way in which reasoning and remembering were measured. Brainerd and Kingma (1985) evaluated this relationship using separate, serially produced problem-solving and memory responses that were subjected to a relatively simple conditional probability analysis. In our research, we used a more sensitive mathematical model that permitted the simultaneous measurement and evaluation of memory and problem success from a single response. We return to the importance of adequate measurement of the resources construct shortly.

Third, much of the data purported to favor a resource hypothesis are actually theoretically neutral because multiple interpretations of these outcomes are available (e.g., see Hirst & Kalmar, 1987, for a skills interpretation; Navon, 1985, for a response competition interpretation). To illustrate, consider the recent controversy that has arisen concerning the interpretation of dual-task deficits. Brainerd and Reyna (1989) raised the possibility that the performance deficits observed when finger-tapping and memory tasks are conjoined occur at the output stage and not during central processing. That is, dual-task deficits are not the result of competition for scarce resources, but rather, are the result of output interference between independent processes. To see why, recall that central processing can be assumed to occur in parallel, whereas output processes are serially organized. Accordingly, different responses (from potentially independent central sources) queue at the output stage creating a response bottleneck. Which response is output, and when, is determined by a decision mechanism. In the dual-task paradigm, performance of the decision mechanism is less than optimal because of the demand to perform two responses in parallel rather than in the preferred serial mode. It is this conflict at the decision stage, not the central processing stage, that gives rise to interference. Developmental trends in dual-task performance are said to occur because of age changes in children's susceptibility to interference. Specifically, developmental differences in dual-task interference arise from corresponding changes in the articulation of the response-selection mechanism.

Although a number of problems also exist with this interpretation of dual-task deficits (e.g., Bjorklund & Harnishfeger, 1989), Howe and Rabinowitz (1989) argued that either interpretation is compatible with dual-task findings. In fact, it turns out that the use of the dual-task procedure to study the relationship between the development of strategy deployment and processing resources is counterproductive. This is because unlike single-output tasks in which interference can be reasonably associated with resource competition (e.g., Rabinowitz et al., 1989), dual-output tasks, with their additional dual response demands, necessarily confound the locus of interference (Howe & Rabinowitz, 1989).

Whether dual-task deficits occur because competition arises for scarce resources in a common pool or arises at the output stage is indeterminant given the generally inadequate operationalization of these theoretical constructs. Thus, rather than continue the debate at a theoretical level, Howe and Rabinowitz (1989) argued that what is needed is a more adequate operationalization of the psychological processes (generic or dedicated resources, response mechanisms, and the mapping between them) under study. This includes knowledge of the appropriate measurement scales corresponding to the theoretical components underlying each of the individual tasks, how they conjoin in the dual-task environment, and how central (e.g., resources) and peripheral (e.g., responses) aspects of processing configure to determine behavior. It is only when these issues have been adequately addressed that the distinct role played by resources (common or dedicated) and output interference can be evaluated and their contribution to cognitive development determined. Perhaps through the use of formal modeling techniques, implemented as mathematical models or computer programs (see Howe & Rabinowitz, 1989; Rabinowitz et al., 1989), these issues will soon be resolved and we can get on with the business of building theories.

CONCLUSION

We have suggested that strategic behavior be reconceptualized to incorporate both automatic and effortful aspects of mnemonic performance regardless of its status in (potential) awareness. Throughout this chapter, we have pointed out that the contribution of strategic operations to memory development must be considered in the broader perspective of changes in underlying cognitive structures (in particular, knowledge structures) and the efficiency with which cognitive processes are executed. We have argued that most, if not all, children engage in behaviors that are strategic given the appropriate task conditions. Whether or not strategic behavior is observed, as well as the effectiveness of that behavior, depends in large measure on the relationship between the child's knowledge base (which includes declarative, procedural, strategic, and metamemorial knowledge) and its relevance on a given task. As development proceeds, children's knowledge base is continually updated, affording greater speed and accuracy in accessing the relevant strategy as well as the content it operates on. Moreover, as children gain wider experience through diverse mnemonic encounters, the number of strategies available increases, permitting greater flexibility in strategy use. Thus, changes in the contents and structure of the knowledge base are directly related to increases in the number of strategies within the strategy pool and the efficiency with which strategies are applied. Similarly, to the extent that practice and expertise are correlated with age, increases in the efficiency of processing occur with development, making various steps involved in the execution of organized behaviors (strategies) relatively effortless. What this means is that, with age, more resources are freed so that more sophisticated cognitive operations can be performed as development proceeds.

Where we need to concentrate our future efforts is on providing reliable measures of the content and structure of children's knowledge base (declarative, procedural, strategic, and metamemorial components) and how the knowledge base changes as development proceeds. As noted, considerable progress has been made in areas related to the accessibility of information in the knowledge base. However, in order to understand the complex relations between growth in mnemonic effectiveness and the dynamic changes in the knowledge base that serve as an important source of these improvements, more effort needs to be allocated to measuring how knowledge is reorganized, and how the different aspects of the knowledge base become integrated to function effectively, across development.

In a similar vein, we close by emphasizing that the central problem facing researchers attempting to diagnose memory development in terms of changes in strategies, knowledge, metamemory, and processing efficiency is to operationalize effectively the constructs *automatic*, *effortful, knowledge base*, and *processing resources*. It is only when these constructs are made measurable (through formal and/or computer models) that we will be able to assess their relative contribution to the development of strategic memory. Indeed, it is our contention that theoretical progress in the area of memory development is contingent on these factors being differentiated so that their status can change from simple heuristic devices to explanatory constructs.

ACKNOWLEDGMENTS

Preparation of this chapter was supported by grant OGP0003334 to Mark L. Howe from the Natural Sciences and Engineering Research Council of Canada.

REFERENCES

Ackerman, B. P. (1987). Descriptions: A model of nonstrategic memory development. In H. W. Reese (Ed.), *Advances in child development and behavior* (Vol. 20, pp. 143–183). New York: Academic Press.

Baddeley, A. (1986). *Working memory.* London: Clarendon Press.

Baker–Ward, L., Ornstein, P. A., & Holden, D. J. (1984). The expression of memorization in early childhood. *Journal of Experimental Child Psychology, 37,* 555–575.

Bjorklund, D. F. (1985). The role of conceptual knowledge in the development of organization in children's memory. In C. J. Brainerd & M. Pressley (Eds.), *Basic processes in memory development: Progress in cognitive development research* (pp. 103–142). New York: Springer–Verlag.

Bjorklund, D. F. (1987). How age changes in knowledge base contribute to the development of children's memory: An interpretive review. *Developmental Review, 7,* 93–130.

Bjorklund, D. F. (1988). Acquiring a mnemonic: Age and category knowledge effects. *Journal of Experimental Child Psychology, 45,* 71–87.

Bjorklund, D. F., & Bernholtz, J. F. (1986). The role of knowledge base in the memory performance of good and poor readers. *Journal of Experimental Child Psychology, 41,* 367–393.

Bjorklund, D. F., & Harnishfeger, K. K. (1987). Developmental differences in the mental effort requirements for the use of an organizational strategy in free recall. *Journal of Experimental Child Psychology, 44,* 109–125.

Bjorklund, D. F., & Harnishfeger, K. K. (1989). In defense of resources. *Journal of Experimental Child Psychology, 47,* 19–25.

Borkowski, J. G. (1985). Signs of intelligence: Strategy generalization and metacognition. In S. Yussen (Ed.), *Development of reflection in children* (pp. 104–144). New York: Academic Press.

Borkowski, J. G., Carr, M., & Pressley, M. (1987). "Spontaneous" strategy use: Perspectives from metacognitive theory. *Intelligence, 11,* 61–75.

Brainerd, C. J., & Kingma, J. (1984). Do children have to remember to reason? A fuzzy-trace theory of transitivity development. *Developmental Review, 4,* 311–377.

Brainerd, C. J., & Kingma, J. (1985). On the independence of short-term memory and working memory in cognitive development. *Cognitive Psychology, 17,* 210–247.

Brainerd, C. J., Kingma, J., & Howe, M. L. (1986). Spread of encoding and the development of organization in memory. *Canadian Journal of Psychology, 40,* 203–223.

Brainerd, C. J., & Reyna, V. F. (1988). Generic resources, reconstructive processing, and children's mental arithmetic. *Developmental Psychology, 24,* 324–334.

Brainerd, C. J., & Reyna, V. F. (1989). Output-interference theory of dual-task deficits in memory development. *Journal of Experimental Child Psychology, 47,* 1–18.

Brown, A. L. (1978). Knowing when, where, and how to remember: A problem in metacognition. In R. Glaser (Ed.), *Advances in instructional psychology* (pp. 77–165). Hillsdale, NJ: Lawrence Erlbaum Associates.

Brown, A. L., Bransford, J. D., Ferrara, R. A., & Campione, J. C. (1983). Learning, remembering, and understanding. In J. H. Flavell & E. M. Markman (Eds.), *Handbook of child psychology* (4th ed., Vol. III, pp. 77–166). New York: Wiley.

Case, R. (1985). *Intellectual development: Birth to adulthood.* Orlando: Academic Press.

Cavanaugh, J. C., & Perlmutter, M. (1982). Metamemory: A critical examination. *Child Development, 53,* 11–28.

Chapman, M. (1987). Piaget, attentional capacity, and the functional implications of formal structure. In H. W. Reese (Ed.), *Advances in child development and behavior* (Vol. 20, pp. 289–334). New York: Academic Press.

Chi, M. T. H. (1981). Knowledge development and memory performance. In M. P. Friedman, J. P. Das, & N. O'Connor (Eds.), *Intelligence and learning* (pp. 221–230). New York: Plenum.

Chi, M. T. H. (1985). Interactive roles of knowledge and strategies in the development of organized sorting and recall. In S. F. Chipman, J. W. Segal, & R. Glaser (Eds.), *Thinking and learning skills* (Vol. 2, pp. 457–483). Hillsdale, NJ: Lawrence Erlbaum Associates.

Chi, M. T. H., & Ceci, S. J. (1987). Content knowledge: Its role, representation, and restructuring in memory development. In H. W. Reese (Ed.), *Advances in child development and behavior* (Vol. 20, pp. 91–142). New York: Academic Press.

Chi, M. T. H., & Koeske, R. D. (1983). Network representation of a child's dinosaur knowledge. *Developmental Psychology, 19,* 29–39.

Corsale, K. (1978). *Factors affecting children's use of organization in recall.* Unpublished doctoral dissertation. University of North Carolina at Chapel Hill.

Corsale, K., & Ornstein, P. A. (1980). Developmental changes in children's use of semantic information in recall. *Journal of Experimental Child Psychology, 30,* 231–245.

DeLoache, J. S., Cassidy, D. J., & Brown, A. L. (1985). Precursors of mnemonic strategies in very young children's memory. *Child Development, 56,* 125–137.

DeLoache, J. S., & Todd, C. M. (1988). Young children's use of spatial categorization as a mnemonic strategy. *Journal of Experimental Child Psychology, 46,* 1–20.

Flavell, J. H. (1971). First discussant's comments: What is memory development the development of? *Human Development, 14,* 272–278.

Flavell, J. H. (1979). Metacognition and cognitive monitoring: A new area of cognitive-developmental inquiry. *American Psychologist, 34,* 906–911.

Flavell, J. H., & Wellman, H. M. (1977). Metamemory. In R. V. Kail & J. W. Hagen (Eds.), *Perspectives on the development of memory and cognition* (pp. 3–33). Hillsdale, NJ: Lawrence Erlbaum Associates.

Friedman, A., Polson, M. C., & Dafoe, C. G. (1988). Dividing attention between the hands and the head: Performance trade-offs between rapid finger tapping and verbal memory. *Journal of Experimental Psychology: Human Perception and Performance, 14,* 60–68.

Guttentag, R. E. (1984). The mental effort requirement of cumulative rehearsal: A developmental study. *Journal of Experimental Child Psychology, 39,* 546–561.

Guttentag, R. E. (1985). Memory and aging: Implications for theories of memory development during childhood. *Developmental Review, 5,* 56–82.

Halford, G. S., Maybery, M. T., & Bain, J. D. (1986). Capacity limitations in children's reasoning: A dual-task approach. *Child Development, 57,* 616–627.

Hirst, W., & Kalmar, D. (1987). Characterizing attentional resources. *Journal of Experimental Psychology: General, 116,* 68–81.

Howe, M. L., Brainerd, C. J., & Kingma, J. (1985). Development of organization in recall: A stages-of-learning analysis. *Journal of Experimental Child Psychology, 39,* 230–251.

Howe, M. L., O'Sullivan, J. T., Brainerd, C. J., & Kingma, J. (1989). Localizing the development of ability differences in organized memory. *Contemporary Educational Psychology, 14,* 336–356.

Howe, M. L., & Rabinowitz, F. M. (1989). On the uninterpretability of dual-task performance. *Journal of Experimental Child Psychology, 47,* 32–38.

Kail, R. (1988). Developmental functions for speeds of cognitive processes. *Journal of Experimental Child Psychology, 45,* 339–364.

Kee, D. W., & Davies, L. (1988). Mental effort and elaboration: A developmental analysis. *Contemporary Educational Psychology, 13,* 221–228.

Klapp, S. T., Marshburn, E. A., & Lester, P. T. (1983). Short-term memory does not involve the "working memory" of information processing: The demise of a common assumption. *Journal of Experimental Psychology: General, 112,* 240–264.

Lange, G. (1978). Organization-related processes in children's recall. In P. A. Ornstein (Ed.), *Memory development in children* (pp. 101–128). Hillsdale, NJ: Lawrence Erlbaum Associates.

Naus, M. J., & Ornstein, P. A. (1983). The development of memory strategies: Analysis, questions, and issues. In M. T. H. Chi (Ed.), *Trends in memory development research* (Vol. 9, pp. 1–30). Basel: Karger.

Navon, D. (1985). Attention division or attention sharing? In M. I. Posner & O. S. M. Marin (Eds.), *Attention and Performance XI* (pp. 133–146). Hillsdale, NJ: Lawrence Erlbaum Associates.

Ornstein, P. A., & Naus, M. J. (1985). Effects of the knowledge base on children's memory strategies. In H. W. Reese (Ed.), *Advances in child development and behavior* (Vol. 19, pp. 113–148). New York: Academic Press.

Pascual-Leone, J. (1970). A mathematical model for the transition rule in Piaget's developmental stages. *Acta Psychologica, 32,* 301–345.

Pressley, M., Borkowski, J., & O'Sullivan, J. T. (1985). Children's metamemory and the teaching of memory strategies. In D. L. Forrest–Pressley, G. E. MacKinnon, & T. G. Waller (Eds.), *Metacognition, cognition, and human performance* (Vol. 1, pp. 111–153). San Diego, CA: Academic Press.

Pressley, M., Borkowski, J., & Schneider, W. (1987). Cognitive strategies: Good strategy users coordinate metacognition and knowledge. In R. Vasta & G. Whitehurst (Eds.), *Annals of Child Development* (Vol. 4, pp. 89–129). Greenwich, CN: JAI.

Pressley, M., Cariglia-Bull, T., Deane, S., & Schneider, W. (1987). Short-term memory, verbal competence, and age as predictors of imagery instructional effectiveness. *Journal of Experimental Child Psychology, 43,* 194–211.

Pressley, M., Forrest–Pressley, D. L., Elliot-Faust, D., & Miller, G. (1985). Children's use of cognitive strategies, how to teach strategies, and what to do if they can't be taught. In M. Pressley & C. J. Brainerd (Eds.), *Cognitive learning and memory in children: Progress in cognitive development research* (pp. 1–47). New York: Springer–Verlag.

Pressley, M., Heisel, B. E., McCormick, C. G., & Nakamura, G. V. (1982). Memory strategy instruction with children. In C. J. Brainerd & M. Pressley (Eds.), *Verbal processes in children: Progress in cognitive development research* (pp. 125–159). New York: Springer–Verlag.

Rabinowitz, F. M., Howe, M. L., & Lawrence, J. A. (1989). Class inclusion and working memory. *Journal of Experimental Child Psychology, 48,* 379–409.

Rabinowitz, M. (1988). On teaching cognitive strategies: The influence of accessibility of conceptual knowledge. *Contemporary Educational Psychology, 13,* 229–235.

Rabinowitz, M., & Chi, M. T. H. (1987). An interactive model of strategic processing. In S. J. Ceci (Ed.), *Handbook of cognitive, social, and neuropsychological aspects of learning disabilities* (Vol. 2, pp. 83–102). Hillsdale, NJ: Lawrence Erlbaum Associates.

Recht, D. R., & Leslie, L. (1988). Effect of prior knowledge on good and poor readers' memory of text. *Journal of Educational Psychology, 80,* 16–20.

Rushton, J. P., Brainerd, C. J., & Pressley, M. (1983). Behavioral development and construct validity: The principle of aggregation. *Psychological Bulletin, 94,* 238–247.

Ryan, E. B., Ledger, G. W., & Weed, K. A. (1987). Acquisition and transfer of an integrative imagery strategy by young children. *Child Development, 58,* 443–452.

Salthouse, T. A. (1988). The role of processing resources in cognitive aging. In M. L. Howe & C. J. Brainerd (Eds.), *Cognitive development in adulthood: Progress in cognitive development research* (pp. 185–239). New York: Springer–Verlag.

Sternberg, R. J. (1985). *Beyond IQ: A triarchic theory of human intelligence.* Cambridge, MA: Cambridge University Press.

Wellman, H. M. (1983). Metamemory revisited. *Contributions in human development, 9,* 31–51.

Wellman, H. M., Ritter, K., & Flavell, J. H. (1975). Deliberate memory behavior in the delayed reactions of very young children. *Developmental Psychology, 11,* 780–787.

CHAPTER 6

The Development of Strategies of Selective Attention

Patricia H. Miller
University of Florida

Developmental change in how children gather information for further processing is a fundamental component of cognitive development. As Gibson (1988, p. 7) comments, "Intellectual development is built on information-gathering, and this is what young creatures (not only human ones) are predestined to do." This behavior eventually becomes strategic: Children planfully use procedures to select certain information in a systematic, organized way. Because this chapter focuses on the selection of task-relevant information from a larger set of available information, the strategies discussed here are closely related to the process of selective attention. These strategies of selective attention are particularly important in real-life situations, where typically only some, not all, of the available information should be attended to and processed further. Strategies of attention are much less studied than are strategies of memory such as rehearsal, organization, and elaboration in situations in which the relevant stimuli already have been identified. Although much of this chapter examines selective attention in the context of memory tasks, the emphasis is on the initial step of information processing, the selection of information.

The chapter begins with a description of developmental changes in attentional strategies and of influences on producing these strategies. Then, children's knowledge about these strategies is considered. Next is a look at whether spontaneously produced appropriate strategies immediately reap benefits for the child's recall or cognitive judgments. An observed "utilization deficiency" suggests that often they do not, or, they at least benefit younger children less than older. Various explanations for this utilization deficiency are explored, particularly the role of the effortfulness of strategy production. Finally, the notion of a utilization deficiency is placed in the context of previous work on the development of strategies.

A DESCRIPTION OF THE DEVELOPMENT OF ATTENTIONAL STRATEGIES

It is well documented that during the preschool and grade-school years children's attention becomes increasingly efficient and flexible. For example, older children are more likely than younger to attend to the most relevant information, explore objects systematically, and tailor their attention to the unique demands of each situation (e.g., Day, 1975; Gibson & Rader, 1979; Lane & Pearson, 1982; Pick, Frankel, & Hess, 1975). This improvement is attributed, in part, to the acquisition of strategies of attention. Two types of attentional strategies are examined: selective attention and spatial organization.

Strategies of Selective Attention

The reliance of researchers on indirect assessments of children's attentional strategies has limited the study of these strategies. Strategies usually are inferred from errors (e.g., Hagen & Hale, 1973), reaction time (e.g., Pick & Frankel, 1974), sorting speed (e.g., Well, Lorch, & Anderson, 1980), verbal reports (e.g., Miller & Weiss, 1981), and eye movements (e.g., Vurpillot, 1968). Although these indirect assessments have produced useful information, all have certain limitations. Error analysis does not permit a separation of the strategy per se from its facilitation of recall because the former is inferred from the latter. Measures of speed usually do not permit the identification of any systematic, but inadequate, strategies. Verbal reports probably underestimate the use of strategies in young children because these children not only have limited verbal abilities but also have little access to their own cognitive processes. Accurate measures of eye movements require uncomfortable and unnatural restraints that are unsatisfactory with young children. Also, eye movements may be unduly influenced by salient physical aspects of the stimuli. Given that strategies usually are defined as intentional, organized, planful procedures, a response that more clearly reflects decision making is more desirable.

One directly observable behavior that can be used for assessment is a child's hand movements. A rudimentary strategy of selective attention appears in simple memory situations, where preschool children touch one object (the one to be remembered) when other objects not to be remembered are present (Wellman, Ritter, & Flavell, 1975). This simple touching strategy, directed to a small amount of information, may be a precursor for a more advanced strategy involving a temporal-spatial pattern of responses that direct attention to a set of relevant information. We have used such a pattern of responses in our assessments of strategies of selective attention in recent years. This procedure and the description of development produced by it now will be described in detail. The apparatus we developed (Miller & Weiss, 1981) is an adaptation of the selective memory task used to study children's attention in the 1960s and 1970s (e.g., Hagen, 1967).

The drawings of objects that the children can choose to examine are inside a box with 12 doors on top arranged into two rows and six columns. Children can view an object by opening the door that conceals it. On the surface of half of the doors is a drawing of a cage, indicating an animal underneath. The other 6 doors contain a drawing of a house, indicating a household object (e.g., chair, plate) below. Each row of doors covers some animal drawings and some household objects. The object under each door changes from trial to trial. There is a practice trial and checks to ensure that the children understand the instructions. During a study period, typically a half-minute long, children are free to open any of the doors they wish, one at a time, as often as they wish. They know that they are supposed to remember only one of the two types of objects, animals for half of the children and household objects for the other half. After this study period on each trial, children attempt to recall the locations of the relevant objects. They point to the location of the drawing shown on a card by the experimenter or, in other studies, place each card on top of the door covering that object.

Children's strategies are inferred by their pattern of door opening during the study periods, that is, which doors they open and the order in which they open them. For a selective memory task such as this one, the most efficient strategy is to open only relevant doors (covering objects to be remembered, such as animals) so that all one's resources can be devoted to remembering the important material.

This procedure has several advantages. First, strategies are inferred from patterns of observable behaviors rather than more indirectly from other measures. Second, the procedure permits the separate assessment of the production of the strategy and its utilization for recall, that is, its benefit for the child. Third, the procedure reveals any partial strategy use which might reflect informative transitional periods in strategy development. Fourth, it can be used to assess what children are doing when they are not using the appropriate strategy. Both random responses and inappropriate strategies can be detected. Fifth, the procedure can be used with a wide age range. We have used children as young as 32 months and as old as 13 years.

Several studies with this procedure (DeMarie-Dreblow & Miller, 1988; Miller, Haynes, DeMarie-Dreblow, & Woody-Ramsey, 1986; Miller & Weiss, 1981; Woody-Ramsey & Miller, 1988) have revealed a developmental sequence of strategy production during the preschool and grade-school years. This sequence is based on age differences in the occurrence of four steps and on changes in strategies from the earlier to later trials within a session. The particular ages for each step depend on several variables, as described later.

In the first step, young children do not produce the selective strategy. Instead, they follow the spatial organization of the apparatus, usually opening first one row then the other. A much smaller group opens doors column by column in an up-down, left-to-right or right-to left pattern. Control groups told to open the doors "just for fun, to see what is inside" also use these spatial patterns. Thus, these early patterns probably are not strategic because they are used in situations with or without a problem-solving goal. It is noteworthy that young children rarely open the doors randomly; their behavior is systematic, but not necessarily strategic.

In the second developmental step, children partially produce the selective strategy. That is, they tend to open the relevant doors, but do not reach the criterion for the fully selective strategy which requires that at least 75% of the doors opened be relevant or all but one of the doors opened be relevant, depending on the particular study. In the third step children produce the selective strategy, but the strategy does not yet help their recall of the locations of the objects. This utilization deficiency, in which there is a developmental lag between spontaneously producing the strategy and receiving any benefit from it, is discussed more fully in a later section. Although a utilization deficiency is plausible in that it is consistent with the view that younger children make less efficient use of their skills than do older children, it also is counterintuitive because it suggests that many children are continuing to do something effortful that does not help them. Finally, in the fourth step, children both produce the selective strategy and benefit from it in their recall.

There are two additional categories that cannot yet be placed into this developmental sequence. On some trials, children partially produce one of the spatial strategies, which may be evidence for movement out of the first step. In addition, a few children occasionally switch from one strategy to another on a single trial, which may also reflect a transitional state. Longitudinal data are needed to clarify the developmental position of these behaviors as well as to more fully support the sequential nature of the four steps.

Strategies Involving Spatial Organization

In the selective-attention task young children tended to adopt a spatial pattern suggested by the array, a pattern that was not efficient. However, such strategies are efficient for certain other types of tasks. In the next section is a description of our work on spatial strategies in a same–different task. Then, spatial strategies appearing in work by other researchers is examined.

Same–Different Judgments

To determine whether a developmental sequence similar to that just described would appear on another task, we examined the strategies children use when asked to judge whether two arrays are the same or different (Miller & Harris, 1988; Miller et al., 1986). We used the apparatus previously described, except that drawings of cages and houses were removed from the doors. Children were asked to decide whether the two rows were exactly the same—the same objects in the same spatial positions such that the first vertical pair was two chairs, the second pair two monkeys, and so on. The most appropriate strategy, labeled the "vertical-pairs" strategy, involved opening the first pair at one end, then the pair next to it, and so on across the rows. Note that this is one of the inappropriate spatial patterns for the selective attention task. This strategy is efficient for the same–different task because it makes modest demands on the children's memory. They can perceptually compare the members of the pairs and continue until they find a pair that differs or complete the row without finding a different pair. In contrast, any other pattern of door opening requires them to remember the locations of all of the objects and then to mentally compare them, a much more taxing process. Previous research that assessed eye movements on a same–different task (Vurpillot, 1968) found that older children are more likely than younger ones to compare corresponding pairs.

The developmental sequence paralleled that on the selective-attention task. As on that task, the youngest children (usually age 3) typically opened the doors in a horizontal spatial pattern, opening first one row then the other. Their frequency of producing the vertical-pairs strategy was not greater than that of a control group opening the doors for fun. The second step was a partial vertical-pairs strategy and the third step a fully vertical-pairs strategy (vertical pairs comprised at least 75% of the door openings). The latter more often led to better recall in 4-year-olds than 3-year olds, thus supporting the utilization deficiency hypothesis. By age 6 children reached the fourth step and both produced, and were helped by, the vertical-pairs strategy. It is notable that these 6-year-olds were appropriately strategic on the same–different task, but not on the selective-attention task in the one study that gave both tasks to each child (Miller et al., 1986). That is, they used a vertical-pairs strategy on the same–different task but followed a horizontal spatial pattern on the selective-attention task. Thus, a child can be in two different developmental levels of strategy use on two different tasks. The possibility that this reflects differences in task difficulty is discussed later when effortfulness is considered.

Our research thus documents a developmental sequence of strategy use on two tasks during the preschool and elementary school years. Strategy development is a gradual process extending over several years. In addition, the production of a strategy does not guarantee that it immediately will help the child. Furthermore, spatial patterns of response appear to be easier, perhaps because they are perceptually supported by the visual array. In contrast, the selective strategy is logic based. To apply it, children must overcome their tendency to use a spatial strategy because the two are incompatible. A spatial pattern may or may not be appropriate, depending on the demands of the task (same–different judgments versus selective memory).

Other Tasks

Young children's facility with spatial strategies also emerges in other investigators' research. DeLoache and Todd (1988) found that preschoolers can spatially organize objects as a strategy in the service of future retrieval. The children watched the experimenter hide either candies or small wooden pegs inside a variety of small opaque containers, took each container as it was handed to them, and placed it on the table. They had been told that they would need to remember which of the 12 containers held the candies. By age 5, children spontaneously separated into two groups the containers holding candies and small wooden pegs. They did not do this in a control condition in which no recall was required, suggesting that their behavior on the memory task had in fact been strategic. In a subsequent study, when the two categories of containers were made perceptually distinctive (e.g., paper clip boxes held candies and film canisters held pegs), children aged 2 to 4 were also able to use the spatial categorization used by the 5-year-olds in the first study. DeLoache and Todd concluded that only the 5-year-olds were able to construct categories based on an internal representation rather than simply use the perceptual differentiation already present in the two sets.

Other researchers (e.g., Wellman, 1985) have found considerable competence in young children's search strategies in larger environments. For example, preschoolers can conduct nonredundant, comprehensive searches (i.e., looking for an object in each location only once).

Although young children naturally adopt a spatial organization, they have more trouble imposing this organization on arrays that resist it. An example is children's naming of pictures of objects scattered over a page. With increasing age, children are more likely to impose a systematic, spatially based pattern of naming (e.g., Elkind & Weiss, 1967; Gottschalk, Bryden & Rabinovitch, 1964).

Conclusions

Thus, investigators using several different paradigms have concluded that young children are adept at spatial, perceptually supported strategies but less successful at producing strategies that require a more logical analysis of the task. Moreover, these earlier spatial strategies may serve as precursors for the more demanding strategies that emerge later. The next question is which variables influence whether children produce an appropriate strategy. This section has suggested that perceptual supports for a spatial strategy encourage its use, but other variables also may be important, especially for tasks in which a spatial strategy is inappropriate. The next section includes studies that more directly and systematically explored influences on strategy production, particularly on the selective attention task.

INFLUENCES ON STRATEGY PRODUCTION

The ages of the four steps of strategy production on the door-opening task can be moved downward under certain conditions. The most dramatic change came when we introduced a story in the selective-attention task (Woody-Ramsey & Miller, 1988). Preschoolers were told to pretend to be the child in the story and to try to do what that child was told to do. The vignette involved a child at nursery school who was instructed daily to put the toys in the proper toy boxes at the end of the day. One day after storing the toys she was told to look in the boxes in order to remember the locations of the animal toys (or toys for playing house for half the subjects), because these toys would need to be found quickly for a special game the next morning. Thus, the child in the story was to memorize which toy box contained which animal toy. This manipulation increased the selectivity of the 4- and 5-year-olds to 76%, which is even greater than the 63% for children 2 years older in an earlier study without the story (Miller et al., 1986). In the Woody-Ramsey and Miller study, two other manipulations produced increased selectivity over the story-alone condition when both, but not each alone, were added to the story condition. They were a reduced number of items (4 out of 8 were relevant rather than 6 out of 12) and increased salience of the animal and household categories from outlining the cages in one color and the houses in another.

There are several possible explanations for the facilitating effect of the story. The most likely is that relating the task to a meaningful context enabled young children to see the implications of the task goal (remembering locations of objects) for their activities during the study period. Without the story, children do not produce this strategy they have available, even though checks have ensured that they understand the goal of the task. Thus, there appears to be increased access of the appropriate strategy when the domain is highly articulated. When there is scripted knowledge, in this case a script for putting away and finding toys at nursery school, this supportive context makes access relatively automatic. This general argument has been advanced with respect to other strategies in other types of memory tasks (Bjorklund, 1987; Ornstein & Naus, 1985). However, other explanations have merit as well. In particular, the story may simply have increased the child's motivation by making the memory task more interesting. Regardless of the reason for the increased use of the selective strategy when the story is added, the important finding is that 4-year-olds can, under certain conditions, produce a selective strategy, which is contrary to their natural inclination to use a spatial strategy.

The added facilitation when other cues are added to the story suggests processes other than those related to the knowledge base. The effect of reducing the number of items (and doors) is consistent with previous research on other tasks (e.g., Spungen & Goodman, 1983). This manipulation may have reduced the capacity required to use the strategy by decreasing the amount of information in the task. The other manipulation, adding distinctive color borders to the two categories, may have increased the perceptual differentiation of the two categories and, consequently, their conceptual differentiation. This should help children keep track of the relevant items as they seek them out during the study period. Young children typically may come to the task with less sensitivity to the categorical nature of the relevant and irrelevant items than older children.

In conclusion, young children apparently possess several strategies that can be applied to cognitive tasks. They are adept at using simple spatial strategies and tend to do so unless there is conceptual or perceptual support for using more difficult strategies. With this support, many 4-year-olds can produce a selective strategy on a selective-attention task.

One central question is what causes developmental changes or individual differences in strategy production. One possible cause, suggested in this section, is the child's growing knowledge base. Several other possible causes, such as decreases in the effortfulness of strategy production or increases in metacognition concerning attentional strategies, are discussed later. Another likely influence, about which we have little information, is parental teaching of attentional strategies (e.g., Wertsch, McNamee, McLane & Budwig, 1980). Finally, observed cross-cultural (Florida versus Puerto Rico) differences in producing the selective attention strategy (Miller & Jordan, 1982) should be explored further.

DEVELOPMENTAL CHANGES IN KNOWLEDGE ABOUT ATTENTIONAL STRATEGIES

Thus far this chapter has examined strategic behavior. Another aspect of development involves knowledge about strategies. Part of our research on metaattentional knowledge (summarized in Miller, 1985) has involved strategies of selective attention. Whether children appear to be naive or sophisticated regarding these strategies depends to a great extent on one's method of assessing this knowledge. Children generally do not spontaneously verbalize good strategies in open-ended interviews until late in the grade-school years (Miller & Bigi, 1979). For example, in a task of finding which drawing of a ski cap is different from the others, few first graders suggested looking at all the tops, middles, and bottoms of the hats in sequence or even looking selectively at certain parts (e.g., all the bottoms). These answers were more common among third and fifth graders. However, when asked to choose the best strategy from several presented, nearly all of the children in all grades selected an appropriate strategy. Thus, recognition of a good strategy of selective attention emerges earlier than the ability to verbalize such a strategy spontaneously, an outcome replicated with other tasks, assessments, and ages (Miller & Bigi, 1979; Miller, Haynes, & Weiss, 1985; Miller & Weiss, 1981, 1982). This result suggests that these strategies are more accessible to the older children.

Subsequent studies examined children's knowledge about what variables affect attempts to attend selectively. Even 3-year-olds understand that it is harder to focus one's attention on one source of stimulation (e.g., instructions from one's mother) when the room is noisy rather than quiet and when one is uninterested rather than interested in the information (Miller & Zalenski, 1982). The assessment was a nonverbal forced-choice procedure requiring a child to choose the one of two arrays (of rooms with toy furniture, people, and other objects) more conducive to attention. For example, on one trial the two rooms differed only in noise level (e.g. whether there were noisy appliances). When noise was pitted against interest, interest was considered more important. This latter outcome was replicated with older children aged 5 through 10 and with other assessment procedures, such as rating scales (Miller, 1982; Miller & Shannon, 1984). Moreover, with increasing age children are more likely to combine information about noise level and interest level according to rules that are more complex than simply adding together the two pieces of information (Miller, 1982).

Several of our studies focus on our selective-attention task described earlier in this chaper. When children estimated the recall of relevant items under various levels of selective attention (looking at only relevant items, looking at relevant and irrelevant items, and looking at only irrelevant items), second graders, but not kindergartners, recognized the most appropriate strategy (Miller & Weiss, 1982). However, children of all ages understood that verbal rehearsal and looking at the relevant items systematically (left to right rather than randomly or partially systematic) should facilitate recall. It is interesting that they perceived more effect of strategy variables and person variables (e.g., motivation) than task variables (e.g., salience of relevant items) on recall. In addition, there was a dramatic developmental increase in the ability to offer a psychological explanation for why the good strategies benefit performance (e.g., prevent distraction from irrelevant items).

Finally, several studies of metaattention regarding visually searching for a particular object are relevant to the visual exploration on our same–different task. There is a fragile, rudimentary knowledge about what variables affect the difficulty of this search (e.g., distractors of colors or shapes similar to the target, number of distractors) at age 3.

This knowledge, however, improves throughout the grade-school years or even later (Miller & Bigi, 1977; Miller et al., 1985).

Although there clearly are age differences in metaattention, it is not clear what causal role, if any, this knowledge plays in the development of the production and utilization of strategies described earlier. Studies finding a relationship between metamemory and strategies or recall (e.g., Beuhring & Kee, 1987; Fabricius & Hagen, 1984) suggest that such a line of research might be fruitful. For our purposes, it would be particularly interesting to know whether metaattentional knowledge plays a role with respect to utilization deficiencies.

EVIDENCE FOR A STRATEGY UTILIZATION DEFICIENCY

It has been assumed that strategies are desirable because they help the child's performance on cognitive tasks. Hundreds of studies have shown that this generally is true with respect to group performance. What is less clear is whether this conclusion accurately characterizes all subgroups. We present evidence that younger children have a utilization deficiency, a transitional phase in strategy development when *spontaneously* producing a strategy results in no benefit for performance (e.g., recall, same–different judgments), less benefit than for older children, or even a decline in performance. Others have noted this phenomenon and have referred to it as a "faulty strategy" (Wellman, 1988) or a lack of "strategy effectiveness" (e.g., Ornstein, Baker–Ward, & Naus, 1988; Schneider & Sodian, 1988; Waters, 1982). Because our apparatus permits us to clearly separate strategy production and subsequent cognitive performance, this section begins with our evidence concerning utilization deficiencies. Then, evidence from other paradigms involving memory is summarized.

Evidence From the Door-Opening Apparatus

The strongest evidence for a utilization deficiency emerges on the selective-attention task. The selective strategy is measured by a selective score, a proportion score based on the number of relevant doors opened divided by the total number of doors opened. The evidence regarding a utilization deficiency is of several types. First, young children have high selectivity but low recall (Woody-Ramsey & Miller, 1988). Second, regression analyses show that the degree of spontaneous selectivity during the study period is a stronger predictor of recall for older children than younger (Miller et al., 1986). The third type of evidence is based on individual trials rather than all trials combined. Conditional probabilities and chi-square analyses reveal that for older children, spontaneously producing the selective strategy on a particular trial is more likely to lead to a correct answer on that trial than is not producing the strategy (Miller et al., 1986). Younger children are less likely to show this pattern of facilitation. Fourth, when spontaneous selectivity is controlled for statistically, older children recall more than younger children (DeMarie-Dreblow & Miller, 1988; Miller et al., 1986; Miller, Woody-Ramsey, & Aloise, 1989). Fifth, analyses of correlations between spontaneous strategy production and recall over trials suggest a pattern consistent with a utilization deficiency (DeMarie-Dreblow & Miller, 1988). Specifically, in this study children received three trials with animals relevant, then three trials with household items relevant (or vice versa). This switch in items relevant may temporarily disrupt the effectiveness of the strategy. For the youngest children, second graders, the correlations between selectivity and recall were significant on Trials 2, 3 and 6 only. The lack of significant correlations for these younger children on the first trial and the first two trials after the switch in which items were relevant suggests a lag in the benefit from a strategy. Stated differently, selectivity continued to improve over the six trials, but recall did not. This microgenetic change from lesser facilitation to greater facilitation within each set of the three trials may parallel the observed developmental change over a longer period of time.

Turning now to a study using the same–different task (Miller & Harris, 1988), we also find a utilization deficiency, though a weaker one than in the selective-attention task. In particular, it is less clear that there ever is a phase with *no* facilitation at all. For the 3-year-olds, the youngest children tested, some analyses detected significant, though moderate, relationships between spontaneously producing the vertical-pairs strategy and judging the arrays correctly, whereas others showed no significant relationship. Four-year-olds more clearly were helped by the strategy. The use of the vertical-pairs strategy accounted for more of the variance in the performance of the 4-year-olds (48%) than the 3-year-olds (22%), an outcome consistent with the utilization deficiency hypothesis.

The less striking utilization deficiency for young preschoolers on the same–different task than the selective-attention task is informative because it suggests possible bases for the utilization deficiency. Because young children tend to explore the array spatially, on the same–different task the appropriate vertical-pairs strategy, a spatial strategy, may be less effortful than the nonspatial selective strategy on the selective attention task. Thus, on the selective-attention task insufficient capacity may remain for mnemonic activities concentrated on the items selected. This second step may require a resource-demanding strategy, such as verbal rehearsal. In contrast, on the same–different task, the second step need not require a strategy because the same–different judgment is minimally demanding. It derives almost automatically from the vertical-pairs strategy. This possible role of effort is considered later in a more general discussion of the causes of the utilization deficiency.

Evidence from Other Research

Only a subset of studies on strategies provides tests of the utilization deficiency hypothesis. Either two ages must be included or the single age included must show no facilitation of recall from the strategy. Including only a single age and finding benefit from the strategy is not informative because it is not possible to determine whether an even younger age group would have a utilization deficiency. Unfortunately, in many articles on children's memory, even if two ages are included the data are not presented in such a way that the utilization deficiency hypothesis can be tested. Most importantly, the performance of different ages of strategic children is not analyzed separately (e.g., Yussen, 1974). However, several studies of children's memory with the appropriate analyses report a pattern of results suggesting a utilization deficiency. For example, Baker-Ward, Ornstein, and Holden (1984) found that spontaneous mnemonic strategies enhanced recall for 6-year-olds but not 4-year-olds. In another study (Bjorklund & Harnishfeger, 1987), both third and seventh graders employed an organizational strategy, but this strategy improved recall only for the older children. The correlation between recall and strategy use was much higher for strategic seventh graders than strategic third graders. An increase, with age, in the effectiveness of a strategy is found not only for these encoding strategies but also for retrieval strategies (e.g., Heisel & Ritter, 1981). It is clear from the various ages of children demonstrating a utilization deficiency in these studies that it is not limited to young children. Instead, the match or mismatch between the task and/or strategy difficulty and the child's developmental level is likely to be more important than age per se.

Greater benefit from strategy use for older than younger children often also emerges in studies in which children are *instructed* to use a strategy. For example, Beuhring and Kee (1987) found that 12th graders benefited more than 5th graders from instructions to use rehearsal and elaboration memory strategies in the paired-associate learning of nouns. Others have reported a similar effect with children aged 7 through 12 instructed to use a rehearsal strategy on a free recall task (Guttentag, 1984, Experiments 2 and 3), and children aged 8 and 12 instructed to organize items into categories (Bjorklund & Harnishfeger, 1987, Experiment 2). Although a developmental lag in the full benefit of a strategy sometimes includes instructed as well as spontaneous strategies, we are focusing on the latter, which we call a utilization deficiency, because it is a more surprising and less discussed phenomenon.

Thus, several types of cognitive tasks from our laboratory and those of others provide evidence that a utilization deficiency may be a fairly general phenomenon. The next question is what causes this deficiency.

PROCESSES UNDERLYING THE UTILIZATION DEFICIENCY

Hypotheses concerning the processes underlying the utilization deficiency are presented. The most attention is given to an effort hypothesis because more relevant evidence is available than for the other hypotheses. According to this hypothesis, there is a lag between producing a strategy and benefiting from it because producing the strategy is so effortful that little capacity remains for encoding per se. After critically examining this hypothesis, we suggest other hypotheses. Both memory and selective attention tasks provide relevant evidence.

Initially Strategies Are Very Effortful

Recent evidence in a wide variety of domains implicates capacity as playing a central role in cognitive development (e.g., Bjorklund, 1987; Case, 1985; Dempster, 1985). Considerable research with both children and adults shows that as a person uses a newly acquired skill it gradually becomes more automatic and requires less effort. Thus, during development as cognitive operations are performed more efficiently, the amount of freed mental capacity available for other information processing should increase. Several developmental researchers (e.g., Bjorklund & Harnishfeger, 1987; Guttentag, 1984) have proposed that if one assumes that (a) strategies are effortful skills that become more automatic, and (b) that there is a fixed amount of real (as opposed to functional) capacity throughout development, then strategies should use more of the available capacity of younger children than older. The implication for the utilization deficiency hypothesis is that a utilization deficiency would occur if the total amount of capacity needed both to produce the strategy and to process the chosen items well enough to recall them later exceeds that available to the younger children. In this argument, younger children have enough capacity to produce the strategy but not enough to also apply additional information-processing activity needed for storage. This activity could include rehearsing the items or applying some other mnemonic strategy. Anything that reduces the effort of producing the strategy, such as practice with the strategy during development or experimental manipulations described later, should decrease or eliminate the utilization deficiency. In an earlier phase, before the utilization deficiency, children may not even attempt to produce the appropriate strategy, even though they could produce it, because it is so effortful. This would be considered a production deficiency (Flavell, 1970). This reluctance to produce strategies that are highly effortful has been suggested by other researchers as well (e.g., Guttentag, 1984). One implication is that the nonsignificant or low correlations between strategy production and recall in younger children, mentioned earlier, actually could reflect two phenomena. First, appropriately strategic children (utilization deficient children) are not recalling as well as they should because of the effortfulness of the strategy. Second, nonstrategic children or children using an easier, inappropriate strategy recall better than they should because of the savings in capacity from deciding not to use a strategy or to use a less effortful strategy.

There is evidence that, as hypothesized, strategies are more effortful for younger children than older. This evidence comes from four sets of studies of the interference of various strategies on a concurrent finger-tapping task. Guttentag (1984) found that second and third graders instructed to use cumulative rehearsal showed more interference (slowing) on a simultaneously performed finger-tapping task than did sixth graders. A second experiment eliminated the possibility that the effect could be due simply to developmental differences in time-sharing performance. Moreover, an easy strategy (rehearsing one word at a time) was less effortful than a more difficult strategy (cumulative rehearsal) for the younger children. A third study revealed that the less capacity required to produce the strategy when subjects are instructed to rehearse, the larger the rehearsal set size during spontaneous rehearsal. In Studies 2 and 3, when putting forth equal strategic effort older children rehearsed more and recalled more than the younger. Thus, the overall pattern of results is consistent with the effort hypothesis. When strategy production and recall are equivalent across age, younger children require more mental capacity to produce the strategy than do older children (Study 1). When there are no age differences in the effort devoted to producing the strategy, older children show superior strategy production and/or recall (Studies 2 and 3).

A pattern of results similar to Guttentag's first study was found when sixth graders and college students were asked to use an elaboration strategy, that is, to generate silently a sentence depicting the two nouns to be associated (Kee & Davies, 1988). The finger tapping of older subjects was reduced less than that of younger. This result was not obtained when the elaboration was done aloud or when verbal rehearsal was used instead of elaboration. However, there was an age-related decline in the effortfulness of rehearsing a set of noun triplets when younger children were examined (Kee & Howell, 1988).

Also using a dual-task paradigm with finger tapping, Bjorklund and Harnishfeger (1987) examined the effortfulness of an organizational strategy (clustering) in free recall. Consistent with Guttentag's second and third study, equivalent effort was used by Grades 3 and 7, but strategy production and recall were greater for the older children. Thus, they benefited more from an equal allocation of effort. The authors explained this developmental lag in benefit in terms of the more elaborated semantic memories in older children, which require less effort for the activation of relations among items than in younger children. Similarly, in a second study, instructing children to use the strategy produced equal strategy effortfulness for the two ages but significant benefit for recall for only the older children. This unequal benefit suggests that when young children must devote considerable effort to the strategy they do not have the necessary resources for mnemonic processing, but older children do.

It should be noted that in most of the studies in the papers just cited, children were instructed to use the strategy. It generally was assumed that the younger children would not have spontaneously produced these strategies but the older ones often would have (though this assumption usually was not tested). Our argument regarding the utilization deficiency is that there also are differences in the recall of younger and older children due to the differences in the effortfulness of *spontaneously* producing equivalent strategies. For utilization deficient children, who spontaneously produce the selective strategy, the interference of finger tapping should be greater and result in lower recall than in older children who have more experience with producing the strategy. We currently are testing this prediction.

If a strategy is so simple that it requires little effort, even young children are helped by the strategy. In the DeLoache and Todd (1988) study described earlier, the preschoolers who separated containers into two piles according to whether they held candies or pegs during the encoding phase subsequently had nearly perfect recall of which containers held candies. Furthermore, Guttentag (1984) found that a simple single-word rehearsal strategy caused little interference with finger tapping in either Grade 2 or 6. That is, it required little effort at either age. In contrast, as described earlier, a more complex strategy of cumulative rehearsal was more effortful for younger children than older.

If it is true that younger children have a utilization deficiency because it is more effortful for them to produce the strategy, then age differences should be eliminated by removing the effortfulness of the strategy. We did this in one study (DeMarie-Dreblow & Miller, 1988) by having the experimenter carry out the selective strategy for the child (i.e., open only the relevant doors). As predicted, the children in Grades 2, 3, and 4 did not differ in the number of relevant items recalled. In contrast, in an earlier session there had been age differences in recall when *spontaneous* selectivity was controlled for statistically. This earlier session was like our initial studies in which children choose which doors to open, which requires more effort. To sum up this study, when the effortful spontaneous strategic behavior of younger and older children is equated through statistical control there are age differences in recall. However, there are no age differences if the strategy production is not effortful (because the experimenter executed the strategy). This age difference in recall when strategy production is effortful does not simply reflect broad differences in the abilities of younger and older children because it does not appear between younger and older children who do not spontaneously produce the appropriate strategy or who have this strategy executed for them. Also, this effect was not due simply to supplying a strategy that the younger children did not have. Most of the children had spontaneously produced the selective strategy in the first session.

Recently, we attempted to tease apart the effort of two components of strategy production—accessing and carrying out the selective strategy (Miller et al., 1989). The effort of accessing was eliminated by showing these kindergarteners and first graders the selective strategy (child opens condition). The effort of both accessing and carrying out the selective strategy was eliminated by having the experimenter perform the strategy as the child watched (adult opens condition). Both could be compared with an initial baseline of spontaneous strategy use. Results were as predicted. The child opens condition did not improve the performance of the children who had been selective spontaneously on the baseline, presumably because they already were accessing the strategy. However, the adult opens condition, which both supplied the appropriate strategy and eliminated the effortfulness of executing the strategy, did improve their recall. Thus, their utilization deficiency was reduced by reducing the effortfulness of executing the strategy. The children who were nonselective on the baseline, in contrast, were helped by both conditions.

This study shows that it is not enough to know which strategy is appropriate and to produce it on one's own. If it is effortful to execute the strategy, then recall may still be low. Executing, as opposed to accessing, the strategy could be effortful because the child has to search for the relevant doors, inhibit the tendency to open adjacent doors (the child's spatial pattern of door opening preferred in his earlier years), and monitor his strategic behavior.

Another way to examine the role of effort in strategy development is to analyze the relationship between children's capacity and their strategy production and subsequent recall. In a recent doctoral dissertation, Woody-Ramsey (1988) assessed the short-term memory capacity of kindergarteners and first graders with five measures: forward digit span, backward digit span, word span, Mr. Cucumber (a test used by Case, 1985, which involves recalling the locations of colored body parts on a clown figure), and an objects-location task (a task developed for this study which involves recalling the locations of a row of line drawings of objects). These capacity measures did not predict how selectively the children opened doors on the selective attention task. Thus, at least for children aged 5 and 6, possessing a larger memory capacity does not encourage children to produce the appropriate strategy. The fact that the children generally were fairly selective (mean = 77%) suggests that most of them had enough capacity to access the selective strategy and to execute it fairly successfully. The individual differences in capacity had an effect, however, on recall. The two memory-for-locations capacity measures (Mr. Cucumber and objects locations tasks) together significantly predicted recall in the selective attention task for the subject group as a whole. Thus, only when capacity was assessed on spatial recall capacity tasks was it related to the selective attention task which also involves spatial recall. A more intriguing result was that the forward digit-span and word-span tasks together predicted recall only for children who consistently produced the selective strategy on the selective attention task. This pattern is interesting because these latter two tasks are verbal, which may implicate verbal rehearsal in recall. That is, the ability to process and store verbally encoded information would be useful for verbal rehearsal. Thus, a child's verbal span becomes important only if she already has selected out the relevant items and needs to conduct further mnemonic processing, such as verbal rehearsal. Of this strategic group, only children with a large verbal span may have enough capacity to engage in verbal rehearsal. A child who does not produce the selective strategy apparently is not helped by having a large verbal span.

This study also revealed that when effortfulness was reduced by telling the child which doors to open or by opening the doors for him, memory capacity predicted recall less well. Thus, when the capacity required to produce the strategy is reduced or eliminated, individual differences in capacity also become less influential. Only the objects location measure predicted recall in all conditions, regardless of the degree of effort required. This may reflect the fact that the objects location and selective attention tasks have a similar task structure and goal—remembering the locations of objects.

This relationship between capacity and recall on the selective-attention task is consistent with findings from the memory literature. Correlations have been found between measures of capacity and recall when children are attempting to use an effortful strategy (e.g., Pressley, Cariglia-Bull, Deane, & Schneider, 1987).

A final source of evidence concerning effort comes from the session in which spontaneous strategy production was assessed in the DeMarie-Dreblow and Miller (1988) study. The items that were to be recalled (animals or household objects) were switched between the first three and second three trials. The trials in which producing the selective strategy should have been most effortful (i.e., when beginning to use the selective strategy with the first set of relevant items and beginning to open different doors after the relevant items changed) resulted in similar recall for young children who had or had not been selective on those trials. On other trials, there were differences favoring the more selective children. Thus, the utilization deficiency emerged on the trials assumed to be more effortful.

Although there is some evidence to support the hypothesized role of capacity in the development of strategic behavior, the observed relationships have been very global. The next step is to examine several more refined questions about their relationship. First, exactly where in the process of strategic problem solving does capacity have an effect? In the selective-attention task, there are several possibilities. One is accessing the selective strategy (choosing from among one's available strategies after analyzing the goal of the task and utilizing one's metacognitive knowledge about tasks and strategies). Another is executing the strategy—actually carrying it out and monitoring one's motoric behavior. Other processes include accessing a mnemonic strategy such as verbal rehearsal, executing it, and retrieving the items. A main goal of future research is to identify more specifically where capacity demands play an important role.

Second, does the site of this influence differ for children of different developmental levels with respect to strategy development? We have focused on children who are just beginning to produce appropriate strategies spontaneously, because of our interest in the utilization deficiency. The processes most sensitive to capacity limitations may be different for nonstrategic children or more experienced strategic children who are beyond the utilization deficiency.

Third, what specific processes underlie the decrease in capacity required for strategy production or utilization? It has been suggested (Bjorklund, 1987; Kee & Davies, 1988) that a greater accessibility of relevant knowledge may be a process mediating reduced effort. This hypothesis is especially likely for organizational strategies in free recall or elaboration strategies in associating unrelated noun pair members. Bjorklund and Harnishfeger (1987) found that comparable effort produced better recall of related than unrelated items, suggesting that "relations among items from the same conceptual category are activated with less mental effort than are relations between unrelated items. Thus, less effort is required to retrieve series of categorically related items than series of unrelated items, leaving more of one's limited mental capacity available for the retrieval of other items" (p. 117). In an earlier section, a dramatic increase in the selective strategy was noted when a meaningful context was created by a scriptlike story. During development, as children become familiar with a wider variety of contexts, including school lessons that call for memorization much like our experimental task with no story, they may become more adept at strategic behavior. A meaningful context may, for example, reduce the effort of access by clarifying which strategy is most efficient for the goal of the task. Or, it may operate in the final step of retrieval by providing an organized knowledge base in which the items to be recalled are embedded. In this case, items may be accessed faster. Our research with preschoolers who became strategic when the story was added, but still did not recall well, suggests that the first process (accessing the strategy) may have been involved in the context effect. If older, spontaneously strategic children were tested, a different process might be involved. We currently are examining whether adding a story moves children from not producing to producing the selective strategy and/or from producing the selective strategy but not benefiting from it to both producing and benefiting from it.

Another possible process underlying the developmental decrease in capacity required for strategic behavior is increased automaticity from practice with a skill. The literature on skill development and the novice-to-expert shift suggests that as a strategy is practiced, it requires less capacity to execute. Thus, if children are given practice with executing the selective strategy (i.e., finding and opening the relevant doors), capacity should be freed for mnemonic processing of the relevant items and recall should improve. We also are testing this hypothesis.

Another process that could underlie the effect of a decrease in the effortfulness of strategy production is more indirect. If capacity is freed when the production (accessing and executing) of the selective strategy requires less and less effort during development, then this freed capacity can be devoted to a second strategy such as verbal rehearsal. The Woody-Ramsey (1988) study is consistent with this hypothesis because the verbal measures of capacity were most predictive of recall among children spontaneously producing the selective strategy. The problem is not that children are *unable* to produce the second strategy, aimed toward mnemonic processing. When children aged 7 through 9 are simply given only the relevant items, so that a selective strategy is not needed, and plenty of effort is available for a mnemonic strategy, there are no age differences in recall (DeMarie-Dreblow & Miller, 1988). But when they must spontaneously produce the selective strategy there may be little capacity remaining for the second strategy and, as a result, age differences in recall emerge, even when controlling for selectivity. The possibility that the utilization deficiency reflects a failure to link together two strategies is also suggested by a study (Baker-Ward et al., 1984) in which 6-year-olds, but not 4-year-olds, linked visual inspection of objects with naming them and were helped by these strategies in subsequent recall. Also consistent with the two-strategy hypothesis is the finding that when there is little or no need for a second strategy, there is much less evidence for a utilization deficiency (DeLoache & Todd, 1988; Miller & Harris, 1988). Research on capacity and strategies should continue to examine all of the preceding processes because the processes that are particularly sensitive to capacity may differ for different developmental levels.

A fourth question regarding capacity concerns whether it is a single, common pool of information-processing resources or a set of independent capacities, each specific to particular processes. This issue currently is being debated (Brainerd & Kingma, 1985; Klapp, Marshburn & Lester, 1983; Rugg, 1986) but no agreement among researchers has been reached. The outcome is important to the effort hypothesis regarding the utilization deficiency because the freed capacity that results from a reduction in effortfulness of strategy production may be limited in what it can be used for if capacity is not domain general or process general.

A final question about the role of capacity in strategy development concerns how best to assess the capacity required by a strategy at different developmental levels or to assess the effect of the capacity requirement for subsequent recall. One approach is to increase the effort required for total performance by introducing a second task and observing whether performing the strategy interferes with the second task more for younger children than older (e.g., Bjorklund & Harnishfeger, 1987; Guttentag, 1984). Investigators conclude from this outcome that the strategy is more effortful for younger children than older. This dual-task paradigm is a promising procedure, but there is disagreement over how clearly interpretable the results are (Brainerd & Reyna, 1989; Guttentag, 1989a, 1989b). We currently are using this procedure to assess the effortfulness of the various strategies used by children on the selective-attention task. In a second type of design, the capacity needed for producing a strategy can be reduced or eliminated by executing it for the child (DeMarie-Dreblow & Miller, 1988; Miller et al., 1989). If this manipulation (a) eliminates the age differences in recall found with spontaneously strategic children or (b) increases recall among spontaneously strategic children, then the role of effort is supported. A third type of assessment of capacity includes various tests of working memory, such as digit span (e.g., Pressley et al., 1987; Woody-Ramsey, 1988). In this design, individual differences in capacity are correlated with differences in strategy production and/or recall of the relevant items. At this early point in the research in this area, multiple assessments of capacity seem desirable.

Other Possible Causes of the Utilization Deficiency

Although most of our research has examined effort as a possible cause of the utilization deficiency, other causes may be involved as well. When younger and older children apparently are producing the same strategy but benefiting from it to different degrees, other differences correlated with age may be important. Possibilities include metacognitive knowledge about strategies, metacognitive skills such as orchestrating a series of strategic behaviors, the ability or tendency to produce a second strategy such as verbal rehearsal, increased speed of accessing information in general, increased skill at simultaneously performing two activities (attentional and mnemonic strategies), and motivation. These developmental differences are involved in strategy development, but their possible role regarding the utilization deficiency has not yet been examined.

The best developed of these alternative hypotheses (Baker-Ward et al., 1984) involves age-related changes in the patterns of co-occurrence of strategies. Four-year-olds, whose recall was not helped by their strategic mnemonic behavior, tended to name the objects while physically manipulating them during the study time. In contrast, 6-year-olds, whose recall was helped by strategies, usually named objects while visually examining them. This latter linking of strategies may be more likely to create an association between visual images of objects and their names, which would facilitate retrieval. In other words, the same strategy, naming, may serve different covert functions at different ages because it is combined with different processes or strategies. A similar argument, that a utilization deficiency may reflect the failure to produce a second strategy, was proposed with respect to our research, but we interpreted this in terms of the effortfulness of the first strategy. However, it may be that the younger children in our studies do not produce the second appropriate strategy, verbal rehearsal, because they cannot verbally rehearse or do not tend to produce that strategy, rather than because they do not have enough capacity to do so.

CONCLUSION

The research reviewed here suggests certain modifications in the traditional account of the development of strategies. Since Flavell's work, beginning in the 1960s, unsuccessful strategic behavior has been classified as a production deficiency, production inefficiency, or mediation deficiency. A production deficiency refers to the failure to spontaneously produce a strategy that would help recall. The improved recall when children are instructed to produce the strategy provides evidence for this phenomenon. Production inefficiencies are incomplete productions of the strategy, for example, the partial strategies in our research. A mediation deficiency, much less often observed than a production deficiency, refers to the child's inability to benefit from a strategy that he produces. Evidence would come from demonstrations that instructing a child to use a strategy does not help his recall. It is not entirely clear where a utilization deficiency fits into this framework because the experimental procedure for demonstrating the existence of a utilization deficiency differs from that used by Flavell and others to study production and mediation deficiencies (Seier, 1988). In our viewpoint, a utilization deficiency has been demonstrated when the *spontaneous* (uninstructed) production of a strategy provides little or no facilitation of recall. In contrast, mediation and production deficiencies are demonstrated primarily with respect to the impact of *instructed* strategy production. That is, production and mediation deficiencies typically are inferred from the demonstration that a child who does not spontaneously produce the strategy does or does not benefit from a strategy when instructed to produce it (Flavell, 1970). Thus, a mediation deficiency and utilization deficiency are defined similarly (i.e., little or no benefit from the strategy), but are demonstrated under different conditions (instructed versus spontaneous strategy production). Consequently, there are two possible conceptualizations of the utilization deficiency. If one considers a mediation deficiency to be demonstrated *whenever* strategy production (spontaneous or instructed) leads to little or no facilitation of recall, then a utilization deficiency is one type of mediation deficiency, a type occuring with spontaneous rather than instructed strategies. In this case, our work (a) further refines the notion of mediation deficiency and (b) suggests that this deficiency is more prevalent than is indicated by the many studies of *instructed* strategy use, which tend to reveal production, rather than mediation, deficiencies. On the other hand, if one follows the operational definition of mediation deficiency (i.e., failure of *instructed* strategies to facilitate recall), then a utilization deficiency is distinct from a mediation deficiency. We favor the latter view at this point because the fact that the two deficiences are demonstrated under different conditions suggests that they may reflect different cognitive limitations.

Because of the concern with production deficiencies, investigators have given little attention to a developmental phase in which a utilization deficiency occurs. As noted earlier, data typically are not analyzed in such a way that a utilization deficiency could be identified. We consider the utilization deficiency to be complementary with, rather than contradictory to, the mediation and production deficiencies.

The research described in this chapter provides a more differentiated picture of the course of strategy development. First, it identifies developmentally earlier patterns of behavior that may be precursors to the later appropriate strategies. Nonrandom responses supported by the spatial layout of the array and partial, incomplete appropriate strategies constitute one transitional period in strategy development. A later transitional period includes the utilization deficiency when producing a strategy may not immediately lead to improved recall. These transitional periods could be identified because the door-opening procedure permitted (a) the direct observation of strategic behaviors and (b) the separation of the production of a strategy from its facilitation of recall.

The main unanswered questions that need to be addressed by future research include the following. What is the temporal and psychological relationship among mediation, production, and utilization deficiencies? Is each type of deficiency more prevalent in certain types of tasks? Does the strain on capacity account for both the failure to produce a strategy at one developmental level and a utilization deficiency at another developmental level? What processes underlie the utilization deficiency? Are there some tasks in which the utilization deficiency never occurs? Recent findings concerning the importance of the developing knowledge structures and decreases in the capacity required for strategic operations may contribute to the answers to these questions.

ACKNOWLEDGMENTS

Work on this chapter was supported by NSF grant #BNS-8710264.

REFERENCES

Baker-Ward, L., Ornstein, P. A., & Holden, D. J. (1984). The expression of memorization in early childhood. *Journal of Experimental Child Psychology, 37*, 555–575.

Beuhring, T., & Kee, D. W. (1987). The relationships between memory knowledge, elaborative strategy use and associative memory performance. *Journal of Experimental Child Psychology, 44*, 377–400.

Bjorklund, D. F. (1987). How age changes in knowledge base contribute to the development of children's memory: An interpretive review. *Developmental Review, 7*, 93–130.

Bjorklund, D. F., & Harnishfeger, K. K. (1987). Developmental differences in the mental effort requirements for the use of an organizational strategy in free recall. *Journal of Experimental Child Psychology, 44*, 109–125.

Brainerd, C. J., & Kingma, J. (1985). On the independence of short-term memory and working memory in cognitive development. *Cognitive Psychology, 17*, 210–247.

Brainerd, C. J., & Reyna, V. F. (1989). Output-interference theory of dual-task deficits in memory development. *Journal of Experimental Child Psychology, 46*, 1–18.

Case, R. (1985). *Intellectual development: Birth to adulthood.* Orlando, FL: Academic Press.

Day, M. C. (1975). Developmental trends in visual scanning. In H. W. Reese (Ed.), *Advances in child development and behavior* (Vol. 10, pp. 154–193). New York: Academic Press.

DeLoache, J. S., & Todd, C. M. (1988). Young children's use of spatial categorization as a mnemonic strategy. *Journal of Experimental Child Psychology, 46*, 1–20.

DeMarie-Dreblow, D., & Miller, P. H. (1988). The development of children's strategies for selective attention: Evidence for a transitional period. *Child Development, 59*, 1504–1513.

Dempster, F. N. (1985). Short-term memory development in childhood and adolescence. In C. J. Brainerd & M. Pressley (Eds.), *Basic processes in memory development: Progress in cognitive development research* (pp. 209–248). New York: Springer–Verlag.

Elkind, D., & Weiss, J. (1967). Studies in perceptual development, III. Perceptual exploration. *Child Development, 38,* 553–561.

Fabricius, W. V., & Hagen, J. W. (1984). Use of causal attributions about recall performance to assess metamemory and predict strategic memory behavior in young children. *Developmental Psychology, 20,* 975–987.

Flavell, J. H. (1970). Developmental studies of mediated memory. In H. W. Reese & L. P. Lipsitt (Eds.), *Advances in child development and behavior* (Vol. 5, pp. 181–211). New York: Academic Press.

Gibson, E. J. (1988). Exploratory behavior in the development of perceiving, acting, and the acquiring of knowledge. In M. R. Rosenzweig & L. W. Porter (Eds.), *Annual review of psychology* (Vol. 39, pp. 1–41). Palo Alto, CA: Annual Reviews.

Gibson, E. J., & Rader, N. (1979). Attention: The perceiver as performer. In G. A. Hale & M. Lewis (Eds.), *Attention and cognitive development* (pp. 1–21). New York: Plenum.

Gottschalk, J., Bryden, M. P., & Rabinovitch, M. S. (1964). Spatial organization of children's responses to pictorial display. *Child Development, 35,* 811–815.

Guttentag, R. E. (1984). The mental effort requirement of cumulative rehearsal: A developmental study. *Journal of Experimental Child Psychology, 37,* 92–106.

Guttentag, R. E. (1989a). Dual-task research and the development of memory. *Journal of Experimental Child Psychology, 46,* 26–31.

Guttentag, R. E. (1989b). Age differences in dual-task performance: Procedures, assumptions, and results. *Developmental Review, 9,* 146–170.

Hagen, J. W. (1967). The effect of distraction on selective attention. *Child Development, 38,* 685–694.

Hagen, J. W., & Hale, G. A. (1973). The development of attention in children. In A. D. Pick (Ed.), *Minnesota Symposia on Child Psychology* (Vol. 7, pp. 117–140). Minneapolis: University of Minnesota Press.

Heisel, B. E., & Ritter, K. (1981). Young children's storage behavior in a memory for location task. *Journal of Experimental Child Psychology, 31,* 250–264.

Kee, D. W., & Davies, L. (1988). Mental effort and elaboration: A developmental analysis. *Contemporary Educational Psychology, 13,* 221–228.

Kee, D. W., & Howell, S. (1988). Mental effort and memory development. In F. Dempster (Chair), *Attentional and Capacity Constraints on Strategy Utilization: Analysis of Individual and Developmental Differences.* Symposium conducted at the meeting of the American Educational Research Association, New Orleans.

Klapp, S. T., Marshburn, E. A., & Lester, P. L. (1983). Short-term memory does not involve the "working memory" of information processing. *Journal of Experimental Psychology: General, 112,* 240–264.

Lane, D. M., & Pearson, D. A. (1982). The development of selective attention. *Merrill–Palmer Quarterly, 128,* 317–337.

Miller, P. H. (1982). Children's integration of information about noise and interest levels in their judgments about learning. *Journal of Experimental Child Psychology, 33,* 536–546.

Miller, P. H. (1985). Metacognition and attention. In D. L. Forrest-Pressley, G. E. MacKinnon, & T. G. Waller (Eds.), *Metacognition, cognition, and human performance: Vol. 2. Instructional practices* (pp. 181–221). Orlando, FL: Academic Press.

Miller, P. H., & Bigi, L. (1977). Children's understanding of how stimulus dimensions affect performance. *Child Development, 48,* 1712–1715.

Miller, P. H., & Bigi, L. (1979). The development of children's understanding of attention. *Merrill–Palmer Quarterly, 25,* 235–250.

Miller, P. H., & Harris, Y. R. (1988). Preschoolers' strategies of attention on a same–different task. *Developmental Psychology, 24,* 628–633.

Miller, P. H., Haynes, V., DeMarie-Dreblow, D., & Woody-Ramsey, J. (1986). Children's strategies for gathering information in three tasks. *Child Development, 57,* 1429–1439.

Miller, P. H., Haynes, V. F., & Weiss, M. (1985). Metacognitive components of visual search in children. *Journal of Genetic Psychology, 146,* 249–259.

Miller, P. H., & Jordan, R. (1982). Attentional strategies, attention, and metacognition in Puerto Rican children. *Developmental Psychology, 18,* 133–139.

Miller, P. H., & Shannon, K. (1984). Young children's understanding of the effect of noise and interest level on learning. *Genetic Psychology Monographs, 110,* 71–90.

Miller, P. H., & Weiss, M. G. (1981). Children's attention allocation, understanding of attention, and performance on the incidental learning task. *Child Development, 52,* 1183–1190.

Miller, P. H., & Weiss, M. G. (1982). Children's and adults' knowledge about what variables affect selective attention. *Child Development, 53,* 543–549.

Miller, P. H., Woody-Ramsey, J., & Aloise, P. A. (1989, April). A strategy utilization deficiency in children. Paper presented at the meeting of the Society for Research in Child Development, Kansas City, MO.

Miller, P. H., & Zalenski, R. (1982). Preschoolers' knowledge about attention. *Developmental Psychology, 18,* 871–875.

Ornstein, P. A., Baker-Ward, L., & Naus, M. J. (1988). The development of mnemonic skill. In M. Weinert & M. Perlmutter (Eds.), *Memory development: Universal changes and individual differences* (pp. 31–50). Hillsdale, NJ: Lawrence Erlbaum Associates.

Ornstein, P. A., & Naus, M. J. (1985). Effects of the knowledge base on children's memory strategies. In H. W. Reese (Ed.), *Advances in child development and behavior* (Vol. 19, pp. 113–148). New York: Academic Press.

Pick, A. D., & Frankel, G. W. (1974). A developmental study of strategies of visual selectivity. *Child Development, 45,* 1162–1165.

Pick, A. D., Frankel, D. G., & Hess, V. L. (1975). Children's attention: The development of selectivity. In E. M. Hetherington (Ed.), *Review of child development research* (Vol. 5, pp. 325–384). Chicago: University of Chicago Press.

Pressley, M., Cariglia-Bull, T., Deane, S., & Schneider, W. (1987). Short-term memory, verbal competence, and age as predictors of imagery instructional effectiveness. *Journal of Experimental Child Psychology, 43,* 194–211.

Rugg, M. D. (1986). Constraints on cognitive performance: Some problems with and alternatives to resource theory. In G. R. J. Hockey, A. W. K. Gaillard, & M. G. H. Coles (Eds.), *Energetics and human information processing* (pp. 391–394). Dordrecht, Netherlands: Martinus Nijhoff.

Schneider, W., & Sodian, B. (1988). Metamemory-memory behavior relationships in young children: Evidence from a memory for location task. *Journal of Experimental Child Psychology, 45,* 209–233.

Seier, W. (1988). *The development of children's memory strategies: Evidence for a utilization deficiency.* Unpublished manuscript, University of Florida, Gainesville.

Spungen, L. B., & Goodman, J. F. (1983). Sequencing strategies in children 18–24 months: Limitations imposed by task complexity. *Journal of Applied Developmental Psychology, 4,* 109–124.

Vurpillot, E. (1968). The development of scanning strategies and their relation to visual differentiation. *Journal of Experimental Child Psychology, 6,* 632–650.

Waters, H. (1982). Memory development in adolescence: Relationships between metamemory, strategy use, and performance. *Journal of Experimental Child Psychology, 33,* 183–195.

Well, A. D., Lorch, E. P., & Anderson, D. R. (1980). Developmental trends in distractibility: Is absolute or proportional decrement the appropriate measure of interference? *Journal of Experimental Child Psychology, 30,* 109–124.

Wellman, H. M. (1985). *Children's searching: The development of search skill and spatial representation.* Hillsdale, NJ: Lawrence Erlbaum Associates.

Wellman, H. M. (1988). The early development of memory strategies. In P. Weinert & M. Perlmutter (Eds.), *Memory development: Universal changes and individual differences* (pp. 3–29). Hillsdale, NJ: Lawrence Erlbaum Associates.

Wellman, H. M., Ritter, K., & Flavell, J. R. (1975). Deliberate memory behavior in the delayed reactions of very young children. *Developmental Psychology, 11,* 780–787.

Wertsch, J. V., McNamee, G. D., & McLane, J. B., & Budwig, N. A. (1980). The adult–child dyad as a problem-solving system. *Child Development, 51,* 1215–1221.

Woody-Ramsey, J. (1988). *Children's production and utilization of a selective attention strategy: Effects of memory capacity.* Unpublished doctoral dissertation, University of Florida, Gainesville, FL.

Woody-Ramsey, J., & Miller, P. H. (1988). The facilitation of selective attention in preschoolers. *Child Development, 59,* 1497–1503.

Yussen, S. (1974). Determinants of visual attention and recall in observational learning by preschoolers and second graders. *Developmental Psychology, 10,* 93–100.

CHAPTER 7

Strategic Processing in Children's Mental Arithmetic: A Review and Proposal

Mark H. Ashcraft
Cleveland State University

In the early 1970s the term *strategy* had a fairly fixed connotation in our discipline. It referred to a conscious, deliberate process or procedure for rehearsing the items to be learned in a memory experiment. Sometimes these procedures were traditional mnemonic devices, for instance, the venerable method of loci (e.g., Bower, 1970). More commonly, however, they were specific rehearsal procedures, say cumulative or clustered rehearsal, that improved recall. Adults were found to be quite adept at first ascertaining the nature or structure of a list, then generating rehearsal strategies tailored to those specific features. For example, Kellas, Ashcraft, Johnson, and Needham (1973) found that adults, when given control over the rate of presentation, quickly learned to rehearse the four contiguously presented members of a category as a unit, with predictable beneficial effects on accuracy and completeness of recall.

Flavell's (1970) crucial statement concerning children's strategies— that children often fail to produce rehearsal strategies *spontaneously*— guided researchers in the area of cognitive development for a good many years (see Harnishfeger & Bjorklund's introductory chapter in this volume for a concise treatment of this research tradition). As an example, Kellas, McCauley, and McFarland (1975a) found an increase in spontaneous cumulative rehearsal across Grades 3, 5, and 7; Kellas, Ashcraft, and Johnson (1973) found that mildly retarded adolescents exhibited no spontaneous rehearsal of a systematic nature, but were able to rehearse effectively with appropriate instructions; and Ashcraft and Kellas (1974) found that fifth graders and retarded adolescents profited from clustering instructions, whereas uninstructed subjects showed little spontaneous generation of tailored rehearsal. (In all of these studies, subjects controlled the rate of presentation, allowing us to infer rehearsal strategies based on their study times.)

Nowadays, as shown by the varied contents of this volume, the term *strategy* has a considerably broader connotation, loosely "how some task is performed mentally." Though some current research preserves the notion that a strategy is a deliberate and conscious mental procedure, an equally valid case can be made that strategies need not be deliberate or conscious in order for that term to be applied meaningfully. Indeed, this change in connotation is almost literally forced upon us by the evidence that formerly conscious or controlled mental processes could achieve a substantial degree of automaticity with practice (Posner & Snyder, 1975; Shiffrin & Schneider, 1977). Thus, in order to accommodate the far broader range of behavior and mental processing now being investigated in the area of cognitive development, and to accommodate empirical effects such as the growth of automaticity, the term *strategy* must be redefined. It must be liberalized to include not only the deliberate and conscious but also the nondeliberate and automatic processes and procedures by which various mental events take place.

An especially good example of such a broad definition, and of the usefulness of thinking about strategies, is provided by the area of mental arithmetic performance, the topic of this chapter. To be sure, we all are introspectively aware of various idiosyncratic strategies we use in troublesome or confusing mathematical situations. Some of these strategies are personally invented, on an as-needed basis, and some are explicitly taught during schooling (e.g., adding 10 then subtracting 1 as a simple alternative to adding 9; "casting out the 9s" as a method of checking a multiplication answer). From a more empirical standpoint, the strategies by which individuals solve arithmetic problems have been the primary concern since the very beginnings of research interest in this topic. These strategies have been—and continue to be—the primary battleground for theoretical statements concerning "how people do arithmetic" (e.g., Ashcraft, 1982, 1987; Baroody, 1983; Groen & Parkman, 1972). Indeed, the most persuasive recent model of this performance, Siegler's Distribution of Associations model (e.g., Siegler, 1988b; Siegler & Shrager, 1984) features strategy choice as one of its most prominent characteristics.

The purpose of this chapter is to discuss the notion of strategies as it applies to research on mental arithmetic performance. A review of this research, and the accompanying theories, is presented in order to highlight the various strategies of arithmetic that have been investigated. Following this, I discuss some difficulties in extending current work to older children and adults, then offer three suggestions that seem to hold some promise for future research. These include a focus on strategies as a function of subject characteristics, and on strategies in more complex arithmetic and mathematics situations; the latter of these represents an important potential contribution that our field can make to education and society. The chapter concludes with a consideration of the construct of *strategies*, and the ways in which this construct has been altered by the study of children's mental arithmetic processes.

A REVIEW

Concern with the strategies children use to perform arithmetic dates back at least into the early part of this century (e.g., Browne, 1906; Thorndike, 1922; see Resnick & Ford, 1981, chap. 2, for a review). The more recent cognitive approach to this topic, however, is generally agreed to have begun with the influential work of Groen and Parkman (1972; Parkman, 1972; Parkman & Groen, 1971). Working within an information-processing framework, these investigators conducted several reaction time (RT) tests of arithmetic performance, using both first graders and adults as subjects. Their evidence, reviewed following, led them to propose the first chronometric model of children's arithmetic performance, known widely as the *min* model of mental addition. Equally important for the present topic was the model they advanced to explain adults' performance, which might be called the "Direct Access plus Backup model." This model contains an important notion that is central to several more recent models, that multiple strategies may be used in solving simple arithmetic problems.

Briefly, the evidence Groen and Parkman (1972) presented on first graders' addition performance is as follows. In a multiple regression analysis that tested five structural variables in the problems (first and second addend, minimum and maximum addend, and sum), the best predictor of RT was the minimum addend, the *min*. This variable accounted for nearly 80% of the RT variance in the first graders' performance to simple addition facts.[1] The slope of the RT function across *min* was approximately 400 msec. These results suggested that

---

[1] The simple facts are those with one-digit answers, i.e., sums less than or equal to 9. The terms *basic facts* and *whole number facts* refer to the entire set of 100 addition problems from $0 + 0$ through $9 + 9$, as well as the comparable problems in subtraction, multiplication, and division.

first graders solve these problems by means of a simple yet efficient counting strategy in which the value of the maximum addend is registered into a mental counter and is then incremented by ones the number of times specified by the *min*. Thus, a first grader was said to add 4 + 3, for example, by setting the counter to 4, then mentally counting on "5 . . . 6 . . . 7," at a 400 msec rate.

That counting is a common and important (and, incidentally, rather sophisticated) strategy in children's arithmetic performance cannot be doubted; countless demonstrations of the role of counting in early number and arithmetic tasks exist (see treatments by Fuson, 1982, 1988; Gelman & Gallistel, 1978; Ginsburg, 1977; Resnick & Ford, 1981). Nonetheless, more recent evidence, as well as an important aspect of Groen and Parkman's own data, indicate that counting by *min* is far less than universal in even first graders' performance.

The Groen and Parkman evidence concerns "ties," problems in which a number is added to itself (e.g., 3 + 3). Even their first graders showed a relatively flat, that is, nonincreasing, RT pattern for these problems, as distinct from the linearly increasing RT profile for nontie problems. Groen and Parkman suggested that first graders had already stored the tie problems in memory and, therefore, could retrieve them directly, without need for the *min*-counting process.

This interpretation, that retrieval coexists with counting, was then extended to account for the results from adult subjects. In a RT task that tested all 100 basic facts, Groen and Parkman's adults demonstrated a 20 msec slope in RT across *min*, far in excess of any reasonable estimate of the speed of mental counting. Although they entertained the possibility that adults were indeed using the *min*-counting strategy, albeit at an extremely rapid counting rate, Groen and Parkman also suggested that a rather different explanation might characterize adult performance.

In particular, they suggested that the 20 msec slope, and the overall significance of the *min*, was an artifact of averaging across two distinct strategies, Direct Access and Backup Counting. The bulk of an adult's performance involves direct access to stored addition facts, they claimed, where such direct-access retrieval would require only some constant amount of time. Upon occasion, however, direct-access retrieval would be expected to fail. In such an event, Groen and Parkman suggested that adults use a backup strategy for solving the problems, the simple *min*-counting strategy. Thus, the 20 msec slope for adults was viewed as a mixture of two strategies, direct access on some 95% of all trials, with a slope of 0, averaged together with *min*-counting, with a slope of 400 msec, on the remaining 5% of trials that experienced retrieval failure.

Two general research themes have come from this initial work by Groen and Parkman. The earlier one has concerned itself largely with the notion of retrieval of arithmetic information, focusing especially on the form of the mental representation of arithmetic knowledge and relying heavily on evidence from adult subjects as well as older children. In anticipation of the outcome of this program of research, this theme is termed the *network retrieval research*. The more recent trend has built on this base and has added the important evidence that network retrieval is but one of several strategies used routinely in children's arithmetic processing. For lack of a better term, this is labeled the *multiple strategy research*. Considering each of these in turn completes the review of current evidence on children's strategic processing in simple arithmetic and sets the stage for the discussion of some difficulties in investigating strategy use and a description of strategies in more complex situations.

Network Retrieval Research

In an early challenge to Groen and Parkman's theoretical interpretations, Ashcraft and Battaglia (1978) objected to two aspects of Groen and Parkman's models. The first objection is directed toward the possibility that adults continue to rely exclusively on the *min*-counting strategy: "From an intuitive standpoint alone, the assumption that addition problems are always counted or computed, even after years of experience, seems unlikely" (p. 528). Concerning the more sophisticated Direct Access plus Backup model, we argued that the assumption of constant retrieval time for the basic addition facts was unreasonable. Citing related research on retrieval time effects in long-term memory, we suggested that "time-consuming search and/or decision processes are assumed to be required for verification in semantic tasks, and, by analogy, similar processes may be assumed to operate during the processing of simple addition problems" (p. 529).

Several aspects of our early results disconfirm predictions from Groen and Parkman's models. At a general level, the strongest prediction of both the *min*-counting and the Direct Access plus Backup model is that RT increases linearly with the size of the minimum addend. Inspection of our data reveal an exponentially increasing function, rather than a linear function.[2] The more specific prediction

---

[2] Although an exponential trend in Groen and Parkman's data may have gone unnoticed, an equally likely explanation for the discrepancy in results is that Groen and Parkman averaged performance over the last 4 days of a 5-day experiment, whereas we tested subjects in only one session.

of the Direct Access model, that performance should be a mixture of direct access trials along with counting trials, was examined in Ashcraft and Stazyk (1981). We divided each subject's RTs into two sets, "faster" trials that should correspond to direct-access retrieval, and "slower" trials that should reflect *min*-counting performance. This was done using Groen and Parkman's retrieval-failure estimate of 5%, as well as an estimate derived from our overall analyses, 18%. In both cases, the "faster" trials, those supposedly characterized by constant-time direct access, continued to show the typical problem-size effect, that is, increases in RT as the size of the problem increases. In fact, a retrieval failure rate of 50% had to be assumed in order to eliminate the significant problem-size effect from our data.

Our theoretical proposal, given these results, is that adults have stored the basic addition facts in a network representation in long-term memory, and that retrieval of the facts depends on a spread of activation through this network. Retrieval time is viewed as due to a semantic distancelike effect, or, equivalently, to the strength with which problems were represented in the network: for example, "elapsed retrieval time [is] proportional to the distance traversed during the search" (Ashcraft & Stazyk, 1981, p. 186); "normal retrieval from a subjectively organized network structure depends heavily on accessibility or mental distance in that structure" (Stazyk, Ashcraft, & Hamann, 1982, pp. 334–5).

Subsequent research has confirmed several important predictions of this network approach, including the predictive power of normative measures of problem difficulty (Hamann & Ashcraft, 1986) and confusability (Campbell, 1987; Campbell & Graham, 1985). Particularly convincing have been demonstrations of network relatedness effects, such as that reported by Stazyk et al. (1982). In brief, Stazyk et al. found that adults' performance is slowed significantly when they are shown "confusion" problems, in which an answer is multiplicatively related to the problem (e.g., $4 \times 7 = 21$). Our interpretation here is that, because the arithmetic facts are stored in interrelated networks, significant activation would accrue at related nodes during retrieval. This would have the effect of slowing down the eventual decision process because of the competing nodes that had received activation during search.

The foregoing results suggest, of course, that the predominant strategy for performing mental arithmetic changes across development, from *min*-based counting to retrieval. Our research with children has documented this change in several ways. Briefly, Ashcraft and Fierman (1982) found that approximately half of their third graders generated RTs that were best fit by the *min* model, but that the other half showed the exponentially increasing pattern typical of adults. Children in Grades four and six, in the same report, showed the typical adult RT patterns as well. In Ashcraft, Fierman, and Bartolotta (1984), the results of an adjunct counting task, along with the standard addition task, suggested a significant degree of memory retrieval at the second grade level; specifically, counting rates were too rapid to account for the speed of addition, and counting on the 5s string indicated reliance on memorized sequences. And in Hamann and Ashcraft (1985), two aspects of the results indicated that even first graders relied somewhat on memory retrieval, as opposed to processing the problems entirely by means of *min* counting. First, the speed of responding to the simple addition facts, compared to responses for the larger basic facts and multicolumn addition problems, suggested memory retrieval rather than counting. The average RT to the simple problems here was about 3.5 seconds, compared to means of about 9 seconds for the larger facts and the two-column addition problems. Since two-column addition problems (e.g., 14 + 12) clearly could not have been performed solely by retrieval, we concluded that the large facts (e.g., 7 + 9), with the same mean RT, were also being computed or reconstructed. Second, the *min* failed to be the best predictor of RTs to the basic facts, by a fairly small amount in Grade 1, but quite dramatically so at Grades 4, 7, and 10. Instead, a normatively derived measure of problem difficulty, based on Wheeler's (1939) study of fact mastery, provided the best prediction.

The most recent theoretical integration of these results is the Distribution of Associations model, by Siegler and Shrager (1984; see also Siegler, 1987, 1988b). A major strength displayed by this model is that it unifies several different perspectives and bodies of evidence into a cohesive account of children's (and adults') long-term memory network for arithmetic knowledge. Its second major strength, discussed in the next section, is a deliberate consideration of multiple-processing strategies.

Siegler's model assumes that all of a child's early experience with number and arithmetic leaves its trace in memory, in the form of problem-specific bonds or associations. The strength of these associations is the factor most directly responsible for the observed RTs to these problems, as well as to the child's use of retrieval versus some other strategy for problem solution. For instance, a preschool child is likely to have discovered for him or herself that 2 + 1 = 3, based on counting and other experiences. As such, the addends 2 and 1 have an association with 3 that is stored in memory. Because this correct answer is easily achieved by counting, and because counting up by one is quite accurate, the bond between 2 + 1 and 3 should achieve substantial strength. In contrast, a more difficult problem such as 3 + 4 is less likely to have been discovered by the child, and is more likely to have competing, incorrect associations stored in memory. For example, if the child had attempted 3 + 4, and gotten the answer 6 by faulty counting, then the answer 6 would be associated with these addends at some nontrivial level of strength in memory. Likewise, the number 5 is often advanced as the answer to 3 + 4, presumably because of its "next number" association in the counting string. This too would lead to increased strength of an incorrect association.

All such experiences, correct or not, leave their imprint on the stored network of associations, as do the child's encounters with the elementary school mathematics curriculum (see Hamann & Ashcraft, 1986) and other informal experiences with number. The upshot of this is that some problems have relatively few associations other than the bond to the correct answer, or the competing associations are of a low enough strength to generate retrieval difficulties only infrequently. In Siegler and Shrager's estimate, the 2 + 1 = 3 bond has a strength of .79 (a probability of being retrieved), with the next strongest association of only .07 (estimates derived from a sample of 4-year-olds). Such problems are characterized as having a "peaked" distribution of associations. These are the problems that are most commonly found to be retrieved from memory, as opposed to being reconstructed by some other strategy.

Other problems, alternately, may have relatively low-strength associations with the correct answer, and several competing associations with nontrivial strength; in their estimates, 3 + 4 = 7 has a strength of .29, and 3 + 4 = 5 has a strength of .23 (again for 4-year-olds). For such problems, said to have a relatively "flat" distribution of associations, accessing the network is more likely to yield an incorrect answer, or a correct answer that fails to reach the response criterion. In such situations, the subject must either ignore the response criterion and state the most recently retrieved answer as a "sophisticated guess," or must revert to some backup strategy for reconstructing the correct answer.

Several lines of support exist for the retrieval aspect of Siegler's model. First, Siegler and Shrager's data reveal that retrieval is the most common processing strategy for problems with peaked distributions of associations, and is certainly the most rapid of the strategies available to young children. In their data, retrieval trials averaged around 4 seconds for first graders, compared to means of 7 seconds or more for various reconstructive strategies; the 4 second average corresponds quite closely to the results reported elsewhere in the literature (e.g., Hamann & Ashcraft, 1985). The associative strength values for children's multiplication, obtained from third and fourth graders (Siegler, 1988b), likewise, have been found to provide the best prediction of RT for adults (Siegler, 1988b), and for children in Grades 3, 5, 7, and 9 (Koshmider & Ashcraft, 1988). This suggests that the associative strengths of the basic facts, once established in early grade school, maintain their relative standings to one another across later education and experience (see Table 7.4 in Siegler, 1988b, and Hamann & Ashcraft, 1986, for evidence that elementary school texts present the various basic facts with seriously unequal frequencies). Finally, Koshmider and Ashcraft have also reported that the confusion effect for multiplication is significant beginning in Grade 7, a further confirmation of the hypothesized interrelatedness of information stored in a network representation.

In summary, research since Groen and Parkman's (1972) paper has documented the presence and importance of retrieval as a major strategy of mental arithmetic performance. Concern with the underlying mental representation of the arithmetic facts has led to the conclusion that this knowledge is stored in an interrelated network representation, one that contains not only the correct answers, but also incorrect associations, all of these stored with some specifiable strength (Campbell, 1987; Campbell & Graham, 1985; Miller, Perlmutter, & Keating, 1984). Retrieval from this network is assumed to involve a process of spreading activation, with the problem-size effect due to slower access to facts with lower strength. Furthermore, retrieval is found to be the most rapid strategy to execute, to be the most common strategy in adults, and to show greater and greater predominance over counting across the elementary school ages. On Siegler's (1988b) view, retrieval may be considered to be an innate process in humans, certainly simpler than any reconstructive method by which arithmetic or other problems might be solved. By extension, retrieval would also be the most likely candidate strategy for achieving automatic status in information processing, although direct evidence for automatic retrieval processing in arithmetic is still sparse (but see Koshmider & Ashcraft, 1988; LeFevre, Bisanz, & Mrkonjic, 1988).

Multiple-Strategy Research

An early demonstration that children may use more than one arithmetic processing strategy was presented by Woods, Resnick, and Groen (1975) in their study of subtraction. They found that second grade children performed simple subtraction by means of a flexible counting process. In particular, two counting methods can be used for simple subtractions such as 7 − 2 or 6 − 4, either counting down from the larger value (7) the number of times specified by the smaller value (2), or counting up from the smaller value (4) to the larger (6). Woods et al. found that their subjects flexibly alternated between these two strategies, such that the strategy that was used on a problem minimized the number of counts required (e.g., for 7 − 2, subjects counted down 2 from 7, yielding the answer 5; instead of counting down for 6 − 4, however, they counted up from 4 to 6, with the number of counts equalling the answer 2). Because these two methods differ—one involves counting down a stated number of times, the other keeping track of counts going from a start to a stop number—they represent two distinct (though similar) strategies. Although subsequent research (Siegler & Shrager, 1984) has suggested that neither of these strategies provides a complete account of children's subtraction, it is clear from this study that having multiple strategies available for performance is not uncommon in the early grade school years.

As stated in the previous section, several reports have documented that both counting and retrieval are commonly found in young children's performance. More recent research, especially by Siegler and his colleagues, has explicitly assessed the use of multiple strategies in children's arithmetic. Two of the more important outcomes of this work are, first, the evidence that multiple strategies coexist in the mental processing of small children, as opposed to superceding one another across ages, and second, that the use of overt, reconstructive strategies is determined by the strength of fact representation in memory (e.g., Siegler, 1987; Siegler & Robinson, 1982; Siegler & Shrager, 1984).

In the earliest of these reports, Siegler and Robinson (1982) tested 4- and 5-year-old children on simple addition facts presented as story problems. Performance was both timed and videotaped. The videotapes revealed clear-cut evidence of no fewer than four strategies. The simplest, most rapid, and most common was retrieval; this strategy was scored when the child displayed no overt evidence of relying on any deliberate strategy. Retrieval accounted for 64% of the trials, had a mean solution time of 4.0 seconds, and an accuracy of 66%. A second strategy, termed *fingers,* was scored when the child held up fingers corresponding to the two addends but then proceeded to answer the problem without overt counting. This strategy accounted for 13% of the trials, took 6.6 seconds on the average, and yielded an 89% accuracy level. A third strategy, *counting,* simply involved counting aloud or silently (with lip movements) with no external referent such as fingers; this strategy occurred on 8% of the trials, with a mean latency of 9.0 seconds, and only a 54% level of accuracy. Finally, "counting fingers" was scored when the child not only held up his or her fingers but then also counted them, either silently or aloud; this accounted for 15% of the trials, with a mean solution time of 14.0 seconds, and an accuracy level of 87%.

In an extension of this work, Siegler (1987) tested children in grades K through 2, on problems ranging from 4 + 1 to 17 + 6, again timing and videotaping the sessions. As before, performance that was unaccompanied by overt strategic behavior (e.g., counting on fingers) was classified as retrieval, with other trials being classified according to the nature of the overt strategy used. Retrieval was found to account for 16% of the kindergartners' trials on these problems, and *min* counting 30%. By Grades 1 and 2, however, retrieval trials clearly outnumbered *min*-counting trials, with frequencies of 44% versus 38% for first grade, and 45% versus 40% for second grade. Other strategies were also now in evidence, although at lower frequencies. These were decomposition (e.g., 12 + 2 is decomposed to 10 + 2 + 2), count all (e.g., for 4 + 2, counting 1,2,3,4,5,6,), and guessing.

Several aspects of these results deserve emphasis. First, as distinct from the implication of Groen and Parkman's (1972) *min* model, even young children appear to rely heavily on retrieval; note that Siegler and Robinson's subjects were approximately a year younger than Groen and Parkman's first graders, yet gave evidence of a more sophisticated strategy, retrieval.[3] Second, the results clearly demonstrated that each child used multiple strategies across the problem set. For example, in Siegler (1987), 99% of the children used at least two strategies, and 62% used three or more. Finally, and quite critical to the Distribution of Associations model, children's processing strategies seemed quite tailored to the problem being solved. That is, simple problems were usually solved by retrieval, whereas difficult problems, those that require longer solution times, tended to be solved by overt strategies. In other words, "[the] children had some systematic way of choosing when to use overt strategies" (Siegler & Shrager, 1984, p. 239).

According to Siegler, this method of choosing a strategy depends critically on the strength of the individual arithmetic facts in memory. That is, facts stored with high associative strength are routinely, rapidly, and accurately retrieved from memory. Those with lower

---

[3.]Siegler's (1987) elegant reanalysis suggests that the significance of *min* is a statistical artifact of averaging across multiple strategies, an ironic finding given that Groen and Parkman themselves interpreted their adult data as being a misleading average of two distinct processing strategies. Siegler's more general point, an important one for the area of mental arithmetic as well as other areas, is that the common practice of averaging across stimuli and subjects often yields misleading results, especially when different processing strategies underlie performance.

associative strengths, that is, those with relatively "flat" distributions of associations, are more prone to solution via some overt strategy. Thus, in Siegler's model, the basic retrievability of an arithmetic fact determines how likely a child is to use a given strategy in solving a problem. Problems with sufficiently high strength are retrieved. Problems that experience retrieval failure due to low strength are subject to renewed attempts at retrieval, and, if these are unsuccessful, by more deliberate and conscious strategies.

To be sure, other strategies have been suggested by other researchers, for example the rules for the special cases of adding or multiplying with 0 or 1 (e.g., Baroody, 1983). Indeed, even our earliest speculation on the network basis for addition (Ashcraft & Battaglia, 1978) contained the notion that a procedural body of knowledge, separate from the declarative network of facts, provided the basis for such processes as estimating magnitudes, carrying or borrowing, and counting (e.g., Ashcraft, 1982). Nonetheless, no other model has stressed strategic processing quite as clearly as Siegler's.

Because Siegler's research is specifically directed toward multiple strategies in children's arithmetic processing, a summary of this research is largely equivalent to a summary of the assumptions in the Distribution of Associations model. There appear to be four general assumptions of greatest importance. First, retrieval is a processing strategy in its own right, despite its nondeliberate and increasingly (across ages) automatic nature. As stated previously, Siegler (1988b) has even suggested that retrieval is an innate process. Second, several other reconstructive strategies coexist with retrieval in the child's repertoire. All of these (except guessing) are derived from one of two sources, the child's knowledge of counting, or, in the case of decomposition, knowledge of other stored facts. Third, selection among the processing strategies is a fairly low level process, *mindless* in Siegler's term, rather than a conscious, metacognitively based decision. In other words, a reconstructive strategy is selected not because of a deliberate assessment or realization on the part of the child that a problem is difficult. Instead, overt strategies are used because a retrieval attempt has failed to yield an acceptable answer.

The fourth point neatly explains the transition from counting in younger children to retrieval in older children and adults. Successful retrieval, as well as successful reconstructive processes, have the effect of strengthening the problem-to-answer associations in memory, thus increasing the overall frequency of retrieval in performance. As Siegler (1988b) put it, "Backup strategies contribute to the transition process in ways that lead to their own demise; retrieval contributes in ways that lead to its own increased use" (p. 274).

SOME DIFFICULTIES IN ASSESSING STRATEGY USE

Siegler's work has clearly documented the presence of multiple strategies in children's arithmetic performance (Siegler, 1988b; Siegler & Shrager, 1984) and some of the theoretical and statistical pitfalls of averaging across multiple strategies (Siegler, 1987). Although it could be argued that the evidence used to diagnose retrieval, the *absence* of overt strategic behavior, is rather weak in his classification method, the unequivocal nature of children's overt behavior is certainly reassuring. Furthermore, other aspects of the data buttress the classification method and help determine which trials were solved via retrieval. In particular, error rates for the different strategies, and analyses of the problem-size effect on retrieval trials, indicate clearly that these trials differ from those solved by overt strategies.

Despite these obvious strengths, however, the strategy-choice model will not be easily extended to older children and adults, certainly not within the domain of simple arithmetic, and probably not within more complex domains either. A variety of empirical and methodological reasons can be offered to support this pessimistic view; three particularly salient ones are discussed following. A fourth difficulty, also discussed later, cuts to the heart of any research program that attempts to assess the strategies that underlie performance. After these four difficulties are described, I then present three suggestions for conducting research on strategies in arithmetic and mathematics, with accompanying examples. These proposed solutions to the problem of assessing strategy use also chart a possible future for research on arithmetic and mathematics performance.

1. Strategic Processing Becomes More Automatic

Siegler's model as well as the available literature indicate that, across development, retrieval becomes the predominant processing strategy for simple addition, subtraction, and multiplication. A corollary point is that, for older children and adults, retrieval of basic arithmetic facts becomes largely automatic as well (see especially Kaye, 1986). As previously noted, a few sources of support for this conclusion exist in the area of mental arithmetic. LeFevre et al. (1988) found explicit evidence that the activation of arithmetic facts is "obligatory," that is, automatic and unavoidable, for adults. Similarly, Koshmider and Ashcraft (1988) found the confusion effect in multiplication RTs, beginning at the seventh grade level; as in the Stazyk et al. (1982) paper, such a result indicates automatic activation of related information within the mental network.

Although such evidence is in no way damaging to the Siegler model, it does create problems for the investigator who wishes to assess strategy use in older subjects. That is, almost by definition, processes that operate at an automatic level are neither open to awareness nor slow enough to report on (e.g., Posner & Snyder, 1975). Consequently, subjects are generally unable to verbalize any useful information about their automatic processing. Although there is now a rather significant literature on using verbal reports as data (e.g., Ericsson & Simon, 1980), it is generally accepted that more rapid, hence (probably) automatic processes cannot be reliably de-scribed by subjects. Therefore, as older subjects are tested, there will be less and less overt behavior with which to diagnose the strategies being employed.

Notice that this difficulty applies both to straightforward retrieval as well as to reconstructive strategies in arithmetic. That is, retrieval clearly becomes automatic in older subjects. But imagine a situation in which some substantial proportion of the basic facts, say $N + 1$ or $N + 9$ problems, are repeatedly solved by a rule, that is, a reconstructive strategy. Siegler predicts that in such a circumstance, the network association for those problems should be strengthened, leading to more frequent retrieval. It seems just as likely, however, that the reconstructive strategy itself might be strengthened, or *compiled* to use Anderson's (1983) term. In such a case, mature performance could reflect more or less automatic execution of a reconstructive strategy, but the subject would be unable to report any useful information on the strategy. Indeed, the subject would presumably be unaware that any strategic processing had occurred at all (see, e.g., Stazyk et al.'s (1982) evidence on $N \times 0$ problems).

2. Performance Becomes More Rapid and Accurate

A related point is that, across development, performance becomes both more rapid and more accurate. Whether these changes are due to an increase in automaticity, a speed up of some central-processing mechanism, or other factors (Kail, 1986) is immaterial to the present argument. The point is simply that time and accuracy differences are critical indicators of different strategies. As information processing becomes more rapid across ages, then, the empirical differences we use to determine reliance on various strategies will disappear, or at a minimum will become quite subtle (Baroody, 1983, has made a similar point).

A clear-cut case for the possibility of multiple strategies exists when the distribution of scores within a condition or treatment is unusual. For example, Siegler (1987) noted that in one subset of his data, where the value of the smaller addend was quite large (e.g., 8 + 6), solution times fell into two clusters; that is to say, the RT distribution was bimodal. The cluster of long solution times was generated by the *min*-counting strategy, and the cluster of shorter times by retrieval. This pattern of times would be expected from these two strategies and would be relatively easy to detect for young children. For older children and adults, however, the temporal characteristics of the different solution strategies are more similar. Although we might still expect nonretrieval strategies to be somewhat slower, or to show differences in accuracy (Ashcraft, 1982), clear cases of nonnormal distributions would be much more difficult to detect. Thus, researchers who are concerned that they might be averaging across multiple strategies might be incorrectly reassured by an examination of their underlying time or accuracy distributions. (The same careful researchers might be doubly reassured, but just as incorrectly, by the evidence in verbal protocols that no other strategies were being used.)

3. Verbalization May Distort or Disrupt Normal Processing

A commonly voiced complaint about subjects' verbalizations is that they may bear little resemblance to the actual mental processes under scrutiny (e.g., Nisbett & Wilson, 1977); of course, this complaint is particularly valid when the processes are operating more or less automatically. A standard solution to this complaint is to refrain from collecting "retrospective protocols," and instead to probe subjects either during or immediately after the experimental trial (e.g., Ericcson & Simon, 1980). Siegler (1987) noted that these methods are not notably easy to apply or interpret, yet concluded that they may nonetheless be useful in detecting multiple strategy use.

The point is not simply that a more automatic strategy such as retrieval will be unavailable for verbalization, though that is the case. The point, rather, is that required verbalization may change the strategy being used, and that with increasing age, there seems to be an increased inability to verbalize *any* useful indications of strategy use. Older children and adults either cannot be believed when they report strategies that operate rapidly, or their strategies may change under instructions to verbalize.

Two examples should suffice to make this argument. Shortly after Rundus's (1971) work on the rehearsal–recall relationship, Kellas, McCauley, and McFarland (1975b) reported that instructions to rehearse aloud led to a change in rehearsal processing. In particular, when their adult subjects had to rehearse out loud, they engaged in considerably more serial or cumulative rehearsal than the silent rehearsal group; this conclusion was based on group differences in study time, using the subject-paced learning task mentioned in the introduction. Thus, when rehearsal was externalized, the nature of the rehearsal strategy itself was changed.

The second example comes directly from the literature on children's arithmetic processing. Hamann and Ashcraft (1985) presented the basic addition facts as well as more complex addition problems to children in Grades 1, 4, 7, and 10. We tested performance both in a RT task and a tape-recorded interview session. The interviews tapped "concurrent verbalizations," rather than retrospective reports, in order to maximize their usefulness. Nonetheless, our 7th and 10th graders gave rather lengthy verbalizations about their solution strategies to all problems, while showing quite rapid RT performance (for instance, all 10th-grade means were under 2 seconds). The mismatch between the protocol and RT data prompted us, in fact, to describe these verbalizations as "blackboard solutions," solutions a student might verbalize at the blackboard while working problems for a math teacher (Ashcraft & Hamann, 1981). In short, "the automaticity of the mental processes, coupled with the experimental demand of the interview session" (Hamann & Ashcraft, 1985, p. 69) made the interview task quite uninformative for these older subjects.

These kinds of results certainly sound a discouraging or at least cautionary note for those who investigate strategy use by means of instructions to verbalize. To a subject who is asked to verbalize his or her mental processes when solving $6 + 3$, saying "I know this equals 9" may seem quite feeble and insufficient to the implied demand characteristics of the interview. At minimum, then, such results certainly recommend the practice of collecting several different measures or coindicators of performance, however thorny deciding which of these has greater validity might be in specific circumstances.

4. The Strategy × Challenge Interaction

A final difficulty in investigating strategy use, apparent in the performance of Hamann and Ashcraft's (1985) younger subjects, gives even further reason to be cautious in interpreting results from verbal protocol methods. As previously described, our subjects performed in both RT and interview tasks, solving problems such as $4 + 3$ and $14 + 13$. Two distinct solution strategies, counting and retrieval, were identified when subjects were shown the basic facts of addition. Two thirds of the 1st graders' scorable protocols verbalized a counting strategy on these problems, compared with only 22% of the 4th graders' protocols, and 0% of the 7th and 10th graders'. Thus, based on the interview session, the bulk of 1st graders' performance to simple addition appeared to rely on counting; "I go 4,5,6,7."

A completely different picture emerged when subjects responded to more challenging problems. When two-column addition problems were presented, only one of the 62 scorable protocols from 1st graders gave any evidence of counting. The remaining 61 either simply stated the fact ("4 and 3 is 7") or referred to memory and retrieval ("I know in my head that 4 + 3 makes 7"). This proportion was approximately the same in the older three groups as well. Such an outcome, of course, indicates that our 1st graders were solving the embedded basic facts by means of retrieval, not counting (our analyses of RT performance led to the same conclusion).

Notice the inconsistency here. The typical 1st grader, when shown 4 + 3, claimed to have counted in "5,6,7" fashion to get the answer. When the same problem was embedded in the more challenging problem 14 + 13, the same 1st grader verbalized a retrieval solution for the one's column ("4 and 3 is 7, then the 1 plus 1 makes 2").

How can this discrepancy be explained? Hamann and Ashcraft concluded, modestly, that the results were inconsistent with purely reconstructive or counting models, but supported models that explicitly contain both retrieval and reconstructive strategies. In terms of the present discussion, I suggest a much stronger conclusion. When relatively unchallenging problems are presented, verbalized solutions may not reflect the subject's true solution strategy, but merely one that is somewhat easier to verbalize. Conversely, when more challenging problems are presented, subjects' verbalizations may be more reflective of their underlying strategies. Part of this Strategy × Challenge interaction might simply be due to the mixture of deliberate and automatic processes, and the degree of automaticity involved. Subjects may be able to verbalize use of carrying, decomposition, and so forth when these less automatic strategies co-occur with retrieval, whereas with simpler problems, solutions may involve only relatively automatic, hence, nonverbalizable processes. Another part of the interaction may be due to the notion of demand characteristics; less "needs" to be said about 4 + 3 when it is a component in a larger problem such as 14 + 13.

SOME PROPOSED SOLUTIONS

It has been argued that existing research supports several important generalizations concerning strategies in arithmetic performance, among them, the existence of multiple strategies and the growing predominance and automaticity of retrieval across ages. It has also been argued that there are several important difficulties in extending strategy-use research to older children and adults, that is, the nonverbalizable nature of automatic retrieval, the speed of information processing in older subjects, the possibility that verbal protocol methods disrupt the very processes under investigation, and the dwindling usefulness of protocol methods with older subjects and/or relatively unchallenging tasks. The proper course of action, given these difficulties, is not to abandon the investigation of children's and adults' strategies in arithmetic, however. Instead, a more appropriate decision would be to consider alternative research questions and methods that are likely to yield useful results. Three such alternatives are described below (see also LeFevre & Bisanz, this volume).

Individual or Subgroup Differences

Although multiple-processing strategies may be present for all subjects, regardless of age, a few recent reports suggest that at least some individuals or subgroups may rely more heavily on one or another strategy, may execute some strategies differently, or may even lack some strategies. Identifying the strategies that are more characteristic of certain individuals or subgroups, then, represents one way of investigating strategy use.

Two recent examples serve to illustrate this point. Siegler (1988a) found that three subgroups characterized his first grade sample of children, referred to as "good students," "not-so-good students," and "perfectionists." These subgroups exhibited rather different performance characteristics on simple addition and subtraction problems (also on a word identification task). Whereas the good students and perfectionists had equally superior knowledge of the arithmetic problems, the perfectionists apparently adopted a considerably higher threshold for stating a retrieved answer than was adopted by the good students. Although one consequence of this higher threshold was relatively slow retrieval performance, this subgroup also demonstrated extremely high accuracy on retrieval trials, compared to the other two groups.[4]

[4.]A similar finding was reported by Hamann and Ashcraft (1985), whose fourth grade sample consisted of equal numbers of low, intermediate, and high ability students. The problem-size effect, for addition problems with sums up to 30, was 1500 msec for the low ability group, 1200 msec for the intermediate, and 800 msec for the high group. These effects, as well as the absolute levels of RTs, indicated that the low ability fourth graders were relying on the same kinds of strategies as our first grade group, and that the high ability fourth graders were quite similar to our seventh graders. Related work by Geary and Burlingham-DuBree (1989) has shown a relationship between strategy choice and children's scores on mathematics subtests of the WISC.

In a rather different kind of investigation, Faust (1988; see also Ashcraft & Faust, 1988) examined adults' performance as a function of assessed levels of mathematics anxiety. Groups that were higher in measured anxiety tended to perform more slowly on the basic addition facts, although all groups were best described by the straightforward retrieval strategy. Performance to false problems, however, as well as performance to more complex addition problems, showed group differences that appeared to depend on a decision-stage processing strategy. All subjects were slow, as predicted, on the most difficult false problems, those stating an answer very close to the correct value (e.g., $7 + 8 = 16$); interestingly, the two highest anxiety groups were especially slow on these problems. When the stated answer was wrong by an extreme amount (e.g., $7 + 8 = 38$), however, the groups differed substantially. The low anxious subjects were extremely rapid and accurate on these problems (mean RT was approximately 800 msec, with a 1% error rate). High anxious subjects were somewhat slower (950 msec) but considerably more inaccurate (10%) in this condition.

Previous research on this effect (e.g., Ashcraft & Stazyk, 1981) has suggested that subjects rely on a magnitude estimation process in such situations, whereby they can quickly reject answers that fall well outside of an estimated range. The overall pattern of results in Faust's study suggests that high mathematics-anxious subjects either lack this strategy, or that they neglect its outcome during processing.

Direct Manipulation of Strategies

A second approach involves manipulating subjects' processing strategies directly, rather than relying on after-the-fact techniques to identify which strategies operated on which trials. This approach, almost of necessity, dictates that we test somewhat more difficult problems than the basic arithmetic facts. That is, we must examine problem-solving performance in situations where processing does not already rely on well known and automatic strategies (e.g., Charness & Campbell, 1988, taught an algorithm for squaring numbers in the range 1 to 99).

As an example, Ashcraft, Koshmider, Roemer, and Faust (1985) reported the results of a pilot study on the effects of strategy instruction and practice (a full-scale replication of this study is in progress). We presented subjects with difficult multiplication problems, from $12 \times 7 = 84$ up to $28 \times 16 = 448$, in an eight-session experiment. Three treatment conditions were evaluated, one that stressed memorization of the answers, one that urged application of a rule, and one with no specific instructions. Daily drill sessions, with required verbalization, reinforced the manipulation of instructions; the "memorize" subjects were drilled with flashcards, and the "rule" subjects had to verbalize the application of the rule to the same flashcard problems. (The rule we taught was a variation on the decomposition strategy. For problems such as 12 × 7, the rule was to break the 12 into 10 and 2, multiply 10 × 7 and 2 × 7, then add the two values. For 28 × 16, the rule was to multiply 30 × 16, then subtract the solution to 2 × 16.)

Aside from the predictable effects of problem size, we found that subjects instructed to memorize the answers achieved very rapid performance by the end of the eight sessions; mean RT was less than 3 seconds at all problem sizes, and errors dropped from about 20% on pretest to 10% on posttest. Their speed advantage also generalized to a similar set of problems that had not been drilled during daily practice (e.g., 28 × 16 appeared in daily practice, but 28 × 15 appeared only as a "transfer" problem on the posttest). In dramatic contrast, subjects who were taught the decomposition rule showed far less benefit from practice, and never achieved the speed or accuracy demonstrated by the "memorize" or control groups; in the final session, large problems such as 28 × 16 = 448 still required nearly 10 seconds, and error rates increased from about 20% on pretest to nearly 30% on posttest. Furthermore, there was no evidence in the RTs of any generalization effect to the set of "transfer" problems. These group differences were particularly striking because the daily practice sessions had presented the same problems to all subjects. Thus, manipulating the processing strategy led to marked group differences in processing speed and accuracy (and, for that matter, in the pattern of practice effects).

Siegler (1987) suggested that "the most basic approach [in strategy use research] is to perform a task analysis, imagine possible strategies for performing the task, and examine the raw data to see if subsets fit different strategies" (p. 261). The present suggestion goes one step further: The possible strategies that are identified in the task analysis can sometimes be manipulated directly by means of instructions. The data can then be examined (and compared to an uninstructed control group) for evidence of strategy compliance and effectiveness.

Complex Arithmetic and Mathematics

As implied in the previous section, the future of research on strategy use in children's arithmetic lies, at least in part, in tests of more complex arithmetic and mathematics situations. Given that retrieval of the basic facts becomes the norm, and that such retrieval becomes largely automatic, a shift in focus to more complex arithmetic processes would seem to be called for.

Two other reasons for such a shift may be stated as well. First, because basic counting and simple addition processes have been rather extensively investigated, further research efforts along those lines may yield relatively few new insights. A possible exception to this advice, notice, involves studies such as Siegler's (1988a) and Faust's (1988), where differences among defined subgroups may stand out in bolder relief when well known arithmetic tasks are used. Second, as a variety of reports (e.g., the recent national assessment of mathematics achievement by Dossey, Mullis, Lindquist, & Chambers, 1988) indicate there is a critical need in this country for research on higher mathematics performance. Our current insights, models, and techniques of investigation seem particularly well suited for studying what older children learn (or don't learn) about more complex arithmetic and mathematics.

Of course, a strong tradition of problem-solving research already exists for topics such as physics and geometry (e.g., Larkin, McDermott, Simon, & Simon, 1980), often relying heavily on verbal protocol methods. The present suggestion, however, is to extend our reach to more complex mathematics situations while maintaining continuity with the existing literature in terms of research methods and theoretical models. Putting it bluntly, we need not abandon our time and accuracy measures as we attempt to study more complex strategies (although combining these with interview and verbal protocol methods is probably wise, especially when a strategy or skill is being acquired and mastered).

As a brief example, Ashcraft and Miller (1983) used a technique for testing different solution "paths" in complex mathematical reasoning. We presented algebralike problems, such as $2 + (4 + 3) =$ and $5 (4 \times 9) =$, with one of three kinds of answers, either the equivalent expression [e.g., $5 (4 \times 9) = 5 (4 \times 9)$], the final answer [e.g., $5 (4 \times 9) = 180$], or an intermediate answer [e.g., $5 (4 \times 9) = 5 \times 36$]. Subjects were timed as they responded either true of false. The purpose of this design, of course, was to determine whether the stated intermediate answer was on the solution path normally taken when the entire problem is solved. This conclusion would be supported when RT to the intermediate solution was less than RT in the final answer condition. If the intermediate answer took longer to verify than the final answer, then this would be evidence that the normal solution path did not pass through the problem state represented by the intermediate answer.

When the answer on the right side of the equation was identical to the problem on the left, RTs averaged about 2 seconds, and did not vary as a function of the size of the numbers or the manipulation of operations (adding or multiplying either inside or outside of the parentheses). When the final answer was stated on the right, RT varied both as a function of problem size and arithmetic operation.

The key condition was the intermediate answer condition. Some of these trials expressed an intermediate solution achieved by solving the parenthetical expression first, and these trials were generally faster than the corresponding final answer trials. For example, the problem $5 + (4 \times 9) = 5 + 36$ required 3.5 seconds; when 41 was the stated answer, RT averaged 4.3 seconds. Other problems stated intermediate solutions that violated the "parenthesis first" rule, and these were usually considerably slower than the corresponding final answer trials. For example, $5 (4 + 9) = 20 + 45$ required 7 seconds, compared with 6 seconds when the stated answer was 65; presumably, 5×13 was on the solution path, but $20 + 45$ was not. This slowing even characterized intermediate answers that would be expected to be far simpler to compute than the "parenthesis first" values. For instance, intuition suggests that $5 (4 \times 9)$ should be considerably easier to solve mentally by the 20×9 path. Yet our data show that the "parenthesis first" answer of 5×36 (RT = 3.5 seconds) was on the path to the final answer of 180 (RT = 6.5 seconds).

The mathematics in this situation pitted the distributive law of multiplication against the "parenthesis first" strategy; with few exceptions, the "parenthesis first" strategy won. The more general point being illustrated is that many of the more complex and sophisticated processing strategies for higher mathematics may be amenable to investigation with current research tasks and methods. An additional benefit here is that we can chart the developmental course of such strategies quite carefully, first because we can determine when instruction begins on these rules, and second because there is little reason to expect children to invent this knowledge prior to formal instruction.

Lest this last point be misunderstood, let me clarify my references to "more complex" or "higher" mathematics. I am not suggesting that the future of this research area necessarily lies in assessments of processing strategies in, say, trigonometry or calculus. The evidence, instead, is that mathematics achievement of American students beyond a fairly basic level is distressingly low (Dossey et al., 1988). For example, only 51% of 17-year-olds performed adequately on "Moderately Complex Procedures and Reasoning" (sample item: Which of the following is true about 87% of 10? It is greater than, less than, or equal to 10, Can't tell, or I don't know). And only 6.4% of the

17-year-olds performed the "Multi-step Problem Solving and Algebra" adequately (sample item: The square root of 17 is between which of the following pairs of numbers? 4 and 5, 8 and 9, 16 and 18, 288 and 290, I don't know). Our current methods are clearly sufficient to examine processing in such situations.

CONCLUSION

The construct of a "strategy" has changed substantially in recent years, from its original connotation, a rehearsal device, to its present connotation, any mental process or procedure in the stream of information-processing activities that serves a goal-related purpose. The research area of mental arithmetic has participated fully in this change of connotation, and as I have argued, provides particularly good illustrations of many of those changes.

The most fundamental change in connotation appears to involve the notion of deliberate versus automatic execution of the strategy. When viewed from the more traditional perspective of metacognition, strategy use provides evidence that people are aware of their cognitive systems, that they monitor their processing, and that they alter their processing when performance is less than adequate. The commonly observed facts of rehearsal fit well into this metacognitive framework; young children fail to generate rehearsal strategies spontaneously, whereas older children are increasingly able to do this in an effective and tailored way.

This metacognitive and deliberate view of strategies does not match the state of affairs in mental arithmetic research. This mismatch is partly due to the classification of retrieval as a bona fide strategy. The evidence is that retrieval is a very early mechanism, far earlier than spontaneous rehearsal, with possibly default or innate, as opposed to deliberate, status. But even if we disregard retrieval, the evidence still forces us to reevaluate young children's abilities to generate useful strategies. Siegler and Robinson's (1982) kindergartners exhibited three deliberate strategies aside from retrieval, all based on counting skill; Siegler's (1987) first and second graders also used a decomposition strategy, based not on counting but on knowledge of related facts. Thus, the picture that emerges in mental arithmetic research is that children are considerably more flexible at generating and using strategies than formerly believed, that they demonstrate this flexibility at much younger ages, and that the choice among strategies need not be considered a deliberate, metacognitive act.

If we restrict our view to the current literature on simple arithmetic, then we find that retrieval becomes more dominant, and more automatic, in children's strategic repertoires; in a sense, its increasing effectiveness "crowds out" the more deliberate, reconstructive strategies. One conclusion that might be drawn from this—probably mistaken—is that multiple strategies *decrease* as children grow older, that their processing becomes more homogenous rather than more flexible and varied. I think this appears to be the case only because we have yet to investigate the richer domains of complex arithmetic and mathematics. Across the broader range of knowledge and skills that needs to be tested, we should see an increase in the number of strategies available and clarification of the role of basic retrieval as a component of that performance. Aside from their basic value to the study of cognitive development, such investigations also have the potential to improve mathematics education and achievement.

ACKNOWLEDGMENTS

Some of the research reported in this chapter was supported in part by National Science Foundation grant SED-8021521. I would like to thank Machelle McNeal and G. A. Radvansky for their helpful comments during the drafting of this chapter. Mailing address: Department of Psychology, Cleveland State University, Cleveland, Ohio, 44115. BITNET: r0599@CSUOHIO

REFERENCES

Anderson, J. R. (1983). *The architecture of cognition*. Cambridge, MA: Harvard University Press.

Ashcraft, M. H. (1982). The development of mental arithmetic: A chronometric approach. *Developmental Review, 2*, 213–236.

Ashcraft, M. H. (1987). Children's knowledge of simple arithmetic: A developmental model and simulation. In J. Bisanz, C. J. Brainerd, & R. Kail (Eds.), *Formal methods in developmental psychology: Progress in cognitive development research* (pp. 302–338). New York: Springer–Verlag.

Ashcraft, M. H., & Battaglia, J. (1978). Cognitive arithmetic: Evidence for retrieval and decision processes in mental addition. *Journal of Experimental Psychology: Human Learning and Memory, 4*, 527–538.

Ashcraft, M. H., & Faust, M. W. (1988). *Mathematics anxiety and mental arithmetic performance: A preliminary investigation*. Manuscript submitted for publication.

Ashcraft, M. H., & Fierman, B. A. (1982). Mental addition in third, fourth, and sixth graders. *Journal of Experimental Child Psychology, 33*, 216–234.

Ashcraft, M. H., Fierman, B. A., & Bartolotta, R. (1984). The production and verification tasks in mental addition: An empirical comparison. *Developmental Review, 4*, 157–170.

Ashcraft, M. H., & Hamann, M. S. (1981, November). *Children's strategies for solving simple and complex addition problems.* Paper presented at the meetings of the Psychonomic Society, Philadelphia.

Ashcraft, M. H. & Kellas, G. (1974). Organization in normal and retarded children: Temporal aspects of storage and retrieval. *Journal of Experimental Psychology, 103,* 502–508.

Ashcraft, M. H., Koshmider, J. W. III, Roemer, J. M., & Faust, M. (1985, November). *Automaticity and practice in mental arithmetic.* Paper presented at the meeting of the Psychonomic Society, Boston.

Ashcraft, M. H., & Miller, W. R. (1983, November). *The processing of complex arithmetic expressions.* Paper presented at the meeting of the Psychonomic Society, San Diego.

Ashcraft, M. H., & Stazyk, E. H. (1981). Mental addition: A test of three verification models. *Memory & Cognition, 9,* 185–196.

Baroody, A. J. (1983). The development of procedural knowledge: An alternative explanation for chronometric trends of mental arithmetic. *Developmental Review, 3,* 225–230.

Bower, G. H. (1970). Analysis of a mnemonic device. *American Scientist, 58,* 496–510.

Browne, C. E. (1906). The psychology of the simple arithmetical processes: A study of certain habits of attention and association. *American Journal of Psychology, 17,* 2–37.

Campbell, J.I.D. (1987). Production, verification, and priming of multiplication facts. *Memory & Cognition, 15,* 349–364.

Campbell, J.I.D, & Graham, D. J. (1985). Mental multiplication skill: Structure, process, and acquisition. *Canadian Journal of Psychology, 39,* 338–366.

Charness, N., & Campbell, J.I.D. (1988). Acquiring skill at mental calculation in adulthood: A task decomposition. *Journal of Experimental Psychology: General, 117,* 115–129.

Dossey, J. A., Mullis, I.V.S., Lindquist, M. M., & Chambers, D. L. (1988). *The mathematics report card: Are we measuring up?* Princeton, NJ: Educational Testing Service.

Ericsson, K. A., & Simon, H. A. (1980). Verbal reports as data. *Psychological Review, 87,* 215–251.

Faust, M. W. (1988). *Arithmetic performance as a function of mathematics anxiety: An in-depth analysis of simple and complex addition problems.* Unpublished master's thesis, Cleveland State University, Cleveland, OH.

Flavell, J. H. (1970). Developmental studies of mediated memory. In H. W. Reese & L. P. Lipsett (Eds.), *Advances in child development and behavior* (Vol. 5, pp. 181–211). New York: Academic Press.

Fuson, K. C. (1982). An analysis of the counting-on solution procedure in addition. In T. P. Carpenter, J. M. Moser, & T. A. Romberg (Eds.), *Addition and subtraction: A cognitive perspective* (pp. 67–82). Hillsdale, NJ: Lawrence Erlbaum Associates.

Fuson, K. C. (1988). *Children's counting and concepts of number.* New York: Springer-Verlag.

Geary, D. C., & Burlingham-DuBree, M. (1989). External validation of the strategy choice model for addition. *Journal of Experimental Child Psychology, 47,* 175–192.

Gelman, R., & Gallistel, C. R. (1978). *The child's understanding of number.* Cambridge, MA: Harvard University Press.

Ginsburg, H. (1977). *Children's arithmetic: The learning process.* New York: Van Nostrand.

Groen, G. J., & Parkman, J. M. (1972). A chronometric analysis of simple addition. *Psychological Review, 79,* 329–343.

Hamann, M. S., & Ashcraft, M. H. (1985). Simple and complex mental addition across development. *Journal of Experimental Child Psychology, 40,* 49–72.

Hamann, M. S., & Ashcraft, M. H. (1986). Textbook presentations of the basic addition facts. *Cognition and Instruction, 3,* 173–192.

Kail, R. (1986). Sources of age differences in speed of processing. *Child Development, 57,* 969–987.

Kaye, D. B. (1986). The development of mathematical cognition. *Cognitive Development, 1,* 157–170.

Kellas, G., Ashcraft, M. H., & Johnson, N. S. (1973). Rehearsal processes in the short-term memory performance of mildly retarded adolescents. *American Journal of Mental Deficiency, 77,* 670–679.

Kellas, G., Ashcraft, M. H., Johnson, N. S., & Needham, S. (1973). Temporal aspects of storage and retrieval in free recall of categorized lists. *Journal of Verbal Learning and Verbal Behavior, 12,* 499–511.

Kellas, G., McCauley, C., & McFarland, C. E., Jr. (1975a). Developmental aspects of storage and retrieval. *Journal of Experimental Child Psychology, 19,* 51–62.

Kellas, G., McCauley, C., & McFarland, C. E., Jr. (1975b). Reexamination of externalized rehearsal. *Journal of Experimental Psychology: Human Learning and Memory, 104,* 84–90.

Koshmider, J. W. III, & Ashcraft, M. H. (1988). *Development of children's mental multiplication skills.* Unpublished manuscript.

Larkin, J., McDermott, J., Simon, D. P., & Simon, H. A. (1980). Expert and novice performance in solving physics problems. *Science, 208,* 1335–1342.

LeFevre, J. A., Bisanz, J., & Mrkonjic, L. (1988). Cognitive arithmetic: Evidence for obligatory activation of arithmetic facts. *Memory & Cognition, 16,* 45–53.

Miller, K. F., Perlmutter, M., & Keating, D. (1984). Cognitive arithmetic: Comparison of operations. *Journal of Experimental Psychology: Learning, Memory, and Cognition, 10,* 46–60.

Nisbett, R. E., & Wilson, T. D. (1977). Telling more than we can know: Verbal reports on mental processes. *Psychological Review, 84,* 231–259.

Parkman, J. M. (1972). Temporal aspects of simple multiplication and comparison. *Journal of Experimental Psychology, 95,* 437–444.

Parkman, J. M., & Groen, G. J. (1971). Temporal aspects of simple addition and comparison. *Journal of Experimental Psychology, 89,* 335–342.

Posner, M. I., & Snyder, C.R.R. (1975). Facilitation and inhibition in the processing of signals. In P.M.A. Rabbitt & S. Dornic (Eds.), *Attention and Performance V* (pp. 669–682). New York: Academic Press.

Resnick, L. B., & Ford, W. W. (1981). *The psychology of mathematics for instruction.* Hillsdale, NJ: Lawrence Erlbaum Associates.

Rundus, D. (1971). Analysis of rehearsal processes in free recall. *Journal of Experimental Psychology, 89,* 63–77.

Shiffrin, R. M., & Schneider, W. (1977). Controlled and automatic human information processing: II. Perceptual learning, automatic attending, and a general theory. *Psychological Review, 84,* 127–190.

Siegler, R. S. (1987). The perils of averaging data over strategies: An example from children's addition. *Journal of Experimental Psychology: General, 116,* 250–264.

Siegler, R. S. (1988a). Individual differences in strategy choices: Good students, not-so-good students, and perfectionists. *Child Development, 59,* 833–851.

Siegler, R. S. (1988b). Strategy choice procedures and the development of multiplication skill. *Journal of Experimental Psychology: General, 117,* 258–275.

Siegler, R. S., & Robinson, M. (1982). The development of numerical understandings. In H. Reese & L. P. Lipsitt (Eds.), *Advances in child development and behavior* (Vol. 16, pp. 241–312). New York: Academic Press.

Siegler, R. S., & Shrager, J. (1984). A model of strategy choice. In C. Sophian (Ed.), *Origins of cognitive skills* (pp. 229–293). Hillsdale, NJ: Lawrence Erlbaum Associates.

Stazyk, E. H., Ashcraft, M. H., & Hamann, M. S. (1982). A network approach to simple multiplication. *Journal of Experimental Psychology: Learning, Memory, and Cognition, 8,* 320–335.

Thorndike, E. L. (1922). *The psychology of arithmetic.* New York: MacMillan.

Wheeler, L. R. (1939). A comparative study of the difficulty of the 100 addition combinations. *Journal of Genetic Psychology, 54,* 295–312.

Woods, S. S., Resnick, L. B., & Groen, G. J. (1975). An experimental test of five process models for subtraction. *Journal of Educational Psychology, 67,* 17–21.

CHAPTER 8

Strategic and Nonstrategic Processing in the Development of Mathematical Cognition

Jeffrey Bisanz
University of Alberta

Jo-Anne LeFevre
Carleton University

The concept of strategy is important for describing and understanding cognitive processing because it pertains to aspects of cognition that are flexible, goal directed, and often oriented toward efficiency (Underwood, 1978). Consider a 5-year-old child who decides to count on his or her fingers to calculate the sum for a difficult arithmetic problem. In observing the child's actions, we probably would conclude that his or her knowledge of arithmetic has helped to select an approach to this particular problem that will maximize the probability of success. A few years later, after much practice with arithmetic problems, the child might obtain the answer to the same problem very quickly and with no obvious external cues or actions, in much the same way as recalling his or her middle name. We would conclude that the child's solution process has changed, and we could attempt to identify precisely what the child did to obtain an answer.

An investigation of this sort can provide insights about the development of arithmetic skill and, more generally, about how flexible, goal-oriented aspects of information processing change with development. Certainly research designed to identify the solution methods used by children at different ages or at different levels of skill acquisition has been central to the study of cognitive development for over two decades and will continue to be important. Does this type of research, however, inform us about the development of strategies?

Examination of past research on strategies reveals two characteristics that are problematic. First, definitions of strategy vary widely (see, e.g., Pressley, Forrest-Pressley, Elliot-Faust, & Miller, 1985). In many studies and reviews, *strategy* is not defined at all, as if the meaning were self-evident. In others, *strategy* refers to any procedure or series of operations used to accomplish a task. In still others, *strategy* is defined in terms that are ambiguous, difficult to operationalize, or contentious. The result is semantic chaos. For example, many researchers define *strategy* in terms of voluntary initiation, deliberateness, or conscious control, whereas others describe high levels of strategic skill in terms of the *absence* of these characteristics!

The second problem is that *strategies* are often described as if they were isolated processes, and consequently the relation between a particular strategy and other aspects of information processing is not always clear. Cumulative rehearsal, for example, is an effective mnemonic device under some conditions, and it has been studied intensively (e.g., Kail, 1984). Nevertheless, attempts to describe possible relations between rehearsal and the specific contents of semantic memory, internal decision processes, and other processes are rare. Most researchers would agree that cognitive performance is best understood in terms of complex interactions among a variety of processes and information structures, but research on the development of strategies rarely reflects this view.

In this chapter we illustrate these problems by examining recent research and theories on cognitive processing in a single content domain, mental arithmetic. Research in this domain is particularly useful for considering concepts of strategy and strategy development because many of the empirical phenomena have been specified clearly and the types of knowledge involved have been described fairly well (Ashcraft, 1982; Campbell, 1987a, 1987b; Campbell & Graham, 1985; Fuson, 1982; Gelman & Gallistel, 1978; Siegler, 1987, 1988a, 1988b, 1989). Moreover, detailed information-processing models exist (Ashcraft, 1983, 1987; Siegler & Shrager, 1984) in a form that allows us to consider likely interactions between processes and information structures. Our contention is that the specificity of these models provides a meaningful context for defining strategy in a useful and unambiguous way.

Because our initial goal is to describe an integrative, information-processing account of metal arithmetic, our review of recent research and theories is very selective. First, we outline three types of knowledge that are used to solve arithmetic problems: procedural knowledge, factual knowledge, and conceptual knowledge. Next, we describe the ways in which procedural and factual knowledge interact to generate answers to arithmetic problems, we outline some developmental characteristics of this interaction, and we provide some ideas about how conceptual knowledge might become involved in this interaction. Throughout these sections we avoid using the term *strategy*, so as not to prejudice a judgment about the optimal definition for the term.

Finally, we settle on a definition of *strategy* and identify some implications for the study of strategic development. We conclude that research on development of strategies, as we define them, is barely under way in the study of mental arithmetic, and we indicate some directions that we believe are important for future research.

DEVELOPMENT OF MENTAL ARITHMETIC

Types of Arithmetic Knowledge

It is useful to distinguish three types of knowledge in the study of mental arithmetic: procedural, factual, and conceptual. *Procedures* are mental activities, or sequences of activities, that occur over time, accomplish a goal, and can be stored in memory. Procedures may be arranged hierarchically, in the sense that components of procedures may be procedures themselves. The operation of a procedure (its start and finish) may be discrete in principle, but in practice procedures may co-occur and interact, making them difficult to identify and measure as discrete entities.

Fortunately, solution procedures in arithmetic often can be inferred from the answers or explanations provided by children (e.g., Siegler, 1987), from patterns in solution latencies (e.g., Groen & Parkman, 1972), or from observations of certain physical correlates, such as the way in which children count on their fingers (e.g., Siegler & Shrager, 1984). A great deal of research has been devoted to describing the procedures individuals use to solve arithmetic problems. Consider, for example, the procedures used by young children to answer simple addition problems of the form $a + b$ (see Fuson, 1982; Houlihan & Ginsburg, 1981; Siegler, 1987). In some cases children simply *retrieve* the answer from memory, much as they would remember their own names.

In many cases, however, children construct or generate an answer. For instance, they may use a *count-all* (or *sum*) procedure, in which some fingers are counted and designated to represent a, others are counted and designated to represent b, and all the designated fingers are counted to obtain the sum. Alternatively, children may use a *count-on* procedure, in which they start counting with a and then increment b times, thus eliminating the need to count the fingers representing *a*. A particularly efficient version of the count-on procedure is the *min* procedure, in which the child always counts on from the larger of the two addends, thus minimizing the number of increments required. *Decomposition* is a more sophisticated procedure in which a problem is transformed into an easier version before being solved (e.g., 7 + 9 is transformed to 7 + 10 − 1). More complex procedures in the domain of arithmetic include multiplication of fractions and decimal addition (Hiebert & Wearne, 1985).

Of particular relevance to understanding cognitive development is research on the ways in which procedures change. For example, Secada, Fuson, and Hall (1983) have examined the transition from the count-all procedure to the count-on procedure, Groen and Resnick (1977) have investigated acquisition of the *min* procedure, and Ashcraft and Fierman (1982) have studied the change from counting-based procedures to retrieval.

Factual knowledge consists of memorized information about arithmetic relations among numbers (e.g., 2 + 2 = 4 or 3 × 9 = 27). Knowledge of arithmetic facts usually improves with development and, in combination with procedural knowledge, forms the core of the arithmetic knowledge that children typically are expected to acquire. Facts are accessed only by retrieval, a procedure that involves relatively direct and rapid access to memory representations.

Conceptual knowledge is somewhat more difficult to define than factual or procedural knowledge. Hiebert and Lefevre (1986), for example, defined conceptual knowledge as "knowledge that is rich in relationships. It can be thought of as a connected web of knowledge, a network in which the linking relationships are as prominent as the discrete pieces of information" (p. 3). Baroody and Ginsburg (1986) defined *meaningful* (conceptual) knowledge as "semantic knowledge with implicit or explicit knowledge of concepts or principles" (p. 75), a definition that would include principles such as associativity and commutativity, the part–whole schema (Riley, Greeno, & Heller, 1983), and knowledge about the underlying decimal structure of arithmetic (Resnick, 1983).

These notions of conceptual knowledge are intuitively appealing but difficult to operationalize, especially without detailed representations of the webs, links, concepts, or principles. Silver (1986) suggested that the relations between conceptual and procedural knowledge are of central importance. More specifically, he noted that successful execution of a particular procedure is often what allows the inference that a person possesses conceptual knowledge. In accord with this view and with that of Baroody and Ginsburg (1986), we define conceptual knowledge in arithmetic as the principles that reflect the underlying structure of mathematics and that can be inferred from the selective use of effective procedures under conditions where those principles apply.

Silver's (1986) point about the importance of relations among different types of knowledge deserves emphasis. In many respects, the three types of arithmetic knowledge have been treated as if they are completely independent. In developmental research the focus on procedures is pervasive and the development of mental arithmetic has been, until recently, very nearly synonymous with the development of solution procedures. Educational researchers have been more interested in conceptual knowledge, and teachers often seem to be especially concerned with factual knowledge. Few researchers have studied interactions among the three types of knowledge in mental arithmetic. In the following sections we describe some recent research that highlights the importance of these interactions for understanding developmental changes in arithmetic and, more generally, the nature of strategies.

Interactions Between Procedural and Factual Knowledge

Research on the development of procedures in mental arithmetic has led to two general conclusions that are of particular interest for present purposes. First, procedures change dramatically as children become more skilled. In particular, the trend is from use of counting-based procedures (e.g., count-all, count-on, min) in young children to use of retrieval in older children and adults (Ashcraft, 1982; Achcraft & Fierman, 1982). Second, even young children use a variety of procedures, counting based and retrieval, in an adaptive manner that depends on task demands and on the availability of factual knowledge (Siegler, 1987; Siegler & Shrager, 1984).

This second conclusion has three interesting implications for understanding the development of procedures. One is that age and level of development, where level is defined in terms of a single procedure, do not necessarily proceed jointly in a lockstep manner (Siegler, 1989). In other words, it is simplistic and misleading to conclude that children in level n use procedure x exclusively, that children in level n + 1 use y, and so on. Another implication is that if children are capable of using a wide variety of procedures and use them in predictable, nonrandom ways, then understanding the process by which procedures are selected becomes crucial to understanding mental arithmetic and its development (Siegler & Shrager, 1984). Finally, if selection of a procedure depends in part on the state of a child's factual knowledge, then the interaction between these two types of knowledge must be understood.

Current views about the interaction between procedural and factual knowledge are represented most clearly in two relatively detailed theories, one by Ashcraft (1983, 1987) and the other by Siegler (1986, 1989; Siegler & Shrager, 1984). Each theory was developed to account for certain behavioral data, each includes an explanation of how solution processes change with age, and each has been formalized as a computer simulation to determine whether the proposed components of solution provide a reasonable fit to existing data. The foci of the two theories are overlapping but not identical, and several aspects of the two theories are complementary. Siegler's theory is focused on the selection of procedures, and we describe it first because it provides a general framework for understanding arithmetic processes. Ashcraft's theory contains more explicit hypotheses about retrieval, a procedure that is fundamental to both models, and we describe those hypotheses and some empirical research on retrieval second. Finally, we describe the nature of development as it is represented in these theories.

Selection of Procedures

In Siegler's model, solution of arithmetic problems is considered to be a two-phase process. In the first phase, an individual attempts to retrieve an answer to a problem directly from his or her knowledge base of arithmetic facts. If that attempt fails, then he or she proceeds to a second phase in which a slower, backup procedure, such as the *min* procedure, is used to generate or construct an answer. As described later, feedback concerning the answer influences a person's knowledge of arithmetic facts and, consequently, the selection of procedures on subsequent occasions.

The success or failure of the retrieval phase depends to a large extent on knowledge of arithmetic facts. In characterizing this type of knowledge, Siegler made three assumptions. First, knowledge about arithmetic facts is assumed to be represented mentally in terms of associative strengths between specific problems and various answer alternatives. In an experienced older child or adult, for example, 4 + 5 may be strongly associated with 9 but only weakly associated with other numbers, such as 6 or 10. In a younger child, however, the associations between 4 + 5 and possible answers 6, 9, and 10 all may be approximately equal. Second, retrieval is assumed to be probabilistic, so that even weakly associated answers may be retrieved on some occasions. Third, the probability of retrieving a particular answer is assumed to be directly related to the associative strength between that answer and the presented problem.

Given these assumptions, knowledge of arithmetic facts can be represented in terms of the probabilities of retrieving various answer alternatives. For example, the numbers in Table 8.1 can be considered as a representation of young children's knowledge about arithmetic facts. Each associative strength in the table was estimated from the performance of 4-year-olds who were instructed to answer each problem within a strict time limit (approximately 4 seconds) and without the use of overt backup procedures (Siegler & Robinson, 1982; Siegler & Shrager, 1984). Under these conditions, for example, children who were presented with 4 + 5 responded with 9 on only 18% of all trials, and with 7 on 9% of all trials. Thus 4 + 5 is weakly associated with 9 and even more weakly associated with 7.

An important property of this form of representation is that associative strengths may vary from problem to problem in terms of *peakedness*. In the left panel of Fig. 8.1, for example, the distribution of associative strengths is peaked in the sense that most of the strength related to 5 + 1 is concentrated on a single answer, 6. In contrast, the distribution of associative strengths related to 4 + 5 is relatively flat in that several answers are associated weakly and at similar levels.

As just noted, the general process that operates on this representation of factual knowledge consists of two general phases. First, the individual encodes the addends of an addition problem and attempts

TABLE 8.1   Associative Strengths for Selected Combinations of Problems and Possible Answers for 4-Year-Olds

Problem	Answer									
	2	3	4	5	6	7	8	9	10	Other
4 + 1	.04	.02	.09	.68	.02	.02	.07			.07
4 + 2	.07	.09		.20	.36	.13	.07		.02	.07
4 + 3		.05	.18	.09	.09	.38	.09		.02	.11
4 + 4		.02	.02	.29	.07	.07	.34		.04	.17
4 + 5			.04	.09	.16	.09	.11	.18	.11	.24
5 + 1	.04		.04	.07	.71	.04	.04		.04	.04
5 + 2	.05	.20	.02	.18	.27	.25	.02		.02	
5 + 3	.02	.11	.09	.18	.05	.16	.23		.05	.11
5 + 4			.11	.21	.16	.05	.11	.16	.04	.16
5 + 5				.07	.25	.11	.02	.04	.34	.19

Note. Values are from "Strategy Choices in Addition and Subtraction: How Do Children Know What to Do?" by R. S. Siegler and J. Shrager, 1984, *Origins of Cognitive Skills* (p. 240). Hillsdale, NJ: Lawrence Erlbaum Associates.

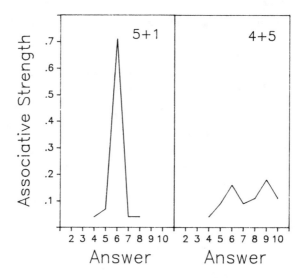

FIG. 8.1.   An example of a relatively peaked distribution (left panel) and a relatively flat distribution (right panel) of associative strengths.

to retrieve an answer. If the associative strength of the retrieved answer exceeds a threshold called the *confidence criterion,* then the answer is stated. If the retrieved answer does not exceed the confidence criterion, then the retrieval operation will be repeated until an answer that exceeds the criterion is retrieved or until a limit is reached on the number of retrievals or the time spent retrieving. If retrieval is unsuccessful, then a second phase is initiated in which one of a series of backup procedures is invoked to generate an answer. Given the distributions of associative strengths depicted in Figure 8.1 and a confidence criterion of .25, a young child who attempts to solve 5 + 1 would be likely to retrieve and state the correct answer without the aid of a backup procedure. On the problem 4 + 5, however, the same child would have to use a backup procedure, such as one of the counting-based routines.

This model accounts for a variety of empirical data, including correlations among accuracy rates, solution latencies, and use of retrieval and backup procedures. For example, Siegler and Shrager (1984) found that overall error rates correlated highly (.91) across problems with the frequency of using overt backup procedures. It is tempting to explain this correlation by assuming that children make errors while executing backup procedures, perhaps due to miscounting. Thus the more frequently a backup procedure is used on a problem, the higher the error rate should be. The model provides a basis for a more subtle alternative, however. According to the model, the distribution of associative strengths directly influences both the frequency of backup trials and the error rates on retrieval trials; both variables depend on the peakedness of the distributions. Thus these two variables should be highly correlated, and indeed they were (.92). In contrast, the error rate on backup trials depends on other factors (such as the accuracy of counting), and so the correlation between it and frequency of backup trials should be lower. In fact, the correlation was significantly lower (.38). Moreover, when Siegler and Shrager examined performance on individual problems, they found that children were more accurate when backup procedures were used than when retrieval was used on 24 of 25 problems.

One limitation of Siegler's model is that, although it accounts for the use of retrieval versus backup procedures, it does not effectively address the issue of how one of several backup procedures is selected. Recently Siegler has revised the model to incorporate a more general mechanism for selection of procedures (Siegler, 1989; Siegler & Jenkins, 1989). In the revised model, problems are associated, in varying degress of strength, with specific procedures as well as with specific answers. According to this model, a person first attempts to retrieve a solution procedure. The success of this attempt depends on the distribution of associative strengths between problems and procedures, as well as the confidence criterion. If implementation of the selected procedure fails to yield an answer, then processing returns to the mechanism for selecting procedures until another procedure is chosen. Describing the details of this new model is beyond the scope of this chapter, but it is important to note that the same sorts of mechanisms proposed in the old model have been maintained in the new model in a way that increases its power and flexibility.

The Process of Retrieval

In Siegler's model, retrieval is a fundamental and pervasive procedure: The results of retrieval may provide an answer or determine whether other procedures will be used. Siegler's theory, however, includes relatively few insights about the psychological representation of number facts or about the process by which number facts might be activated. Number facts are "represented" only in terms of probabilities, rather than in terms of more theoretical descriptors that pertain to the relations among numbers. Similarly, the processes by which numbers are linked to each other in real time are not specified clearly. Details of this type are not entirely necessary for Siegler's model to accomplish its main tasks effectively, but they are potentially important for a complete understanding of mental arithmetic and for linking research in this domain with theories and results in other areas of cognitive investigation (LeFevre, Bisanz, & Mrkonjic, 1988). Although Ashcraft (1982, 1983, 1987) has had less to say than Siegler about procedural knowledge and selection procedures, he has provided more specific hypotheses about representation of factual knowledge and the process of retrieval.

Ashcraft's initial studies were designed to examine the finding that solution latencies for simple addition problems generally increase as the magnitude of the addends increases. For example, 6 + 5 generally is solved more quickly than 6 + 7 (Miller, Perlmutter, & Keating, 1984). This finding, known as the problem-size effect, is robust and pervasive in research on mental arithmetic (Ashcraft, 1982; Groen & Parkman, 1972). The effect of problem size is easily understood in young children who use counting-based procedures to solve simple problems: Children must count more to solve problems with larger addends, and thus more time is required. For adults, solution latencies also increase with problem size, but the slope of the increase is very shallow.

Ashcraft (Ashcraft & Battaglia, 1978; Ashcraft & Fierman, 1982; Ashcraft & Stazyk, 1981) discovered that, for adults, increases in latency as a function of problem size were not entirely consistent with what would be expected if counting-based procedures were used. For children younger than 8 or 9 years, however, the problem-size effect appeared to correspond reasonably well to predictions based on counting procedures. (See, however, Siegler, 1987, for evidence that this conclusion is misleading.) Ashcraft also noted that adults' performance on mental arithmetic tasks resembled their performance on semantic memory tasks. For instance, adults sometimes exhibit a form of semantic confusion in mental arithmetic (Winkelman & Schmidt, 1974; Zbrodoff & Logan, 1986): They take longer to reject an equation that is incorrect as stated but that would be correct for another operation (e.g., $4 \times 3 = 7$) than to reject a more neutral, incorrect equation (e.g., $4 \times 3 = 10$). For these reasons, Ashcraft proposed that younger children primarily use counting-based procedures, whereas older children and adults primarily respond on the basis of retrieval from a semantic network of arithmetic facts (Ashcraft, 1982; Ashcraft & Fierman, 1982).

According to Ashcraft (1983, 1987), numbers are represented as nodes in a network of associative links. When the addends of a problem are encoded, activation spreads from these nodes to related nodes. The amount of activation at any particular node depends on a number of factors, but most importantly on the "strength" of the association between that node and the addend nodes. During a single act of retrieval, activation spreads throughout the network. When the process of retrieval is completed, one node will be more activated than all the others. If the activation level of that node exceeds a certain threshold, it will be selected as the answer. If the activation level of the most activated node does not exceed threshold, then retrieval is unsuccessful and another procedure must be used.

Ashcraft (1987) tested the plausibility of his notions by developing a computer simulation that embodies his assumptions about the structure of the number network and the rules of spreading activation. The strengths of associations between problems and answers were estimated on the basis of adults' ratings of the subjective difficulties of simple arithmetic problems. The simulation was generally successful in predicting latencies and problem-size effects that are consistent with adults' data.

An important characteristic of retrieval, according to Ashcraft (1987), is that activation spreads *automatically* among nodes. The term *automatic* is often used to refer to processing that is fast, unconscious, unintentional, highly skilled, autonomous, and/or effortless (Hasher & Zachs, 1979; Logan, 1980; Posner & Snyder, 1975; Zbrodoff & Logan, 1986). In mental arithmetic, as in other domains (e.g., Logan, 1985), automatic processing is often viewed as an important aspect of, and possibly as a prerequisite for, highly skilled performance (Goldman, Pellegrino, & Mertz, 1988; Kaye, 1986; Resnick & Ford, 1981). Evidence for automaticity is critical for understanding mental arithmetic and its development.

A relatively direct test of whether retrieval in mental arithmetic is automatic in adults was provided by LeFevre et al. (1988). Individuals were presented with a cue consisting of two addends (e.g., 5 + 1). After a delay, the cue disappeared and a target digit was presented. Subjects had to indicate whether the target digit matched one of the cue digits by pressing an appropriate key as quickly and as accurately as possible. Notice that subjects had no reason to compute the sum of the cue digits in this task; mental arithmetic was unnecessary. LeFevre et al. reasoned that the cue digits are activated when they are encoded, and that subjects evaluate whether the target digit is one of the cues by comparing the target to the set of activated digits. When the cue 5 + 1 is followed by 5, for example, the nodes for 5 and 1 are activated, the target is compared to this set, and a match is found. When 5 + 1 is followed by the target 3, no match is found. When 5 + 1 is followed by its sum, 6, however, the matter may be more complicated. If activation spreads automatically to sums, then 6 will be at least partially activated at some point following encoding of the addends. When the target is compared with the set of activated digits, a match is possible, and the subject will either answer incorrectly or will perform additional processing to resolve the ambiguity. In the latter case, automatic computation of the sum will interfere with processing and will result in slower latencies.

As indicated in Fig. 8.2, LeFevre et al. (1988) found clear evidence of interference with very brief delays (stimulus onset asynchrony, or SOA) between cue and target. That is, responses were significantly slower when the target digit was the sum of the cue digits than when it was not directly related to the cue digits. Activation at such brief intervals usually is interpreted as being automatic in nature, whereas activation effects at longer intervals may be subject to intentional control (e.g., Neely, 1977). Thus the pattern in Fig. 8.2 is consistent with the view that activation requires a brief period of time to spread from addends to sums, and that this spread of activation is automatic. This conclusion has been confirmed more recently in priming studies by LeFevre, Pilon, Yu, and Bisanz (1989). Presentation of number pairs (i.e., primes) facilitated performance on a digit-identification task when the target was the sum of the initial pair. As in LeFevre et al. (1988), mental arithmetic was unnecessary in this task.

LeFevre and Bisanz (1987) conducted an exploratory study with 7- and 11-year-olds to determine whether retrieval of sums was an automatc procedure for children at these two age levels, using the digit-matching task developed by LeFevre et al. (1988). Results for the 11-year-olds were very similar to those for adults, but the data for

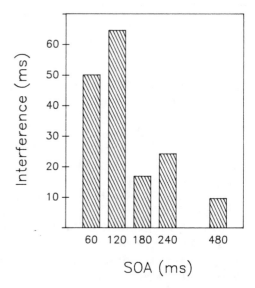

FIG. 8.2. Interference due to the computation of sums as a function of delay (stimulus onset asynchrony, or SOA, between cue and target). Interference is estimated by subtracting latencies for the neutral condition from latencies for the sum condition (see text). *Note.* Based on data from "Cognitive Arithmetic: Evidence for Obligatory Activation of Arithmetic Facts" by J. Le-Fevre, J. Bisanz, and L. Mrkonjic, 1988, *Memory and Cognition, 16*, p. 49.

7-year-olds were somewhat variable and difficult to interpret. Thus older children appear to retrieve sums to simple addition problems in an automatic fashion that is similar to adults, whereas the same conclusion cannot be supported for younger children.

This research on retrieval mechanisms should not be interpreted as implying that automatic spreading activation is the *sine qua non* of retrieval. Traditionally, retrieval has been defined as a combination of search and recognition processes, where search refers to any method of exploring memory to generate candidate answers on a recall task and recognition refers to the process of identifying the correct or best answer (Kintsch, 1970). Spreading activation may be one search mechanism, but it need not be the only one operating in mental arithmetic. Children may use a variety of mnemonic devices to help them find an answer to an arithmetic problem. For example, the 5-year-old son of one of the authors is an aficianado of anything automotive. When asked for the sum of 2 + 3, he thought for a few seconds and then answered correctly. He showed no signs of count-ing, and it was unlikely that he would have memorized the answer on previous occasions because he had not been asked many addition problems in the past. Bewildered, his father asked how he knew the answer. The boy replied that the family car held two people in front and three in back, and he knew very well that it held five people, so he knew that 2 + 3 was 5! Thus the answer appears to have been based on analogical reasoning from a related domain of knowledge. Spread-ing activation may have been involved, but clearly the links between addends and answer were not direct. To our knowledge, no research has been conducted on the mnemonics young children might use to learn and remember arithmetic facts.

To summarize, retrieval is a fundamental and pervasive procedure in mental arithmetic. For skilled individuals, retrieval may be accom-plished by means of automatic spreading activation, but other mech-anisms are possible. More generally, the work of Ashcraft and Siegler establishes that procedural and factual knowledge systems interact continuously in the process of generating an answer to an arithmetic problem. In the next section we examine how these two systems interact to produce developmental change.

Development

Developmental changes can be described for factual and pro-cedural knowledge separately. Children's factual knowledge becomes increasingly accurate and extensive. Children also show changes in the range of procedures available and in the choice of procedures.

More specifically, young children have few procedures available to them. They attempt retrieval, but it is rarely effective and so they must rely on primitive, counting-based procedures (e.g., count-all) that they have learned by means of imitation or direct instruction. As children become more skilled, they acquire a larger repertoire of procedures that are potentially applicable to arithmetic problems. As their repertoire grows, however, they tend to become increasingly likely to use a single procedure, retrieval, at least on simple problems (see Ashcraft, chap. 7).

Although factual and procedural changes can be described separately, development is better understood by examining interactions among these types of knowledge. Two components of change are incorporated in both Ashcraft's (1987) and Siegler's (1989; Siegler & Shrager, 1984) accounts of the development of arithmetic. The first component is a learning process that strengthens associations between stimuli (i.e., arithmetic problems) and responses (i.e., answers). In Siegler's model, for example, the associative strength between two addends and a possible answer increases every time the child states that answer, and the increase is greater for correct responses than for incorrect responses. Presumably a child's answer is often confirmed or disconfirmed by parents, peers, and teachers, or by other sources of feedback, so that some answers "grow" in strength relative to others. This type of learning is represented by increasing peakedness in the distribution of associative strengths, which in turn influences the probability of selecting subsequent procedures, the accuracy of response, and the latency of response.

The second component of change is the frequency with which arithmetic problems are encountered and attempted. Siegler and Shrager (1984) reported data on how often simple arithmetic problems are presented to preschoolers by parents, and Hamann and Ashcraft (1986; Ashcraft, 1987) compiled counts of the frequency with which simple addition problems are presented to children in elementary school textbooks. One conclusion is that problems with smaller addends generally are presented more often. Moreover, problems with other special characteristics are presented more frequently than might be expected. For example, addition problems of the form $n + 1$ are presented more commonly than problems of the form $1 + n$.

A reasonable assumption about early learning of problem-answer pairs is that frequency of exposure to specific problems influences the rate at which these associations are strengthened and, consequently, the use of retrieval or backup procedures. Both Ashcraft and Siegler used computer simulations to test the plausibility of this assumption.

Ashcraft (1987) expected that if his hypothesis about developmental change is correct, then it ought to be possible to predict the growth of associative strengths across years. He used Siegler and Shrager's empirical estimates of strength values for young children as a starting point (see Table 8.1), and he forecast changes in these values by means of a standard equation representing the effects of incremental learning. Increments in strength values for particular problem–answer associations were weighted with a variable reflecting the frequency of exposure to particular problems, as estimated by the text-book data. Thus the predicted strengths varied considerably as a function of age. For example, problem–answer associations for small-addend problems showed a faster rate of growth in early development than associations for problems with larger addends. When the strength values generated by the equation for students in Grades 1, 4, 7, 10, and college were inserted into Ashcraft's simulation of mental arithmetic, the simulation predicted solution latencies and problem-size effects that were very similar to the actual data obtained for each of the groups (Ashcraft, 1987).

Siegler and Shrager's (1984) test was even more ambitious. They presumed an initial state of knowledge in which the distributions of associative strengths (see Table 8.1 and Fig. 8.1) for all problem–answer combinations were flat and near zero. In this state, the sim-ulation's performance did not resemble the performance of children at all. Siegler and Shrager then simulated the effects of learning in a simulation that incorporated a number of assumptions about, for example, increments in associative strengths, the frequency of expo-sure to certain problems, and the likelihood of making a counting error when a backup procedure is used. After a large number of simulated learning trials, Siegler and Shrager found that the pattern of peakedness for the simulated knowledge base varied in expected ways for many problems. More importantly, correlations between children's behavior and the model's performance were high ($rs \geq .80$) for the frequency of errors, for solution times, and for the frequency with which backup procedures were used.

In summary, the view offered by both Siegler and Ashcraft is that changes in factual knowledge occur as a function of (a) a mechanism that increments associative strengths and (b) children's experience with problems. Several points need to be emphasized about the view of development exemplified by Ashcraft's and Siegler's work. First, factual knowledge and the use of procedures are subject to change with experience. In contrast, the process by which procedures are implemented and the learning mechanism itself are both *developmen-tally invariant*. These invariant aspects of the cognitive system work in a way that produces *adaptive* change in knowledge and performance, in the sense that children become more efficient and accurate in mental arithmetic. Thus invariant mechanisms can, in principle, produce at least some types of developmental changes in performance. In Ashcraft's words, "development is learning" (1987, p. 332).

Second, the simulations conducted by Ashcraft and by Siegler offer compelling evidence for the *plausibility* of the mechanisms they describe, but by themselves they do not constitute conclusive evidence. The use of simulations with very specific mechanisms and with explicit assumptions is an appealing and compelling alternative to the very verbal, very imprecise descriptions about developmental change to which psychologists have become accustomed (Klahr, 1976; Neches, Langley, & Klahr, 1987; Rabinowitz, Grant, & Dingley, 1987). The simulations show that certain assumptions are reasonable because, when implemented and synthesized in a package, they are sufficient for producing output that imitates observed aspects of development. Thus the simulations are a good source of hypotheses for future investigations, but they should not be viewed as surrogates for empirical research with children. The task of identifying testable assumptions and collecting relevant data remains, as does the problem of determining the boundary conditions of the proposed mechanisms. (See Ashcraft, 1987; Bisanz & Bisanz, 1988; Rabinowitz et al., 1987.)

Third, one of the two factors that combine to produce learning appears to be internal to the cognitive system and the other appears to be external, but this distinction is more illusory than real. In the proposed models, internal and external factors must interact to produce change. In particular, the associative mechanism is ostensibly internal, but it cannot operate without practice and feedback in a problem-filled environment. Similarly, the frequency of exposure to specific problems, an "environmental" variable, may be under the control of the cognitive system to some extent. It is entirely possible, for example, that parents and teachers select certain problems more than others *because* children respond more effectively, or learn better, with certain types of arithmetic "diets." Thus the cognitive system, in combination with parental beliefs and judgments, may exert control over an apparently external variable such as frequency of exposure. The ways in which these two factors interact remain to be explicated.

Fourth and finally, the current view of mental arithmetic represented by Siegler's and Ashcraft's work has a number of implications for understanding development, as noted already, but it is decidedly less clear about other important aspects of development. Missing entirely, for example, is a compelling account of how an entirely new procedure is acquired. Siegler and Shrager (1984) briefly alluded to possible roles for direct instruction and imitation, but no detailed account is provided in either model for these types of learning. Similarly, neither model is capable of inventing, discovering, or constructing new procedures. Evidence for such a capacity in children is provided in numerous descriptions of discovery, invention, and construction of procedures (e.g., Groen & Resnick, 1977; Resnick, 1980, 1983), and certainly no developmental theory of mental arithmetic is complete unless these qualitative aspects of developmental change can be accommodated. We suspect that a better understanding of how new procedures are acquired will emerge as researchers begin to focus more carefully on the interaction of procedural and conceptual knowledge, a topic to which we now turn.

The Role of Conceptual Knowledge

To this point our account of mental arithmetic includes no mention of how conceptual knowledge might influence performance. Ashcraft (1987) speculated that some types of conceptual knowledge might be implemented as principles and rules (e.g., "anything times zero is zero"), that these rules might be processed in parallel with retrieval, and that in some cases rules might yield answers before retrieval is completed. Clearly, however, the primary emphasis in Ashcraft's work, as in Siegler's, has been on interactions between factual and procedural knowledge. Given the importance of conceptual knowledge in any definition of what it means to "understand" arithmetic (Hiebert & Lefevre, 1986), integrating conceptual knowledge into an information-processing account of mental arithmetic must be a major priority.

One problem with past research on conceptual knowledge is that investigators have attempted to infer whether children have a concept without attempting to specify relations among conceptual, factual, and procedural knowledge. For example, Starkey and Gelman (reported in Starkey & Gelman, 1982) studied the principle of inversion, that is, that addition and subtraction of the same quantity leaves the original quantity unchanged (i.e., $a + b - b = a$). They found that 3- to 5-year-olds could answer such simple problems as $1 + 1 - 1$ and $3 + 1 - 1$ correctly, and they concluded that these children showed some evidence of understanding the inversion principle. Unfortunately, Starkey and Gelman examined only accuracy data and did not systematically compare performance on noninversion problems to inversion problems. Thus the results could have reflected use of procedures that do not involve conceptual knowledge of inversion. For example, the children may have been using covert counting procedures, or they simply might have chosen a whenever they did not know what else to do! To determine whether children "understand" inversion in any sense, it is critical that their problem-solving procedures be identified before determining whether, or in what sense, conceptual knowledge has influenced performance.

In a recent series of studies we examined the role of conceptual knowledge in the performance of children and adults (Bisanz, Le-Fevre, & Gilliland, in preparation). We reasoned that one way to operationalize understanding of an arithmetic concept is to determine whether children selectively use that concept when it is appropriate and helpful to do so. We presented two types of three-term problems in which all the numbers were single digits: inversion problems $(a + b - b)$ and standard problems $(a + b - c)$. We also manipulated problem size by altering the magnitudes of b and c.

If a subject simply uses the familiar algorithm of adding the first two digits and then subtracting the third from the sum, then performance should be similar on inversion and standard problems. More specifically, the problem-size effect for inversion problems should be the same as that for standard problems. In contrast, a subject could use a shortcut procedure on inversion problems that would obviate computation. For example, a subject who noticed that the principle of inversion applies to inversion problems could respond without calculating any sums or differences. Such a procedure would yield a flattened problem-size effect on inversion problems because no computation (retrieval or counting-based procedures) would be involved. Thus individuals who use an inversion-based procedure selectively on inversion problems would show a diverging interaction in solution latencies as a function of problem type and problem size: Latencies for standard problems should increase as a function of problem size, but latencies for inversion problems should not.

We have used this approach with both verification (i.e., $a + b - b = d$; true or false?) and production (i.e., $a + b - b = ?$) methods, and the results are very similar. The youngest children tested, 6-year-olds, showed the diverging interaction in their latency data; that is, the problem size effect for inversion problems was relatively small and nonsignificant, whereas for standard problems it was quite large. Thus the latency data appear to support the hypothesis that young children use a logical shortcut selectively. Such data may be misleading, however, because they may mask individual differences in the procedures used. Consequently, we observed children as they solved a subset of standard and inversion problems, and we asked them to describe the procedures they used to solve these problems. Self-reports of this type have proved to be very useful in identifying young children's solution procedures (e.g., Siegler, 1987), but because self-reports can be influenced in a variety of ways by demand characteristics of the experiment, it is critical that they be corroborated with other data (see also Ashcraft, chap. 7).

The results of these analyses showed substantial individual differences in 6-year-old children. Based on observations and self-reports, about 40% of the 20 children tested appeared to use a knowledge-based shortcut and 25% appeared to use a standard, left-to-right algorithm. These characterizations are supported with latency data, as illustrated in Fig. 8.3. Children who used conceptually based short-cuts (left panel) showed the diverging interaction and no problem-size effect on the inversion problems, in contrast to a substantial effect on standard problems. Children who used a standard algorithm (right panel) showed parallel problem-size effects for both types of problems.

The remaining children appeared to use a third option that we did not anticipate and that we refer to as the *negation* procedure. On inversion problems, these children typically used an abbreviated version of the standard algorithm. Specifically, they started by computing the sum of $a + b$, usually on their fingers. Then, instead of subtracting b from the sum by counting down, they quickly withdrew

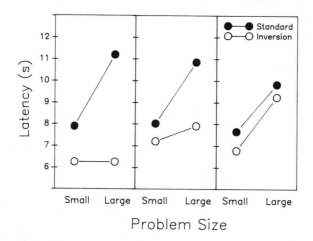

FIG. 8.3.   Latencies for 6-year-olds as a function of group and problem size. On inversion problems, children in the left panel used a conceptually based shortcut, children in the middle panel used negation, and children in the right panel used a standard algorithm.

b fingers all at once and answered *a*. It appeared that they were able to negate the last counting action, rather than going through the laborious procedure of computing the difference between *sum(a + b)* and *b*.

The latency data for negation users clearly reflect this procedure (Fig. 8.3, middle panel). On standard problems their latencies are comparable to the data for the other groups, but on inversion problems their latencies show an intermediate problem-size effect. In the latter case, they did compute *a + b* and so a problem-size effect would be expected, but their efficient method of obtaining the final answer resulted in less of a problem-size effect than for children who used a completely standard algorithm. Thus this group of children used a computational shortcut, but it is not at all clear that the shortcut was based on an understanding of inversion or any other logical principle. Instead, they seem to have kept track of their previous counting operations, then they were able to negate or withdraw the last operation in an efficient manner.

Thus a number of 6-year-olds showed clear evidence of using a shortcut based on a logical principle of arithmetic. We also tested 7-, 9-, and 11-year-olds, as well as adults. Interestingly, the proportion of children who used conceptually based shortcuts did not increase between 6 and 9 years, despite the fact that overall latencies decreasd dramatically. This result is surprising because, during this period in school, children have extensive practice with simple arithmetic problems. Apparently the result of all this practice is improved efficiency in computation, probably due to more frequent use of retrieval (Ashcraft & Fierman, 1982). This improved efficiency is not due to changes in the flexibility with which computational procedures are selected, however. Children may experience a form of *cognitive inertia* in which they continue to use a tried-and-true algorithm even when a conceptually based shortcut would be more efficient. In contrast, a majority of 11-year-olds showed clear evidence for use of a conceptually based procedure, as did nearly all of the adults. Many adults, in fact, also employed a shortcut on the standard problems that was based on the principle of associativity and that reduced solution latencies considerably.

In summary, we found an increasing tendency to use a conceptually based procedure selectively with increasing age, but only from middle childhood to adulthood. At earlier ages, children showed increased efficiency in computation, but not because of greater use of conceptual knowledge. Importantly, substantial individual differences were evident at all ages. The results conform to the view that information processing becomes more efficient with development (e.g., Kail & Bisanz, 1982), but they show that the *manner* in which this change takes place can vary with development. In particular, in earlier phases of skill acquisition increased efficiency appears to result from replacing counting-based procedures with retrieval, which in turn depends on changes in factual knowledge (Siegler & Shrager, 1984). Later, improved efficiency appears to result from increased use of conceptual knowledge in the selection of solution procedures. The generality of this conclusion about developmental changes in acquisition remains to be ascertained.

Our studies have convinced us that it is not sufficient to try to describe the development of conceptual knowledge separately from factual and procedural knowledge. Rather, the role of conceptual knowledge must be incorporated into the type of interactive, information-processing system just described. The details of how conceptual knowledge might interact with factual and procedural knowledge would require considerable elaboration, but we can sketch some possibilites.

Consider performance on three-term inversion problems. We might suppose that conceptual knowledge consists, in part, of productions that detect certain conditions and effect certain actions. For example, knowledge of inversion might be represented on this particular task as "if $a + b - b$, then the answer is a," where a and b are variables that can be bound to any number. If this production is activated more quickly than other procedures and if its associative strength exceeds the confidence criterion, then the subject would respond "a." No computation would be necessary and response latencies would be unaffected by problem size, thus producing the pattern of solution latencies characteristic of individuals who use a conceptually based procedure.

We suspect, however, that people normally do not retain such a specific procedure in long-term memory unless, of course, they participate daily in our inversion experiments. A more likely possibility is that conceptual knowledge about inversion is represented more generally as "if the same number is supposed to be added and subtracted, then do neither operation." If subjects encode the fact that, on some problems, the same number is added and subtracted, then this production would be activated. Procedural knowledge might contain a production that constructs or modifies specialized procedures when conceptual productions are frequently activated, such as "If a conceptual production is activated frequently, then construct a new procedure that incorporates a specific form of that production." On initial trials individuals may detect that many problems (50% in our studies) satisfy the condition of this production, and consequently they construct a specific procedure for use on subsequent trials. Such a procedure might consist of the following components: "Scan the problem and encode all three terms. If $a + b - b$, then the answer is a." Being new and probably temporary, this procedure might be activated more strongly than otherwise, which in turn would increase its probability of being selected (see Siegler's, 1989, notion of "novelty points").

A system with these features would be capable of storing conceptual knowledge about arithmetic and using it to generate efficient task-specific procedures. These new procedures would then compete with other procedures on the basis of associative strengths, according to the selection mechanisms already outlined by Siegler (1989; Siegler & Jenkins, 1989). Failure to use procedures based on conceptual knowledge could be due to a variety of factors, including lack of an appropriate conceptual production or failure to activate a conceptual production sufficiently. Alternatively, individuals could lack an appropriate procedure-building production that detects frequent activations of a conceptual production, or they might fail to activate the procedure-building production. Finally, a newly constructed procedure might be available but not be activated strongly enough to be selected. (See Ohlsson, 1987, for a detailed model in which propositions reflecting logical knowledge contribute to the development of new procedures.)

To summarize, we have described some data pertaining to developmental changes and individual differences in the influence of conceptual knowledge on solution procedures, and we have provided a preliminary sketch of how conceptual knowledge might interact with other forms of arithmetic knowledge. The role of conceptual knowledge clearly needs to be integrated into a more complete information-processing account of mental arithmetic. Much additional work, both empirical and theoretical, needs to be initiated to identify precisely how such a system would work and develop.

STRATEGIES RECONSIDERED

In our synopsis of current, information-processing views of mental arithmetic and its development, we have avoided use of the term *strategy*. Instead, we have reviewed theories and data selectively with the intent of describing development in this domain. We now can consider which of these procedures might be considered strategies and, more generally, which aspects of processing might be considered strategic.

A Definition of Strategy

We begin by imposing two constraints on the definition of *strategy* in research on cognitive development. First, use of the term should be generally consistent with common, dictionary definitions and with previous uses of the term in research. The tendency to develop technical meanings for common words is unavoidable, but adopting connotations or denotations that are substantially different from common usage is counterproductive for communication. Second, a reasonable definition of *strategy* should not be completely redundant with other terms and should be useful for highlighting particular types of procedures and particular types of cognitive processing. These constraints serve to narrow the class of procedures that might be considered strategic, a result that contrasts sharply with a trend toward broader definitions of the term *strategy* (e.g., Ashcraft, chap. 7).

Dictionary definitions of *strategy* and *strategic* include terms such as *planful, skillful in management, flexible,* and *adaptive.* The clear implication is that a strategy is a decision made prior to certain actions when more than one option is available. In fact, the term is derived from the Greek word *strategos,* a general in the military, and one technical definition of *strategy* is "the science of planning and directing large-scale military operations, [and] specifically . . . of maneuvering forces into the most advantageous position prior to actual engagement with the enemy" (*Webster's New Twentieth Century Dictionary,* 1978, p. 1799). Similar ideas, minus the military overtones, are implied in some of the definitions used by developmental psychologists. For example, Kail (1984) and Flavell (1970) defined strategies as planful, goal-oriented activities.

The connotations associated with these definitions can be illustrated with an example. Consider the sport of ice hockey and, specifically, a situation in which a player has the puck and is skating at top speed toward the opposing team's goal. Imagine that no defenders are in the way except for the goalie, who will try to block the shot. The player with the puck must quickly decide how to deceive the goalie and shoot the puck into the net. He might consider which of his moves is most reliable, which shooting position is optimal for him, the reputed strengths and weaknesses of the goalie, the speed with which the goalie's teammates are approaching, the condition of the ice around the net, and so on. The player makes a decision that will optimize his chances of scoring, he shoots the puck toward a certain area of the goal, and he hopes for the best.

The process by which the player arrives at his decision is clearly strategic in many respects. The process involves *selection:* A skilled player has many different maneuvers and shots that could be used, but he must select one option. The process is *goal-oriented,* not only literally, but also in the sense that the selection process is constrained so that the probability of a successful outcome is maximized. The process is also *flexible* in that a skilled player can alter the choice and *implementation* of maneuvers in response to a variety of inputs (e.g., the movements of the goalie, recent threats by the coach, sudden pain in one arm). Finally, the process involves activities that occur "prior to engaging the enemy." What the puck does once it is shot may determine the outcome of the game, but its flight is a product of the strategy, not the strategy per se. Similarly, the execution of the shot is not the strategy. Instead, the strategy consists of the process that results in the decision to shoot the puck in a particular direction with a particular speed.

With these connotations and constraints in mind, we propose that strategy be defined as a *procedure that is invoked in a flexible, goal-oriented manner and that influences the selection and implementation of subsequent procedures.* In the following section we explore some implications of this definition for understanding mental arithmetic.

Strategic Processing in Mental Arithmetic

Given our definition, which procedures in mental arithmetic are considered to be strategic? Solution procedures such as retrieval, count all, *min,* and the conceptually based shortcut used on inversion problems commonly are referred to as strategies (e.g., Siegler & Shrager, 1984), just as rehearsal and other mnemonic activities typically are considered as memory strategies (e.g., Brown, Bransford, Ferrara, & Campione, 1983). We reject equating *strategy* with *procedure,* however, because it violates the two general constraints just described. First, the terms would be completely redundant, and thus the term *strategy* would denote no special characteristics that would highlight particularly interesting or distinctive features of strategic procedures.

Second, the solution procedures used in mental arithmetic violate several of the connotations associated with the term *strategy.* For example, recall the constraint that strategies be prior activities that influence the selection or implementation of subsequent procedures. By this criterion, using a counting-based procedure or retrieval to obtain an answer is not any more strategic than the execution of the shot or the flight of the puck.

Moreover, the manner in which these solution procedures are

implemented sometimes does not really involve flexible selection from alternatives. If the hockey player had only one move and one way of shooting in his repertoire, his "choice" of that shot would not be strategic at all because no alternatives were available. In mental arithmetic, initial use of retrieval is a fundamental property of the cognitive system; it is not an optional procedure, and hence it is not strategic. Similarly, a child who has only one backup procedure in his or her repertoire is not being strategic when that procedure is invoked, again because there are no alternatives from which to choose. Finally, an adult who, after dozens of previous trials, executes a conceptually based shortcut on every inversion trial is not being strategic. More generally, if there is no flexibility in optimizing the selection for special conditions on a particular occasion, no matter how momentary those conditions may be, then the process is not strategic. Thus solution procedures in mental arithmetic often are not strategic.

A point of clarification is critical here. The distribution-of-associations model is indeed adaptive in the sense that the strengths of associations change in a manner that optimizes performance over many trials. This characteristic clearly is an appealing virtue of the model. Long-term adaptivity is not the same as flexibility, however. The point is that the model is not very flexible on a trial-by-trial basis, in part because the aspects of knowledge that are capable of change (i.e., strengths of association between problems and answers in the old model, or between problems and both answers and procedures in the revised model) do so only in a very gradual fashion over the course of many trials. No option exists for altering processing in significant ways on a trial-by-trial basis.

If solution procedures such as *min* and retrieval are not strategies, and even the selection process is not strategic in some cases, what could be considered strategic in mental arithmetic? We must look for procedures that could influence selection or implementation of subsequent procedures in a flexible way. Based on our considerations of the interactions among procedural, factual, and conceptual knowledge, we can suggest three illustrative possibilities.

First, procedures that set confidence criteria or that alter limits on retrieval attempts would be considered strategic. For example, a child might set his or her confidence criterion especially high for a teacher who rewards accuracy and lower for another teacher who rewards speed. Indeed, Siegler has interpreted some individual differences in arithmetic performance as being due to stable differences in criterion levels (Siegler, 1988a), but the issue of how criterion levels might change for an individual as a function of task conditions has yet to be addressed. Certainly it would not be difficult to incorporate procedures that alter particular processing parameters, such as confidence criteria, but the issue has received little empirical or theoretical attention.

Second, procedures that alter activation levels or associative strengths in dramatic ways, either momentarily or permanently, also would be considered as strategies when they are invoked to optimize performance. Consider, for example, a child who is capable of using either the *min* or count-all procedures but generally selects the latter. Under conditions in which speed is rewarded, the child might momentarily increase the activation level for the *min* procedure so that performance is optimized. Again, such a procedure could be implemented relatively easily in existing models (see the hypothesis about awarding "novelty points" in Siegler, 1989).

Third, procedures that create new procedures or alter old procedures in flexible ways also could be considered strategic. For example, we presume that children and adults who solve many inversion and standard problems in an experimental session do not invent or construct an inversion-based procedure anew on each trial. Similarly, when children switch from count-all to *min* procedures, they do not have to discover or invent the *min* procedure anew on each and every trial thereafter. In a developmental system, procedures must exist that detect nonoptimal characteristics of other procedures and modify those other procedures (Klahr, 1976). Some general characteristics of these procedure-modifying procedures are described in Kail and Bisanz (1982), and specific models are described by Wallace, Klahr, and Bluff (1987), Ohlsson (1987), and Neches (1987). To the extent that such self-modifying procedures operate to optimize other procedures, processing would be called *strategic*.

The procedures we describe as being strategic might be considered as metacognitive because they control processing in various ways. The concept of metacognition has a number of different meanings (Wellman, 1983), however, and its value for clarifying the nature of strategies is questionable (see Siegler & Shrager, 1984, for an empirical evaluation of a metacognitive explanation in arithmetic). For example, many theories about metacognition have a distinctly hierarchical structure in which executive procedures control subordinate routines (e.g., Sternberg, 1984). An alternative view, and one that is consistent with the research described in this chapter, is that control of one procedure by another may depend on associative strengths or activation speeds, such that strategies and other procedures compete with each other for selection (Lawler, 1981; Siegler, 1989). This latter view has a number of advantages for conceptualizing development, as compared with the hierarchical view of metacognition. Thus we see no clear benefit in defining strategies in terms of metacognition.

In contrast to many previous views (see Pressley et al., 1985), we have not referred to consciousness in our definition of strategy. Subjects may be consciously aware of some strategies, but the ambiguity of the concept of consciousness limits its utility. Methods exist for measuring constructs that may be correlates of consciousness, such as effort and controlled processing (e.g., Schneider & Shriffrin, 1977), but the degree to which these methods measure consciousness is not clear. Moreover, some procedures can become increasingly automatic and, presumably, less conscious with extensive practice (Schneider & Shiffrin, 1977). We know of no compellng reason to suspect that well practiced strategies might not follow a similar course. Indeed, one might suspect that our hockey player might be more conscious of some aspects of his decision than others, depending on his level of experience and skill. We prefer to define a strategic procedure in terms of its hypothesized function, rather than by the presence or absence of an attribute (consciousness or metacognition) that is itself not well defined.

Implications for the Study of Strategic Development

Our consideration of the literature on the development of mental arithmetic and our definition of strategy have four implications for studying strategic development. First, the development and selection of strategies in mental arithmetic typically involve an interaction among different types of knowledge. One tendency in research has been to examine only changes in procedural knowledge, with little concern for the roles of factual and conceptual knowledge. Changes in procedures are often considered equivalent to changes in strategies. When strategies are defined as a subset of procedures that select and implement subsequent procedures, however, understanding the interaction of different types of knowledge becomes essential for understanding how procedures change. The generality of this implication beyond arithmetic remains to be demonstrated, but we suspect that it is likely to hold in other domains.

Second, detailed models of performance at different points of development are necessary to clarify ambiguities in concepts and to pinpoint potentially different loci of development change. In mental arithmetic, our present understanding of developmental change is made possible only by the availability of relatively precise models of how procedures are selected (Siegler & Shrager, 1984) and how retrieval operates (Ashcraft, 1987). This degree of precision is essential if progress is to be made toward identifying information-processing mechanisms that account for developmental change (Kail & Bisanz, 1982; Klahr, 1976).

Third, existing models of mental arithmetic do not include many details that are specifically relevant to strategic processing, as we use the term. Instead, the focus has been on identifying specific solution procedures and a process for determining whether retrieval or some counting-based procedure is to be invoked. Nevertheless, the general design and mechanisms of existing models seem entirely amenable to incorporation of processes that would be more directly relevant to strategic development.

Fourth, consideration of strategic development in the context of mental arithmetic has helped to highlight aspects of performance that need to be more thoroughly investigated if we are to understand development. The implication is not just that the term *strategy* needs to be redefined, but rather that the focus of cognitive developmental research needs to include additional questions about the genesis of problem-solving procedures. In mathematical cognition, considerable progress has been made in identifying solution procedures, so that changes in the use of procedures can be described. With the contributions of Ashcraft and Siegler, a very compelling explanation of how procedures are selected is beginning to emerge. The next step is to account for the modification and creation of procedures. Over the next decade we expect increased attention to this missing piece of the puzzle, growing emphasis on understanding strategies as we have defined them, and greater concern with the mechanisms that enable discovery, invention, and construction of new procedures.

ACKNOWLEDGMENTS

Research conducted by the authors and described in this chapter was supported by the Natural Sciences and Engineering Research Council of Canada. We thank Gay Bisanz, Maria Dunn, Robert Kail, Daniel Pilon, Monique Senechal, Robert Siegler, and Alice Yu for their helpful comments on an earlier version of this manuscript.

REFERENCES

Ashcraft, M. H. (1982). The development of mental arithmetic: A chronometric approach. *Developmental Review, 2,* 213–236.
Ashcraft, M. H. (1983). *Simulating network retrieval of arithmetic facts.* Learning Research and Development Center Publication Series, University of Pittsburgh, 1983/10.

Ashcraft, M. H. (1987). Children's knowledge of simple arithmetic: A developmental model and simulation. In J. Bisanz, C. J. Brainerd, & R. Kail (Eds.), *Formal methods in developmental psychology: Progress in cognitive development research* (pp. 302–338). New York: Springer–Verlag.

Ashcraft, M. H., & Battaglia, J. (1978). Cognitive arithmetic: Evidence for retrieval and decision processes in mental addition. *Journal of Experimental Psychology: Human Learning and Memory, 4,* 527–538.

Ashcraft, M. H., & Fierman, B. A. (1982). Mental addition in third, fourth, and sixth graders. *Journal of Experimental Child Psychology, 33,* 216–234.

Ashcraft, M. H., & Stazyk, E. H. (1981). Mental addition: A test of three verification models. *Memory and Cognition, 9,* 185–196.

Baroody, A. J., & Ginsburg, H. P. (1986). The relationship between initial meaningful and mechanical knowledge of arithmetic. In J. Hiebert (Ed.), *Conceptual and procedural knowledge: The case of mathematics* (pp. 75–112). Hillsdale, NJ: Lawrence Erlbaum Associates.

Bisanz, J., & Bisanz, G. L. (1988). New directions in the study of human learning and development, or the subgoal that ate Pittsburgh? [Review of *Production system models of learning and development*]. *Contemporary Psychology, 33,* 943–945.

Bisanz, J., LeFevre, J., & Gilliland, S. (in preparation). *Development of conceptual knowledge in arithmetic: The case of inversion.*

Brown, A. L., Bransford, J. D., Ferrara, R. A., & Campione, J. C. (1983). Learning, remembering, and understanding. In J. H. Flavell & E. M. Markman (Eds.), P. H. Mussen (Series Ed.), *Handbook of child psychology: Vol. 4. Cognitive development* (pp. 77–166). New York: Wiley.

Campbell, J. I. D. (1987a). Network interference and mental multiplication. *Journal of Experimental Psychology: Learning, Memory, and Cognition, 13,* 109–123.

Campbell, J. I. D. (1987b). Production, verification, and priming of multiplication facts. *Memory and Cognition, 15,* 349–364.

Campbell, J. I. D., & Graham, D. J. (1985). Mental multiplication skill: Structure, process, and acquisition. *Canadian Journal of Psychology, 39,* 338–366.

Flavell, J. H. (1970). Developmental studies of mediated memory. In H. W. Reese & L. P. Lipsett (Eds.), *Advances in child development and behavior* (Vol. 5, pp. 181–211). New York: Academic Press.

Fuson, K. C. (1982). An analysis of the counting-on solution procedure in addition. In T. P. Carpenter, J. M. Moser, & T. A. Romberg (Eds.), *Addition and subtraction: A developmental perspective* (pp. 67–81). Hillsdale, NJ: Lawrence Erlbaum Associates.

Gelman, R., & Gallistel, C. R. (1978). *The child's understanding of number.* Cambridge, MA: Harvard University Press.

Goldman, S. R., Pellegrino, J. W., & Mertz, D. L. (1988). Extended practice of basic addition facts: Strategy changes in learning-disabled students. *Cognition and Instruction, 5,* 223–265.

Groen, G. J., & Parkman, J. M. (1972). A chronometric analysis of simple addition. *Psychological Review, 79,* 329–343.

Groen, G. J., & Resnick, L. B. (1977). Can preschool children invent addition algorithms? *Journal of Educational Psychology, 69,* 645–652.

Hamann, M. S., & Ashcraft, M. H. (1986). Textbook presentations of the basic arithmetic facts. *Cognition and Instruction, 3,* 173–192.

Hasher, L., & Zacks, R. T. (1979). Automatic and effortful processes in memory. *Journal of Experimental Psychology: General, 108,* 356–388.

Hiebert, J., & Lefevre, P. (1986). Conceptual and procedural knowledge in mathematics: An introductory analysis. In J. Hiebert (Ed.), *Conceptual and procedural knowledge: The case of mathematics* (pp. 1–27). Hillsdale, NJ: Lawrence Erlbaum Associates.

Hiebert, J., & Wearne, D. (1985). A model of students' decimal computation procedures. *Cognition and Instruction, 2,* 175–205.

Houlihan, D. M., & Ginsburg, H. P. (1981). The addition methods of first- and second-grade children. *Journal for Research in Mathematics Education, 12,* 95–106.

Kail, R. (1984). *The development of memory in children* (2nd ed.). New York: Freeman.

Kail, R., & Bisanz, J. (1982). Information processing and cognitive development. In H. W. Reese (Ed.), *Advances in child development and behavior* (Vol. 17, pp. 45–81). New York: Academic Press.

Kaye, D. B. (1986). The development of mathematical cognition. *Cognitive Development, 1,* 157–170.

Klahr, D. (1976). Steps toward the simulation of intellectual development. In L. B. Resnick (Ed.), *The nature of intelligence* (pp. 99–133). Hillsdale, NJ: Lawrence Erlbaum Associates.

Kintsch, W. (1970). *Learning, memory, and conceptual processes.* New York: Wiley.

Lawler, R. W. (1981). The progressive construction of mind. *Cognitive Science, 5,* 1–30.

LeFevre, J., & Bisanz, J. (1987, April). *Cognitive arithmetic: Evidence for the development of automaticity.* Presented at the biennial meeting of the Society for Research in Child Development, Baltimore. (ERIC Document Reproduction Service No. ED 286 732)

LeFevre, J., Bisanz, J., & Mrkonjic, L. (1988). Cognitive arithmetic: Evidence for obligatory activation of arithmetic facts. *Memory and Cognition, 16,* 45–53.

LeFevre, J., Pilon, D. J., Yu, A., & Bisanz, J. (1989). *Priming of sums in digit naming: Implications for mental arithmetic.* Manuscript submitted for publication.

Logan, G. D. (1980). Attention and automaticity in Stroop and priming tasks: Theory and data. *Cognitive Psychology, 12,* 523–553.

Logan, G. D. (1985). Skill and automaticity: Relations, implications, and future directions. *Canadian Journal of Psychology, 39,* 367–386.

Miller, K., Perlmutter, M., & Keating, D. (1984). Cognitive arithmetic: Comparison of operations. *Journal of Experimental Psychology: Learning, Memory, and Cognition, 10,* 46–60.

Neches, R. (1987). Learning through incremental refinement of procedures. In D. Klahr, P. Langley, & R. Neches (Eds.), *Production system models of learning and development* (pp. 163–219). Cambridge, MA: MIT Press.

Neches, R., Langley, P., & Klahr, D. (1987). Learning, development, and production systems. In D. Klahr, P. Langley, & R. Neches (Eds.), *Production system models of learning and development* (pp. 1–53). Cambridge, MA: MIT Press.

Neely, J. H. (1977). Semantic priming and retrieval from lexical memory: Roles of inhibitionless spreading activation and limited-capacity attention. *Journal of Experimental Psychology: General, 106,* 226–254.

Ohlsson, S. (1987). Truth versus appropriateness: Relating declarative to procedural knowledge. In D. Klahr, P. Langley, & R. Neches (Eds.), *Production system models of learning and development* (pp. 287–327). Cambridge, MA: MIT Press.

Posner, M. I., & Snyder, C. R. R. (1975). Attention and cognitive control. In R. L. Solso (Ed.), *Information processing and cognition* (pp. 55–85). Hillsdale, NJ: Lawrence Erlbaum Associates.

Pressley, M., Forrest-Pressley, D. L., Elliot-Faust, D., & Miller, G. (1985). Children's use of cognitive strategies, how to teach strategies, and what to do if they can't be taught. In M. Pressley & C. J. Brainerd (Eds.), *Cognitive learning and memory in children* (pp. 1–47). New York: Springer–Verlag.

Rabinowitz, F. M., Grant, M. J., & Dingley, H. L. (1987). Computer simulation, cognition, and development. In J. Bisanz, C. J. Brainerd, & R. Kail (Eds.), *Formal methods in developmental psychology: Progress in cognitive development research* (pp. 263–301). New York: Springer–Verlag.

Resnick, L. B. (1980). The role of invention in the development of mathematical competence. In R. Kluwe & H. Spada (Eds.), *Developmental models of thinking* (pp. 110–149). New York: Academic Press.

Resnick, L. B. (1983). A developmental theory of number understanding. In H. P. Ginsburg (Ed.), *The development of mathematical thinking* (pp. 109–151). New York: Academic Press.

Resnick, L. B., & Ford, W. W. (1981). *The psychology of mathematics for instruction.* Hillsdale, NJ: Lawrence Erlbaum Associates.

Riley, M. S., Greeno, J. G., & Heller, J. I. (1983). Development of children's problem-solving ability in arithmetic. In H. P. Ginsburg (Ed.), *The development of mathematical thinking* (pp. 153–196). New York: Academic Press.

Schneider, W., & Shiffrin, R. M. (1977). Controlled and automatic human information processing: I. Detection, search, and attention. *Psychological Review, 84,* 1–66.

Secada, W. G., Fuson, K. C., & Hall, J. W. (1983). The transition from counting all to counting on in addition. *Journal for Research in Mathematics Education, 14,* 47–57.

Siegler, R. S. (1986). Unities in strategy choices across domains. In M. Perlmutter (Ed.), *Minnesota symposium on child development* (Vol. 19, pp. 1–48). Hillsdale, NJ: Lawrence Erlbaum Associates.

Siegler, R. S. (1987). The perils of averaging data over strategies: An example from children's addition. *Journal of Experimental Psychology: General, 116,* 250–264.

Siegler, R. S. (1988a). Individual differences in strategy choices: Good students, not-so-good students, and perfectionists. *Child Development, 59,* 833–851.

Siegler, R. S. (1988b). Strategy choice procedures and the development of multiplication skill. *Journal of Experimental Psychology: General, 117,* 258–275.

Siegler, R. S. (1989). How domain-general and domain-specific knowledge interact to produce strategy choices. *Merrill-Palmer Quarterly, 35,* 1–26.

Siegler, R. S., & Jenkins, E. A. (1989). *How children discover new strategies.* Hillsdale, NJ: Lawrence Erlbaum Associates.

Siegler, R. S., & Robinson, M. (1982). The development of numerical understandings. In H. Reese & L. P. Lipsett (Eds.), *Advances in child development and behavior* (Vol. 16, pp. 241–312). New York: Academic Press.

Siegler, R. S., & Shrager, J. (1984). Strategy choices in addition and subtraction: How do children know what to do? In C. Sophian (Ed.), *Origins of cognitive skills* (pp. 229–293). Hillsdale, NJ: Lawrence Erlbaum Associates.

Silver, E. A. (1986). Using conceptual and procedural knowledge: A focus on relationships. In J. Hiebert (Ed.), *Conceptual and procedural knowledge: The case of mathematics* (pp. 181–198). Hillsdale, NJ: Lawrence Erlbaum Associates.

Starkey, P., & Gelman, R. (1982). The development of addition and subtraction abilities prior to formal schooling in arithmetic. In T. P. Carpenter, J. M. Moser, & T. A. Romberg (Eds.), *Addition and subtraction: A cognitive perspective* (pp. 99–116). Hillsdale, NJ: Lawrence Erlbaum Associates.

Sternberg, R. J. (1984). Mechanisms of cognitive development: A componential approach. In R. J. Sternberg (Ed.), *Mechanisms of cognitive development* (pp. 163–186). New York: Freeman.

Underwood, G. (1978). Concepts in information processing theory. In G. Underwood (Ed.), *Strategies of information processing* (pp. 1–22). New York: Academic Press.

Wallace, I., Klahr, D., & Bluff, K. (1987). A self-modifying production system model of cognitive development. In D. Klahr, P. Langley, & R. Neches (Eds.), *Production system models of learning and development* (pp. 359–435). Cambridge, MA: MIT Press.

Webster's new twentieth century dictionary of the English language (2nd ed., unabridged). (1978). Collins-World.

Wellman, H. M. (1983). Metamemory revisited. In M. T. H. Chi (Ed.), *Contributions to human development: Trends in memory development research* (Vol. 9, pp. 31–51). Basel, Switzerland: S. Karger.

Winkelman, J. H., & Schmidt, J. (1974). Associative confusions in mental arithmetic. *Journal of Experimental Psychology, 102,* 734–736.

Zbrodoff, N. J., & Logan, G. D. (1986). On the autonomy of mental processes: A case study of arithmetic. *Journal of Experimental Psychology: General, 115,* 118–130.

CHAPTER 9

Children's Use of Strategies in Reading

Ruth Garner
Washington State University

When adults read, we often engage in activities that enhance our understanding and remembering of information. If the text we are reading matters to us, we might stop periodically and inquire of ourselves, "Am I getting this?" We allocate extra time and effort to reading and studying text segments that may be difficult, perhaps because of lack of topic familiarity, length, new vocabulary, or anxiety we have about the task awaiting us after reading. We backtrack to earlier parts of text if we sense that something we just read conflicts with our recollection of something already read. We select important information from the array of main ideas and details, and we re-hearse the important points. We might create a short summary, in our own words, of just the important information that we have read; we try to decide if this synopsis is adequate or if we should reread the material to get a better grasp of the author's message.

All of these activities are "strategic." Before I begin to discuss children's use of strategies in reading, let me be very explicit about what makes some of the behaviors children and adults engage in while reading strategic, and others not.

STRATEGIES: WHAT ARE THEY?

Strategies Are Goal Oriented

At the very least, if we are engaged by the reading task, we are trying to comprehend. If a task awaits us after the reading, we may also be trying to remember. (The common school tasks, in this regard, are tests, class discussions, and worksheets.) To these ends, we employ activities that assist us.

Paris, Lipson, and Wixson (1983) noted that a reader's reading only the topic sentence in a paragraph and thus happening upon the main idea is lucky, but not strategic. To be considered strategic, that same reader would choose an action to reach a goal (in order to find the important information in a paragraph, perhaps reading the initial sentence in the paragraph and paying close attention to it because the first sentence is a conventional location for important information). Goals can be specified by the reader or by someone else.

Flavell (1979) proposed some time ago that some of our goals are cognitive, some metacognitive. The categories can be differentiated as follows: A reader does not know the content of the history chapter on the Louisiana Purchase well, so she rereads the chapter, taking notes on points the author has italicized. Two cognitive strategies—rereading and creating an external record for possible further study—are aimed at the straightforward cognitive goal of improving her knowledge base. Later, the reader wonders if she is ready for the next day's test, and she quizzes herself, using questions from the end of the chapter. This metacognitive strategy is aimed at the metacognitive goal of assessing her knowledge. (Presumably, if she decides that her knowledge base is still deficient, she would reread the material yet again or try an alternative cognitive strategy.) In Flavell's scheme, cognitive strategies are invoked to *make* cognitive progress, metacognitive strategies to *monitor* it.

Flavell (1971) also pointed out that sometimes the goal that the strategic behavior is invoked to achieve is at some distance from the behavior. He gave the example of deliberate memorizing. When you deliberately memorize, you intentionally do something now that will only pay off later, at recall time. Flavell compared memorizing to storing nuts for the winter. When readers memorize pairs of events and dates from their social studies textbooks or chemical formulas from their science textbooks, or long names of characters in their English anthologies, they are planning to use this information in subsequent reading and in test situations.

Strategies Are Intentionally Invoked

When readers use strategies, they do so deliberately. It is true that certain activities that were once deliberate, conscious, intentional (and cumbersome) become automated, but I would argue, as others have (see, for instance, Paris, 1988) that these automatic activities are then better labeled *skills,* reserving the label *strategies* for activities that retain some amount of deliberateness. Strategies are judicious actions undertaken to reach goals.

I have noted elsewhere (Garner, 1987a, 1988) that, because strategies are consciously invoked, they require attentional resources that are not limitless and they can be examined, reported, and modified. This is a classic "bad news/good news" situation. It is when strategic subroutines become automatic after extensive reading practice that a variety of strategies can be engaged simultaneously without the process being overloaded (van Dijk & Kintsch, 1983).

For commentary on the alternative perspective that the descriptor *deliberate* should not be used in defining strategies, one can consult the work of Pressley and his colleagues (e.g., Pressley, Forrest-Pressley, Elliott-Faust, & Miller, 1985). They argued that strategies are almost always potentially controllable, behaviors that *could be* deployed deliberately. They cite relatively mindless, reflexive (but effective) processing of text of the sort academics engage in when they survey a research article in their field as an example of nondeliberate, but strategic, processing.

My own introspection about my performing this academic ritual yields the insight that either I read journal articles in a manner where I mindfully and effectively employ a repertoire of text-processing strategies *or* I read the articles mindlessly and ineffectively, usually in a state of fatigue. Though, as Langer (1985) noted, it is surely maladaptive to suffer cognitive overload because of an inability to reduce the amount of cognitive activity in which we engage, I cannot imagine reading articles in my field and not intentionally invoking steps of my processing strategy (e.g., checking the reference list for conceptual overlap with my current work, underscoring the salient details about method for possible rereading, making counterinterpretive comments in the margin of the Discussion section for future reference). All of this strikes me as conscious cognition.

It should be noted that intentional activity implies selection. That is, from a repertoire of possible activities, one selects those that seem most likely to enhance performance. For instance, one employs a story schema to remember the key components of a narrative text— what precipitated a character's action, what the character did, what resulted from the character's action (Yussen, Mathews, Buss, & Kane, 1980)—whereas one employs a model of a macroproposition followed by a series of supportive micropropositions (Kieras, 1982, 1985) to remember the important information in an expository text. In my conceptualization of strategies, behavior must be engaged in discriminatively to support the claim that the behavior is strategic (see also DeLoache, Cassidy, & Brown, 1985).

Strategies Are Effortful

As Paris et al. (1983) pointed out, readers might judge a particular activity to be useful in reaching a particular goal, but they might not employ the activity because they perceive it to be too demanding of time and effort. Paris et al. gave the examples of readers failing to use context, analyze word parts, skim, or reread because the costs appear too high given general classroom valuing of task completion. Paris and his colleagues suggested that skilled readers make choices about costs of using various strategies and benefits of the goals to be achieved.

I have argued (Garner, 1987b) that, given the frenetic pace of most classrooms, students are unlikely to slow down their activity flow to incorporate unpracticed cognitive and metacognitive strategies. It is quicker for them to copy some sentences and delete others, rather than work at a reduced, coherent summary that integrates important ideas. It is quicker to respond to some questions and leave other response spaces blank than to reread text to locate unrecalled information. Strategies that are not yet routinized to some degree are likely to be abandoned in the classroom.

Reading to remember (i.e., studying text) outside the classroom is also effortful (Thomas & Rohwer, 1986). It must be self-instigated and it is often unrewarding. It is isolated and individual. Learners must supply their own feedback about the success of the enterprise. As Thomas and Rohwer noted, studying test requires volition, the disposition to exert effort, to persist, to seek out and transform information. This is hard work.

As Pressley, Borkowski, and O'Sullivan (1985) reminded us, one way to make effortful strategies more palatable to students is to make certain that they understand the benefits of strategy execution. The burden for use, then, falls on the instructor or competent adult who, if he or she is able to persuade children that extra effort is warranted and that the strategic actions are worthwhile, may expect to see maintenance of strategies without duress (Paris, Newman, & Jacobs, 1985).

Strategies Enhance Performance
In Some Instances and Not In Others

I mentioned the notion of repertoire earlier. It is clear that no single text-processing strategy works in all situations. Readers will find that looking for story components such as setting, initiating events, and consequences will be of little use when reading about Newtonian laws of motion, content likely to be organized as a series of principles with exemplars, attributes, and properties that support the principles (Dee-Lucas & Larkin, 1987). Assessing one's knowledge of battles of the American Civil War with a self-quiz on battles and dates from the text will prove to be of little use if a student is then tested with an essay question about prewar economic contrasts between the North and the South. Finally, it is not necessary for an expert on baseball to read glossary entries inserted in text defining *hit, run, error, sacrifice,* and the like. In each of these cases, because of text, task, or learner factors, strategies that would be very useful in some instances are not particularly useful here.

Paris et al. (1983) have introduced the term *conditional knowledge* to capture this dimension of knowing when to apply various strategies. They propose that skilled readers have three sorts of knowledge about strategies: (a) declarative, knowing *that;* (b) procedural, knowing *how;* and (c) conditional, knowing *when.* Our research on the text reinspection strategy (e.g., Garner, Macready, & Wagoner, 1984) supports that adept strategy users have all three sorts of knowledge. They know *that* reinspecting text for information once read, but no longer remembered, aids in question answering. They know *how* to skim the text, using vague spatial memory and key words in the question to locate relevant information to be reread. They know *when* to utilize this strategy: when questions cue access to text, not to general knowledge base. As Paris et al. (1983) noted, conditional knowledge describes the circumstances for strategy application. Someone with only declarative and procedural knowledge does not adjust behavior to changing text and task demands.

It is failure to adjust behavior to changing text and task demands that Frese and Stewart (1984) described in their example of an undergraduate student falling into a "skill trap" by thinking that the highly practiced routine of memorizing content from textbooks will produce success in graduate school, where, instead, integration of information and original ideas are expected. A related example is Bransford and Heldmeyer's (1983) example of students who use "flowery" language, not scientific prose, as they move from composition in one domain to composition in a new, unrelated one.

Learner factors can be as important as text and task factors in making a strategy inappropriate in a particular context. The most important learner factor is domain knowledge. It has been well documented that experts and novices in a particular domain differ in amount, organization, and accessibility of information in that domain (Glaser, 1984; Gobbo & Chi, 1986; Rabinowitz, 1984; Voss, 1984).

The importance of these differences is apparent in the following scenario: A word or group of words is encountered in text. A concept in memory is (or is not) activated. Activation spreads automatically from that concept to many (or few) related concepts in the network. Stronger associative links lead to stronger activations beyond the original concept.

Simply put, if a reader knows a great deal about a topic, then strategies are likely to play minor roles in determining the quality of comprehension and recall performance (Borkowski, Carr, & Pressley, 1987). That is, the professor of biology seldom needs to stop for comprehension evaluation, to backtrack for information checks, to rehearse important points, or to deliberately summarize to assess comprehension/recall when reading a text on the topic of effects of acid rain on plants and animals. The biology novice may need to engage in much more effortful activity to understand and remember this information. Suppose, however, that the biology novice is an expert on Renaissance art, whereas the professor of biology has never seen or read about Renaissance masterpieces. When reading an art history text, the likelihood of strategy use would be reversed for the two readers. This compensatory aspect of strategy use, the use of general strategies in domains where background knowledge is low, allows readers to be what Brown and Palinscar (1985) called "intelligent novices," readers who may not possess background knowledge needed in a field, but who know how to go about getting that knowledge, often from text. The relation between strategies and knowledge is necessarily an interdependent one (Chi, 1985).

Having established what counts as a strategy and what does not for the purposes of this chapter, I now turn to the topic of children's use of strategies in reading. Rather than presenting a myriad of discrete strategies that are known or not known, used or not used by children, I shall try to present a list of conditions under which children generally *do not* employ effective strategies to enhance understanding and remembering of information in text. My assumption is that for most reading situations that present at least a moderate degree of challenge to the reader, a single strategy or a set of strategies would assist readers in processing information effectively. It becomes clear, as we examine the research on children's use of strategies in reading, that sometimes children fail to employ any routines to improve understanding and remembering and sometimes they employ maladaptive routines that do not enhance performance.

CHILDREN'S FAILURE TO USE STRATEGIES IN READING UNDER A VARIETY OF CONDITIONS

Poor Comprehension Monitoring

If children do not notice that they are not understanding information that they are reading, they are unlikely to seek a strategic remedy. Ideal self-regulation by a reader has been described by Brown (1980): A reader proceeds merrily through a relatively easy reading task with rapid construction of meaning until a comprehension failure occurs and is detected. This situation can be characterized as cognitive failure (information processing is impaired) but metacognitive success (the reader notices this). The reader takes action, perhaps continuing to read, but more slowly and attentively; perhaps rereading material already read; perhaps consulting an external source. In any case, if the problem is serious enough to disrupt ongoing meaning construction, some strategic remedy is applied. The ideal reader continuously evaluates the success of the reading operation and provides remedies as needed (Baker, 1985).

Poor comprehension monitoring in a reading context has been aptly described by Markman (1981). She remarked that occasionally while she is reading, her mind begins to wander. As she becomes more engrossed in her daydream, she understands less and less of what she is "reading." If she continues to turn pages, she is engaging in profitless activity—"reading" without understanding. If she had noticed that she was not understanding, she could have taken action, perhaps putting the book aside until she was more alert, perhaps strengthening her resolve to finish the task and making a deliberate attempt to concentrate on the task.

We know from a great deal of recent research that children, particularly younger children and less skilled readers, often do not engage in comprehension monitoring while they read. Two examples from the literature demonstrate this.

Harris, Kruithof, Terwogt, and Visser (1981) asked 8- and 11-year-old children to read short texts that were exposed line by line with a window card. When titles were manipulated, one line in the text became anomalous. One short text, with both possible titles and the resulting anomalies, follows:

Title 1:   At the hairdresser's
Title 2:   At the dentist's

John is waiting.
There are two people before him.
After a while, it is his turn.
He sees his hair getting shorter (anomaly, Title 2).
Luckily, there are no cavities this time (anomaly, Title 1).
After a while he can get up.
John puts his coat on.
He can go home.

Reading times for each line were recorded. After reading each passage, the children were asked to identify the line that did not belong in the story; they were permitted to reinspect the text to do so. Harris et al. found that the older children were more likely to identify the anomalous lines than the younger children. However, both age groups were equally likely to read the anomalous lines more slowly than the appropriate lines.

The finding of longer reading times for anomalous lines for both age groups indicates that the 8-year-olds were evaluating the comprehensibility of the short text at some level, despite the fact that they generally did not identify the anomalous sentences. The discrepancy between nonverbal and verbal measures of comprehension monitoring has been found in other studies (e.g., Flavell, Speer, Green, & August, 1981; Patterson, Cosgrove, & O'Brien, 1980). Flavell et al. (1981) suggested that young children may have only fleeting and semiconscious experiences of comprehension difficulties which, to a degree surprising to an adult, they seem to ignore or to dismiss as unimportant. Having ignored these experiences, they would naturally fail to employ comprehension fix-up strategies.

Additional evidence of children's propensity for ignoring comprehension difficulties emerges from August, Flavell, and Clift's (1984) work. August and her colleagues asked skilled and less skilled fifth-grade readers to read five eight-page stories that were presented page by page on a computer terminal. In this study, anomalous material resulted not from single-line logical inconsistency with earlier text, but from a large gap in information; in three of the five stories a portion of the story was omitted, rendering the narrative confusing.

Reading times for acceptable text and for text immediately following gaps were recorded. Reinspection of text for acceptable and unacceptable text segments was also recorded. After reading, the children were asked about textual problems and any remedies they might have employed. Skilled readers detected problems, located them appropriately, and reported repair strategies with higher frequency than less skilled readers. In addition, the skilled readers spent more time on unacceptable texts than less skilled readers. Very few readers in either group used text reinspection, and a great many in both groups generated inferences to create an acceptable story from unacceptable input.

Inferential resolution of information gaps or inconsistencies in text is a common finding in the comprehension monitoring research literature. Readers seem intent on making sense of nonsense. Unless told that the text they are reading is unacceptable in some way, they will go to great lengths to fix problems inserted by researchers.

Surely this is the result of our getting meaning from flawed messages in the real world of written communication. Children and adults work with scribbles, ambiguity, lack of coherence, distracting detail, and scores of other features of "inconsiderate text" (Armbruster & Anderson, 1981). To construct meaning from inconsiderate texts, we expend extra cognitive effort to compensate for authors' failures. It seems that children who participate in comprehension-monitoring experiments do much the same thing. They work very hard to construct meaning. They take texts such as the Markman (1979) "Fish" text and make sense of nonsense. The text that Markman presented to "editorial consultants" in Grades 3, 5, and 6 was as follows:

> Fish must have light in order to see. There is absolutely no light at the bottom of the ocean. It is pitch black down there. When it is that dark the fish cannot see anything. They cannot even see colors. Some fish that live at the bottom of the ocean can see the color of their food; that is how they know what to eat.

Adults found the discrepancy in fish needing light (and having none) versus seeing the color of their food anomalous. Nearly half of the children at each grade level did not. When I have presented this same text to elementary school children without telling them that it is flawed, they tell me, when prompted, how they have resolved the apparent contradiction: "Oh, the ocean at the beginning of the paragraph is a different one from the ocean at the end of the paragraph," "These fish that are talked about live at the bottom of the ocean, but they come to the top to eat," and so on. These children are working hard to make sense of nonsense. Having fixed up the text they have encountered with inferences (that were clearly unintended by the researcher/author of the text), they have little need of additional comprehension fix-up strategies.

There is evidence that comprehension monitoring improves rather dramatically with age and experience. The classic demonstration of development of monitoring skill has come from Markman (1977) who presented a listening task to young children.

Children in Grades 1 through 3 were asked to serve as "editorial consultants." They were given game and magic-trick instructions from which critical information had been deleted. Children were told to tell the investigator if she had failed to clarify something or had forgotten to give them information. The measure of whether the children monitored their comprehension was whether or not they asked a question or requested additional information of the investigator. A series of 10 probes about the adequacy of the instructions was used. At the point of the 8th probe, the children were actually asked to try to play the game or try the magic trick.

First grade children differed from third grade children in the point at which they realized instructions were incomplete. It took an average of 9, 6, and 3 probes for children in Grades 1, 2, and 3, respectively, to note the missing information. Of the eight first grade children who asked a clarification question, all but one had to attempt to play the game and fail before posing the question. Markman pointed out that these youngest children probably failed to execute the instructions mentally, and therefore did not notice the problems until they attempted to follow the instructions.

Informing children that there *is* something wrong with an oral or written message makes a difference, but again there are age differences. When Markman (1979) asked children in Grades 3 and 6 to be "editorial consultants" for a set of essays (the "Fish" text presented earlier is one example), she told some of them that "there is something tricky about each of the essays. Something which does not make any sense. Something which is confusing. I would like you to try and spot the problem with each essay and tell me what it was that did not make any sense" (p. 651).

Children given this information were more likely to note the problem than children who were not given the information, but sixth graders outperformed third graders, even when uninformed. Rates for "spotting the problem" were as follows: 6 of 16 informed third graders, 14 of 16 informed sixth graders, 4 of 16 uninformed third graders, and 8 of 16 uninformed sixth graders.

We also know that older children are more proficient than younger children at a number of specific aspects of comprehension monitoring. For instance, Baker (1984) decomposed monitoring into application of lexical acceptability, internal consistency, and external consistency standards for text and found that 9-year-olds were more successful at identifying all three types of problems than 7-year-olds, who, in turn, were more successful at identifying all problems than 5-year-olds.

Evidence that very young children can monitor their comprehension *in some situations* comes from Revelle, Wellman, and Karabenick (1985). Revelle et al. (1985) asked preschool children to participate in two natural play interactions with an adult (sandbox play and preparations for a pretend tea party). In the course of the play sessions, the adult made a series of requests of the child, some of which posed comprehension or compliance dilemmas.

Comprehension problems were of three types: referential ambiguity, unintelligibility, and memory overload. Compliance problems were of two types: unbringable items and absent items. These problem requests were embedded in a relatively spontaneous, unstructured conversation.

Transcripts were made of all verbalizations. Nonverbal compliance attempts and search behaviors were coded as well. Seven categories of verbalizations that could indicate a child's detection of a comprehension or compliance problem (e.g., requests for repetition, requests for elaboration) were identified.

Though there were age effects, both 3- and 4-year-old children discriminated between requests that posed problems and those that did not. Both verbally and nonverbally, the younger and older children demonstrated that they evaluated the unbringable item mentally, instead of trying to comply and then discovering that they could not.

Revelle and her colleagues accounted for the apparent difference in results in this study and in Markman's (1977) study by noting that familiar and simple stimuli, natural interactions, and a familiar setting in their study may account for some of the variation. In addition, the relatively easy task of trying to comply with an adult's request to bring an object surely induced different responses than the difficult task of stating that an oral or written message is problematic and then specifying what is wrong with it.

What is it that develops? How can we account for the finding that most young children are not skilled at monitoring their own comprehension when reading?

I agree with Wellman (1985) that understanding of human cognition is acquired and nurtured. A child develops a theory of mental processes (a "theory of mind") that includes information such as the following: people possess minds, there are distinct mental processes, one can "read" one's mental state. At early points of development, children know very little about illusions, beliefs, certainties, hunches, mistakes, guesses, or deceptions. Notions of the internal mental world are often less salient than notions of the external, observable world. Small wonder then that at these early points, children are not adept at noting comprehension failure, an event in the internal mental world.

These young children may be able to act in the external world of pretend tea parties in a manner that displays a rudimentary theory of mind, but they are unlikely, in the absence of schooled information about language, to be very successful at analyzing and explaining how the mind works or fails to work when processing text. Older children, with a more sophisticated theory of mind and acquired proficiency at "treating language itself as an object of thought" (Tunmer, Nesdale, & Pratt, 1983) can use their knowledge about their own cognitions to direct their cognitive activity. That is, they can seek strategic remedies for comprehension failure (Flavell, 1981).

Low Efficacy Expectations

It is clear that children and adults are unlikely to invoke procedures that are demanding of time and effort if they believe that the procedures will not make any difference, that they will fail to perform successfully despite the use of strategies. A number of recent papers make the point that one's perception of one's ability to perform a task may be a more critical influence on behavior than task incentives or actual personal skill (Brown, Bransford, Ferrara, & Campione, 1983; Corno & Mandinach, 1983; Pressley, Goodchild, Fleet, Zajchowski, & Evans, 1989). Without high self-esteem, an internal locus of control, and the tendency to attribute success to effort, both children and adults are unlikely to initiate or persist at strategic processing, of text or any other input.

Attributions may be particularly important. For children, a major cultural context is the school and the agenda it sets (Yussen, 1985). If children in school believe that failure on academic tasks is a result of low ability, rather than of insufficient effort or application of the wrong strategy, they are unlikely to invoke the same (or different) strategies the next time they encounter a similar set of tasks. On the contrary, they are likely to assume that performance is not something in their control. They are likely to abandon strategies.

Nicholls (1983) put the critical contrast in attributions well. A child can: (a) be task involved; (b) ask in a failure situation, "What must I do differently to succeed?"; and (c) focus on effort to improve performance. On the other hand, a child can, instead: (a) be ego involved; (b) ask in a failure situation, "Am I stupid?"; and (c) focus on uncontrollable ability as the sole determinant of performance.

Clearly, competitive classrooms support children's ability attributions (Ames, 1984). In such classrooms, as Covington (1985) noted, though teachers label students who appear indifferent to learning as *lazy* or *unmotivated,* these students are often engaging in self-protective behaviors that emerge because of their feelings of failure. The stress of expecting to look stupid, and avoiding situations where that is most likely to occur, can lead ego-involved students to give up.

Even very capable students become involved in these self-defeating dynamics. Dweck (1986) singled out bright female students who, despite early, consistent, and abundant success, do not relish the prospect of challenge. Dweck documents the presence of shaky expectations and frequent failure attributions to lack of ability among bright girls.

Attributions can be changed. Borkowski et al. (1987) reported recent work where some hyperactive children were given detailed procedural information and self-control training plus attribution retraining. Attribution retraining was designed to enhance both antecedent and program-generated self-attributions. To change antecedent attributions, instructors discussed general, pervasive beliefs about the causes of success and failure; children were given the opportunity to perform previously failed items. To influence program-generated attributions, instructors provided feedback about the relation between strategic behavior (or its absence) and performance; individual items were shown to be correct or incorrect depending upon whether the appropriate strategy had been used as instructed.

Children in this attribution retraining condition used the instructed strategies 3 weeks after training ended and maintained use 10 months later. In addition, attributional beliefs were permanently altered.

Ames and Archer (1988) sounded a critical caution about adult expectations for children's strategy use in a recent paper. They argued that interventions aimed at training learning strategies and modifying attributions may not have any lasting effects if the classroom does not support children's strategy use. Ames and Archer follow Nicholls' contrast of individual attributions with a contrast between classroom goal orientations. They propose that classrooms either display a predominantly "performance goal orientation" (where students are concerned about being able, about outperforming others, about achieving success with little effort) or a predominantly "mastery goal orientation" (where students are concerned about acquiring new skills, about the process of learning, about using effort).

Ames and Archer (1988) asked academically talented junior high and high school students to complete performance scale items (e.g., "Only a few students can get top marks," "Students feel bad when they do not do as well as others") and mastery scale items (e.g., "Students are given a chance to correct mistakes," "I work hard to

learn"), rating each item on a 5-point scale ranging from strong
disagreement to strong agreement. The students also reported their
strategy use on 15 items adapted from the Learning and Study Strategies Inventory (Weinstein, Schulte, & Palmer, 1987) and responded
to questions about attributions and perceived ability.

When students perceived an emphasis on mastery goals in their
classroom, they reported using more learning strategies. As might be
expected, a student's perceived ability was also a significant predictor
of strategy use. Students used strategies if they thought that performance might be enhanced and strategic activity might be valued.

The question of when attributions and goal orientations begin to
affect children's strategy use has not received much attention in the
research literature. Certainly the expectation that we are likely to
succeed at any given task (or the alternative one, that we are likely to
fail) is derived from social learning, some of which occurs in the early
years of school in academic settings that support self-assessing behavior, and some of which occurs in the home, between parent and
child. Research examining the onset and change of self-defeating
attributions and behaviors before and during the school years is much
needed. As Miller (1983) noted, present versions of social learning
theory do not adequately address development.

A Weak Textual Schema

Particularly when reading exposition, young readers may be prepared to invoke a set of strategies to find and remember the most
important information in text, but they may not know where to look.
They may be uninformed about expository text structure (Garner, in
press), partially at least because of a steady diet of simple stories in the
early grades (Anderson, Hiebert, Scott, & Wilkinson, 1985).

To expand this point, I provide a short text about insects that we
have used recently. Note the "semantic signaling" of important information (van Dijk, 1979) in the first sentence:

> Some insects live alone, and some live in large families. Wasps that live
> alone are called solitary wasps. A Mud Dauber Wasp is a solitary wasp.
> Click Beetles live alone. Ants live in large families. There are many
> kinds of ants. Some ants live in trees. Black Ants live in the ground.

If the semantic signal were not present and the text began with the
second ("Wasps . . .") sentence, there is reason to believe that sorting
"big" ideas from less important details would be more difficult. Readers would be likely to mistake details for main ideas until enough

information would be available from which an appropriate main idea could be induced: "Ah, this is about wasps, wasps that live alone. Oops, I guess it's about lots of different insects that live alone, wasps and beetles. Oh wait, ants don't live alone. I guess this says that some insects live alone and some live in families."

Given the importance of a semantic signal of this sort, it is critical that readers accord special attention to it, when authors are considerate enough to provide a signal. Unfortunately, the evidence is that relatively young readers do no such thing. For instance, Williams, Taylor, and Ganger (1981) found that fourth- and sixth-grade readers asked to select the best title for short texts from among a set that included the specific topic of the text, the general topic of the text, a detail in the text, and an unrelated topic did not perform better for texts for which a semantic signal of this sort was provided than for texts where no signal was given.

In two recent studies (Garner et al., 1986; Garner & Gillingham, 1987), we examined children's lack of knowledge about structural features of text a bit more. We asked third, fifth, and seventh grade students to "build" expository texts, either by manipulating sentence strips or by ordering sentences on a microcomputer screen. They were given seven randomly ordered sentences, such as those below:

4. In the past, it was common for families and friends to hold "quilting bees" to make quilts together.
2. A quilt usually has a top piece and a bottom piece.
1. Quilts are special kinds of blankets made of scraps of cloth.
7. Worms eat plants in the soil.
5. However, today, these gatherings of families and friends are less common.
3. It also has some stuffing in between.
6. Blankets are often made of synthetic materials that are machine washable.

The first sentence is a definitional topic sentence. Sentences 2 and 3 are cohesively tied by pronoun reference. Sentences 4 and 5 are tied by conjunction. The 6th sentence presents information related to the *general* topic of the paragraph (blankets), but not to the *specific* topic (quilts). The 7th sentence presents information totally unrelated to the topic of the paragraph, information from an alternate text.

Graduate students in psychology all performed the "building" task virtually flawlessly. They eliminated topically unrelated sentences, kept cohesively tied sentences adjacent, and—the point of interest for our present discussion—they placed the topic sentence in the conventional "initial mention" position (Kieras, 1980). Only about three in five of the third graders and fifth graders placed the topic sentence in its conventional location. About four in five of the seventh graders performed as the adults had. It seems that children do not know as much as adults know about conventional locations for important information in expository text. Without this knowledge, they are ill equipped for invoking any strategy (e.g., text summarization) that requires readers to distinguish important and unimportant information in expositions.

Further evidence that knowledge of structural features of expository text develops comes from a recent study of children's writing. Englert, Stewart, and Hiebert (1988) asked third graders and sixth graders at three ability levels per grade to act as "editors." The children read a stimulus idea and then generated two relevant details to complete a paragraph *and* read details and generated an appropriate main idea statement. The older children were more able to generate both textually consistent details and main ideas. Composing main ideas was much more difficult than composing relevant details for the less able children at both grade levels.

Considering this finding with the reading results mentioned earlier, we can be fairly confident in claiming that readers and writers get better with age and experience in their ability to comprehend and compose "big" ideas and supporting details in expository paragraphs. As I mentioned earlier, the relative inability of young children to sort out important and unimportant information in text handicaps them in any attempts to perform a number of text-processing strategies well.

Rejection of Imposed Activities

Flavell (1978) commented that coming to cognitive maturity in cultures such as ours may involve learning how to think effectively even when motivation and meaningfulness are low, learning to learn things we would not have chosen to learn. If Flavell is correct, it should not be surprising to us that less mature thinkers (i.e., young children) are less likely than more mature thinkers (i.e., older children and adults) to behave strategically while learning things they would not have chosen to learn. On the other hand, children may be very strategic about tasks they have selected.

Findings from recent studies seem to speak to this very point. For instance, we know from DeLoache and her colleagues' work involving spontaneous manipulation of objects that children under 2 years old exhibit primitive mnemonic strategies for retrieving a hidden object (DeLoache, Cassidy, & Brown, 1985) and that children ranging in ages 18 to 42 months employ correction strategies in attempts to nest five cups graded by size so that all fit one into the other (DeLoache, Sugarman, & Brown, 1985). However, we also know from recent work on a number of academic text-processing strategies (see Garner, 1987a; Scardamalia & Bereiter, 1984, for summaries of this work) that most of these strategies are not employed by children spontaneously, and that they are often abandoned when adult inducement to continue them is no longer present. As DeLoache, Sugarman, and Brown (1985) said about their task, there is no inducement other than the presence of the cups, and children's highly goal-directed, persistent behavior to solve the problem seems motivated by their own sense of discovery and achievement. This could not be said of any of the academic strategies reviewed in Garner (1987a).

King's (1979) interviews with kindergarten children about what constitutes "work" and "play" may be relevant to our understanding of inducements to use strategies. In four classrooms in New England and the Midwest, King observed children's directed and undirected activity and then asked them about some of the activities she had observed. All classes were taught by experienced teachers, but the four classrooms varied dramatically in amount of structure for the children's activities (i.e., in one, undirected activity was interrupted only rarely by the teacher, whereas in another, the opportunity for "free play" was available only to children who had finished assigned work; the other two classrooms fell somewhere in between).

When children being interviewed clearly recalled an activity from the day before, they were asked whether the activity was an instance of classroom work or classroom play. They were also asked about the relative importance of work activities and play activities, both to them and to the teacher.

The kindergarten children had no difficulty distinguishing work and play activities. In all four classrooms, they described most of their classroom experiences as work. All play activities were voluntary. The children believed that the activities they labeled *work* were more important to the teacher than the activities they labeled *play*. The children did not indicate that work was boring or tiresome, but it was involuntary, other-directed activity.

Given that strategy theorists talk about self-control as a key component of strategic activity (Brown & DeLoache, 1978; Garner, 1987a; Paris et al., 1983), it may be that tasks that are not selected by children may not evoke much strategic processing at early ages. One move that young learners may make to make an induced strategy more "theirs" is the modification and personalization that has been documented to occur (Adams, Carnine, & Gersten, 1982).

Adams et al. (1982) taught some elementary school students an explicit routine for studying textbook material for four days. The day after training was completed and again 2 weeks later, students were asked to read textbook material, to retell the content, and to answer questions about the content. Trained students outperformed untrained students for question answering in both immediate and delayed testing. The trained students also studied longer for the tests. However, in the finding of most interest here, only 50% of the trained students were observed using the instructed routine for the immediate test. This figure dropped to 20% for the delayed test. A large proportion of the trained students did use an observable study strategy, if not the instructed one. Adams et al. (1982) suggested that by the second test session many of the trained students had adopted more personalized study methods with which there was no decrement in performance.

When a child alters an instructed strategy to suit himself or herself, it may work in favor of the learner, but it may not. Perkins (1985) pointed out that even adults experience strategy "drift," or the sense that one is using the effective strategy adopted some days before, but discovering that the behavior has shifted substantially, often away from effective action. A number of intermediate steps may have been deleted, thus reducing cognitive load *and* effectiveness.

Primitive Strategies as an Impediment

Some children have acquired routines that at least to some degree enhance their reading performance. Given that these partially effective strategies are deployed, more effective strategies are not (Brown et al., 1983).

Perhaps the best example of partially effective strategies are those used to generate a short summary of what has been read. Elsewhere (Garner, 1987b), I have discussed a development from *strategic deficiency* to *strategic inefficiency* to *strategic efficiency* for this academic task. It is children at a strategic inefficiency level who display partially effective strategies, strategies that operate as an impediment to deployment of more effective routines.

Strategically deficient children are likely to make a single pass through a text segment, not stopping to assess relative importance of information or to attempt a restatement of any of the information (Scardamalia & Bereiter, 1984). They test individual statements against their world knowledge to assess accuracy. Integration of information is minimal (Markman, 1981). When pressed to select important information in text, strategically deficient summarizers rate structural importance differently from expert adult readers (Brown & Smiley, 1977; Garner, 1985; Winograd, 1984), often mistaking information of high interest to them for information with high textual relevance.

Strategically inefficient readers do know that distinguishing important and unimportant information is critical, but they perform this activity in a maladaptive manner. Brown and Day (1983) described their postreading summarizing strategy, which operates something like this: Copy, verbatim, ideas that are important; do not deviate from the surface structure of the text; do not paraphrase; do not combine ideas; stop when you run out of space. Brown and Day called this ineffective strategy "copy-delete."

This routine is very different from the routine invoked by efficient summarizers, who select only the most important information in text for their summaries, use rules for condensing text, and produce succinct and coherent texts as summaries. They revise the products if their summaries are insufficiently reduced or unintegrated (Hare & Borchardt, 1984). They employ the six rules identified by Brown and Day (1983): (a) delete unnecessary material, (b) delete redundancy, (c) substitute a superordinate term for a list of items, (d) do the same for a list of events, (e) select a topic sentence if one is provided in text, and (f) invent a topic sentence if none appears in text.

It is apparent how the intermediate level, the point at which children are copying and deleting, can block refinement of the summarizing strategy. Children at this level label what they are doing *summarizing*. They resist instruction, even into the high school and college years (Brown et al., 1983).

It is my hunch (data are meager on this point) that most young children formulate primitive strategies. These strategies probably disappear or are changed with instruction or with performance failure that leads to spontaneous generating of new routines (note that this change scenario requires comprehension monitoring and high motivation to complete a task successfully, two factors that I have already said are not always present). Research that examines transitional learners—children moving away from a primitive strategy and toward a more sophisticated one—is much needed.

CONCLUSION

Expert adult readers read text strategically. They try to understand and remember information, and to assist them in doing so, they intentionally invoke fairly complex routines. Sometimes the routines are very demanding of time and effort. Sometimes they do not improve performance. Yet, for text that presents at least a moderate degree of cognitive challenge, expert readers persist at strategic processing.

Children, for a number of reasons, tend to be less strategic about their text processing. Five conditions under which children generally do not employ strategies have been discussed in this chapter: (a) when they fail to monitor their comprehension; (b) when they believe that strategies will not make a difference in their performance; (c) when they lack knowledge about text features, particularly structural features of exposition; (d) when they are unwilling to employ strategies to learn things they have not chosen to learn; and (e) when they deploy primitive routines in lieu of more efficient strategies. This list is surely not exhaustive, and I suggest that continuing to investigate these conditions is an important activity for psychologists and educators. Results from such empirical activity can inform efforts to teach strategies to children.

REFERENCES

Adams, A., Carnine, D., & Gersten, R. (1982). Instructional strategies for studying content area texts in the intermediate grades. *Reading Research Quarterly, 18,* 27–55.

Ames, C. (1984). Achievement attributions and self-instructions under competitive and individualistic goal structures. *Journal of Educational Psychology, 76,* 478–487.

Ames, C., & Archer, J. (1988). Achievement goals in the classroom: Students' learning strategies and motivation processes. *Journal of Educational Psychology, 80,* 260–267.

Anderson, R. C., Hiebert, E. H., Scott, J. A., & Wilkinson, I.A.G. (1985). *Becoming a nation of readers: The report of the commission on reading.* Washington, DC: National Institute of Education.

Armbruster, B. B., & Anderson, T. H. (1981). *Content area textbooks* (Rdg. Ed. Rep. No. 23). Urbana: University of Illinois, Center for the Study of Reading.

August, D. L., Flavell, J. H., & Clift, R. (1984). Comparison of comprehension monitoring of skilled and less skilled readers. *Reading Research Quarterly, 20,* 39–53.

Baker, L. (1984). Children's effective use of multiple standards for evaluating their comprehension. *Journal of Educational Psychology, 76,* 588–597.

Baker, L. (1985). How do we know when we don't understand? Standards for evaluating text comprehension. In D. L. Forrest-Pressley, G. E. MacKinnon, & T. G. Waller (Eds.), *Metacognition, cognition, and human performance* (Vol. 1, pp. 155–205). Orlando, FL: Academic Press.

Borkowski, J. G., Carr, M., & Pressley, M. (1987). "Spontaneous" strategy use: Perspectives from metacognitive theory. *Intelligence, 11,* 61–75.

Bransford, J. D., & Heldmeyer, K. (1983). Learning from children learning. In J. Bisanz, G. L. Bisanz, & R. Kail (Eds.), *Learning in children: Progress in cognitive development research* (pp. 171–190). New York: Springer–Verlag.

Brown, A. L. (1980). Metacognitive development and reading. In R. J. Spiro, B. C.

Bruce, & W. F. Brewer (Eds.), *Theoretical issues in reading comprehension* (pp. 453–481). Hillsdale, NJ: Lawrence Erlbaum Associates.

Brown, A. L., Bransford, J. D., Ferrara, R. A., & Campione, J. C. (1983). Learning, remembering, and understanding. In J. H. Flavell & E. M. Markman (Eds.), *Handbook of child psychology* (Vol. 3, pp. 77–166). New York: Wiley.

Brown, A. L., & Day, J. D. (1983). Macrorules for summarizing texts: The development of expertise. *Journal of Verbal Learning and Verbal Behavior, 22,* 1–14.

Brown, A. L., & DeLoache, J. S. (1978). Skills, plans, and self-regulation. In R. S. Siegler (Ed.), *Children's thinking: What develops?* (pp. 3–35). Hillsdale, NJ: Lawrence Erlbaum Associates.

Brown, A. L., & Palincsar, A. S. (1985). *Reciprocal teaching of comprehension strategies: A natural history of one program for enhancing learning* (Tech. Rep. No. 334). Urbana: University of Illinois, Center for the Study of Reading.

Brown, A. L., & Smiley, S. S. (1977). Rating the importance of structural units of prose passages: A problem of metacognitive development. *Child Development, 48,* 1–8.

Chi, M.T.H. (1985). Interactive roles of knowledge and strategies in the development of organized sorting and recall. In S. F. Chipman, J. W. Segal, & R. Glaser (Eds.), *Thinking and learning skills* (Vol. 2, pp. 457–483). Hillsdale, NJ: Lawrence Erlbaum Associates.

Corno, L., & Mandinach, E. B. (1983). The role of cognitive engagement in classroom learning and motivation. *Educational Psychologist, 18,* 88–108.

Covington, M. V. (1985). Strategic thinking and the fear of failure. In J. W. Segal, S. F. Chipman, & R. Glaser (Eds.), *Thinking and learning skills* (Vol. 1, pp. 389–416). Hillsdale, NJ: Lawrence Erlbaum Associates.

Dee-Lucas, D., & Larkin, J. H. (1987). *Novice importance rules: Definitions and equations* (Report No. 18). Pittsburgh: Carnegie–Mellon University, Department of Psychology.

DeLoache, J. S., Cassidy, D. J., & Brown, A. L. (1985). Precursors of mnemonic strategies in very young children's memory. *Child Development, 56,* 125–137.

DeLoache, J. S., Sugarman, S., & Brown, A. L. (1985). The development of error correction strategies in young children's manipulative play. *Child Development, 56,* 928–939.

Dweck, C. S. (1986). Motivational processes affecting learning. *American Psychologist, 41,* 1040–1048.

Englert, C. S., Stewart, S. R., & Hiebert, E. H. (1988). Young writers' use of text structure in expository text generation. *Journal of Educational Psychology, 80,* 143–151.

Flavell, J. H. (1971). First discussant's comments: What is memory development the development of? *Human Development, 14,* 272–278.

Flavell, J. H. (1978). Comments. In R. S. Siegler (Ed.), *Children's thinking: What develops?* (pp. 97–105). Hillsdale, NJ: Lawrence Erlbaum Associates.

Flavell, J. H. (1979). Metacognition and cognitive monitoring: A new area of cognitive-developmental inquiry. *American Psychologist, 34,* 906–911.

Flavell, J. H. (1981). Cognitive monitoring. In W. P. Dickson (Ed.), *Children's oral communication skills* (pp. 35–60). New York: Academic Press.

Flavell, J. H., Speer, J. R., Green, F. L., & August, D. L. (1981). The development of comprehension monitoring and knowledge about communication. *Monographs of the Society for Research in Child Development, 46* (5, Serial No. 192).

Frese, M., & Stewart, J. (1984). Skill learning as a concept in life-span developmental psychology: An action theoretic analysis. *Human Development, 27,* 145–162.

Garner, R. (1985). Text summarization deficiencies among older students: Awareness or production ability? *American Educational Research Journal, 22,* 549–560.

Garner, R. (1987a). *Metacognition and reading comprehension*. Norwood, NJ: Ablex.

Garner, R. (1987b). Strategies for reading and studying expository text. *Educational Psychologist, 22,* 299–312.

Garner, R. (1988). Verbal-report data on cognitive and metacognitive strategies. In C. E. Weinstein, E. T. Goetz, & P. A. Alexander (Eds.), *Learning and study strategies: Issues in assessment, instruction, and evaluation* (pp. 63–76). San Diego, CA: Academic Press.

Garner, R. (in press). Skilled and less skilled readers' ability to distinguish important and unimportant information in expository text. In S. R. Yussen & M. C. Smith (Eds.), *Reading across the life span*. New York: Springer–Verlag.

Garner, R., Alexander, P., Slater, W., Hare, V. C., Smith, T., & Reis, R. (1986). Children's knowledge of structural properties of expository text. *Journal of Educational Psychology, 78,* 411–416.

Garner, R., & Gillingham, M. G. (1987). Students' knowledge of text structure. *Journal of Reading Behavior, 19,* 247–259.

Garner, R., Macready, G. B., & Wagoner, S. (1984). Readers' acquisition of the components of the text-lookback strategy. *Journal of Educational Psychology, 76,* 300–309.

Glaser, R. (1984). Education and thinking: The role of knowledge. *American Psychologist, 39,* 93–104.

Gobbo, C., & Chi, M. (1986). How knowledge is structured and used by expert and novice children. *Cognitive Development, 1,* 221–237.

Hare, V. C., & Borchardt, K. M. (1984). Direct instruction of summarization skills. *Reading Research Quarterly, 20,* 62–78.

Harris, P. L., Kruithof, A., Terwogt, M. M., & Visser, T. (1981). Children's detection and awareness of textual anomaly. *Journal of Experimental Child Psychology, 31,* 212–230.

Kieras, D. E. (1980). Initial mention as a signal to thematic content in technical passages. *Memory and Cognition, 8,* 345–353.

Kieras, D. E. (1982). A model of reader strategy for abstracting main ideas from simple technical prose. *Text, 2,* 47–81.

Kieras, D. E. (1985). Thematic processes in the comprehension of technical prose. In B. K. Britton & J. B. Black (Eds.), *Understanding expository text: A theoretical and practical handbook for analyzing explanatory text* (pp. 89–107). Hillsdale, NJ: Lawrence Erlbaum Associates.

King, N. R. (1979). Play: The kindergartners' perspective. *The Elementary School Journal, 80,* 80–87.

Langer, E. J. (1985). Playing the middle against both ends: The usefulness of adult cognitive activity as a model for cognitive activity in childhood and old age. In S. R. Yussen (Ed.), *The growth of reflection in children* (pp. 267–285). Orlando, FL: Academic Press.

Markman, E. M. (1977). Realizing that you don't understand: A preliminary investigation. *Child Development, 48,* 986–992.

Markman, E. M. (1979). Realizing that you don't understand: Elementary school children's awareness of inconsistencies. *Child Development, 50,* 643–655.

Markman, E. M. (1981). Comprehension monitoring. In W. P. Dickson (Ed.), *Children's oral communication skills* (pp. 61–84). New York: Academic Press.

Miller, P. H. (1983). *Theories of developmental psychology*. San Francisco, CA: Freeman.

Nicholls, J. G. (1983). Conceptions of ability and achievement motivation: A theory and its implications for education. In S. G. Paris, G. M. Olson, & H. W. Stevenson (Eds.), *Learning and motivation in the classroom* (pp. 211–237). Hillsdale, NJ: Lawrence Erlbaum Associates.

Paris, S. G. (1988). Models and metaphors of learning strategies. In C. E. Weinstein, E. T. Goetz, & P. A. Alexander (Eds.), *Learning and study strategies: Issues in assessment, instruction, and evaluation* (pp. 299–321). San Diego, CA: Academic Press.

Paris, S. G., Lipson, M. Y., & Wixson, K. K. (1983). Becoming a strategic reader. *Contemporary Educational Psychology, 8,* 293–316.

Paris, S. G., Newman, R. S., & Jacobs, J. E. (1985). Social contexts and functions of children's remembering. In M. Pressley & C. J. Brainerd (Eds.), *Cognitive learning and memory in children: Progress in cognitive-development research* (pp. 81–115). New York: Springer–Verlag.

Patterson, C. J., Cosgrove, J. M., & O'Brien, R. G. (1980). Nonverbal indicants of comprehension and noncomprehension in children. *Developmental Psychology, 16,* 38–48.

Perkins, D. N. (1985). General cognitive skills: Why not? In S. F. Chipman, J. W. Segal, & R. Glaser (Eds.), *Thinking and learning skills* (Vol. 2, pp. 339–363). Hillsdale, NJ: Lawrence Erlbaum Associates.

Pressley, M., Borkowski, J. G., & O'Sullivan, J. (1985). Children's metamemory and the teaching of memory strategies. In D. L. Forrest-Pressley, G. E. MacKinnon, & T. G. Waller (Eds.), *Metacognition, cognition, and human performance* (Vol. 1, pp. 111–153). Orlando, FL: Academic Press.

Pressley, M., Forrest-Pressley, D. L., Elliott-Faust, D., & Miller, G. (1985). Children's use of cognitive strategies, how to teach strategies, and what to do if they can't be taught. In M. Pressley & C. J. Brainerd (Eds.), *Cognitive learning and memory in children: Progress in cognitive development research* (pp. 1–47). New York: Springer-Verlag.

Pressley, M., Goodchild, F., Fleet, J., Zajchowski, R., & Evans, E. D. (1989). The challenges of classroom strategy instruction. *The Elementary School Journal, 89,* 301–342.

Rabinowitz, M. (1984). The use of categorical organization: Not an all-or-none situation. *Journal of Experimental Child Psychology, 38,* 338–351.

Revelle, G. L., Wellman, H. M., & Karabenick, J. D. (1985). Comprehension monitoring in preschool children. *Child Development, 56,* 654–663.

Scardamalia, M., & Bereiter, C. (1984). Development of strategies in text processing. In H. Mandl, N. L. Stein, & T. Trabasso (Eds.), *Learning and comprehension of text* (pp. 379–406). Hillsdale, NJ: Lawrence Erlbaum Associates.

Thomas, J. W., & Rohwer, W. D., Jr. (1986). Academic studying: The role of learning strategies. *Educational Psychologist, 21,* 19–41.

Tunmer, W. E., Nesdale, A. R., & Pratt, C. (1983). The development of young children's awareness of logical inconsistencies. *Journal of Experimental Child Psychology, 36,* 97–108.

van Dijk, T. A. (1979). Relevance assignment in discourse comprehension. *Discourse Processes, 2,* 113–126.

van Dijk, T. A., & Kintsch, W. (1983). *Strategies of discourse comprehension.* New York: Academic Press.

Voss, J. F. (1984). On learning and learning from text. In H. Mandl, N. L. Stein, & T. Trabasso (Eds.), *Learning and comprehension of text* (pp. 193–212). Hillsdale, NJ: Lawrence Erlbaum Associates.

Weinstein, C. E., Schulte, A. C., & Palmer, D. R. (1987). *Learning and study strategies inventory.* Clearwater, FL: H & H Publishing.

Wellman, H. M. (1985). The child's theory of mind: The development of conceptions of cognition. In S. R. Yussen (Ed.), *The growth of reflection in children* (pp. 169–206). Orlando, FL: Academic Press.

Williams, J. P., Taylor, M. B., & Ganger, S. (1981). Text variations at the level of the individual sentence and the comprehension of simple expository paragraphs. *Journal of Educational Psychology, 73,* 851–865.

Winograd, P. N. (1984). Strategic difficulties in summarizing texts. *Reading Research Quarterly, 19,* 404–425.

Yussen, S. R. (1985). The role of metacognition in contemporary theories of cognitive development. In D. L. Forrest-Pressley, G. E. MacKinnon, & T. G. Waller (Eds.), *Metacognition, cognition, and human performance* (Vol. 1, pp. 253–283). Orlando, FL: Academic Press.

Yussen, S. R., Mathews, S. R., Buss, R. R., & Kane, P. T. (1980). Developmental change in judging important and critical elements of stories. *Developmental Psychology, 16,* 213–219.

CHAPTER 10

The Development of Analogical Problem Solving: Strategic Processes in Schema Acquisition and Transfer

Barry Gholson
David Morgan
Andrew R. Dattel
Karen A. Pierce
Memphis State University

The transfer of existing knowledge to new but closely related problems and situations has been a topic of continuing interest to psychologists throughout the 20th century. Historically, this kind of transfer, here called *analogical reasoning*, has been studied in diverse theoretical contexts under a variety of labels. For example, generalization due to identical (or common) elements (e.g., Cantor, 1965; Hull, 1939; Spence, 1937, 1942; Thorndike, 1923; Thorndike & Woodworth, 1901), resonance effects of signals (e.g., Dunker, 1945; Luchins, 1942; Sobel, 1939), and the mapping of structural relations from the known to the new (e.g., Inhelder & Piaget, 1958; Judd, 1908; Spearman, 1923). More recently, researchers in three relatively insular disciplines have focused on analogical reasoning. First, cognitive scientists have proposed that analogy plays a principal role in the induction mechanisms of intelligent systems, both biological and electronic. Thus models and simulations have appeared with increasing frequency in that literature (e.g., Burstein, 1986; Carbonell, 1986; Falkenhainer, Forbus, & Gentner, 1986; Holland, Holyoak, Nisbett, & Thagard, 1986; Sweller, 1988; Winston, 1980, 1984). Second, the role of analogy in mathematical problem solving has attracted considerable attention (e.g., Cooper & Sweller, 1987; Kintsch & Greeno, 1985; Novick, 1988; Reed, 1987; Read, Dempster, & Ettinger, 1985; Ross, 1987; Silver, 1981). Finally, some psychologists have focused their research efforts on attempts to understand the *development* of analogical reasoning processes (e.g., Alexander,

Willson, White, & Fuqua, 1987; Brown, Kane, & Echols, 1986; Gentner, 1977; Gentner & Toupin, 1986; Gholson, Eymard, Morgan, & Kamhi, 1987; Holyoak, 1984; Holyoak, Junn, & Billman, 1984; Sternberg, 1985; Sternberg & Rifkin, 1979). This convergence of research and theory reflects an emerging theoretical consensus in which analogical reasoning is taken as an essential feature of learning and problem solving (Brown & Campione, 1984; Gentner, 1989; Gholson, Eymard, Long, Morgan, & Leeming, 1988), playing an important role in, among other things, classroom learning (Brown, 1989; Brown et al., 1986; Sternberg, 1985) and the various enterprises of science (Gentner, 1983; Hesse, 1966; Nersessian, 1984).

Lest we mislead the reader regarding the convergence just noted, two caveats are in order. These are concerned with the issues addressed and the subject populations studied by researchers in the three disciplines. Cognitive scientists are primarily concerned with computer models in the artificial intelligence tradition, with little emphasis on data from human subjects. Researchers studying mathematics have focused most of their attention on how young adults apply newly learned formulas to related problems. And much of the work reported by developmentalists has aimed at demonstrating the conditions under which young children are capable of analogical transfer in simple problems. Thus there are many gaps in our current understanding of analogical reasoning processes.

Before beginning our discussion of the dynamics of analogical reasoning, it will be useful to define the term *strategy*. A *strategy* is a deliberate goal-directed activity on the part of the child. According to this definition, training conditions (or experimental arrangements) requiring children to engage in specific activities that facilitate analogical transfer are *not* strategic. If the activities became part of the child's own repertoire and generalized to new situations, however, they would be. Similarly, activities or processes that are so well practiced they are completely automatic (Shiffrin & Schneider, 1977) are not considered strategic. We realize that many, including contributors to this volume, prefer a broader definition and we take no issue with them. Our preference is due mostly to pragmatic considerations specifically associated with the domain of analogical reasoning.

ANALOGICAL REASONING PROCESSES

In order to provide an explicit context for the present discussion, we begin by describing an *isomorphic* transfer task (i.e., one in which the problems have identical goal structures). A problem called the "genie," has been used in several studies of children's analogical reasoning. In this problem a genie is presented with the task of transferring jewels from one bottle to another, with the latter located on the other side of a barrier (a wall) that the genie itself cannot cross. The child is told the genie solved the problem by commanding a magic carpet to shape itself into a hollow tube through which the jewels could be rolled from the first bottle to the second (Holyoak, 1984; Holyoak et al., 1984). Various procedures are then used to assure that the child understands both the problem and the solution. For example, in some studies the child and experimenter jointly enacted the solution by folding a large sheet of paper into a hollow tube through which beads were transferred from one container to another (Brown, 1989; Brown et al., 1986). Then the child is immediately presented with an isomorphic transfer task in which, for example, a bunny must transfer Easter eggs across a barrier (a river) which, of course, the bunny cannot cross. The child is presented with a variety of props (e.g., cups, paper clips, scissors, in addition to a large sheet of paper). The analogical solution is to fold the large sheet of paper into a hollow tube and then roll plastic Easter eggs from one river bank to another.

Now consider the *component* processes that are required for successful isomorphic transfer. First, the solution to the genie problem, called the *base*, must be learned (e.g., Gholson, Eymard, Long et al., 1988; Gholson, Eymard, Morgan, & Kamhi, 1987; Reed, Ernst, & Banerji, 1974). Second, the base must be *represented* in terms of structural features of a generalizable mental model, rather than in terms of specific surface details, such as object attributes (Brown et al., 1986; Gentner, 1983; Holland et al., 1986; Johnson-Laird, 1980). One may think of structural features as representing how the entities in a problem are causally interrelated, whereas surface details refer to the entities themselves and their properties (Brown et al., 1986; Chi, Feltovich, & Glaser, 1981; Holyoak, 1985; Novick, 1988). Third, the child must *notice* the correspondence between the *target* (bunny) problem and base, *retrieving* the base in terms of its generalizable structure, rather than in terms of specific surface details, such as bottles, jewels, and a wall. Fourth, the one-to-one correspondence between structural features of the base and target must be *mapped* (Brown et al., 1986; Carbonell, 1986; Gentner, 1983; Holyoak, 1984; Winston, 1980) and any appropriate problem-solving activities carried out.

When children successfully execute a *global* strategy in isomorphic transfer, then, we may reasonably assume that three conditions held: (a) the one-to-one correspondence between the target and base was noticed, (b) a high quality base was retrieved, and (c) critical structural features of the base were mapped to the target. When analogical transfer fails, the focus shifts to one or more of the components. Thus, more *specific* strategies that affect base quality, retrieval, and mapping processes also need to be considered. Specific strategic activities include those that facilitate the acquisition of a base representation composed of structural features. Similarly, both base retrieval and mapping processes may involve specific strategies.

Much of the existing research on analogical reasoning processes in humans, and most of the research involving children, has focused on isomorphic transfer. When the target problem is not isomorphic (nonisomorphic) to the base, however, the four processes previously described do not provide a complete account of what is necessary for successful analogical transfer. To help clarify what is meant by *nonisomorphic* transfer, consider a child trained on the genie problem (with the magic-carpet solution), but transferred to a new problem that required using a rakelike implement to pull objects across a barrier. In general, when a given base is mapped to a nonisomorphic target problem the mapping is, by definition, incomplete. That is, because there is not a one-to-one correspondence between structural features of the base and target, a complete mapping is not possible.

If the child attempts to solve a nonisomorphic transfer problem using analogical reasoning processes, one of three very different strategies might be adopted. First, the child might, at the outset, represent both the base and target problems correctly in terms of the structural features, notice what the differences are, and then modify the procedures in the base (see Carbonell, 1986, pp. 144–145), making whatever changes are required to yield a one-to-one mapping between the (now modified) base and the target. If this *procedural adaptation* (Novick, 1988) is carried out correctly, it results in perfect transfer, an error-free solution in the transfer task. Second, the child might immediately assume the target is isomorphic to the base, blithely applying structural features in the base to the new problem without any further attempt at understanding. This would, of course, at some point lead to error(s) during the attempt to solve the new problem. When an error occurs, this child might try one of the following: (a) Attempt to delineate the differences between the target and structural features of the base, adapting the procedures accordingly before proceeding; (b) make a new attempt at isomorphic transfer; or (c) abandon the attempt at applying analogical reasoning processes altogether. Third, a strategy involving some combination of the other two might also be expected to occur, particularly in complex problem-solving tasks. The child might, for example, recognize at the outset that a one-to-one mapping between the base and target is not possible, but be unable to modify structural features of the base to bring them into correspondence with the target. Any attempts at procedural adaptation, then, would be expected to take place while the problem-solving activities themselves were being carried out. Unfortunately, little is currently known about procedural adaptation in subjects of any age.

Work on procedural adaptation has been reported in the artificial intelligence literature (e.g., Burstein, 1986; Carbonell, 1986; Falkenhainer et al., 1986; Holland et al., 1986; Sweller, 1988; Winston, 1980, 1984), but the relevance of that work to the performance of human subjects, and particularly children, is unknown. These models generally assume, for example, that most (or all) object-to-object or structure-to-structure mappings between the base and target are known at the outset. The best analogical interpretation is then the one that places the most structural features and/or objects in correspondence. A difficulty with this approach is that complete representations of both the base and target must be available at the outset, which seems unlikely, particularly among young children.

It will be useful to digress briefly to point out that what is being addressed in this chapter is the use of analogical reasoning processes during problem-solving and related activities. We are not concerned with the processes involved in solving verbal analogies of the form $A:B::C:D$, where the A, B, and C terms are given with the D term a forced choice among several alternatives. These kinds of verbal analogies, which were widely used historically in intelligence tests, have received considerable attention over the years (e.g., Goldman, Pellegrino, Parseghian, & Sallis, 1982; Inhelder & Piaget, 1958; Levinson & Carpenter, 1974; Spearman, 1923; Sternberg, 1985; Sternberg & Nigro, 1980; Sternberg & Rifkin, 1979). The relationship between that research and the processes involved in analogical reasoning of the kind just described, however, is not clear. The consensus seems to be that children have difficulty solving problems of the form $A:B::C:D$ by analogy until they are about 9 years of age, or even older (Holyoak et al., 1984; Levinson & Carpenter, 1974; Lunzer, 1965; Sternberg, 1985; Sternberg & Nigro, 1980; Sternberg & Rifkin, 1979). Instead, they appear to rely on various types of verbal associations in their attempts to solve (e.g., Achenbach, 1970, 1971; Sternberg & Nigro, 1980).

Many children readily establish a link between A and B, and between C and D, but they cannot establish the relational structure that links $A:B::C:D$. Some have suggested that understanding this latter kind of higher order relational structure requires formal reasoning in the Piagetian sense (Lunzer, 1965; Sternberg & Nigro, 1980). But a number of other variables, for example, specific stimulus factors (Levinson & Carpenter, 1974; Sternberg & Rifkin, 1979), priming (Gentile, Tedesco-Stratton, Davis, Lund, & Agunanne, 1977), and the complexity of the relationship between the *A:B* and the *C:D* terms (Lunzer, 1965) also have been shown to affect children's performance on verbal analogy tasks. In any case, solving verbal analogies requires different processing components than those needed for successful analogical transfer in tasks exemplified by the genie problem (Sternberg, 1977, 1985).

The focus of the present chapter is (a) on the component processes that are required for analogical reasoning during learning and problem solving, and (b) on specific strategic activities that facilitate each of the four component process—all of which are presumed necessary for a global analogical-reasoning strategy to be successfully executed. In the following sections we describe research concerned with the four component processes and identify strategic activities that may affect them. First, how is the base acquired and what variables affect the process? Second, how is the base represented? Although base acquisition and representation are closely interrelated, we keep them separate for purposes of conceptual clarity. Third, under what conditions do children notice that the base corresponds to the target and retrieve it? Fourth, what is involved in mapping the base to the target and modifying the base when procedural adaptation is required? As will be seen below, much more is known about some of these processes than others, particualry from a developmental perspective.

COMPONENT PROCESSES IN ANALOGICAL REASONING

Most research on analogical reasoning processes has focused on performance in transfer tasks, with transfer performance used as a criterion measure to identify variables that affect either the *quality* of the base or the probability it is retrieved and mapped to the target. The *course* of acquisition of the base, however, has received relatively little attention. Thus we begin by describing some of our own research that was specifically designed to explore learning processes during base acquisition (Gholson, Dattel, Eymard, & Morgan, 1989; Gholson, Eymard, Long et al., 1988; Gholson, Eymard, Morgan, & Kamhi, 1987). This is followed by closely related sections on base quality, representation, retrieval, and mapping.

Acquiring the Base

We have employed a common methodology in our research with children of various ages and adults. The materials used in both ac-

·quisition and transfer were relatively complex scheduling problems, mostly of the type illustrated in Tables 10.1 and 10.2. These Tables present analogs of seven-move scheduling problems called the "farmer's dilemma" and "missionaries/cannibals," respectively. An *analog* is simply a specific instance of a given problem type. Each table contains setting/constraint information, a recall instruction, and a numbered set of story units containing all the information required to solve the analog of the particular problem.

Method

During acquisition each *trial* consisted of the following: (a) the child was read setting/constraint information for the particular analog; (b) the recall instruction was presented to the child followed by the seven-story units representing a sequence of moves that solves the problem; (c) recall protocols were obtained from the child and audio recorded; and (d) appropriate physical materials representing the objects in the problem (e.g., fox, goose, corn, man, boat, river, house) were produced from behind a screen and placed in front of the child along with the instruction to solve the problem the way it was done in the story. Each move the child made was recorded.

TABLE 10.1 The Setting/Constraint Information and Story Units Containing Information for the Required Move Sequence in an Analog of the Farmer's Dilemma Problem

---

Farmer's dilemma Problem: Fox/Goose/Corn Analog

Setting/Constraint Information: Once a man bought a fox, a goose, and some corn at the market. He wanted to take them to his house, but his house was on the other side of a river that he had to cross. He had a boat, but it would only carry the man and one other thing over to his house at a time. He knew that if he left the fox alone with the goose, the fox would eat it. He also knew that if he left the goose alone with the corn, the goose would eat it. So he had to figure out how to get them all across the river to his house without anything being eaten.

Recall instruction: Now listen carefully to how they did it, because this is what I want you to remember so that you can say it back to me.

Story units:
1. The man took the goose across the river to his house.
2. The man then went back across the river.
3. The man took the fox across the river to his house.
4. Now the man took the goose back across the river with him.
5. The man took the corn across the river to his house.
6. The man then went back across the river.
7. The man took the goose across the river to his house.

TABLE 10.2   The Setting/Constraint Information and Story Units
Containing Information for the Required Move Sequence in an Analog
of the Missionaries/Cannibals Problem

Missionaries/Cannibals Problem: Dreadnocks/G.I.s Analog

Setting/Constraint Information: Two blue dreadnocks and three white G.I.s were on one side of a river they needed to cross to get to a house. They had a small boat, but it would only carry two people at a time. They all knew that if the blue dreadnocks ever outnumbered the white G.I.s on either side of the river the dreadnocks would harm the G.I.s. What they had to figure out was how to get the two blue dreadnocks and the three white G.I.s across the river to the house safely, without any of the G.I.s being harmed.

Recall instruction: Now listen carefully to how they did it, because this is what I want you to remember so that you can say it back to me.

Story units:
1. First a blue dreadnock and a white G.I. went across the river to the house.
2. Then the blue dreadnock went back across the river.
3. Next a blue dreadnock and a white G.I. went across the river to the house..
4. Then a white G.I. went back across the river.
5. Next a blue dreadnock and a white G.I. went across the river to the house.
6. Then a blue dreadnock went back across the river.
7. Finally, a blue dreadnock and a white G.I. went across the river to the house.

The child was stopped and a trial terminated when either (a) an error was made on the physical task, or (b) the child successfully carried out the seven-move sequence that was required in solving the physical task. If the child made an error, the experimenter indicated what it was, removed the physical task materials, and a new trial began immediately. In most of the research the acquisition *criterion* was two consecutive seven-move solutions on the physical task. In *transfer* only the setting/constraint information was provided; neither the recall instruction nor the story units containing the problem-solving information was presented to the child. That is, the child was read the setting/constraint information, the physical materials were produced, and the child was asked to solve the problem. During transfer the experimenter recorded each move the child made and provided immediate corrective feedback following all moves that resulted in illegal problem states. Some experiments involved only isomorphic transfer, but others included nonisomorphic transfer as well. Further details of specific experiments are described as warranted.

In our evaluation of acquisition processes we focus on three basic sets of data: first, the number of moves per trial prior to an error on the physical task (trial termination); second, the number of relevant story units recalled per trial during both precriterion and criterion trials; third, rank order correlations comparing the order in which the story units were read to the children with the order in which they recalled them. We also analyzed the number of trials to criterion (along with other measures) in each study. The differences between problem types have been small in most cases, for example, among elementary school children the number of trials to criterion was in the range 4.67 to 5.14 in the problems illustrated in Tables 10.1 and 10.2 (Gholson, Eymard, Long et al., 1988).

Learning Processes

In general, backward-learning procedures were used to structure the trial-to-trial data for purposes of tabular presentation and statistical treatment (Gholson, 1980; Kozminsky, Kintsch, & Bourne, 1981; Levine, 1975; Wickens & Millward, 1971). The data are first divided into subgroups based upon the number of trials the children required to reach criterion. These subgroups are then pooled cumulatively for analysis, with subgroups requiring smaller numbers of trials to criterion always cumulatively including appropriate data from children who required larger numbers.

Table 10.3 helps clarify the use of backward-learning procedures. The data are taken from an experiment in which third and sixth graders learned either a single analog or an alternating series of two analogs of the farmer's dilemma problem (Table 10.1) to a criterion of two consecutive seven-move solutions on the physical task (Gholson et al., 1987). An *alternating* series of two analogs means the child received one analog of the farmer's dilemma on the first trial, a second analog on the second, the first analog on the third trial, and so forth, until criterion was met. Table 10.3 presents the mean number of moves per trial (collapsed over age) given cumulatively for 5, 4, and 3 trials to criterion. Trial ST + 1 is the second criterion (i.e., solution) trial, ST (solution trial) is the first criterion trial, −1 is the trial before the beginning of the criterion run, and so forth. The maximum number of moves was, of course, seven. Notice that 28 children were included in the five-trial analysis. Because 16 more children required exactly four trials to achieve criterion, the four-trial analysis was performed on the appropriate four trials of data provided by the cumulative total of 44 children, and so forth.

Analyses of these data reveal no increase in the number of moves per trial prior to trail ST. (A trial was terminated when the child made an error on the physical task.) Stationary performance on trials prior to solution is usually taken to reflect none-to-all learning (Gholson,

TABLE 10.3   The Mean Number of Moves Per
Trial Prior to an Error (Trial Termination) on the
Physical Task, Collapsed over Other Variables

Number of Children	Trial				
	−3	−2	−1	ST^a	$ST+1$
28	2.21	1.93	2.07	7	7
44		1.98	2.23	7	7
61			2.31	7	7

Note. The Data of Individual Criterion Subgroups
are Pooled Cumulatively for Decreasing Numbers of
Trials to Criterion. Tables 10.3 and 10.7 are from
"Problem solving, recall, and isomorphic transfer
among third-grade and sixth-grade children" by B.
Gholson, L. A. Eymard, D. Morgan, and A. G.
Kamhi, 1987, *Journal of Experimental Child Psychology,
43*, p. 227–243. Copyright 1987 by Academic Press.
Reprinted by permission.
[a]Solution Trial (ST)

1980; Levine, 1975; Trabasso & Bower, 1968). Neither the children's
ages, nor whether they learned one analog or the alternating series
of two analogs had any effect on this, or most other *acquisition* measures.

For purposes of developmental comparison we present data from
two other studies. In one experiment the subjects were preschoolers,
half of them were 4-year-olds and half, 5-year-olds. The materials
were analogs of a five-move scheduling problem called "father/sons"
(Gholson, Dattel et al., 1989). A 200-pound man and his two 100-
pound sons must cross a barrier using a vehicle that can carry no
more than 200 pounds and must carry at least one person on each
crossing. The solution is two sons across, one son back, father across,
one son back, two sons across. The various analogs of the problem
that were used all involved cartoon characters, a mother and her two
children in each case. In the second study the subjects were young
adults (Morgan, Gholson, Eymard, Coles, & Leeming, in preparation). The materials were two *11-move* scheduling problems, a mis-
sionaries/cannibals problem with the constraints presented in Table
10.2 (but with three characters of each kind) and a closely related
problem called the "jealous husbands," which involves three husband/
wife pairs. The constraint in the latter problem is that no woman may
ever be in the presence of any man unless her own husband is also
present (Simon & Reed, 1976; Reed et al., 1974).

In the study with preschool children, modeling procedures were used on acquisition trials. As each of the five story units was read to the child, the corresponding move was enacted by the experimenter. In the adult study the start and goal states of the physical task were screened from view throughout. The experimenter moved objects from one side of the barrier to the other following instructions given by the subjects. The subjects saw the objects only as they traversed the barrier. Subjects in both studies either received one analog on consecutive trials during acquisition or an alternating series of two. The mean number of moves per trial for 5, 4, and 3 trials to criterion is presented in Table 10.4. There are no increases in the numbers of moves until trial ST, again reflecting none-to-all learning (cf. Table 10.3). In both the preschool and adult data (Table 10.4) there is a slight increase in the average number of moves on trial −2. This finding is an artifact of the acquisition criterion (Gholson, Dattel et al., 1989; Gholson, Eymard, Long et al., 1988; Gholson, Eymard, Morgan, & Kamhi, 1987). Occasionally a subject solves on one trial, makes an error on the next, and then solves on two consecutive trials, thus meeting the acquisition criterion. The effects is to inflate slightly the scores obtained on Trial −2.

The mean number of relevant story units recalled per trial for the preschoolers, elementary-school children, and adults is presented in Table 10.5. In each case there is a significant incremental increase across precriterion trials, and then a somewhat larger increase in going from Trial −1 to trial ST. There are also some small age differences in favor of older preschoolers and older elementary school children in the precriterion recall data (Gholson, Dattel et al., 1989; Gholson, Eymard, Morgan, & Kamhi, 1987). Similarly, the preschoolers recalled on average about 70% (3.5/5) of the revelant story units on criterion trials, whereas the older children and adults recalled between about 80% and 90% on criterion trials (Table 10.5).

Trial-by-trial analyses of the move and recall data yield strikingly similar patterns across the three age ranges. All three age groups show none-to-all learning in the move data (Tables 10.3 and 10.4). All three age groups, however, show incremental increases in the number of story units recalled across precriterion trials, and a somewhat larger increase on trial ST (Table 10.5). Thus, although subjects of all ages acquired the list of story units piecemeal, one at a time, they consolidated structural features of the base into a coherent whole suddenly, yielding solution to the physical task.

In order to explore the subjects' linguistic representations of structural features of the base, rank-order correlation coefficients were used to compare the order in which the story units were recalled

TABLE 10.4   The Mean Number of Moves Per Trial
Prior to an Error (Trial Termination) on the Physical
Task, for Preschoolers and Adults Collapsed over
Other Variables

	Preschool				
Number of Subjects			Trial		
	−3	−2	−1	ST^a	$ST + 1$
19	1.36	2.68	1.07	5	5
25		2.36	1.04	5	5
36			1.06	5	5

	Adults				
Number of Subjects			Trial		
	−3	−2	−1	ST	$ST + 1$
52	6.06	7.08	5.63	11.23	11.16
63		6.68	5.49	11.19	11.10
71			5.31	11.19	11.08

Note. The data of individual criterion subgroups are
pooled cumulatively for decreasing numbers of trials to
criterion. Data from Tables 10.4, 10.5, and 10.6 are
from Gholson, Eymard, Morgan, & Kamhi (1987);
"Problem solving, recall, and mapping relations in
isomorphic transfer and nonisomorphic transfer
among preschoolers and elementary-school children"
by B. Gholson, A. R. Dattel, D. Morgan, and L. A.
Eymard, 1989, Child Development; and Isomorphic and
Nonisomorphic Transfer: Surface and Structural Similarity
by D. Morgan, B. Gholson, L. A. Eymard, R. Coles, and
F. C. Leeming, in preparation. Adapted by permission
of the authors.
[a]Solution trial (ST)

with the order in which they were presented. The correlations were
computed for each subject on each trial. The mean rank-order coefficients from the three studies are presented in Table 10.6. The numbers of subjects are somewhat reduced (relative to Tables 10.3–10.5),
because some subjects failed to recall the number of relevant units
required to compute correlations on some trials. The patterns of data
yielded by the three age groups are quite different on this measure.
Among the preschoolers, there is a significant increase across trials
only in the three-trial data, and only one score was higher than .75

TABLE 10.5 The Mean Number of Relevant Propositions Per Trial for Preschool (Maximum 5), Elementary School (Maximum 7), and Adult (Maximum 11) Subjects.

Number of Subjects	Preschool				
	Trial				
	−3	−2	−1	ST^a	$ST + 1$
19	2.47	2.69	2.84	3.39	3.11
25		2.68	2.80	3.40	3.36
36			2.75	3.25	3.50
48				3.31	3.72

Number of Subjects	Elementary School				
	Trial				
	−3	−2	−1	ST	$ST + 1$
46	3.41	4.30	4.30	5.67	5.83
62		3.92	4.08	5.55	5.71
69			3.93	5.58	5.75
72				5.47	5.61

Number of Subjects	Adults				
	Trial				
	−3	−2	−1	ST	$ST + 1$
52	7.39	7.71	7.96	8.83	9.82
63		7.56	7.98	8.97	9.96
71			7.75	8.96	9.93
72				8.98	9.94

Note. The data are collapsed over other variables (see text). The data of individual criterion subgroups are pooled cumulatively for decreasing numbers of trials to criterion.
[a]Solution trial (ST)

(this finding is replicated in the seven-move problem illustrated in Table 10.1, Gholson, Dattel et al., 1989). Among the elementary school children, the correlations are stationary in the .75 to .80 range prior to Trial ST and then jump to nearly 1.0. The adults show yet a third pattern. All their scores are above .90, showing only a small increase on Trial ST.

TABLE 10.6   The Mean Rank Order Correlation
Coefficients for Preschool, Elementary School and
Adult Subjects

Preschool					
Number of Subjects	*Trial*				
	−3	*−2*	*−1*	*ST^a*	*ST + 1*
14	.32	.26	.62	.63	.58
19		.35	.44	.71	.67
30			.41	.74	.74
43				.65	.80

Elementary School					
Number of Subjects	*Trial*				
	−3	*−2*	*−1*	*ST*	*ST + 1*
16	.76	.78	.80	.98	1.00
29		.76	.76	.98	1.00
53			.79	.97	1.00
76				.98	.99

Adults					
Number of Subjects	*Trial*				
	−3	*−2*	*−1*	*ST*	*ST + 1*
51	.95	.91	.94	.99	.99
62		.91	.95	.99	.99
71			.95	.99	.99
72				.99	.99

Note. The data are collapsed over other variables (see
text). The data of individual subgroups are pooled
cumulatively for decreasing numbers of trials to criterion.
^{a}Solution Trial (ST)

Thus there are large developmental differences in the rank-order
data on both precriterion and criterion trials. The preschoolers'
linguistic representations improve somewhat over trials but barely
reach the level shown by the older children during precriterion trials.
The preschoolers had clearly acquired the base, as reflected in their
performance on the physical task (Table 10.4), and in their transfer
performance (the following section). They showed nearly perfect

isomorphic transfer, particularly in the two-analog condition, as did the elementary school children (Gholson, Dattel et al., 1989; Gholson, Eymard, Morgan, & Kamhi, 1987), and the college students (Morgan et al., in preparation).

The elementary school children's rank-order data mirrored their performance on the physical task. That is, even though they acquired the story units incrementally (Table 10.5), final consolidation of the units into a coherent linguistic representation of the problem structure occurred abruptly (Table 10.6), mirroring their performance on the physical task (Table 10.3). The college students performance on this measure was nearly perfect throughout (.90 to .99). Thus, although they showed none-to-all learning in the move data (Table 10.4), and incremental acquisition of the story units (Table 10.5), the story units they recalled were ordered nearly perfectly on both pre-criterion and criterion trials (Table 10.6).

Given age-appropriate tasks, then, the course of acquisition of the base is about the same across the age range that was studied. There are large differences, however, in the subjects' abilities to linguistically order structural features of the knowledge embodied in the base. The one clear developmental trend in these acquisition data, then, is in the ability to represent linguistically the ordered knowledge constituting the base, with recall order providing a good reflection of the knowledge represented in the base only among the elementary-school children. Whether this reflects different acquisition strategies remains to be determined.

Base Quality

Number of Analogs

A number of variables have been identified that affect the quality of the base, as reflected in *transfer* data, and we consider these before turning to how the base is represented. One variable that has been shown to dramatically affect the quality of the base is the number of analogs presented during acquisition. Gick and Holyoak (1980, 1983; Holyoak & Koh, 1987) used Dunker's (1945) radiation problem to explore conditions that enhance analogical problem solving among young adults. In this problem a single large source of radiation is available that will destroy a tumor, but it will also destroy healthy tissue on either side of the tumor. The task is to discover a "convergence solution," that is, a solution that involves dividing the single high-level source of radiation into multiple low-level sources that converge on the tumor from different directions.

In a typical study (Gick & Holyoak, 1983) the radiation problem was preceded by some combination of one or two analogs of the radiation problem with the same structure (e.g., divide a large military force into smaller forces that converge on a fortress from different directions), along with comprehension or summarization instructions, diagrams, or explicit statements of the underlying (convergence) principle. One analog in various combinations with diagrams and instructions produced about 40% success in transfer before a hint to attempt to apply the prior (analogous) solution was given, and 60% to 80% after the hint. However, when two analogs preceded transfer, performance was much better and when subjects gave evidence that they understood the underlying principle (inferred from how they related two analogs), performance was nearly perfect. This finding suggests the base that results from learning one analog yields knowledge that is embedded in a specific context (Brown, 1975, 1989; Dunker & Krechevsky, 1939; Holyoak, 1985), but learning two analogs encourages subjects to disembed structural features of the base from specific surface details. Holyoak (1984) suggested that experience with two analogs of a given problem results in an abstract problem-solving *schema* composed of structural features that are separate from the specific surface details of any particular analog. This results in a more flexible base with wider strategic application.

Brown et al. (1986) obtained similar findings among preschoolers in research using analogs of the genie problem (described previously). Following training on one analog, all children immediately received two consecutive isomorphic transfer tasks. All children enacted the folded paper solution jointly with the experimenter in the training problem. In the first transfer task children who failed to transfer (enact the solution by themselves) enacted it jointly with the experimenter for a second time. This led to dramatically better performance on the second transfer task (Brown et al., 1986; p. 112). We obtained corresponding findings among preschoolers in the study with five-move problems that was described previously (Gholson et al., 1989). Children in the one-analog condition required an average of 6.66 moves to solve the five-move isomorphic transfer task, but those in the two-analog condition required only 5.42.

We also obtained better isomorphic transfer in the two-analog condition than in the one-analog in the study involving elementary school children and the farmer's dilemma problem (Table 10.1), described earlier (Gholson, Eymard, Morgan, & Kamhi, 1987). The number of moves required to solve the seven-move transfer task and total amount of time they required in each condition is presented in Table 10.7. The fourth column, labeled *control,* is a condition in which the children received only the transfer task. The differences in both the move and time data are statistically significant from column to column in the table. Thus though the number of analogs experienced during acquisition does not affect the *course* of acquisition of the base (see preceding section "Acquiring the Base"), it does affect the *quality* of the base. We failed, however, to obtain an effect of number of analogs in our study with young adults that was described earlier (Morgan et al., in preparation), but that was probably due to ceiling effects. The subjects in both the one- and two-analog conditions required only about 13 moves to solve the transfer task (minimum was 11).

Rules and Enactment

Whether subjects are required to *state* the rules governing solution during acquisition, *enact* the solution, or both state rules and enact the solution, has also been shown to affect the quality of the base. On the one hand, Gick and Holyoak (1980, 1983; Holyoak, 1985; Holyoak & Koh, 1987), in their work with young adults, argued that concrete experience solving a problem, that is, physically enacting the solution, facilitates analogical transfer relative to experience involving only a more abstract textual or linguistic representation that results from merely stating the solution. On the other hand, Brown and Campione (1984) suggested that requiring children to state the rules governing solution (see "Causal Structure," following), as well as enact it, facilitates both acquisition of the base and transfer. And in a series of studies with preschool children involving the genie problem as well as others, Brown and her colleagues (Brown, 1989; Brown et al., 1986) have shown that prompting children to state the rules governing

TABLE 10.7 The Mean Number of Moves in Transfer and Total Amount of Time in Transfer for Third and Sixth Graders in the Two-Analog, One-Analog, and Control Conditions

	Condition		
	Two Analog	One Analog	Control
Grade 3	8.80 (51)	14.05 (161)	27.65 (499)
Grade 6	9.40 (66)	12.90 (169)	25.80 (488)

Note. Time in seconds is given in parentheses.

solution, as well as *enact* them, leads to dramatically better analogical transfer than simply enacting solutions. They suggested that explicitly stating the solution disembeds the base representation from the surface details of any particular analog, yielding a base that is highly generalizable (Brown et al., 1986, p. 109). An implication is that if the activity of explicitly stating the rules governing solution became part of the child's own problem-solving repertoire, it would constitute a strategy that enhances base quality.

In order to explore the generality of the findings obtained by Brown and her colleagues with preschoolers and by Gick and Holyoak with young adults, we conducted a study with third and fourth graders using the kinds of procedures previously described (Gholson, Dattel et al., 1989). We addressed two basic questions. First, what effect does combining the recall task with the physical task have on performance on the recall task *itself* and on transfer? Second, what effect does combining the recall task with the physical task have on performance on the physical task *itself* and on transfer? The two questions taken together required four groups.

Meeting the acquisition criterion for two of the groups was contingent upon their performance on two consecutive trials on the recall task. They were required to recall at least five story units without reversal in recall order on the first criterion trial and six on the second. One of these groups received both the recall task and the physical task, whereas the other received only the recall task during acquisition. The acquisition criterion for the other two groups was a seven-move solution on the physical task on two consecutive trials. The children in one of these groups received both the recall task and the physical task, whereas the others received only the physical task.

Despite differences in the acquisition criterion, there were no significant differences among the four groups during acquisition. In isomorphic transfer, however, the three groups of children who received the physical task each performed significantly better than the children who received only the recall task. The former groups required means of 7.15 to 7.95 moves and 34 to 53 seconds to solve the transfer task. Children who received only the recall task in acquisition, however, required 10.45 moves and 97 seconds in transfer. Thus enacting the solution in the physical task improved the quality of the base relative to just stating the correct sequence of moves. Transfer performance among all three groups who received the physical task was so good, however, that there was no room for improvement when the children who received *both* the recall and the physical task were compared to those who received *only* the physical task. Consequently, although the findings support the suggestion that requiring subjects to enact solutions improves performance relative to just requiring them to state the rules governing solution (Gick & Holyoak, 1980, 1983), the results do not bear on related findings indicating that both stating the rules and enacting solutions improves performance relative to only enacting solutions (Brown & Campione, 1984; Brown et al., 1986).

Causal Structure

Gentner and Toupin (1986; see also, Brown, 1989) have shown that the degree of causal structure embedded in the acquisition task can have measurable effects on base quality as reflected in isomorphic transfer. In a study with children in the age ranges 5–7 and 8–10 years, they manipulated the amount of explicit causal structure that was provided during acquisition of the base. All children were first told a story about three animals engaged in a play activity. Props were then produced (e.g., the three animals, lake, boat, mountain, etc.), and the children were asked to enact the story line. If any errors were committed the children were corrected and required to enact the story line again, until they could act it out without help. Isomorphic transfer followed immediately. One variable that was manipulated involves what Gentner (1983, p. 14) called "systematicity," with different values reflecting the amount of causal structure among object relations. Half the children at each age level were presented with a thematic statement about one of the animals that provided a coherent rationale for the contents of the story at the outset. In addition, at the conclusion of the story they were presented with a statement that further linked the thematic statement and the contents of the story. Thus, during acquisition these children were explicitly required to causally interrelate structural features of the base. Gentner refers to these kinds of causal relations as "systematic" (Gentner, 1983; Gentner & Toupin, 1986). In the other condition children received unrelated statements at the outset and end of their stories (unsystematic).

The characters and the roles they played in the isomorphic transfer task were varied in terms of their similarity to those in the original story. In one condition both the characters and roles were similar, in a second the characters were different but the roles similar, and in a third the characters were similar but the roles they played were different. Gentner and Toupin referred to these three transfer conditions as involving high, medium, and low *transparency*, respectively. Among the older children transfer was significantly better in the systematic acquisition condition than in the unsystematic. In both age groups performance decreased with transparency. Among the older children in the systematic condition it decreased from about 95% to about 85% in going from the high to the low transparency condition, but the parallel decrease in the unsystematic condition was from about 92% to 60%. Thus, strategic activities directed toward explicitly processing causal relations would be expected to help children in this age range (8–10 years) overcome misleading cues in transfer tasks. Among the younger children there was no effect of systematicity. That is, the systematic condition did not differ significantly from the unsystematic, and performance of both groups dropped precipitously as transparency decreased.

In a related study that may be construed as exploring explicit causal structure, Brown et al. (1986; Brown, 1989) used the genie problem in three experimental conditions with preschoolers: prompted goal structure, free recall, and control. In the prompted condition the children were asked questions that required them to state the four key elements of the "goal structure" (1986, p. 109) of the problem (i.e., protagonist, goal, obstacle, and solution). In free recall the children simply recalled what they could about the story, and in the control condition the children went directly from acquisition to transfer. All children enacted the rolled paper solution (described previously) prior to transfer. Children who were able to state the goal structure showed excellent transfer (70% to 80%), whereas only about 20% of the remaining children solved the transfer problem. Thus, prompting the child to state the four causally related elements of the goal structure enhanced the quality of the base and transfer. These findings, taken together with those of Gentner and Toupin (1986), suggest that a good strategy for children to adopt during learning would be to explicitly state (process) the causal relations among the objects in the problem.

Summary: The Base

What can we conclude, then, concerning acquisition of the base and the variables that affect its quality? First, as measured by the number of moves per trial and the number of relevant story units recalled, the course of acquisition of the base is similar across developmental levels, at least in subjects ranging in age from 4 years to about 20. The move data indicate that the base is acquired suddenly, in an all-or-none fashion (Tables 10.3 and 10.4), but the story units were acquired incrementally, one at a time (Table 10.5). The ability to represent structural features of the base linguistically (Nelson, 1986; Nelson & Gruendel, 1981), however, varies with age and is a good reflection of performance on the physical task only among elementary school children (Table 10.6).

As measured by transfer performance, at least three variables have been identified that affect the quality of the base acquired during original learning. First, experience with two analogs clearly produces better transfer than experience with only one. Holyoak (1984; Gick & Holyoak, 1980, 1983) proposed that when two (isomorphic) analogs are presented during acquisition only their common structural features, called "mapped identities," are preserved in the base, with specific surface details removed through a process called "eliminative induction" (Mackie, 1974, pp. 297–321). When only one analog is presented, however, surface details are preserved in the base, as well as structural features. Thus in transfer, experience with two analogs produces two potential advantages relative to experience with one. Because surface details are eliminated from the base, and only structural features of the problem are retained, it is more probable that correspondences will be noticed and the base retrieved (Ross, 1987). In addition, because surface details are eliminated, they are not there to interfere with the mapping process.

Second, enacting solutions during acquisition results in better isomorphic transfer relative to stating solution rules (Gholson, Dattel et al., 1989; Gick & Holyoak, 1980, 1983). In addition, there is clear evidence that, among young children at least, stating the rules that govern solution, as well as enacting them, enhances performance relative to enactment alone (Brown, 1989; Brown & Campione, 1984; Brown et al., 1986). Thus combining the two activities results in a higher quality base than either activity taken alone. It is possible, of course, that the two different activities result in two different kinds of representations (Paivio, 1979). Some children might rely more on one kind of representation (e.g., linguistic), being more facile at using that kind in transfer, whereas other children might rely more on a second kind (e.g., imagery) for representation and transfer. Given the current state of our knowledge, however, it appears more parsimonious to conclude that combining the verbal and enactment tasks enhances performance through the same mechanism that results in better performance following experience with two analogs relative to one. That is, a strategy of combining the two activities may result in a base with structural features that are more disembedded from context-specific surface details (Holyoak, 1984; Gick & Holyoak, 1983). As just indicated, this improves the quality of the base, which may increase the liklihood that the correspondence between base and target is noticed, and facilitate the mapping process itself.

Explicitly processing causally interrelated object relations in the base (structural features) during acquisition is another strategy that appears to enhance isomorphic transfer (Brown, 1989; Brown et al., 1986; Gentner, 1983; Gentner & Toupin, 1986; see also, Trabasso & Sperry, 1985). Gentner and Toupin (1986) obtained the finding among children 8–10 years old and Brown et al. (1986) obtained it among preschoolers. Gentner and Toupin failed to find significant facilitation among their younger children, that is, performance in both the systematic and unsystematic conditions dropped precipitously as transparency decreased. Why explicit causal structure failed to improve the younger children's performance remains a puzzle. It should be noted though that in both the systematic and unsystematic conditions the children showed about 90% transfer in the high transparency condition, and performance dropped to only about 60% under low transparency.

Gentner and Toupin (1986, p. 296) proposed that increased systematicity, or explicit causal structure, may improve both the quality of the base and the mapping process, the latter by guiding the mapping process and providing a check on its correctness (p. 296). Unfortunately, due to the paucity of relevant data, the relative contribution of explicit causal structure in enhancing the quality of the base versus improving the mapping process cannot be assessed at present. Gentner and Toupin also showed that transparency, or the similarity between specific objects in the base and target, affects transfer, but because transparency presumably has its effect on retrieval and mapping processes, it is discussed further in later sections.

Representing the Base

Gentner (1983, Gentner & Jeziorski, 1989) has given causal structure preeminence in her "structure mapping" theory of analogical reasoning. Predicates are mapped from the base to the target following three rules: (a) surface details, such as object attributes are discarded; (b) relations among objects (structural features) are preserved in the base; and (c) higher-order relations, or relations among relations, are preserved at the expense of lower order relations. The latter embodies the principle of *systematicity* that was described above. The base, then, according to Gentner (1983, 1989), contains a connected system of causal relations, rather than isolated predicates and object attributes. The ideal strategy for analogical transfer, then, involves mapping higher order relations from the base to the target (Gentner, 1989).

Holyoak (1984; Gick & Holyoak, 1980, 1983) proposed that the base representation is a "problem schema," consisting of an initial state (constraints, goals, resources), a solution plan, and an actual or anticipated outcome of using the plan. The initial state is causally related to the solution plan; the goal is the reason for the plan; the resources enable the plan; and the constraints prevent alternate plans (1984, p. 208). Although Holyoak's base appears similar to Gentner's in the emphasis on causal relations, he also emphasized the importance of pragmatic considerations, such as the subject's goals (1985, pp. 60–62).

Brown (1989) has also emphasized causal structure as the critical feature of the base. Brown et al. (1986) found that children who filled the four key slots in a frame (Minsky, 1975) representing the goal (causal) structure of the genie problem showed excellent transfer. Among children in whose recall protocols goal structure elements were not predominant, however, transfer was poor. On the basis of these and related findings, Brown (1989) concluded that the base is a frame representing an abstract situation (van Dijk & Kintsch, 1983) or mental model (Gentner, 1983; Johnson-Laird, 1980) containing slots representing key elements of the goal structure.

Finally, we have proposed (Gholson, Dattel et al., 1989), that the base representation acquired in complex scheduling problems is an event schema (Mandler, 1979, 1983; Nelson, 1986). Like scripts (Schank & Abelson, 1977), event schemas involve temporally and causally connected activities, or events. These events, which occur in a designated sequence, are temporally organized and causally related in the sense that each event (move, state) successively enables the next event in the sequence. Thus, because each event enabled the next, even our preschool subjects were able to carry out and transfer the temporally ordered sequence of events designated by the schema (see "Base Acquisition"). We suggested the reason the preschoolers failed to correctly sequence the story units in their recall protocols (see Table 10.6), even though they solved the physical task and showed nearly perfect isomorphic transfer, was because they lacked the kind of reversible thought processes (Beilin, 1975; Gholson, 1980; Gross, 1985; Inhelder & Piaget, 1964) that are needed to correctly verbalize an alternating (i.e., reversing) move sequence. Consistent with this possibility, Brown (1976) has shown that preschoolers understand temporal sequences before they are able to produce them in a narrative.

Retrieving the Base

Although there is little developmental research concerned with noticing correspondences and base retrieval, Ross (1984, 1987) investigated what he called "reminding" during analogical reasoning by young adults. Noticing a match between information in memory (the base) and a new (analogous) problem constitutes a reminding. In a series of studies, Ross (1984, 1987) provided evidence that similarity among surface details, or superficial similarity, promotes reminding, at least among novices (Gick & Holyoak, 1983; Novick, 1988; Reed, 1987). Gentner and Landers (1985) presented similar evidence. Their (young adult) subjects first read a large set of scenarios, then 2 weeks later they read new ones that were either true analogs or spurious matches that shared only low order predicates. Mere appearance matches, or superficial similarities, were about twice as likely to be noticed as true analogies that lacked surface similarities. Gentner and Landers concluded that *retrieving* the base is governed by surface similarity, but its *usefulness* for purposes of analogical reasoning is governed by the similarity between structural features of the base and the target (Ross, 1987). In their study of transparency (described previously), Gentner and Toupin (1986) obtained corresponding findings. The children showed nearly perfect transfer in the high transparency condition, in which the base and target shared common surface and structural features, but when similar characters played different roles (low transparency), the children had particular difficulty. That is, misleading superficial similarities led to incorrect role assignments.

There is some evidence from tasks in which subjects *classify* problems according to similarity that this reliance on superficial similarity may only hold for novice problem solvers (Chi et al., 1981; Chi, Glaser, & Rees, 1982; Gobbo & Chi, 1986). Novices, for example, classify physics problems by surface features, but physicists group them by physical principles (structural features). Similarly, Silver (1979) reported that among seventh graders, good problem solvers grouped mathematical word problems by their mathematical structure, whereas poor math students grouped them on the basis of surface similarity.

Although we located no research directly concerned with remindings in young children, the aforementioned findings indicate that young children, universal novices, may be particularly dependent on surface cues for base retrieval. There is some evidence, though, that even preschoolers can overcome appearance matches in categorizing objects if they have relevant information (Carey, 1985; Gelman & Markman, 1986). Furthermore, Brown (1989) presented some preliminary findings indicating (a) that children's sets may affect base retrieval, and (b) that children sometimes transfer a modeled solution in ways that overcome superficial similarity. We suggest, then, that deliberate strategic activities directed toward processing structural features of a target problem, rather than processing superficial surface details, would increase the likelihood of a useful base being retrieved. In the absence of research identifying useful strategic activities, however, it seems reasonable to conclude that if one wants to enhance the probability that a well learned base will be retrieved by children or novices, a good first step would be to engineer appearance matches between surface details of the target and base.

Mapping the Base

It is generally agreed that successful analogical reasoning requires mapping structural features of the base to the target (Brown, 1989; Brown et al., 1986; Carbonell, 1986; Cooper & Sweller, 1987; Gentner, 1983, 1989; Gholson, Dattel et al., 1989; Gholson, Eymard, Long et al., 1988; Gick & Holyoak, 1980, 1983; Novick, 1988; Reed, 1984, 1987; Reed et al., 1974; Ross, 1984; 1987; Winston, 1980, 1984). Various researchers have thought about these features of the base in slightly different ways and have labelled them differently, for example, goal structure (Brown, 1989; Brown et al., 1986), higher order relations (Gentner, 1983, 1989), event schemas (Gholson, Dattel et al., 1989), and problem schemas (Holyoak, 1984, 1985). As the literature reviewed in the previous sections demonstrates, there is now considerable evidence that when age-appropriate materials and procedures are used, even preschoolers can map structural features of a base to an isomorphic target, exhibiting nearly perfect transfer (Brown et al., 1986; Brown, 1989; Gentner & Toupin, 1986: Gholson, Dattel et al., 1989). Thus most of this section focuses on the role of analogical reasoning in nonisomorphic transfer, that is, transfer in which there is not a 1:1 correspondence between the base and target. An example might involve training children on analogs of the farmer's dilemma (Table 10.1) and transferring them to analogs of missionaries/cannibals (Table 10.2).

First, however, we briefly restate the important role similarity plays in retrieval and mapping processes during isomorphic transfer. If the base and target share both surface and structural features, both experts and novices show nearly perfect mappings as measured by transfer performance (Chi et al., 1981, 1982; Gholson, Dattel et al., 1989; Gholson, Eymard, Long et al., 1988; Gholson, Eymard, Morgan, & Kamhi, 1987; Gick & Holyoak, 1983; Holyoak, 1984; Holyoak et al., 1984; Holyoak & Koh, 1987; Novick, 1988; Reed, 1987; Simon & Hayes, 1976). This assumes, of course, that the base is of high quality (see preceding section "Base Quality"). When surface features of the target are highly dissimilar to those in the base or are low in transparency and provide misleading cues, however, only experts show much positive transfer (Brown, 1989; Chi et al., 1982; Gentner & Toupin, 1986; Novick, 1988; Reed, 1987; Silver, 1979, 1981). This difference is presumably because surface details predominate in the base representations of novices, whereas the representations of experts contain mostly structural features (Adelson, 1984; Chi et al., 1981; Novick, 1988; Schoenfeld & Herman, 1982; Silver, 1979). Gentner and Toupin (1986) showed that older children overcome most of the detrimental effects of low transparency if there is a high degree of causal structure in the base. This finding appears to be consistent with the findings on experts versus novices. That is, the base representations of older children in the systematic condition, like those of experts (Gentner & Toupin, 1986), may have contained mostly structural features of the problem.

Nonisomorphic Mapping

Reed et al. (1974) studied nonisomorphic transfer in young adults using missionaries/cannibals (MC) and jealous husbands (JH) problems (with three individuals of each type) requiring 11 moves for solution. The constraint in MC is that cannibals may never outnumber missionaries on either side of the barrier (Table 10.2). In JH the only constraint is that no woman may ever be in the presence of any man unless her husband is also present. Because there is no way to distinguish any one missionary or cannibal from another, there are only four distinct 11-move solution paths in that problem, but more than 400 identifiable 11-move solution paths in the JH problem. If wives are substituted for cannibals and husbands for missionaries, however, each of the latter solution paths will map directly to one of the four in MC, a many:one (or homomorphic) mapping (Reed et al., 1974).

In three experiments, Reed et al. (1974) observed little transfer between the two problem types. Transfer occurred only when the JH problem provided the base with MC as the target, and only under conditions in which subjects were explicitly told the substitution rules and how to implement them in the target problem. There was no transfer from MC to JH under any conditions they studied. Thus in the many:one mapping condition, the subjects required explicit instructions in order to map the base to the target, but in the one:many condition even mapping instructions were ineffective in producing nonisomorphic transfer. In related work involving mathematics word problems, Reed (1987) also obtained very little nonisomorphic transfer (cf. Novick, 1988).

We recently conducted research exploring mapping relations in nonisomorphic transfer using the procedures described previously (see "Base Acquisition"). The acquisition and transfer tasks in the first of these studies (Gholson, Eymard, Long et al., 1988) involved analogs of three different seven-move scheduling problems: the farmer's dilemma (Table 10.1), a three-peg/three-disc version of the tower of Hanoi (Kotovsky, Hayes, & Simon, 1985), and the MC problem illustrated in Table 10.2. The tower of Hanoi involves three disks of different sizes stacked on one of three pegs, ordered in terms if size, with the largest on the bottom. The task is to order the three disks the same way on a different specified peg. The constraints are that only one disk may be moved at a time and under no conditions may a larger disk be stacked on top of a smaller disk. One third of the children trained on each problem type were transferred to an isomorphic analog. The remaining children were transferred to an analog of one of the other problem types used in acquisition.

The major finding was that nonisomorphic transfer was asymmetrical. There was good transfer from both the farmer's dilemma and tower of Hanoi to MC. In fact, in the move data there was no difference between these two nonisomorphic transfer conditions and the isomorphic condition. But there was no transfer from MC to either farmer's dilemma or tower of Hanoi. Furthermore, there was no transfer from farmer's dilemma to tower of Hanoi or vice versa relative to controls. There was one noteworthy discrepancy among the three groups transferred to MC. Children in the isomorphic condition required a mean of about 7 seconds per move, but those transferred from farmer's dilemma and tower of Hanoi required about 15 seconds per move (Gholson, Eymard, Long et al., 1988, p. 44). Presumably, this extra time was required because children in the nonisomorphic conditions engaged in procedural adaptation during transfer. That is, they used a strategy that included activities for modifying structural features of the base in order to bring them into one-to-one correspondence with features of the nonisomorphic target problem.

One difficulty in the Gholson, Eymard, Long et al. (1988) study was that the three problems used in acquisition and transfer were so different from each other that neither mapping relations nor constraint differences could be explicitly delineated. Thus, in a second study (Gholson, Dattel et al., 1989) they were made explicit. Conditions were devised in which a complete mapping was possible between the solution path represented in the base and a path in the target problem, but there was only a partial overlap between the problem spaces of the base and target. One acquisition condition involved analogs of MC (Table 10.2). Figure 10.1 presents the nine seven-move solution paths that are possible in the problem space of

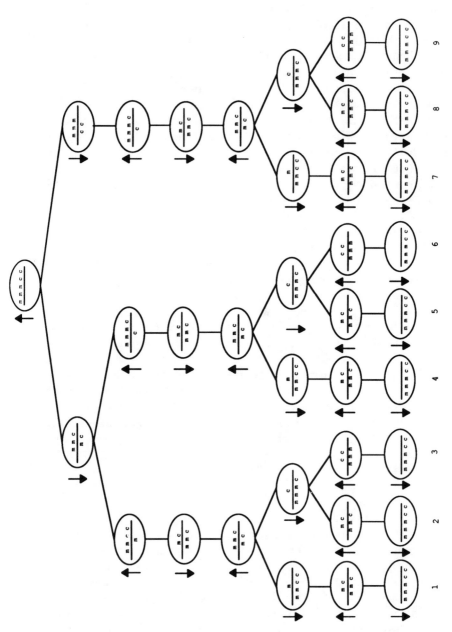

FIG. 10.1. The nine seven-move solution paths in the problem space of the missionaries/cannibals problem. The paths are numbered across the bottom of the figure. The problem cannot be solved in fewer than seven moves.

this version of MC. In the second acquisition condition, children learned analogs of a seven-move version of JH. In this analog of the JH problem (Table 10.8), called "robots/wrestlers" (R/W) there are three Ws and two Rs, with two R/W pairs. There is no constraint on the location of the unpaired W relative to other individuals. There are more than 200 seven-move solution paths in this JH problem space. If Rs are substituted for Cs and Ws are substituted for Ms in Fig. 10.1, many of the solution paths in this analog of the JH problem map to paths in MC.

In addition to the MC and JH problems that were used in both acquisition and transfer, a third problem was used only in transfer. This problem, called "robbits and orcs" (R/O) to distinguish it from the other two, involves three Rs, two Os, and a mixture of MC and JH constraints. The Os may never outnumber Rs on either side of the barrier, and there is one (color-coded) R/O pair, in which the (red) R may never be in the presence of any O unless the paired (red) O is also present. This problem space yields 12 seven-move solution paths, all of which map to paths in Fig. 10.1. Half the children were trained on MC and half on JH analogs, with all trained on the first solution path

TABLE 10.8   The Setting/Constraint Information and Story Units
Containing Information for the Required Move Sequence in an Analog
of the Jealous Husbands Problem

Jealous Husbands Problem: Robots/Wrestlers Analog

Setting/Constraint Information: A green robot with his green wrestler and a purple robot with his purple wrestler and a red wrestler were on one side of a river they needed to cross to get to a house. They had a small boat, but it would only carry two people at a time. They all knew that if the green wrestler or the purple wrestler were ever in the presence of any of the robots without his own robot present, the wrestler would be harmed. What they had to figure out was how to get the green wrestler, the purple wrestler, the red wrestler, the green robot, and the purple robot across the river to the house without the green wrestler or the purple wrestler being harmed.

Recall instruction: Now listen carefully to how they did it, because this is what I want you to remember so that you can say it back to me.

Story units:
1. First a green robot and a green wrestler went across the river to the house.
2. Then the green robot went back across the river.
3. Next the green robot and the red wrestler went across the river to the house.
4. Then the red wrestler went back across the river.
5. Next the purple robot and the red wrestler went across the river to the house.
6. Then the purple robot went back across the river.
7. Finally, the purple robot and the purple wrestler went across the river to the house.

in Fig. 10.1 (Path 1). Transfer was to an isomorphic analog or an analog of one of the other two problem types.

Although children in all six conditions showed good transfer performance (means of 7.08 to 9.42 moves and 47 to 125 seconds), isomorphic transfer was, as expected, better than nonisomorphic. In order to explore specific mappings, the solution paths the children exhibited in the various transfer conditions were mapped to the problem space presented in Fig. 10.1. The way this was done was to map the move sequence under the appropriate substitution rules, for example, substituting Hs for Cs and Ws for Ms in Fig. 10.1, while ignoring the occasional errors or loops (i.e., a move into a legal problem state that is immediately reversed) that occurred. The data are presented in Table 10.9. These data appear to reflect three different patterns of performance. First, children in the two iso-morphic conditions and those transferred from MC to JH showed nearly perfect mappings. That is, they were trained on the first path in Fig. 10.1 and at least 10 of the 12 in each condition exhibited that path in transfer. Second, at least 9 of the children in each of the two RO transfer conditions exhibited move sequences that corresponded to the left branch (Paths 1–3) of Fig. 10.1, indicating that at least the first four moves were directly mapped from the base. Finally, 7 children transferred from JH to MC clustered on the right branch of the tree (Paths 7–9), and only two children were on the left branch

TABLE 10.9   The Number of Children in Each Training/Transfer Condition (maximum = 12) Who Showed Each Solution Path in Fig. 10.1 Under the Appropriate Substitution Rules for each Condition

Training/Transfer	Solution Path in Fig. 10.1								
	1	2	3	4	5	6	7	8	9
MC/JH	11	0	0	0	1	0	0	0	0
MC/RO	6	3	1	1	0	0	0	1	0
MC/MC	10	0	1	0	0	1	0	0	0
JH/JH	12	0	0	0	0	0	0	0	0
JH/RO	2	6	1	1	0	0	2	0	0
JH/MC	1	1	0	1	2	0	1	4	2

Note 1. MC = Missionaries/Cannibals; JH = Jealous Husbands; RO = Robbits/Orcs.

Note 2. From "Problem Solving, Recall, and Mapping Relations in Isomorphic Transfer and Nonisomorphic Transfer Among Pre-schoolers and Elementary-School Children" by B. Gholson, A. R. Dattel, D. Morgan, and L. A. Eymard, 1989. Reprinted by permission.

(children in this condition also showed the worst transfer performance).

We believe this pattern of findings results from structural features and surface details embodied in the event schemas (Mandler, 1979; Nelson, 1986) constituting the bases that resulted from the different acquisition conditions, and the relationships of these to the transfer problems. The base consisted of a temporally and causally connected sequence of events, or moves and states, with each event enabling the next one in the sequence. Despite different constraints and considerable variations in the problem spaces (Newell & Simon, 1972; Simon & Hayes, 1976), the children were expected to map the event sequence constituting the base directly to the nonisomorphic target problems. A *direct* mapping was possible because the solution path the children were trained on was available in each problem space (under appropriate substitution rules). Surface features, however, may have been differentially encoded as part of the base in the two training conditions.

Children trained on MC analogs were required to pair a M of one color with a C of a different color (see Table 10.2) on the first and on three subsequent moves of each training problem. Thus they emphasized the relations of the actors to each other, having no reason to encode color as an important feature in the base. Of the 24 children trained on MC and transferred to JH or RO, 21 made at least the first four moves dictated by their event schema. Children trained on JH analogs, however, were required to pair, for example, a green robot and green wrestler on the first move, and color pairings were important constraints throughout (see Table 10.8). Thus color was a salient feature for them. Those transferred to RO could make a comparable base-dictated and color-paired first move, for example, by moving a red R and red O, which 9 of them did. For those transferred from JH to MC, however, the only color-coded pairs were those in the two-element set (e.g., two blue dreadnocks, see Table 10.2), and 7 of those 12 children made that first move. Thus when color pairing constituted an important feature of the acquisition task, it was encoded as a salient feature of the base. Among children transferred from JH to MC, this feature was mapped to a misleading cue in the target and resulted in a faulty mapping (Gentner & Toupin, 1986). These findings, taken together with those obtained by Gentner and Toupin (1986) in their low transparency condition (see "Base Quality"), suggest a useful strategy for children to adopt would be to direct their activities toward mapping only structural features of the base to the target, while completely ignoring surface details, even those represented in the base.

In describing the Gholson, Dattel et al. (1989) study, we said the children were expected to *directly* map the event schema that constituted the base to the target. We referred to this mapping as direct, because the actors in the acquisition and transfer tasks had similar relations to each other and played similar roles. For example, there were two Cs and three Ms, and two Hs and three Ws. Similarly, Cs constrained the locations of Ms, and Hs constrained the locations of Ws.

We have a study in progress in which this kind of direct mapping was not possible. As part of a larger study, 40 (third and fourth grade) children were trained on analogs of JH in which there were three Hs and two Ws (contrast this with Table 10.8, which includes two Hs and three Ws). All children were trained on the same solution path in Fig. 10.1 (under appropriate substitution rules). They were transferred to MC analogs with three Ms and two Cs. Thus a cross mapping was required (Gentner & Toupin, 1986; Reed, 1987): The locations of the two Ws were constrained by the three Hs in the training problem. But in transfer the locations of the three Ms were constrained by the two Cs. Under these cross-mapped conditions only about half the children (19/40) mapped their base to the appropriate branch in Fig. 10.1, and only 20% (8/40) actually exhibited the solution path they were trained on. The children did, however, show reasonably good transfer, averaging about 9.4 moves at about 15 seconds per move.

In concluding this section, a comment is in order concerning the contrast between the nonisomorphic transfer performance we have obtained from children and the performance of young adults. As previously indicated, past research shows that adults do not perform well in nonisomorphic analogical-reasoning tasks (Novick, 1988; Reed, 1987; Reed et al., 1974; Ross, 1984, 1987), suggesting procedural adaptation may be very difficult for them. Our work shows, however, that elementary school children show reasonably good nonisomorphic transfer (see above, Gholson, Eymard, Long et al., 1988; Gholson, Dattel et al., 1989). We think this discrepancy may be due to differences in the experimental methods that were used during base acquisition. In our research, subjects were given ample opportunity to acquire a base representation consisting of a high quality event schema, through auditory presentation of solution information, recall procedures, and problem-solving activities on each trial.

In the research with adults, however, subjects were usually given only one opportunity to acquire the base (Novick, 1988; Reed, 1984, 1987; Ross, 1984, 1987). In research closely related to ours, for example, Reed et al. (1974) just presented subjects with setting/ constraint information along with the physical materials, recording moves, errors, and the total time required to complete the task in both acquisition and transfer. Thus the subjects may not have actually learned much about the problem except how to avoid illegal problem states. That is, the base that was acquired may have been of very low quality, containing little of use in the transfer task. Sweller (1988) recently argued that in coventional problem-solving tasks, in which subjects are simply presented with a problem and told to solve it, so much cognitive processing capacity is required in (means/ends) problem solving itself that few resources are left for learning, that is, for schema acquisition. He recently presented both a computational model and empirical evidence from 15- and 16-year-olds (solving geometry problems) that offers strong support for this contention (see also, Cooper & Sweller, 1987; Lewis & Anderson, 1985; Mawer & Sweller, 1982; Sweller, 1983; Sweller & Levine, 1982; Sweller, Mawer, & Howe, 1982).

Thus future research on analogical reasoning, particularly research involving nonisomorphic transfer, should include conditions that assure a high quality base representation is available for transfer. More precise experiments are also needed, experiments that provide for fine-grained comparisons of activities dictated by direct mappings of the base with activities that require specific kinds of procedural adaptation. Although further understanding will have to await those experiments, it seems reasonable to speculate that the expanding knowledge foundation that comes with age and experience may include more facile strategies for modifying an existing base, that is, strategies for such activities as creating and inserting new procedures into the base as required in nonisomorphic transfer.

CONCLUSION

In our discussion of *global* strategies for analogical reasoning we draw a distinction between isomorphic and nonisomorphic transfer. When a global strategy is successfully executed in *isomorphic* transfer we may safely assume the correspondence between the base and target was noticed, a high quality base was retrieved, and structural features of the base were mapped to the target. Things are somewhat more complicated in using a global strategy during nonisomorphic transfer. That is, in addition to retrieval and mapping processes, procedural adaptation is required. This involves such activities as deleting, creating, and inserting procedures into the event schema that constituted the original base, in order to modify it and bring it into one-to-one correspondence with the target. We described three strategies children might adopt when they attempt to use analogical reasoning processes to solve nonisomorphic transfer problems: (a) recognize how the base and target differ at the outset, and immediately modify procedures in the base to bring it into 1:1 correspondence with the target; (b) treat the target as though it is isomorphic to the base, which results in errors; or (c) recognize that the base and target differ at the outset, but introduce any modifications into the base as required during problem solving. We also pointed out, though, that there is a paucity of research involving human subjects that illuminates how procedural adaptation is carried out. If what we already know frequently provides a base for new learning, however, procedural adaptation is an integral part of much human activity and requires scientific understanding.

We also draw a sharp distinction between global strategies for analogical reasoning and specific strategies. Specific strategies involve deliberate activities that affect the individual component processes: base acquisition, base quality, retrieval, and mapping. Because these components are very general learning and problem-solving mechanisms, specific strategies are in no sense unique to analogical reasoning. Examples of specific strategies include deliberate activities aimed at (a) acquiring a base of high(er) quality, (b) processing structural features of a target problem so an appropriate base is retrieved, and (c) assuring that correct mappings are carried out. Thus focusing attention on the goal structure of the problem, for example, or stating the critical solution rules while enacting them, would constitute specific strategies for improving the quality of the base representation (Brown, 1989; Brown & Campione, 1984; Brown et al., 1986; Gholson, Dattel et al., 1989). Similarly, it is well established that novices of all ages process new problems in terms of surface details and that superficial similarities tend to dictate which base is retrieved (Gentner & Landers, 1985; Novick, 1988; Reed, 1987; Ross, 1984, 1987). Deliberate activities directed toward processing structural features of new problems, rather than superficial details, then, might constitute specific strategies that increase the likelihood a useful base is retrieved. Finally, because (novice) subjects of all ages have considerable difficulty mapping structural features of a base to a target when surface details provide misleading cues (Gentner & Toupin, 1986; Gholson, Dattel et al., 1989; Novick, 1988; Reed, 1984, 1987; Ross, 1984, 1987), specific strategies that focus on processing structural features (at the expense of surface details) would be expected to enhance the mapping process. Because we consider only deliberate goal-directed activities strategic, we suggest that future research aimed at studying either specific or global strategies should involve training specific activities in one (analogical reasoning) task and evaluating increases in strategic activities in a second.

Where strategies come from, or what develops, may be a key developmental question (Siegler, 1978). Clearly, under ideal circumstances even young preschoolers exhibit excellent isomorphic transfer in relatively complex problems (Brown, 1989; Brown et al., 1986; Crisafi & Brown, 1986; Gentner & Toupin, 1986; Gholson, Dattel et al., 1989). Thus the mechanisms required to acquire and represent a high quality base, retrieve it in appropriate circumstances, and map it to a target are well within the competencies of preschoolers. It is also clear, though, that younger children require considerable assistance, relative to older children and adults, in order to elevate performance to comparable levels (e.g., Brown, 1989; Carey, 1985; Crisafi & Brown, 1986; Gholson, Dattel et al., 1989, Nelson, 1986). Older children accomplish for themselves many activities that younger children need help with. Older children, for example, are much better at correctly mapping structural features of a base when surface details of a target provide misleading cues (Gentner & Toupin, 1986; Novick, 1988; Reed, 1987). And elementary school children quickly construct a base when provided only a linguistic representation of the problem-solving information (Gholson, Eymard, Long et al., 1988; Gholson, Eymard, Morgan, & Kamhi, 1987). Preschoolers find this very difficult, requiring modeling procedures in order to reach comparable levels of performance (Gholson, Dattel et al., 1989; Gentry, Kamhi, Mauer, & Gholson, 1987; Kamhi, Gentry, Mauer, & Gholson, in press). We take these differences to reflect meta-conceptual competence (Borkowski & Kurtz, 1984), with older children, for example, reflecting more on problem solutions, looking for general rules, and knowing more about how to learn. These kinds of metaconceptual competencies, of course, involve exactly the kinds of activities we have identified as reflecting the use of specific strategies.

ACKNOWLEDGMENTS

We express our sincere appreciation to Dr. Kathy E. Pruett of the Memphis City Schools Division of Research and Planning for her helpful cooperation in this program of research. We also thank Arthur C. Graesser and David F. Bjorklund for very constructive comments on earlier versions of the manuscript.

REFERENCES

Achenbach, T. M. (1970). The children's associative responding test: A possible alternative to group IQ tests. *Journal of Educational Psychology, 61,* 340–348.

Achenbach, T. M. (1971). The children's associative responding test: A two-year followup. *Developmental Psychology, 5,* 477–483.

Adelson, B. (1984). When novices surpass experts: The difficulty of a task may increase with expertise. *Journal of Experimental Psychology: Learning, Memory, and Cognition, 10,* 483–495.

Alexander, P. A., Willson, V. L., White, C. S., & Fuqua, J. D. (1987). Analogical reasoning in young children. *Journal of Educational Psychology, 79,* 401–408.

Beilin, H. (1975). *Studies in the cognitive basis of language development.* New York: Academic Press.

Borkowski, J. G., & Kurtz, B. E. (1984). Metacognition and special children. In B. Gholson & T. L. Rosenthal (Eds.), *Applications of cognitive-developmental theory* (pp. 193–213). New York: Academic Press.

Brown, A. L. (1975). The development of memory: Knowing, knowing about knowing, and knowing how to know. In H. W. Reese (Ed.), *Advances in child development and behavior* (Vol. 10, pp. 104–152). New York: Academic Press.

Brown, A. L. (1976). The construction of temporal succession by preoperational children. In A. D. Pick (Ed.), *Minnesota Symposium on Child Psychology* (Vol. 10, pp. 28–83). Minneapolis: University of Minnesota Press.

Brown, A. L. (1989). Analogical learning and transfer: What develops? In S. Vosniadou & A. Ortony (Eds.), *Similarity and analogical reasoning* (pp. 369–412). Cambridge, England: Cambridge University Press.

Brown, A. L., & Campione, J. C. (1984). Three faces of transfer: Implications for early competence, individual differences, and instruction. In M. Lamb, A. L. Brown, & B. Rogoff (Eds.), *Advances in developmental psychology* (Vol. 3, pp. 143–192). Hillsdale, NJ: Lawrence Erlbaum Associates.

Brown, A. L., Kane, M. J., & Echols, C. H. (1986). Young children's mental models determine analogical transfer across problems with a common goal structure. *Cognitive Development, 1,* 103–121.

Burstein, M. H. (1986). Concept formation by incremental analogical reasoning and debugging. In R. S. Michalski, J. G. Carbonell, & T. M. Mitchell (Eds.), *Machine learning: An artificial intelligence approach* (pp. 351–369). Palo Alto, CA: Tioga Publishing.

Cantor, J. H. (1965). Transfer of stimulus pretraining to motor paired-associate and discrimination learning tasks. In L. P. Lipsitt & C. C. Spiker (Eds.), *Advances in child development and behavior* (Vol. 2, pp. 19–58). New York: Academic Press.

Carbonell, J. G. (1986). Learning by analogy: Formulating and generalizing plans from past experience. In R. S. Michalski, J. G. Carbonell, & T. M. Mitchell (Eds.), *Machine learning: An artificial intelligence approach* (pp. 137–161). Palo Alto, CA: Tioga Publishing.

Carey, S. (1985). *Conceptual change in childhood.* Cambridge, MA: Bradford Press.

Chi, M. T. H., Feltovich, P. J., & Glaser, R. (1981). Categorization and representation of physics problems by experts and novices. *Cognitive Science, 5,* 121–152.

Chi, M. T. H., Glaser, R., & Rees, E. (1982). Expertise in problem solving. In R. J. Sternberg (Ed.), *Advances in the psychology of human intelligence* (Vol. 1, pp. 7–75). Hillsdale, NJ: Lawrence Erlbaum Associates.

Cooper, G., & Sweller, J. (1987). Effects of schema acquisition and rule automation on mathematical problem-solving transfer. *Journal of Educational Psychology, 79,* 347–362.

Crisafi, M. A., & Brown, A. L. (1986). Analogical transfer in very young children: Combining two separately learned solutions to reach a goal. *Child Development, 57,* 953–968.

Dunker, K. (1945). On problem solving. *Psychological Monographs, 58* (Whole No. 270).

Dunker, K., & Krechevsky, I. (1939). On solution achievement. *Psychological Review, 46,* 1034–1039.

Falkenhainer, B., Forbus, K. D., & Gentner, D. (1986). *The structure-mapping engine* (Tech. Rep. No. UIUCDS-R86-1275). University of Illinois.

Gelman, S., & Markman, E. (1986). Categories and induction in young children. *Cognition, 23,* 183–209.

Gentile, J. R., Tedesco-Stratton, L., Davis, E., Lund, N. J., & Agunanne, B. A. (1977). Associative responding versus analogical reasoning by children. *Intelligence, 1,* 369–380.

Gentner, D. (1977). Children's performance on a spatial analogies task. *Child Development, 48,* 1034–1039.

Gentner, D. (1983). Structure-mapping: A theoretical framework for analogy. *Cognitive Science, 77,* 155–170.

Gentner, D. (1989). The mechanisms of analogical learning (pp. 199–241). In S. Vosniadou & A. Ortony (Eds.), *Similarity and analogical reasoning.* Cambridge, England: Cambridge University Press.

Gentner, D., & Jeziorski, M. (1989). In B. Gholson, W. R. Shadish, Jr., R. A. Neimeyer, & A. C. Houts (Eds.), *Psychology of science: Contributions to metascience* (pp. 296–325). Cambridge, England: Cambridge University Press.

Gentner, D., & Landers, R. (1985, November). Analogical reminding: A good match is hard to find. *Proceedings of the International Conference on Systems.* Tucson, AZ.

Gentner, D., & Toupin, C. (1986). Systematicity and surface similarity in the development of analogy. *Cognitive Science, 10,* 277–300.

Gentry, B., Kamhi, A., Mauer, D., & Gholson, B. (1987). *Problem solving in language-impaired children: "Doing but not saying."* Paper presented at the American Speech and Hearing Association Meetings, New Orleans.

Gholson, B. (1980). *The cognitive-developmental basis of human learning: Studies in hypothesis testing.* New York: Academic Press.

Gholson, B., Dattel, A. R., Morgan, D., & Eymard, L. A. (1989). Problem solving, recall, and mapping relations in isomorphic transfer and nonisomorphic transfer among preschoolers and elementary-school children. *Child Development, 60,* 1172–1187.

Gholson, B., Eymard, L. A., Long, D., Morgan, D., & Leeming, F. C. (1988). Problem solving, recall, isomorphic transfer, and nonisomorphic transfer among third-grade and fourth-grade children. *Cognitive Development, 33,* 37–53.

Gholson, B., Eymard, L. A., Morgan, D., & Kamhi, A. G. (1987). Problem solving, recall, and isomorphic transfer among third-grade and sixth-grade children. *Journal of Experimental Child Psychology, 43,* 227–243.

Gick, M. L., & Holyoak, K. J. (1980). Analogical problem solving. *Cognitive Psychology, 12,* 306–355.

Gick, M. L., & Holyoak, K. J. (1983). Analogical induction and analogical transfer. *Cognitive Psychology, 15,* 1–38.

Gobbo, C., & Chi, M. T. H. (1986). How knowledge is structured and used by expert and novice children. *Cognitive Development, 1,* 221–237.

Goldman, S. R., Pellegrino, J. W., Parseghian, P., & Sallis, R. (1982). *Child Development, 53,* 550–559.

Gross, T. F. (1985). *Cognitive Development.* Monterey, CA: Brooks/Cole.

Hesse, M. B. (1966). *Models and analogies in science.* Notre Dame, IN: University of Notre Dame Press.

Holland, J. H., Holyoak, K. J., Nisbett, R. E., & Thagard, P. R. (1986). *Induction: Processes of inference, learning, and discovery.* Cambridge, MA: MIT Press.

Holyoak, K. J. (1984). Analogical thinking and human intelligence. In R. J. Sternberg (Ed.), *Advances in the psychology of human intelligence* (Vol. 2, pp. 199–230). Hillsdale, NJ: Lawrence Erlbaum Associates.

Holyoak, K. J. (1985). The pragmatics of analogical transfer. In G. H. Bower (Ed.), *The psychology of learning and motivation* (pp. 59–87). New York: Academic Press.

Holyoak, K. J., Junn, E. N., & Billman, D. O. (1984). Development of analogical problem-solving skills. *Child Development, 55,* 2042–2055.

Holyoak, K. J., & Koh, K. (1987). Surface and structural similarity in analogical transfer. *Memory & Cognition, 15,* 332–340.

Hull, C. L. (1939). The problem of stimulus equivalence in behavior theory. *Psychological Review, 46,* 9–30.

Inhelder, B., & Piaget, J. (1958). *The growth of logical thinking from childhood to adolescence.* New York: Basic Books.

Inhelder, B., & Piaget, J. (1964). *The early growth of logic in the child.* New York: Norton.

Johnson-Laird, P. N. (1980). Mental models in cognitive science. *Cognitive Science, 4,* 71–115.

Judd, C. H. (1908). The relation of special training to general intelligence. *Educational Review, 36,* 28–42.

Kamhi, A. G., Gentry, B., Mauer, D., & Gholson, B. (in press). Analogical learning and transfer in language-impaired children. *Journal of Speech and Hearing Disorders.*

Kintsch, W., & Greeno, J. G. (1985). Understanding and solving word arithmetic problems. *Psychological Review, 92,* 109–129.

Kotovsky, K., Hayes, J. R., & Simon, H. A. (1985). Why are some problems hard? Evidence from tower of Hanoi. *Cognitive Psychology, 17,* 248–294.

Kozminsky, E., Kintsch, W., & Bourne, L. E., Jr. (1981). Decision making with texts: Information analysis and schema acquisition. *Journal of Experimental Psychology: General, 110,* 363–380.

Levine, M. (1975) *A cognitive theory of learning: Research on hypothesis testing.* Hillsdale, NJ: Lawrence Erlbaum Associates.

Levinson, P. J., & Carpenter, R. L. (1974). An analysis of analogical reasoning in children. *Child Development, 45,* 857–861.

Lewis, M., & Anderson, J. (1985). Discrimination of operator schemata in problem solving: Learning from examples. *Cognitive Psychology, 17,* 26–65.

Luchins, A. S. (1942). Mechanization in problem-solving. *Psychological Monographs, 54,*(6, Whole No. 248).

Lunzer, E. A. (1965). Problems of formal reasoning in test situations. In P. H. Mussen (Ed.), European research in cognitive development. *Monographs of the society for Research in Child Development, 30*(2, Serial No. 100), 19–46.

Mackie, J. L. (1974). *The cement of the universe.* London: Oxford University Press.

Mandler, J. M. (1979), Categorical and schematic organization in memory. In C. R. Puff (Ed.), *Memory organization and structure* (pp. 259–299). New York: Academic Press.

Mandler, J. M. (1983). Representation. In P. H. Mussen (Ed.), *Handbook of child psychology: Cognitive development* (Vol. 3, pp. 420–494). New York: Wiley.

Mawer, R., & Sweller, J. (1982). The effects of subgoal density and location on learning during problem solving. *Journal of Experimental Psychology: Learning, Memory, & Cognition, 8*, 252–259.

Minsky, M. (1975). A framework for representing knowledge. In P. Winston (Ed.), *The psychology of computer vision* (pp. 95–128). New York: McGraw–Hill.

Morgan, D., Gholson, B., Eymard, L. A., Coles, R., & Leeming, F. C. (in preparation). *Isomorphic and nonisomorphic transfer: Surface and structural similarity.*

Nelson, K. (1986). *Event knowledge: Structure and function in development.* Hillsdale, NJ: Lawrence Erlbaum Associates.

Nelson, K., & Gruendel, J. M. (1981). Generalized event representations: Basic building blocks of cognitive development. In M. E. Lamb & A. L. Brown (Eds.), *Advances in developmental psychology* (Vol. 1, pp. 131–158). Hillsdale, NJ: Lawrence Erlbaum Associates.

Nersessian, N. J. (1984). Aether/or: The creation of scientific concepts. *Studies in the History and Philosophy of Science, 15*, 175–212.

Newell, A., & Simon, H. A. (1972). *Human problem solving.* Englewood Cliffs, NJ: Prentice–Hall.

Novick, L. R. (1988). Analogical transfer, problem similarity, and expertise. *Journal of Experimental Psychology: Learning, Memory, & Cognition, 14*, 510–520.

Paivio, A. (1979). *Imagery and verbal processes.* New York: Holt, Rinehart, & Winston.

Reed, S. K. (1984). Estimating answers to algebra word problems. *Journal of Experimental Psychology: Learning, Memory, & Cognition, 10*, 778–790.

Reed, S. K. (1987). A structure-mapping model for word problems. *Journal of Experimental Psychology: Learning, Memory, & Cognition, 13*, 124–139.

Reed, S. K., Dempster, A., & Ettinger, M. (1985). The usefulness of analogous solutions for solving algebra word problems. *Journal of Experimental Psychology: Learning, Memory, & Cognition, 11*, 106–125.

Reed, S. K., Ernst, G. W., & Banerji, R. (1974). The role of analogy in transfer between similar problem states. *Cognitive Psychology, 6*, 436–440.

Ross, B. H. (1984). Remindings and their effects in learning a cognitive skill. *Cognitive Psychology, 16*, 371–416.

Ross, B. H. (1987). This is like that: The use of earlier problems and the separation of similarity effects. *Journal of Experimental Psychology: Learning, Memory, and Cognition, 13*, 629–639.

Schank, R. C., & Abelson, R. P. (1977). *Scripts, plans, goals and understanding.* Hillsdale, NJ: Lawrence Erlbaum Associates.

Schoenfeld, A. H., & Herman, D. J. (1982). Problem perception and knowledge structure in expert and novice mathematical problem solvers. *Journal of Experimental Psychology: Learning, Memory, & Cognition, 8*, 484–494.

Shiffrin, R. M., & Schneider, W. (1977). Controlled and automatic human information processing: II. Perceptual learning, automatic attending, and a general theory. *Psychological Review, 84*, 127–190.

Siegler, R. S. (Ed.). (1978) *Children's thinking: What develops?* Hillsdale, NJ: Lawrence Erlbaum Associates.

Silver, E. A. (1979). Student perceptions of relatedness among mathematical verbal problems. *Journal for Research in Mathematics Education, 10*, 195–210.

Silver, E. A. (1981). Recall of mathematical problem information: Solving related problems. *Journal for Research in Mathematics Education, 12*, 54–64.

Simon, H. A., & Hayes, J. R. (1976). The understanding process: Problem isomorphs. *Cognitive Psychology, 8*, 154–190.

Simon, H. A., & Reed, S. K. (1976). Modeling strategy shifts in a problem-solving task. *Cognitive Psychology, 8*, 86–97.

Sobel, B. (1939). The study of the development of insight in preschool children. *Journal of Genetic Psychology, 55,* 381–388.

Spearman, C. (1923). *The natire of 'intelligence' and the principles of cognition.* London: Macmillan.

Spence, K. W. (1937). The different response in animals to stimuli varying within a single dimension. *Psychological Review, 47,* 271–288.

Spence, K. (1942). The basis of solution by chimpanzees of the intermediate size problem. *Journal of Experimental Psychology, 31,* 257–271.

Sternberg, R. J. (1977). Component processes in analogical reasoning. *Psychological Review, 84,* 353–378.

Sternberg, R. J. (1985). *Beyond IQ: A triarchic theory of human intelligence.* Cambridge, England: Cambridge University Press.

Sternberg, R. J., & Nigro, G. (1980). Developmental patterns in the solution of verbal analogies. *Child Development, 51,* 27–38.

Sternberg, R. J., & Rifkin, B. (1979). The development of analogical reasoning processes. *Journal of Experimental Child Psychology, 27,* 195–232.

Sweller, J. (1983). Control mechanisms in problem solving. *Memory & Cognition, 11,* 32–40.

Sweller, J. (1988). Cognitive load durigng problem solving: Effects on learning. *Cognitive Science, 12,* 257–285.

Sweller, J., & Levine, M. (1982). Effects of goal specificity on means-ends analysis and learning. *Journal of Experimental Psychology: Learning, Memory & Cognition, 8,* 463–474.

Sweller, J., Mawer, R., & Howe, W. (1982). Consequences of history-cued and means-ends strategies in problem solving. *American Journal of Psychology, 95,* 455–483.

Thorndike, E. L. (1923). *Educational psychology: The psychology of learning* (Vol. 2). New York: Teachers College, Columbia University.

Thorndike, E. L., & Woodworth, R. S. (1901). The influence of improvement in one mental function upon the efficiency of other functions. *Psychological Review, 8,* 247–261.

Trabasso, T., & Bower, G. H. (1968). *Attention in learning: Theory and research.* New York: Wiley.

Trabasso, T., & Sperry, L. L. (1985). Causal relatedness and importance of story events. *Journal of Memory & Language, 24,* 595–611.

van Dijk, T. A., & Kintsch, W. (1983). *Strategies of discourse comprehension.* New York: Academic Press.

Wickens, T. D., & Millward, R. B. (1971). Attribute elimination strategies for concept identification with practiced subjects. *Journal of Mathematical Psychology, 8,* 453–480.

Winston, P. H. (1980). Learning and reasoning by analogy. *Communications of the ACM, 23,* 689–703.

Winston, P. H. (1984). *Artificial intelligence* (2nd ed.). Reading, MA: Addison–Wesley.

CHAPTER 11

Children's Strategies: Their Definition and Origins

David F. Bjorklund
Katherine Kipp Harnishfeger
Florida Atlantic University

CHILDREN'S STRATEGIES: THEIR DEFINITION

It would seem that in a volume dedicated to the topic of children's strategies, the various contributors would all deal with the same basic issues and mean the same thing when they wrote of *strategies*. In a very broad sense, we think this is true. Each chapter herein deals with children's goal-directed behavior and cognitive processes executed in quest of those goals. The goal-directed nature of behavior is the cornerstone of strategies. But once we try to get beyond this most rudimentary of definitions, the consensus fades.

A TRADITIONAL VIEW OF CHILDREN'S STRATEGIES

Most of the contributors did not stray far from what we call a *traditional* definition of strategies—traditional to the extent that the definitions are similar to the way *strategy* has been used, often implicitly, in the developmental research literature over the past 20 years (e.g., Belmont & Butterfield, 1969; Brown, 1975; Flavell, 1970; Naus & Ornstein, 1983). A precise definition in the "traditional" vein was provided several years ago by Pressley, Forrest-Pressley, Elliot-Faust, and Miller (1985):

A strategy is composed of cognitive operations over and above the processes that are natural consequences of carrying out the task, ranging from one such operation to a sequence of interdependent operations. Strategies achieve cognitive purpose (e.g., comprehending, memorizing) and are potentially conscious and controllable activities. (p. 4)

We place the chapters by Willatts (chap. 2), Folds, Footo, Guttentag, and Ornstein (chap. 3), Bjorklund, Muir-Broaddus, and Schneider (chap. 4), and Miller (chap. 6) in this "traditionalist camp."

The simplest and most straightforward definition is provided by Willatts in his review of problem-solving strategies during infancy. Willatts views strategies as organized problem-solving behaviors that are directed toward a goal. To be strategic does not require planning, only the intention of achieving a goal. Willatts defines intention behaviorally as selecting an action, persisting at the behavior, correcting errors, and stopping when the goal is reached. By keeping to this relatively broad definition of strategies, Willatts's careful observations from well-crafted experiments make it clear that the origins of strategic behavior are found many months before children have the linguistic wherewithall to communicate about their strategies. Even infants in the first 6 months of life behave strategically because they direct their behavior to achieve goals, they can determine success and failure, they redirect activity when failure occurs, and they use information about failure to modify future attempts.

Conscious awareness is not required for a behavior to be considered strategic. Indeed, even if one would wish to attribute conscious awareness to preverbal infants, it is difficult to imagine how such consciousnesss could be assessed with respect to strategies. On all other counts, however, the behavior that Willatts observes in infants falls within the traditional definition of strategies: they are selective, goal directed, and intentional. If not true strategies, they are at least the behavioral antecedents to the covert, problem-solving operations granted the label *strategy* in older children.

A defining characteristic of Willatts's definition of strategy involves the concept of intentionality. As just noted, the intentional, or deliberate, use of an information-processing operation is central to most definitions of strategies. Through Willatts's work, we can see how intentionality on the part of infants can be inferred.

The intentionality of strategies is also a major aspect of chapter 3 by Folds et al. They propose that the child's *intent* to reach a goal, as defined by the awareness of the need for some procedure, is more important in defining strategic behavior than actual execution of the plan. Although intentionality is considered a necessary component for strategic behavior by Folds et al., they also point out that intent is very difficult to document, especially in young children. They suggest that in order to better understand the intentionality of children's endeavors, we must consider changes in profiles of performance across multiple settings.

In a similar vein, Miller defines strategies as "intentional, organized, planful procedures" (p. 158), and Bjorklund et al. define strategies as goal-directed, effort-consuming processes that are potentially conscious. Both Miller and Bjorklund et al. observe that some strategy-like patterns (in strategic attention tasks or organization in recall) are mediated by the relatively automatic activation of information, and thus do not qualify as strategies. Although the surface behavior may appear strategic, it is not intentional. The classification of such behavior as nonstrategic is consistent with the traditional view of strategies.

CONSERVATIVE VIEWS OF CHILDREN'S STRATEGIES

Slightly more conservative views of strategies are provided by Bisanz and LeFevre (chap. 8), Garner (chap. 9) and Gholson, Morgan, Dattel, and Pierce, chap. 10). These authors all emphasize the importance of selecting an effortful operation in the service of some goal.

For example, Bisanz and LeFevre propose that relatively automatic and efficient processes should not be considered strategic. They emphasize the importance of *selectivity* in their definition of strategies, defining *strategy* as "a procedure that is invoked in a flexible, goal-oriented manner and that influences the selection and implementation of subsequent procedures" (p. 236). Thus, for Bisanz and LeFevre, the procedures involved in executing a strategy do not constitute the strategy itself, but merely its products. Strategies are limited to decisions made prior to action, decisions that involve choosing among several alternatives in a flexible fashion to achieve a goal. For example, fact retrieval as a means for solving simple addition and subtraction problems is not considered to be a strategy by Bisanz and LeFevre. They consider fact retrieval to be "a fundamental property of the cognitive system, it is not an optional procedure, and hence it is not strategic" (p. 237). Rather, procedures qualifying as strategies may set confidence criteria, change associative strengths of problems and answers, or produce new procedures, and they need not be conscious to the individual.

By restricting their definition of strategy in this way, Bisanz and LeFevre do not reduce the importance of processes such as fact retrieval or other automatic operations involved in competent cognitive functioning. They emphasize that such operations are central to our understanding of cognition and its development, but that using the umbrella term *strategy* to cover a wide range of diverse operations, obscures critical distinctions among different classes of processes.

Garner, studying the development of reading strategies, also narrows the focus of the term *strategy*. She follows the lead of Paris, Lipson, and Wixson (1983), who differentiated between *skills*, highly efficient and relatively automatic operations, and *strategies*, effortful operations that are "selected by the agent from alternative actions and must be intended to attain the specific goal" (p. 295). The issue of intentionality is key here. Automatic processes, although they may yield high levels of performance, should not be classified as strategies if they are not deliberate and conscious. This is similar to the position taken by Miller and by Bjorklund et al. They refer to early developing processes, such as the relatively automatic activation of information, which may develop *into* efficient strategies. Garner, in contrast, referred to highly practiced processes that may develop *from* the more effort-consuming strategies (cf. Bisanz & LeFevre with respect to fact retrieval in arithmetic). Each of these authors considers these unintentional behaviors to be nonstrategic.

Gholson et al.'s chapter focuses on the importance of child directedness in defining strategic behaviors. In referring to strategies of analogical reasoning, they propose that "training conditions (or experimental arrangements) requiring children to engage in specific activities that facilitate analogical transfer are *not* strategic. If the activities became part of the child's own repertoire and generalized to new situations, however, they would be" (p. 270). Thus, Gholson et al. do not simply emphasize the ability to execute a procedure, but the ability of children to execute a procedure *on their own*. Merely demonstrating that a child can do what he or she is told (with respect to executing the procedures of an adult-defined strategy), does not mean that that child is strategic. A strategy is only demonstrated when the child deliberately engages in some goal-directed processing, without specific prompting from an external agent.

Note that this definition is not far removed from the traditional definition provided by Pressley et al. The importance of Gholson et al.'s definition may be in the extension of their logic to other areas of cognition, which would require that the results of training studies be reappraised. Are children who have been taught a rehearsal strategy, for example, truly strategic, or are they merely following instructions? By Gholson et al.'s definition of strategy, children are rightfully called strategic only when they generalize that strategy or use a strategy without prompting. By training children, we can learn if they are capable of executing the various components of a strategy, but that may not be the same as being strategic.

The views of Bisanz and LeFevre, Garner, and Gholson et al. are more conservative than those of Willatts, Folds et al., Miller, and Bjorklund et al. with respect to declaring what is a strategy and what is not, but the differences are only a matter of degree. All the aforementioned authors would agree that strategies have a deliberate component to them and are selected from alternative operations. Such processes are differentiated from those that are relatively automatic in nature, unavailable to consciousness (with the exception of Bisanz & LeFevre), and/or executed by default (i.e., there is no selection).

LIBERAL VIEWS OF CHILDREN'S STRATEGIES

Although definitions of strategies following in both the traditional and conservative veins have predominated cognitive developmental research in the past 20 years and have served the field well, they are not without challenge. Presently, as reflected by the contributors of this volume, there is controversy concerning the boundaries of strategic behavior that goes beyond the debates of the traditionalists and conservatives.

In part, definitional problems have arisen due to the recognition that relatively automatic (and thus unconscious) processes can result in enhanced levels of performance, often mirroring or exceeding performance attained when deliberate strategies are employed (e.g., Hasher & Zacks, 1979; Shiffrin & Schneider, 1977). In developmental research, strategy-like behavior has been observed in children that was apparently mediated by the relatively automatic activation of semantic memory relations (e.g., Bjorklund, 1985; Lange, 1978), with children having little or no awareness of the presumed techniques observed in their protocols (e.g., Bjorklund & Zeman, 1982). In other work, highly practiced techniques, such as retrieval of addition and subtraction facts from long-term memory (e.g., Ashcraft & Fierman, 1982) and the skills involved in proficient reading (e.g., Paris et al., 1983) are again executed without subjects deliberately selecting among alternative techniques or being conscious of their highly effective processing.

Following both the traditional and conservative definitions of strategies, these activities are not strategic. However, consider the caveat of Pressley et al.'s definition of strategy, that it must be "potentially" available to consciousness. Children may be able to reflect upon their skilled reading or mathematics computation, or may be able to infer their use of an organizational strategy after being queried, even if they were unaware of their highly effective processing while performing the task. In these cases, should children's behavior be described as strategic, or should some other terms be used? Moreover, even if reflection does not yield awareness, why should these efficient, goal-directed, albeit automatic processes not be afforded the label *strategic*? Such arguments are made by Howe and O'Sullivan (chap. 5) and Ashcraft (chap. 7), which we refer to here as liberal views.

Ashcraft proposes that the way *strategy* is used today differs greatly from the way it was used in early memory research. Rather than viewing strategies as deliberate and conscious mental procedures, Ashcraft states that the term today is defined, loosely, as "how some task is performed mentally" (p. 186). More precisely, Ashcraft defines a strategy as "any mental process or procedure in the stream of information processing activities that serves a goal-related purpose" (p. 207).

Although the majority of the authors of this volume continue to hold a traditional or slightly more conservative view of strategies, Ashcraft's claim that the term has a broader connotation today has merit. This is most clearly seen in research on children's arithmetic, the topic of Ashcraft's chapter, in which the relatively automatic retrieval of addition and subtraction facts is classified as an efficient strategy for solving simple arithmetic problems. (This, of course, would not be considered a strategy by Bisanz and LeFevre.) In numerous research articles, as well as review papers that deal with strategies only tangentially, the term tends to be used in the broad way Ashcraft suggests. Thus, for Ashcraft, the definition of strategies must include both conscious, deliberate processes as well as those that achieve automatic status across development, a position at odds with both traditionalists and conservatives.

Howe and O'Sullivan take a very similar position. They define memory strategies as

> task-appropriate behaviors used in the service of maximizing perfor-
> mance. In this context, memory strategies can be defined as specific sets
> of processes (involving both automatic and controlled subcomponents)
> that determine the content and order of execution of essential memory
> operations (e.g., encoding, storage, search, and retrieval). (p. 132)

They argue that distinguishing between "strategic" and "nonstrategic" or between "effortful" and "automatic" processes is counterproductive to developing an understanding of strategies. Furthermore, questions of degree of effortfulness and whether a process is "potentially conscious and controllable" are not important in determining what is and what is not a strategy. Howe and O'Sullivan state that "in order to understand strategic behavior, we must consider both the automatic and purposive components of that behavior in children of all ages, as well as the types of knowledge structures children of different ages (and abilities) possess" (p. 136).

DEFINING STRATEGIES: IS A SYNTHESIS POSSIBLE?

How different are these various definitions of strategies, and do the differences make the term useless as an organizing concept for cognitive development? Can the differences be resolved?

There can be no doubt about the range of opinions concerning what constitutes a strategy and what does not. In this volume, authors writing on the same topics and reviewing similar research have what appear to be opposing definitions of the term (e.g., Bjorklund et al. versus Howe & O'Sullivan for memory; and Bisanz & LeFevre versus Ashcraft for arithmetic). Despite the differences, however, contributors holding seemingly opposing views often share the same concerns.

The major source of difference between those holding what we have called a "liberal" view of strategies and those holding both "traditional" and "conservative" views centers around the issue of automatic cognitive processes. For example, Ashcraft states that, as far as most researchers interested in children's arithmetic are concerned, fact retrieval is a bona fide strategy. Yet, he acknowledges that it is relatively automatic in its nature, not deliberate, and likely innate. Bisanz and LeFevre recognize the same characteristics of fact retrieval, and state quite flatly that the automatic and nonselective way fact retrieval is used should exclude it from consideration as a strategy. It is efficient, develops in effectiveness, and warrants serious study, say Bisanz and LeFevre, but it is not a strategy.

A closer look at the statements of Ashcraft and of Bisanz and LeFevre concerning fact retrieval shows more agreement than disagreement. When they look at fact retrieval, they are looking at the same thing and they both recognize its significance to the development of arithmetic skill. Bisanz and LeFevre do not state that automatic processes are unrelated to strategic functioning. They choose to use the label *strategy* more selectively than Ashcraft.

This, we believe, is true of all of the contributors of this volume. There is a recognition that strategic functioning is synergistic, involving one's knowledge base, automatic processes, as well as deliberate and conscious mental operations. Howe and O'Sullivan state this explicitly, proposing that all such components should be considered strategic, and to do otherwise is counterproductive. A similar claim was made by Bjorklund et al., although they proposed restricting the definition of strategy while studying how factors such as knowledge base and automatic processing influence strategy use and development.

From our understanding of the literature and particularly of the chapters herein, we believe that the definitional problems surrounding the term *strategy* have not made a great difference in how or what researchers study. That is, most researchers acknowledge the importance of multiple factors in mediating task performance, some effortful and conscious, others automatic and unconscious. Whatever a particular researcher chooses as a label, it is clear that many researchers in the field are investigating goal-directed cognitive processing, and that this is the phenomenon of interest.

Despite our belief that research efforts have not been seriously hampered by the various ways "strategy" has been used, the definitional diversity has impeded comprehension and generalization of research findings, making it desirable for a consensus definition of this much used term. We have already taken a position on this in our chapter (Bjorklund et al.), stating that the term should be kept distinct from other words or phrases used as synonyms for cognitive processing, lest it be relegated to a generic word for *thinking*. Bisanz and LeFevre make an even stronger case for this position, arguing that psychologists should not stray far from the standard dictionary definition of the term. However, we do not suppose that our saying this would convince people such as Howe and O'Sullivan or Ashcraft to change their minds. What is needed, we propose, is a broader conception of strategies accompanied by a modified vocabulary.

We suggest the term *strategy complex* in referring to the multiple factors that contribute to performance on complicated tasks. From our perspective, a strategy complex is similar to the definition that Howe and O'Sullivan currently propose for strategy. A strategy complex includes all task-appropriate and goal-directed behaviors used to facilitate task performance. The many components of a strategy complex must be delineated; these include factors associated with the knowledge base, automatic processes, and strategies proper. A *strategy proper* is defined as a conscious and deliberate process executed to achieve a specific goal, similar to the way conservatives currently define strategy. Unconscious cognitive functioning, such as the automatic activation of semantic memory relations in a free-recall task, would be considered as contributing to enhanced performance, and possibly to the development and execution of the strategy proper, but would not be considered strategic. Moreover, highly practiced processes, that once may have been effortful and conscious but are now automatic, would also not be considered as strategies proper. These processes, such as word identification in reading or fact retrieval in arithmetic, would be labeled as *skills* and considered to be components of the strategy complex. In addition to including the highly practiced skills of older children within a strategy complex, strategy complexes could be used to study goal-directed behavior in infancy, as in Willatts's research, without the need of using a definition of strategy that may be at odds with that used by investigators studying older children's cognitions.

Using the idea of a strategy complex may help researchers, who now often talk past one another, to communicate with one another. As developmentalists, we can concentrate on how various aspects of the strategy complex change and interact to produce effective task performance in children of different ages. As we noted previously, we believe that most researchers in the area already take this point of view. However, because of definitional differences, it sometimes appears that investigators studying the same topic are seeing things quite differently. We believe that a slight modification in terminology, as suggested here, may yield substantially improved communication among researchers and thus progress our understanding of children's cognition.

CHILDREN'S STRATEGIES: WHENCE DO THEY COME?

Despite the controversy among the contributors of this volume concerning what constitutes a strategy, there is greater agreement concerning strategy development. None of the authors treat strategies as isolated cognitive operations that develop independently of other aspects of cognition. Rather, strategies proper, adopting our new terminology, are viewed as being comprised of many components, all of which develop. The various components of a strategy proper develop interactively: Changes in one component (e.g., knowledge base) affect other components (e.g., efficiency of processing), which, in combination, influences the development of a strategy proper.

Moreover, all contributors argue that the components of a strategy complex develop continuously and quantitatively. The strategies that children of different ages use do not reflect discrete transitions from one style of information processing to another, but rather changes brought about by quantitative changes in the components of the strategy complex.

THE CONTINUITY OF STRATEGY DEVELOPMENT

The idea that strategies develop gradually and continually was held by researchers investigating children of all ages and for highly diverse tasks. With respect to strategies during infancy, for example, Willatts proposes that development is mainly the expansion of existing strategies to incorporate developing abilities and to apply to new problems. Rather than new strategies suddenly appearing, existing strategies are fine tuned with development. Most of the other contributors to this volume would concur that strategic abilities develop gradually in older children. There is also a great deal of agreement concerning what develops. For example, claims that practice with a procedure results in decreases in the amount of attention necessary for its execution were made by Willatts for infants' strategies, by Folds et al., Bjorklund et al., and Howe and O'Sullivan with respect to the development of memory strategies, Miller for selective attention strategies, and Ashcraft and Bisanz and LeFevre for arithmetic strategies. Similarly, Willatts's suggestion that infants and toddlers become increasingly able to monitor their progress on a task is similar to the claim that increases in metacognition contribute importantly to more efficient strategy use in older children (e.g., Bjorklund et al.; Folds et al.; Garner; Gholson et al.; Howe & O'Sullivan; and Bisanz & LeFevre, although the latter authors avoid the term *metacognition*).

Finally, knowledge of the content to which a strategy is to be applied is generally thought to develop gradually. Developmental differences in the knowledge base, it would seem, are universally agreed upon as important contributors to strategy development. Greater knowledge for the to-be-processed information appears to permit children to use fewer resources in processing that information (Bjorklund et al.; Howe & O'Sullivan; Miller), to identify the nature of the problem and select appropriate strategies (Bisanz & LeFevre; Folds et al.), and to automatize processing, bypassing the need for strategies proper (Ashcraft; Bisanz & LeFevre; Garner).

THE PRECURSORS OF STRATEGIES PROPER

The precursors of the strategies proper used by older children can be observed in younger children as well, although these early strategies and skills are rarely executed with the same degree of proficiency. For example, analogical reasoning, which is often quite poor even in adults (e.g., Reed, Dempster, & Ettinger, 1985), has its roots in the preschool years. Gholson et al. demonstrate that many of the skills of strategic problem solving are available to preschoolers, although improvements continue throughout childhood. They note that older children in general require less assistance to attain high levels of performance than do younger children. Specifically, they propose that older children are advanced in "metacognitive competence," or such skills as "reflecting . . . on problem solutions, looking for general rules, and knowing . . . about how to learn" (p. 303). Nevertheless, the basic components necessary to perform strategically on analogical reasoning tasks are available to preschool children.

Ashcraft made a similar claim for arithmetic strategies, proposing that younger and older children alike possess multiple strategies that may be selected for any particular problem. New strategies are acquired in development, as children face new problems. But equally important in strategy development for Ashcraft are changes in the strategies children prefer to use to solve math problems, from overt methods, to covert counting methods, to fact retrieval. The reason for changes in strategy preference is due to changes in the associative strength of basic arithmetic facts. As facts become better established, children rely less on highly effortful reconstructive strategies, and more on direct and automatic fact retrieval. Bisanz and LeFevre make similar claims of changes in children's arithmetic strategies. The important fact here is that many of the processes involved in efficient arithmetic are available to the young child. Many of the strategies used by older children on complicated problems are the same as those used on simpler problems by younger children.

Despite the similarity of the strategies used by younger and older children, there are considerable differences in the effectiveness of these strategies. Moreover, not all of the strategies used by older children are available to their younger peers, even though components of those strategies may be. For example, Miller proposes a developmental sequence of strategy acquisition including periods of nonproduction, partial production of a selective strategy, production of a strategy without facilitation (utilization deficiency), and finally mature strategy use that facilitates performance. The strategies used by older children emerge from the strategies used earlier in development, making the developmental process continuous. Miller proposes that the processes underlying strategy development are likely quantitative in nature (i.e., changes in efficiency of processing). Yet, in terms of effectiveness, the strategies of the younger children differ substantially from those used by older children. In fact, Miller's period of utilization deficiency refers to a time in development when a strategy of known efficiency (i.e., it facilitates performance of older children) fails to enhance performance of younger children (see also Bjorklund et al.; Folds et al.).

Similarly, Garner proposes that the development of strategic behavior in reading is marked by both an increase in the use of effective strategies and a decrease in the use of inefficient ones. Specific strategies are learned and ineffective routines are gradually dropped. Bisanz and LeFevre make a similar claim, proposing that children acquire with development more procedures for solving problems.

Based on the chapters of this volume, we believe a relatively clear outline of strategy development (or the development of strategy complexes) can be attained. Strategies develop continuously. The primitive and often ineffective techniques of infants and young children serve as the basis for the more mature and effective strategies of older children. Changes in children's goal-directed behaviors are mediated by underlying changes in such continuously developing factors as knowledge base, processing efficiency, and self-monitoring. Changes in these underlying factors make some information-processing techniques more probable than others (fact retrieval in arithmetic, for example). Generally, children become increasingly effective in selecting and implementing strategies with development. Some techniques, such as fact retrieval in arithmetic or the processing of sequences of words in reading, become automatized and unavailable to consciousness. In other situations, however, children become increasingly aware of their information-processing attempts, consciously deciding among alternatives to solve problems. Both of these aspects reflect mature strategy complexes. The former, we and others have labeled *skills,* the latter, *strategies proper.*

THE ROLE OF SELF-AWARENESS IN STRATEGY DEVELOPMENT

One aspect of the development of strategies proper that has been skirted by most of the contributors is the role of self-awareness. Although being conscious of one's actions is a definitional requirement for strategies proper, the issue of the development of self-awareness is rarely addressed with respect to strategy development. In this final section, we speculate how age-related changes in self-awareness may contribute to the development of strategies proper.

For children to behave strategically, they must be aware of themselves as problem solvers. They must realize that their actions influence their progress toward a goal. They must identify a goal they wish to achieve, keep that goal in mind, and then monitor their progress toward that goal. In short, they must be able to conceptualize themselves as active agents who are separable from the objects they act upon.

From this perspective, self-awareness is a characteristic of infants from the time they are able to differentiate objects in the environment from their direct actions on them. Based on Piaget's (1952) interpretations, this separation develops gradually over infancy, although sufficient distinction between self and objects is attained by about 8 months to permit the rudiments of strategic behavior. Based on new research and interpretations, Willatts would move that age back to as young as 3 months.

Self-awareness develops both in the number of circumstances in which it is observed and in quality over childhood. For example, an increasing sense of self is seen between 18 months and 2 years of age as reflected by mirror recognition, the use of a child's own name and possessive pronouns (such as *mine*), and the beginning of embarrassment (e.g., Kagan, 1981; Lewis, 1986; Lewis & Brooks-Gunn, 1979). In recent research by Bullock and Lütkenhaus (1988), differences in problem solving were noted between children 15- and 35-months of age with respect to their attention to producing outcomes, the pleasure they derived from achieving goals, and their tendencies to monitor and correct their performance (see also DeLoache, Sugarman, & Brown, 1985). They interpreted these changes as reflecting the active involvement of the self in actions.

We propose that developmental differences in self-awareness contribute significantly to children's strategy development. In problem-solving situations, children become more cognizant of the outcomes of their actions. This increased awareness of outcomes is accompanied by increased attention to the behaviors they use to achieve the goal. The behaviors begin to be seen as agents in service of a goal rather than as ends in themselves. This produces enhanced awareness of the connection between one's behaviors and the goal. As children's awareness of this relation improves, they will be more likely to monitor their progress toward their goal, further increasing their consciousness of their actions and enhancing the effectiveness of the strategy. With age and experience, children's awareness of this means–ends connection generalizes across situations. Initially, it is limited to familiar contexts or much practiced problems. The reason for this, we propose, is that awareness of means–ends relations requires some of a child's limited resources, and, as we discussed in our chapter (Bjorklund et al.), functional resources vary with experience

and familiarity with the problem-solving situation. As general processing efficiency increases, due both to maturationally paced changes
in myelinization and experience (Bjorklund & Harnishfeger, 1990;
Case, 1985), children will display self-awareness in a broader range of
contexts, increasing the frequency and effectiveness of their strategies.

Developmental differences in self-awareness have been too little
attended to with respect to strategy development. Although consciousness (usually confirmed by verbal reports) has typically been a
criterial feature in the definition of strategies, it has not been systematically investigated as an important developmental factor in strategy
development. Consciousness, or self-awareness, is a slippery concept.
It is difficult to define and study, particularly when our subject
population includes both preverbal infants and articulate adolescents
and adults. Future research attempts should include self-awareness,
along with the other agreed-upon topics such as knowledge base and
efficiency of processing, as components of the strategy complex.

ACKNOWLEDGMENTS

We would like to thank Barbara Bjorklund and Jacqueline Muir-
Broaddus for their comments on this chapter.

REFERENCES

Ashcraft, M. H., & Fierman, B. A. (1982). Mental addition in third, fourth, and sixth
    grades. *Journal of Experimental Child Psychology, 33,* 216–234.
Belmont, J. M., & Butterfield, E. C. (1969). The relations of short-term memory to
    development and intelligence. In L. Lipsitt & H. Reese (Eds.), *Advances in child
    development and behavior* (pp. 30–83, Vol. 4). New York: Academic Press.
Bjorklund, D. F. (1985). The role of conceptual knowledge in the development of
    organization in children's memory. In C. J. Brainerd & M. Pressley (Eds.), *Basic
    processes in memory development: Progress in cognitive development research* (pp. 103–142).
    New York: Springer.
Bjorklund, D. F., & Harnishfeger, K. K. (1990). The resources construct in cognitive
    development: Diverse sources of evidence and a theory of inefficient inhibition.
    Developmental Review.
Bjorklund, D. F., & Zeman, B. R. (1982). Children's organization and metamemory
    awareness in their recall of familiar information. *Child Development, 53,* 799–810.
Brown, A. L. (1975). The development of memory: Knowing, knowing about knowing,
    and knowing how to know. In H. W. Reese (Ed.), *Advances in child development and
    behavior* (pp. 103–152, Vol. 10). New York: Academic Press.
Bullock, M., & Lütkenhaus, P. (1988). The development of volitional behavior in the
    toddler years. *Child Development, 59,* 664–674.

Case, R. (1985). *Intellectual development: Birth to adulthood.* New York: Academic Press.

DeLoache, J., Sugarman, S., & Brown, A. (1985). The development of error correction strategies in young children's manipulative play. *Child Development, 56,* 928–939.

Flavell, J. H. (1970). Developmental studies of mediated memory. In H. W. Reese & L. P. Lipsitt (Eds.), *Advances in child development and child behavior* (pp. 181–211, Vol. 5). New York: Academic Press.

Hasher, L., & Zacks, R. T. (1979). Automatic and effortful processes in memory. *Journal of Experimental Psychology: General, 108,* 356–388.

Kagan, J. (1981). *The second year: The emergence of self-awareness.* Cambridge, MA: Harvard University Press.

Lange, G. W. (1978). Organization-related processes in children's recall. In P. A. Ornstein (Ed.), *Memory development in children* (pp. 101–128). Hillsdale, NJ: Lawrence Erlbaum Associates.

Lewis, M. (1986). Origins of self-knowledge and individual differences in early self-recognition. In J. Suls & A. G. Greenwald (Eds.), *Psychological perspectives on the self* (Vol. 3, pp. 55–78). Hillsdale, NJ: Lawrence Erlbaum Associates.

Lewis, M., & Brooks-Gunn, J. (1979). *Social cognition and the acquisition of self.* New York: Plenum.

Naus, M. J., & Ornstein, P. A. (1983). Development of memory strategies: Analysis, questions and issues. In M. T. H. Chi (Ed.), *Trends in memory development research: Vol. 9. Contributions to human development* (pp. 1–30). Basel: S. Karger.

Paris, S. G., Lipson, M. Y., & Wixson, K. K. (1983). Becoming a strategic reader. *Contemporary Educational Psychology, 8,* 293–316.

Piaget, J. (1952). *The origins of intelligence in children* New York: Norton.

Pressley, M., Forrest-Pressley, D. L., Elliot-Faust, D., & Miller, G. (1985). Children's use of cognitive strategies: How to teach strategies, and what to do if they can't be taught. In M. Pressley & C. J. Brainerd (Eds.), *Cognitive learning and memory in children: Progress in cognitive development research* (pp. 1–47). New York: Springer.

Reed, S. K., Dempster, A., & Ettinger, M. (1985). Usefulness of analogous solutions for solving algebra word problems. *Journal of Experimental Psychology: Learning, Memory, & Cognition, 11,* 106–125.

Shiffrin, R. M., & Schneider, W. (1977). Controlled and automatic human information processing: II. Perceptual learning, automatic attending, and a general theory. *Psychological Review, 84,* 127–190.

Subject Index

Author Index